Portland Community College

D0021814

Southern Illinois University Carbondale

Free for All

CALIFORNIA STUDIES IN FOOD AND CULTURE

Darra Goldstein, Editor

FREE FOR ALL

FIXING SCHOOL FOOD IN AMERICA

Janet Poppendieck

UNIVERSITY OF CALIFORNIA PRESS

Berkeley Los Angeles London

University of California Press, one of the most distin-
guished university presses in the United States, enriches
lives around the world by advancing scholarship in the
humanities, social sciences, and natural sciences. Its activities are supported by the UC Press Foundation and by
philanthropic contributions from individuals and institutions. For more information, visit www.ucpress.edu.

University of California Press
Berkeley and Los Angeles, California

University of California Press, Ltd.
London, England

© 2010 by The Regents of the University of California

Library of Congress Cataloging-in-Publication Data

Poppendieck, Janet, 1945–.
   Free for all : fixing school food in America / Janet
Poppendieck.
      p.   cm. — (California studies in food and
culture; 28)
   Includes bibliographical references and index.
   ISBN 978-0-520-24370-5 (cloth : alk. paper)
   1. National school lunch program.   2. School break-
fast programs—United States.   3. School children—
Food—United States.   4. Children—Nutrition—United
States.   I. Title.   II. Title: Fixing school food in
America.

LB3479.U6P55 2010
371.7'160973—dc22   2009015369

Manufactured in the United States of America

19   18   17   16   15   14   13   12   11   10
10   9   8   7   6   5   4   3   2   1

This book is printed on Cascades Enviro 100, a 100%
post consumer waste, recycled, de-inked fiber. FSC recycled certified and processed chlorine free. It is acid free,
Ecologo certified, and manufactured by BioGas energy.

For my daughter, Amanda

Contents

Acknowledgments

I am grateful to the many people who have helped me along the journey represented by this book. First, I want to thank the food service director and staff at the school I call Any Town High School, who must remain anonymous. Your generosity and candor were essential to helping me understand the realities of school food. And so were the time and insights of all of the people that I interviewed—food service staff, legislators, advocates, innovators, parents, teachers, administrators, students, and the staff and leadership of the School Nutrition Association. Very busy people with many demanding responsibilities took time to teach me about school food. I interviewed many more people than I quoted, so not all of you will find your names in these pages, but rest assured that you all contributed to my understanding.

Between me and the people I interviewed, there were often intermediaries, people who helped me find the folks who could tell me the real story. In this role, I particularly want to thank Mark Winne, Bernie Beaudreau, Bill Flynn, Dorigen Keeney, Frank Fear, Jonathan Osorio, Joyce Lowry, Toni Liquori, Matt Sharp, Ken Hecht, Martha Lee, Sandy Sheedy, and, in Sweden, Annika Wesslen.

Librarians at Hunter College and the University of California, Santa Cruz were unfailingly helpful, and the staff of the wonderful Child Nutrition Archives at the National Food Service Management Institute steered me toward many useful sources in my brief time there. I am also grateful to the staff at USDA who answered my many questions by phone and e-mail, and particularly to John Endahl for finding and sending studies of schools that had withdrawn from the National School Lunch Program. I thank the staff at the Women's Center for Education and Career Advancement in New York City for using the sophisticated computer models of the Self Sufficiency Standard to model school food affordability for me.

Colleagues and students have provided support for this endeavor since its inception. I'm grateful to both the members of the "Agfood" Seminar and to my temporary colleagues in the Community Studies Department, both at the University of California, Santa Cruz, for stimulating and thought-provoking discussions and for encouraging this project during the sabbatical semester I spent there. UC Santa Cruz was where I first asked students to write their school food memories for me, and I am grateful to those who did so, and to Mary Beth Pudup for permitting me to distribute a brief questionnaire in her large class. I continued to collect such memories when I returned to Hunter College, and I am also indebted to Mary Summers at the University of Pennsylvania, Kathleen Gorman at the University of Rhode Island, and Lisa Heldke at Gustavus Adolphus College for arranging for me to collect such memoirs from their students. I want to thank all the students for their candor and humor.

At my home base in New York, I'm grateful to the City University of New York Foodways Seminar organized by Jonathan Deutsch, Annie Hauck Lawson, and Babette Audant for an attentive hearing early in the process. Colleagues at Hunter also listened attentively at a departmental brown bag, asked good questions, and then took the initiative to pass along useful items of interest. Thanks to Nancy Foner, Margaret Chin, Jack Levinson, and Ruth Sidel for such thoughtfulness, to all of my colleagues for a helpful level of interest in this project, to Rick Zdan for stepping up to the plate at a crucial moment, and to my department chair, Robert Perinbanaygam, for a course release when I needed it most. More recently, Nick Freudenburg and colleagues in the Hunter College School of Public Health provided useful feedback and an opportunity to gain insights from colleagues in London through a joint CUNY–London Metropolitan University project on responses to childhood obesity. I am also grateful to the Hunter College Institutional Review Board and the Office of Research Administration under the leadership of Bob Buckley for able administration of grant funds and the protocols for the protection of human subjects.

The W. K. Kellogg Foundation, through the good offices of Gail Imig and Rick Foster, provided generous support for the travel necessitated by this research and for release from teaching at crucial points. I am grateful both for the funds and for the expression of faith in the project that they represented. I am also grateful to the Kellogg Foundation for including me in several of their annual Food and Society convocations, which gave me an opportunity to learn more about innovations in school food and much more about the food system context. And I am grateful to the Kellogg Fellows Leadership Alliance for its ongoing interest in this project.

Those funds from the Kellogg Foundation also made possible some student research assistance, and additional research assistance was provided as part of a course requirement in the nutrition program at Teachers College, Columbia. In alphabetical order, I am grateful to JC Dwyer, Natali Gonzalez, Thomael Joannidis, Cara Nemchek, and Ina Tsagaraskis. I am also grateful to Hunter College graduate students S.M. Burke, Biana Perelshteyn, and Sylwia Struk, who wrote papers on aspects of school food that added to my understanding.

The tapes of my interviews were transcribed with exceptional care, patience, and speed by Christian Peet and Lynn du Hoffmann, both of whom also contributed useful ideas and welcome encouragement.

There comes a time in the creation of any book in which there are drafts of chapters to be read, and I have been fortunate to have many friends and colleagues who have performed this essential service and provided both moral support and exceptionally good advice. Many thanks to Bill Ayres, David Beller, Minna Bloch, Lynn Chancer, JC Dwyer, Tom Forster, Kathy Kilmer, Madeline Levin, Toni Liquori, Marion Nestle, Connie Norgren, Ruth Sidel, Mickey Silverman, Roberta Sonnino, Patty Stotter (whose exceptional turnaround time has made a difference more often than I can count), Deborah Szekely, and Dee Unterbach. The members of the Feast and Famine Colloquium at New York University read a substantial segment and provided helpful feedback. Closer to home, my daughter, Amanda Goldberg, has read parts of the manuscript, and my husband, Woody Goldberg, has read draft after draft of chapter after chapter with unfailingly good humor. Once the manuscript was complete, the anonymous readers selected by the University of California Press provided useful critiques and suggestions, as did the readers who responded to the original book proposal. The remaining errors, oversights, and omissions are my own.

Encouragement has also been provided all along the way by the staff and my fellow board members at World Hunger Year, by the chef and author Ann Cooper, by Kathi Johnson, Martha Lee, and other members of the Kellogg Fellows Leadership Alliance, by long-time child nutrition activists Kathy Goldman, Agnes Molnar, Ken Hecht, and Matt Sharp, by Toni Liquori and the staff of Liquori and Associates, and by New York City school food change agents including Kate McKenzie, Chef Jorge Collazo, Stephen O'Brien, and SchoolFood Director David Berkowitz, and more recently by members of School Food FOCUS.

My editor, Naomi Schneider, at the University of California Press has provided not only good advice at crucial junctures, but also a rapid response time that appears to me to be unmatched in publishing. I feel fortunate to have had her clarity and helpful guidance from the outset of this project. Ellen F. Smith did a wonderfully thoughtful and constructive job of copyediting, improving the manuscript in countless ways.

Finally, my family—my mother while she was still living; my sister, Trudie Prevatt; my sister-in-law Jill Cutler and her partner, Jeremy Brecher; my daughter, Amanda; and my husband, Woody Goldberg—have provided the steady support and tolerance for vacations deferred and visits and celebrations delayed and space disrupted that I needed to bring this project to completion. Thank you.

INTRODUCTION

In Search of School Food

School meals don't have a very good reputation. Mention them and many people think of noisy, crowded cafeterias where children wait too long in line, then have too little time to eat. For people of a certain age, they evoke images of dreary, repetitive, unappetizing menus, airline-style entrees, overcooked vegetables, unripe fruit. For those who have been in a school cafeteria more recently, the imagery is apt to be what one critic has called "carnival fare": corn dogs, french fries, burgers, pizza, offerings high in fat and salt and low in fruits and vegetables, color, flavor, and variety.

It doesn't have to be that way. In place of industrial kitchens turning out frozen entrees to be defrosted and reheated miles from where they are produced, we can have fresh foods, cooked on site in local kitchens. Instead of low-skill, poorly paid "McJobs" in central kitchens and school cafeterias, we can have meaningful work in which culinary trainees develop marketable skills under the direction of talented chefs. In place of surplus commodities purchased by the federal government to support industrial agriculture and then processed into fast food clones, we can have fresh, local, organic, seasonal fruits and vegetables, dairy and meats, produced by family farmers using humane and sustainable farming practices. In place of lunchrooms virtually segregated by social class, where poor children eligible for free food line up for a federally regulated meal while their more affluent peers purchase Taco Bell or Pizza Hut or Burger King items—or leave the campus altogether—we can have common meals, shared by all in an atmosphere of conviviality. In place of

1

noisy, chaotic, dingy, and unattractive cafeterias where teachers are reluctant to set foot, faculty and students can eat together in their classrooms or in comfortable, well-equipped dining rooms. In place of the enormous paperwork burden of determining eligibility for free, reduced price and full price meals, we can provide our school food service departments with budgets adequate to feed all of our children a nutritious and appealing meal at midday—and another in the morning if they want it. In place of meals that reinforce the high-fat, high-sodium, high-sugar food choices promoted by the fast food and snack industries, we can help our students to develop healthy preferences. In place of the increasingly narrow "teach to the test" curriculum, we can reintroduce the study of food and nutrition to our schools, providing opportunities for application of the core skills of reading and math by engaging students in menu planning, food production, and meal preparation.

Pie in the sky? Each of these alternatives is in use and working somewhere in the United States at this moment. Our spectacular failure to provide fresh, appealing, healthy meals for all our children is the result of a series of specific and identifiable social choices that we have made: a massive disinvestment in our public schools, an industrialized food system, an agriculture policy centered on subsidies for large-scale commodity production, a business model rather than a public health approach to school food programs. Concern about obesity among American children and adolescents, however, has created an opportunity to transform the way we feed our children at school. As anxiety about overweight and its attendant health risks has mounted, parents, educators, public health professionals, and legislators have joined school food service personnel, anti-hunger activists, and community food security advocates in demanding better, healthier meals. And we know how to provide them; exemplary programs abound. Of course, we cannot implement such innovations and improvements on a large scale without investing more in our children. There is no such thing as a free lunch makeover. The economics of diet-related disease, however, make it clear that our choice is between doing a better job now or paying much more later for medical care. Now is the time to revise our choice in favor of the health and well-being of our children.

DISCOVERING SCHOOL FOOD

For the past several years, I have been on a journey of discovery, trying to understand the challenges and realities of school food in the United

States. What are school meals like today? How did they get that way? What are program administrators and concerned communities doing to improve them? This book is an eclectic account of my observations; it encompasses firsthand experience in a school kitchen and cafeteria and extensive interviews with school food service personnel, research on the history of school meals in the United States, exploration of current issues in school food, including the menu, the nutritive quality, the factors that deter students who have effective access to school meals from taking advantage of them, and the factors that impede access, especially the dysfunctional three-tier eligibility system. It looks briefly at efforts to improve both access to and quality of meals and concludes with my own prescription for "fixing" school food.

My initial focus was the National School Lunch Program (NSLP) and its younger sibling, the School Breakfast Program (SBP), the federal programs administered by the United States Department of Agriculture (USDA) that subsidize and regulate school meals. Some 94,000 of the nation's public and private schools offer the National School Lunch Program, and in 2008 more than thirty-one million children participated on an average day. The breakfast program, begun in 1966, was permanently authorized in 1975. It is currently available in 84,500 schools, and last year it served more than ten million children on a typical school day.[1] Together, the two programs support more than seven billion meals a year. Large numbers like these have a tendency to wash over us without sinking in. For me it is a major production to prepare a meal for eight or ten; the idea of forty million meals in a day is almost meaningless, seven billion meals unfathomable. I will always be grateful to a speaker at an antiwar convocation who explained to me, in terms that I could comprehend, the difference between a million and a billion. If he could keep us in the auditorium listening to his impassioned arguments for a million seconds, he said, we would be there for a little over eleven and a half days. If, however, he were allocated a *billion* seconds to make his case, we would be there for thirty-one years, eight months, two weeks, one day, eleven hours, sixteen minutes and forty-eight seconds. Seven billion meals is a very large number. Feeding our children at school is an enormous undertaking.

Although I began with the federally sponsored lunch and breakfast programs, I quickly learned that there is a great deal of food bought, sold, and consumed at school that is not part of these programs, and consequently not subject to the nutrition regulations or the burdensome accountability procedures that govern the official "reimbursable" meals.

Increasingly, children with the wherewithal to do so purchase essentially unregulated foods in a la carte lines, food courts, school stores, or vending machines, collectively dubbed "competitive foods" because they are sold in competition with the federally regulated meal. As an article in the *San Francisco Chronicle* put it, "The lunch lady serving a government-approved hot lunch is but a dusty icon. The most popular school lunch is a small pepperoni pizza, nachos, a peanut butter cookie and a diet soda . . . a dietary bomb containing 1,116 calories and 51 grams of fat."[2] A USDA study conducted during the 2004–2005 school year found that competitive foods were available from vending machines in 98 percent of high schools, 97 percent of middle/junior high schools, and 27 percent of elementary schools, and that foods were sold a la carte in the cafeterias of more than 90 percent of middle and high schools and 75 percent of elementary schools.[3] Neither children nor their parents are very good at distinguishing between the nutritionally regulated lunch offered by the NSLP and the other foods waiting at the checkout counter or in the vending machine. For them, it is all part of "school food."

School food service directors and school business officials know the difference, however. The complex financing arrangements that govern the program make the distinction crucial. When I say that more than thirty-one million children "participated" on an average school day, I mean that they selected a federally reimbursable school meal, one that complied with federal nutrition standards, although they may also have purchased a la carte items in the cafeteria or supplemented the official meal with vending machine goodies. All reimbursable meals are subsidized, but the depth of the subsidy and thus the size of the reimbursement depend on income eligibility categories derived from the federal poverty line. Some children eat free; others qualify for a "reduced price," typically 40 cents for lunch and 30 cents for breakfast, and others must pay what is misleadingly referred to as the "full price," a figure that averaged $1.85 in the 2006–2007 school year.[4] Subsidies range from $2.57 per meal for free meals to $0.24 for "full price" or "paid," plus an allocation of commodities based on the total number of lunches served. Nationally, about three-fifths of lunches and four-fifths of breakfasts were served free or at the bargain rates of the reduced price category. The lion's share of the program's federal expenditure of close to $11 billion in fiscal 2007 thus went to fund free and reduced price meals.

The administrative burden created by the three-tier system is substantial; it is complex, prone to error, and difficult to operate. Further, many parents of children who pay the "full price" have no idea that they are, in fact, receiving a subsidy of nearly $0.45 per lunch in cash and commodities combined. The invisibility of the full price subsidy affects the image of the program. In some communities it is normal for most students to eat school meals; in others, however, it is looked down upon as "welfare food." Nearly everywhere, as students reach the middle school and high school years, they begin to attach a stigma to eating free or reduced price meals. As a result, some students who qualify for these meals are deterred from eating them, and others eat a meal soured by embarrassment. Either way, the three-tier system hampers the program from realizing its full potential. We need to rethink it.

Nutrition regulations are another aspect of school food policy clearly in need of revision. Ironically, the regulations designed to protect the quality of school food can end up undermining it. Formal compliance with the federal standards can lead to counterproductive and sometimes downright unhealthy offerings, as when schools add sweetened, flavored milk in order to meet required calorie minimums. Further, the fear of losing reimbursements if the meals are found wanting has driven many systems to heavy use of prefabricated products that have achieved a federal Child Nutrition, or CN, label. Manufacturers of these products guarantee that they provide specified components of the federal meal plan and assume the financial risk if they should be found to fall short. Unfortunately, while this system may guarantee that a product has a particular number of ounces of protein, it does not guarantee that it is truly healthy.

The nutrition regulations are currently under review by a task force of the Institute of Medicine (IOM) of the National Academies of Science. It seems reasonable to hope that such anomalies will be addressed, but the regulations they are revising apply only to the federally reimbursable meal. The situation in which the reimbursable meal must meet nutrition standards but competitive foods have almost none sets children up to shun the healthier meal and select their favorite (heavily advertised) foods, which may be on sale right in the cafeteria. Even where foods are not sold a la carte in the cafeteria itself, candy, cookies, soft drinks, and salty snacks may be available in snack shops and vending machines throughout the day. Some progress in limiting competitive foods has been made over the past few years by state governments and local school districts, but the fundamental situation remains one in which the nutritionally regulated meal must compete with less healthy options.

Principals who permit vending machines and food service directors who offer a la carte snacks are not driven by a secret perverse desire to destroy the teeth and undermine the health of children, but by the need for revenue. Where vending machine revenues accrue to the principal, such funds may be virtually the only unrestricted, discretionary dollars at his or her disposal. They are often used to pay for sports, arts, and enrichment programs or to meet emergencies. And in many cafeterias, as we shall see, the a la carte offerings subsidize the federally reimbursable meal, helping to keep the price down for "full price" children and filling a gap between federal reimbursements and actual costs for free and reduced price meals. The recent escalation of fuel and food prices, especially the price of dairy products, has intensified the cost-price squeeze in the cafeteria. Add school food finance and reimbursement rates to the aspects of federal policy that need a thorough reconsideration. Clearly school food is in need of an overhaul, not only in the local cafeteria, but also in the federal policy arena.

Fortunately, pressures are mounting for just such a transformation. The changes we need in school food will not occur without substantial public effort and concern. As Texas State Secretary of Agriculture Susan Combs memorably declared, "it will take 2 million angry moms to change school food" in America.[5] One reason that I am optimistic about the potential for change is that the school cafeteria represents a kind of intersection, a meeting place, of skilled and motivated change agents with a whole host of worthwhile agendas. New voices and new allies are joining the effort every day. In the last major piece of school food legislation, the Child Nutrition and WIC Reauthorization Act of 2004, Congress accelerated this process by including a Wellness Policy Mandate; essentially this required school districts that receive federal funds for school lunch or breakfast to form committees and establish policies governing physical activity at school and foods sold or served on campus. The latter category includes food in the school lunch and breakfast programs, foods served a la carte, foods in vending machines and school stores, foods served in classrooms at parties or used as rewards, foods sold at bake sales or other fundraisers, and refreshments at school events. The mandate did not specify the content of these policies, but did specify that the committees that established them should include administrators, parents, students, school food service personnel, the school board, and representatives of the public. "Wellness" has become a watchword, and the wellness policy process has drawn many new stakeholders into the school food arena. The anti-hunger activists and school nutrition professionals who have been the protectors of child nutrition programs since the discovery of severe hunger and poverty-related malnutrition rocked the nation in the late 1960s have been joined by advocates of public health and environmental activists, particularly champions of sustainable agriculture. Now is the time for what Kevin Morgan and Roberta Sonnino, writing from a global perspective, have called a "school food revolution."[6]

NOW IS THE TIME

It is not only the convergence of agendas and the addition of new voices that make this the time for school food reform. It is also the urgency of the underlying concerns to which school meals are addressed. Hunger is on the rise. Our children's health is deteriorating. The environment is under assault. School food reform holds the promise of addressing all of these issues. That is why it cannot wait.

Hunger

Despite national wealth that is astounding by historical standards, childhood hunger continues to blight the lives and reduce the potential of too many of our children. USDA's most recent annual "household food security" survey found that 36.2 million Americans were living in households that lacked access to adequate food sometime during 2007 because of poverty. These 13 million households were 11.1 percent of U.S. households, about the same rate as the previous year, although the absolute numbers are larger because the population has grown. The federal government tries to avoid the term "hunger" and instead reports households with "low food security" (at risk of hunger), "very low food security" (formerly known as "food insecurity with hunger"), and the most troubling category, "households with very low food security with children." Talk to any school cafeteria manager in a low-income neighborhood about the rush of children for breakfast on Monday mornings after a long weekend, however, and she will convince you that hunger by any other name hurts just as much. Among the 13 million food-insecure households, 4.7 million had "very low food security," the more severe category. Both the size of this group and its share of the overall population have risen over the last decade. Of particular concern is the fact that the number of children living in households that reported very low food security among children rose by over 60 percent between 2006 and 2007, from 430,000 to 691,000.[7]

There is always a considerable lag between the collection of federal food security data and their release, so currently available data fail to reflect either the dramatic food price increases that have stymied many American households in 2007–8 or the recession officially under way as of this writing. State and local organizations can sometimes process results more quickly. A recent report released by the Massachusetts anti-hunger organization Project Bread, for example, found a sharp increase in the number of food-insecure households. "High food prices combined with the current economic crisis are driving a crisis in food insecurity that is broader and deeper than we've seen before in this state," according to Ellen Parker, the executive director of Project Bread, who predicted that "hundreds of thousands of Massachusetts citizens will need help to cover the basics—including many who have never needed help before."[8]

Recessions hit children particularly hard, in part because younger families are less well positioned to weather the storm. They have lower incomes to begin with, fewer assets, lower savings, and more debt. Younger workers, as parents of young children tend to be, have less seniority; more recently hired and more expendable, they lose their jobs more quickly. And because children are rapidly developing organisms, the effects of deprivation of health care, shelter, and nutrition are more damaging than for mature people. The census figures that will quantify this disaster for families and children have not yet been collected, but other indicators make the trends clear. Case loads in the Supplemental Nutrition Assistance Program, or SNAP, formerly known as Food Stamps, which typically track both poverty rates and unemployment, rose 13 percent between December 2007 and November 2008. School districts around the country are reporting more homeless children. And job loss is leaving more children without health insurance. As Dr. Irwin Redlener, president of the Children's Health Fund in New York City explained, "We are seeing the emergence of what amounts to a 'recession generation.' This includes the children who were already living in poverty, but also millions more whose families had a reasonable chance of making it. Two years ago, they saw themselves as working class and middle class, but now many are unemployed or underemployed, and one of the results is that we're seeing growing numbers of children depending on emergency rooms for health care or going without care." These forms of deprivation pile up and interact; the children who are exhausted from moving from shelter to shelter are the same ones who are delaying needed health care and weakened by inadequate food. As the columnist Bob Herbert has reminded us, "This is a toxic mix for children, a demoralizing convergence of factors that have long been known to impede the ability of young people to flourish."[9]

And nowhere is this failure to flourish more acute than in the classroom. Study after study has shown that hunger interferes with the ability of children to absorb an education. Long-term malnutrition can interfere with brain development, but even short-term bouts of hunger are a problem. Children who do not get enough to eat are listless and withdrawn or irritable and hostile. They find it difficult to concentrate and are easily distracted. They get sick more often and miss school more frequently than well-fed children. They may act out in the classroom and thus interfere with the learning of other children.[10] Experienced principals report that the first question they ask children referred for disciplinary reasons in the morning hours is "Have you had breakfast?" and the answer is usually "No." A reduction in such disciplinary referrals is the single most consistently reported impact of universal breakfast programs. Hunger is the enemy of education.

School meals, along with SNAP, are the front line in efforts to avert hunger, and last year 17.5 million low-income children participated in school meals on an average day, about twice the number of school-aged children served by SNAP. One reason that the school lunch and breakfast programs serve so many more children is that their eligibility standards are more generous and realistic. Families can qualify for the remarkable bargain of reduced price meals with incomes up to 185 percent of the federal poverty line, a figure that in 2008 equals $39,220 annually for a family of four; in order to obtain SNAP, gross income in most states cannot exceed 130 percent of poverty, and income after certain allowable deductions must be under the poverty line itself, or $21,200 for a family of four in 2008. There is no doubt that reduced price meals are a boon to many families in the "near poor" category, though it is equally true that many such families cannot actually afford the reduced price meals for all of their children. Elimination of the charge for reduced price meals is one of the reforms being sought by anti-hunger advocates and school food service organizations.

Economic hardship in the current economy, however, is not limited to those in the lowest income sectors. Many families with incomes above 185 percent of the poverty line are suffering. Sharp reductions in income due to job loss by one earner in a dual income family can place a tremendous strain on the family budget, even if the remaining earner's pay exceeds the cut off. Families struggling to meet mortgage payments or pay for health care can easily find themselves too strapped to take advantage of school meals, even though they are a bargain. The school food eligibility and price structure are ripe for reconsideration. Meanwhile, the rising rate of childhood hunger makes attention to school food programs particularly urgent.

Childhood Obesity

It is not hunger, however, but childhood obesity that has put school food on the national radar screen. By now, nearly everyone has heard the figures. The Centers for Disease Control and Prevention have reported that the prevalence of obesity has more than tripled for children aged 6 to 11 since the 1970s and that it has more than doubled for adolescents aged 12 to 19 in the same period. They estimate that about nine million children over the age of six are obese, another sixteen million are overweight.[11] This is not an aesthetic issue. Overweight in childhood is associated with increases in type 2 diabetes and atherosclerosis, formerly regarded as adult diseases, with asthma and joint problems, and with depression, anxiety, and sleep apnea. It contributes to low self-esteem and increases the likelihood that a child will be bullied or teased. Like hunger, childhood obesity can interfere with children's academic performance and ability to concentrate in school.[12]

I confess that I felt some discomfort about jumping on the childhood obesity bandwagon.[13] It is an issue that seems to me fraught with dangers and ambiguities. I worry that calling more attention to weight will increase the stigmatization of the overweight—and do so in their tender childhood and adolescent years when stigma has such destructive power. I worry that a climate of stigma will drive even more young people to eating disorders such as anorexia and bulimia. I worry that a focus on overweight will inevitably reinforce an unappealing and counterproductive ideology of "personal responsibility." Despite mounting evidence of the importance of advertising and what the Yale University psychologist Kelly Brownell has called a "toxic environment"[14] in which high-calorie foods of limited nutritive value are everywhere convenient, the personal responsibility story is deeply ingrained in our culture. Indeed, when I think about my own extra pounds, I tend to think moralistically in terms of personal choices and will power. I am not surprised that much public discourse about obesity falls into that mode, but I remain convinced that systemic public health approaches will have a far greater impact on the problem than will homilies, just as research suggests that cigarette taxes have done more to encourage smoking cessation than health messages. Finally, I worry that a focus on obesity "problematizes" overeating, directs our attention to this one negative aspect of our food system when in fact the whole system is fraught with hazards and social costs. Nevertheless, childhood obesity has captured the attention of the nation, and as any good teacher knows, one does not lightly forgo the potential for learning inherent in such "teachable moments." Further, it is childhood obesity, more than any other factor, that has induced us to take a closer look at what our children are eating, and that scrutiny can only be a good thing, because our children's diets are in bad shape, whether or not they result in excess weight.

I was impressed when I looked at the figures. The federal government has provided us with a tool for assessing our food consumption: the Food Guide Pyramid. It is not devoid of controversy, yet nearly everyone agrees with its recommendations about fruit and vegetables. Only 2 percent of school-aged children meet the Food Guide Pyramid recommendations for all five of the major food groups.[15] Two percent! One child in six (16 percent) consumes a diet that meets *none* of the recommendations. Less than 15 percent meet the recommendations for fruit, and less than 20 percent for vegetables. Less than 25 percent consume the recommended servings of grains, and only 30 percent meet the milk recommendation on any given day.[16] Thinking in terms of key nutrients, more than 60 percent of U.S. children and adolescents do not eat enough fiber, and 85 percent of adolescent females do not consume enough calcium. No wonder broken bones and joint diseases have become more common among children and adolescents. And what are they consuming when they are not eating the fruits and vegetables, beans and whole grains that could supply the fiber or the green leafy vegetables and dairy products that could provide the calcium? More than three-fifths of U.S. children and adolescents eat too much saturated fat, and during the last twenty-five years, average daily soft drink consumption has almost doubled among adolescent girls and almost tripled among adolescent boys. Nearly a fifth of calories consumed by children and youth come from added sugars.[17] And french fries are the most popular vegetable.

When childhood obesity first captured national attention and people began to focus on school food, many school food service professionals adopted a defensive posture. They felt unfairly blamed for what the veteran journalist Eleanor Randolph has called "The Big Fat American Kid Crisis."[18] They pointed out that even children who eat lunch at school five days a week were eating fewer than a quarter of their meals at school over the course of a year.[19] Further, they argued, schools could not undo what children learned at home. "You can't serve fast food at home and then expect the kids to come to school and make healthy

Portland Community College

choices," declared a dietician with the Arlington, Virginia, school system. But there are very good reasons for starting with school food, even if you don't think school menus are culpable. In the first place, school is where the children are. More than 97 percent of children and youth are enrolled in school, and on an average day, about 90 percent of them are in attendance.[20] Most states require schools to operate 180 days per year. So simple arithmetic suggests that schools are the place to influence children's eating habits. Further, it is much easier for public policy to influence what goes on in schools than it is to affect what happens in the nation's thirty-five million households with children. Overhaul of the menu, restriction of competitive foods, and restoration of nutrition education are all on the school food reform agenda.

There are many caveats. Nutritional advice has been notoriously unstable. Is margarine an improvement over butter because of its lower saturated fat content or a bearer of deadly trans fats? Is coffee bad or good? Do we need more carbohydrates or fewer? And one size does not fit all when it comes to nutrition. Is cow's milk "nature's most nearly perfect food"? Not if your child is lactose intolerant. Further, in addition to errors and "flip-flops," nutritional advice has a reputation for a sort of "holier than thou" or puritanical approach to eating. One has only to read *The Road to Wellville*, T.C. Boyle's hilarious fictional send-up of the extreme eating regimens once promulgated at the Adventist Sanitarium in Battle Creek, Michigan, or Harvey Levenstein's scholarly history of science-based eating, *Revolution at the Table,* to be very wary indeed of telling other people how to eat.

Despite continuing controversies, however, there is enough emerging consensus to permit at least a modicum of dietary guidance in the school curriculum. Marion Nestle was once asked by an interviewer, "Good nutritional advice is notoriously complicated and hard to follow, isn't it?" She replied, "No, it's not complicated. It's simple: eat more fruits and vegetables, and don't eat too much. And be active and don't smoke."[21] The federal government has become sufficiently convinced of a core nutrition message to issue official dietary guidelines. Nutrition education and health education are woefully underresourced in our schools, and the version of accountability imposed by the No Child Left Behind Act has made it difficult for teachers and schools to allocate time to teaching anything that is not going to be tested, but if we are serious about preventing diet-related diseases, we need to make sure that schools can teach healthy food habits. Teaching healthy eating and serving healthy food, however, must go hand in hand. Children are smart;

many have fairly well developed hypocrisy detectors. It does not make any sense at all to teach healthy eating in the classroom and then offer cafeteria fare that is high in fat, sugar, and salt or lacking in fiber and nutrients. Not in the official federally regulated school meal and not as "competitive foods." As a California nutrition advocate put it to me one day, "If a child has a cola and a bag of chips for lunch at school, that *is* her nutrition education for that day."

The eating habits of our children reflect changes in the way we produce, process, and distribute and consume food in this country. Ninety-eight percent of children ages 6 to 18 report eating at least three snacks each day, and more than half report eating five or more snacks.[22] Snack foods tend to include packaged products—chips and cookies and pastries, high in "energy density" calories per ounce, and low in valuable nutrients. Between the snacks and the preassembled microwaveable meals, our children are eating more and more highly processed foods—fabricated foods, food prepared in factories and preserved and "shelf-stabilized" with additives with long, unpronounceable names—and less and less whole food or "minimally processed" food. Behind the shift to hyperprocessed foods are the nature and structure of industrialized agriculture and a series of federal policy decisions, including the decision to subsidize corn and soy, the building blocks of snack foods. Worries about both the health and the environmental impact of this industrialized agriculture have brought a whole new group of actors and concerns to the school food table, the advocates of sustainable agriculture.

Environmental Degradation

Some health concerns lead directly to environmental activism. What begins as an anxiety about pesticide residues on the fruits and vegetables served to my child can quickly become an ardent support for organic as opposed to conventional agriculture because of the toxic burden on our soil and waters, as well as the potential harm to our children. A concern about the safety of ground beef used in school lunches has led many to look more critically at the entire way in which beef is raised and processed in this country. Such scrutiny was fueled by the graphic accounts in Eric Schlosser's *Fast Food Nation* (2001) and rekindled by the dramatic recall sparked in 2008 by the Humane Society video showing workers forcing "downer cows" into the production line, despite federal regulations prohibiting the practice. And beef processing is not the only intersection of animal welfare concerns and human health and environmental concerns.

Animal welfare is a primary motive behind the formation of the vegetarian activist group called the Physicians Committee for Responsible Medicine, which over the last half dozen years has become a significant player in the world of school food, lobbying for inclusion of soy milk among the beverage options and issuing annual "report cards" to school systems, with grades based primarily upon the availability of vegan and vegetarian options in school cafeterias. The annual release of these grades has shown a robust capacity to generate media attention and in many cases to induce change in school menus.

Meanwhile, even for omnivores like myself who may not share the vegetarian's desire to avoid or minimize animal-based foods, the production of meat in huge confined animal feeding operations, or CAFOs for short, presents a whole menu of issues. The crowding of animals has necessitated the use of high doses of antibiotics, raising the specter of the evolution of antibiotic resistant organisms. The widespread use of growth hormones is another downside of CAFOs, with documented effects on human consumers. And the lagoons in which manure from such operations is collected and stored have generated an additional round of environmental degradation and destruction of rural communities. During storms, such lagoons have flooded, contaminating large areas with fecal matter, and even in pleasant weather, the odors from manure lagoons destroy the quality of life for neighbors downwind. The problems associated with CAFOs have persuaded many thoughtful people to take a closer look at the implications of our animal-based diet for the biosphere. Even grass-fed livestock, it turns out, generates a large volume of greenhouse gases. The shift of the school food menu toward more plant-based foods would reduce environmental damage and global warming.

The desire to preserve rural communities and farming as a way of life and to protect the remaining small and mid-sized farms is another aspect of the contemporary food system that has captured the attention of groups and organizations who see school food as a potential part of the solution. The "farm to school" or "farm to cafeteria" movement has grown rapidly in the past decade. Purchasing directly from local or regional farmers and building a relationship between schools and nearby farms in order to help children understand where their food comes from has considerable potential, argue the proponents of this approach, to create stable markets for local and regional farmers who may not be big enough to supply the canneries. Further, direct marketing to schools, rather than to the many layers of brokers and agents, wholesalers, and processors that normally intervene between a grower and the end consumer, can allow farms to earn a sufficient profit to stay in business. In addition, locally grown fruits and vegetables are likely to arrive at the kitchen fresher, because they travel shorter distances, thus preserving flavor, an important factor if the goal is to teach children to enjoy them. And locally grown produce that travels a shorter distance may have a smaller "carbon footprint" than its cross-country or global competition.[23]

This is not a complete list of the environmental issues that have begun to influence school food. What is important here is recognizing that these questions are finally being asked and that energy and environment have now joined health and hunger as important contexts for making school food policy and procurement decisions. Consider, for a moment, whether you have consciously tried to change your own eating habits in the last few years. Perhaps you have worried about cancer or become concerned by the impact of agricultural chemicals like fertilizers and pesticides on the health of our land and water systems, and you have chosen to eat organic produce whenever you can afford it. Or perhaps, alarmed by global warming, you have decided to give preference to foods produced in your own region to reduce the energy expended in transport: "Think Globally, Eat Locally" as the bumper sticker puts it. If you eat three meals a day, you are responsible for about a thousand meals a year—1,095 if you never skip one. It is easy to persuade yourself that your small change has little impact. Suppose, however, that you were responsible for seven billion meals a year. Imagine the impact you could have on the health of our ecosystems, on the economies of rural areas, or the processes used for raising and slaughtering animals. Imagine the impact you could have on the health of our children. Through the school lunch and breakfast programs, of course, we *are* responsible for those seven billion meals, and potentially many more, since overall only a little over half of students who attend participating schools consume the federally subsidized and regulated lunch. There is so much at stake here. School food could be just the lever for change that we need.

There are other agendas and other organizations joining the chorus concerned about school food. Advocates of "slow food" have urged a return to an emphasis on the pleasures of eating and the civility of shared meals, along with the preservation of local and regional culinary traditions. In pursuit of more palatable school fare and less reliance on highly processed foods, many have joined in a call for more "from scratch" cooking and less defrost-and-reheat. People concerned about the commercialization of childhood have called for a halt to marketing to children, especially in schools, envisioning the school as the one place in the child's life where she might be free from advertising pressures and branded products. Minority communities determined to preserve their cultures have asked for accommodations in the school menu, while proponents of multiculturalism have favored inclusion of a wide array of cuisines. The parents of children with food allergies have won the right to labeling of allergens and the provision of alternatives. And advocates of experiential education in the tradition of John Dewey have seen in school gardens and cooking classes an opportunity to engage the full range of youthful intellects and capacities.

It is not just the urgency of the underlying issues or the convergence of diverse agendas, however, that makes this such an important time in the development of school food. It is also the remarkable opportunity created by the interaction of these varied agendas with the great yearning for change now evident in American public life. In order to fully appreciate the current opportunity, it is worth taking a brief look backward. As we shall see in chapter 7, during the last round of school food reform in 2004, school food advocates rallied under the banner of "First, do no harm" to resist an effort by the Bush administration to require extensive income verification procedures that would almost certainly have denied free and reduced price meals to millions of eligible children. Advocates won that issue and enough other gains to regard the Child Nutrition Reauthorization of 2004 as a great victory, an outcome that surprised many observers. As Ellen Teller, the chief lobbyist for the Food Research and Action Center told me, "People keep asking, why was the child nutrition reauthorization bill the only bill coming out of an incredibly poisoned legislative atmosphere this year in Congress . . . the only unanimous legislation coming out of the House and Senate and signed by the president that provided new federal funding to any of the human needs programs."

Teller went on to explain the extent and diversity of support that was enlisted for a statement of principles developed early in the process by the major stakeholders, "and literally thousands of national, state, and local groups signed onto it. . . . And then we built one of the largest coalitions that I've ever been associated with." In addition to the core stakeholders, the anti-hunger advocates and the School Food Service Association, she listed religious groups, direct service providers, education groups, medical and dietetic organizations, various organizations that provide meals and snacks to children as part of their programs, agriculture and farm commodity groups, mayors and state legislatures, immigrant and ethnic associations, and groups working with and on behalf of the homeless. "So everybody wanted to join on, and so when we went for a hill visit, you wouldn't just have FRAC and ASFSA and Second Harvest and the Lutherans at the table—you would have United Fresh Fruit and Vegetable Growers, and you would have the National PTA. It was extraordinary."[24]

It was not just the short-term process, however, or the skill of the advocates who orchestrated this massive turnout. It was also the result of years of hard work. "Well, I think it's interesting that we could have done as well as we did, with the White House and Congress both in Republican hands. One would think that this would have been the *most* difficult reauthorization," Julie Paradis told me in the Washington office of Second Harvest where she represented the food bank network on Capitol Hill. "But I think that something really fundamental has happened over the course of at least the last decade, and that is that we have got truly enormous bipartisan support for programs that address hunger. . . . What it has meant for us is that when we go to the hill and we talk about hunger issues and children, . . . the doors are open for us."

And on Capitol Hill, there are strong leaders on both sides of the aisle who, with their staffs, have been working to improve child nutrition programs for a long while. What is new and hopeful in the current equation is the White House. There is now a president who has publicly committed to ending childhood hunger in the United States by 2015. There is a first lady who has dug up the south lawn to plant a vegetable garden; there are two school-aged children in the White House and a chef who has expressed concern about the quality of school food. If child nutrition advocates could accomplish so much in the unpromising circumstances of 2004, imagine what might be possible now. The way ahead seems bright with promise. Now is indeed the time for a closer look at school food.

METHODS OF STUDY

I have employed a variety of methods to learn about school food in the United States. The core sources for this book are a series of open-ended interviews and brief episodes of participant observation. Over the course of the last several years, I have undertaken a sort of odyssey in the world of school food, a tour through what the comedian Adam Sandler has derisively called "Lunch Lady Land." I worked for a week in a school kitchen, just to get a feel for the job. I attended a series of conferences and similar events sponsored by the School Nutrition Association (SNA, formerly the American School Food Service Association), the 55,000-member professional association of school food service personnel, including an Annual National Conference, an "Industry Boot Camp," and a Child Nutrition Industry Conference. I visited the National Food Service Management Institute (NFSMI) and used its excellent archive, and I interviewed staff at the Alexandria, Virginia, headquarters of the SNA. In various settings, I also interviewed several past presidents of the SNA, and one memorable evening at the NFSMI, I was privileged to sit quietly in a corner while twenty-some past SNA presidents summarized the challenges and accomplishments of their years in office.

Here and there around the country, I interviewed dozens of school food service directors, cafeteria managers, and lunchroom workers at all levels and ate lunch or breakfast in dozens of school cafeterias. Some were typical, others were innovations or exemplary programs. All helped me to understand the complex realities and day-to-day challenges of school food in the United States, but a caveat is in order here. I can certainly say I crossed the country—from Michigan to Mississippi, from New York to California and even Hawaii—but these sites represent targets of opportunity, not a scientific random sample. I went where I heard that something interesting was occurring and where I had connections to open the cafeteria doors. Along the way, I conducted interviews and observed meals in ten states (and I interviewed people from a dozen more), in rural areas, small communities, suburbs, and inner cities. While I feel confident that I have understood a great deal about the reality of school food, I feel equally sure that there are places in the United States where the reality may differ from the picture I've assembled.

In and around and between these experiences inside the world of school food service, I have explored the parallel universe constructed by advocates. I attended conferences and visited offices to interview advocates who are trying to change school food—to make it more accessible, to reduce its stigma, to improve its quality, to integrate it with the curriculum, to resist the commercialization of schools, or to increase the use of school food purchasing power as a means to preserve the family farm and the quality of life in rural America. State legislatures have been in the forefront of efforts to improve school food, and I interviewed state legislators in four states and participated in a lobbying day in Sacramento with California food and fitness activists organized by California Food Policy Advocates. Finally, in hopes of gaining some comparative perspective, I traveled to Sweden to see what school food is like when it is served free of charge to all children. Here, I was able to interview both local and national officials and school food activists and to eat school meals in Stockholm, Uppsala, Gnesta, and Malmoe.

These interviews were transcribed, and excerpts from them appear throughout this book. Any direct quotation not otherwise attributed can be assumed to have come from my interviews.

I have tried, of course, to keep up with the burgeoning literature on school food, and I quickly became aware that the United States Department of Agriculture, which administers the NSLP, the SBP, and a host of other child nutrition programs, has spent literally millions of dollars funding large-scale studies in an effort to assess the health and other impacts of school food and to evaluate a series of pilot programs addressed to everything from new approaches to menu planning to alternate methods of determining eligibility. I am almost overwhelmed by the amount of data that has been collected and analyzed, and I have tried my best to absorb it and incorporate it into my work. Much of it is first-rate, well presented and clear, and it represents just the sort of random sample–based research that permits generalizations with a degree of certainty that I could never attach to my own more impressionistic approach. On the other hand, the scale of these studies is sometimes a deterrent to their use. USDA is not unresponsive to this problem of data overload: each study begins with an executive summary, and most are later boiled down into "issue briefs" that distill the highlights. Further, the Economic Research Service, a branch of USDA, has issued an extremely helpful overview of recent studies.[25] I, for one, am grateful. Nevertheless, as you will see in chapters 4 and 7 of this book, I wonder if there may not be something a bit off kilter here: this much investment in measurement is often a signal that a program is falling short of expectations.

Needless to say, USDA is not the only entity generating research on school food. At the request of Congress, the Government Accountability Office has produced dozens of studies. The inspectors general of the USDA and of several of the state agencies that administer these programs at the state level have been busy. The NFSMI sponsors extensive studies. Several academic and professional journals regularly carry research on school meals. And in the wake of the rising national concern about childhood obesity, several major foundations have been promoting research and study. School food research has become a small industry in its own right.

Two other sources of data that have proven important were more accidental in nature. I wish I could say that I foresaw their utility and built them into my research design, but that would not be quite accurate. The first is a series of "school lunch memories" written for me by college undergraduates at five different academic institutions. It started as a classroom assignment at the University of California, Santa Cruz where I spent my last sabbatical. The responses I received from my students there were so instructive that they became a major factor in my decision to undertake this research. And once I made that decision, a colleague generously offered to distribute a brief questionnaire in her much larger class. This only whetted my appetite, and when I returned to Hunter College of the City University of New York, where I have taught for the past thirty-three years, I began asking my students for a paragraph or two of school food memories as a "writing sample," early in the term. "Writing samples" are a hedge against plagiarism and a means of spotting students who should be referred to the college's writing center for extra help. It has taken me a long while to write this book, and I teach many large classes, so I have, literally, hundreds of these brief memoirs. Students at the University of Pennsylvania, the University of Rhode Island, and Gustavus Adolphus College in Minnesota also completed brief questionnaires for me, full of insight, humor, and information. Since schools draw their students from a variety of hometowns, the school meals thus recalled represent at least twenty-nine states and every conceivable type of American school and community.

A second "accidental" resource for understanding school food began when I mentioned to a youthful friend that I had added an "alert" for school lunch to the alerts for "hunger," "poverty" and "obesity" that I had placed on my online subscription to the *New York Times*. "Oh, just put one on Google," he suggested. (I think it was Margaret Mead who pointed out that in societies characterized by rapid technological change, the young must instruct their elders.) I put two on Google, one for school lunch and one for school breakfast, and every day, ever since, Google has delivered to my desktop at least two and often half a dozen or more links to newspaper articles and television and radio reports that discuss school lunch and breakfast. Occasionally, they are irrelevant—they simply have "school" and "breakfast" in the same article as with an article on a civic organization's pancake breakfast at which a school official has spoken. But most of them are articles about developments in school food—about the need to raise lunch prices to keep pace with soaring costs of fuel and milk or the local school board's decision to contract out the operation of the program to a private food service management company, or to terminate such an arrangement and go back to self-operation. Many have concerned the initiation of prepayment plans and the subsequent controversies over what to do when children's accounts run out of money. Sadly, there are regular stories about automobile accidents involving students from "open" campuses rushing back to school after leaving for lunch at the fast food restaurant or gas station convenience store. An enormous number of reports have dealt with efforts to upgrade the quality of school food and reduce its fat content, especially after the institution of the wellness policy requirement. As I was writing this, there were dozens about the big beef recall. It has been an extraordinary window on these programs as they are perceived by journalists all across America. Unfortunately, I have no way of knowing the basis for their selection, so you will not find in these pages a formal analysis of the shifting content or many generalizations based on this flood of local accounts. I feel I have my finger on the pulse, but I cannot prove it.

Finally, I have found, as I almost always do, that I needed to understand the history of these programs in order to make sense out of the policies that govern them. Therefore a final type of research reflected here is historical and archival. Some of it comes from research I did long ago for my doctoral dissertation and later a book on food assistance in the Great Depression, *Breadlines Knee Deep in Wheat* (1986). And some of it comes from the Child Nutrition Archive at the NFSMI at the University of Mississippi, and from the remarkable collection of historical materials available online through the HEARTH project (the Home Economics Archive: Research, Tradition, and History, Cornell University Library) and other online documents collections.

This research has been a journey, an odyssey in many senses of the word: through space, and cyberspace, through time and through a remarkable and growing literature. You may remember from ninth-grade English that an odyssey is a journey of discovery through unfamiliar territory, fraught with challenges and leading, eventually, back to its starting place. It takes you back home, though both the home and the traveler are very much changed by the time of the homecoming. I realized how much I had been changed—how much I had learned—when I arrived, a bit breathless and trailing luggage, at my afternoon fieldwork seminar at Hunter College one day in March. A plane had been delayed by heavy snowfall in Vermont, and my suitcase evoked the obvious question from my students of where I had been. I had barely started to describe my research on school food when one of my students interrupted. She straightened her shoulders, drew herself up to her full height, and sniffed: "I don't know why they don't just feed them healthier food; it wouldn't have to cost more." As I began to explain some of the complexities and barriers, I was struck by an echo of my own voice; her pronouncement sounded a lot like my thoughts when I began this project, a lot like what many people assume. I have returned home from my journey a wiser critic. I have not surrendered the vision of healthy, nutritious, appetizing, and instructive meals for all our children, but I have come to understand a great deal about what would be necessary to produce them. A central task of this book is to explain the realities of school food and the obstacles to its improvement.

THE PLAN OF THE BOOK

Early in the research process, I arranged to spend a week working in a school kitchen and cafeteria in a small city in the northeastern part of the United States. I hoped it would provide me with enough understanding of the day-to-day mechanics of running a school food program and of the job of preparing and serving school meals that I would be able to ask useful and insightful questions when I began my interviewing. It proved to be, in every way, more stimulating, revealing, and exhausting than I had imagined possible. Chapter 1, "School Food 101," is an account of that week and, through it, an introduction to the basic parameters of the National School Lunch and School Breakfast programs.

My week in the kitchen and cafeteria raised many questions for me, particularly about aspects of public policy that I think most insiders to the world of school food service take for granted. That is one of the values of the "outsider's eye." I turned to history for an explanation: how did the programs get this way? Chapter 2 is a brief history of school food in the United States; it provides a very limited sketch of the origins of the program up through the passage of the National School Lunch act in 1946 and then looks at a series of "wars" that changed the program, sometimes dramatically, from a modest program serving about seven million children on an average day and costing the federal government less than $100 million a year to a pair of programs that serves forty million meals a day and costs some $11 billion a year.

A great deal of the criticism that now surrounds school food, especially in the context of the concern about children's health, is leveled at the menu. Chapter 3 provides an overview of the forces and factors that shape what is served in schools and how it is prepared. If you are reading this book because you are concerned about the food in your own community or your own school, you probably want to know whether or not school food is nutritious. Chapter 4 looks at the massive body of research that has been done to answer this question and raises some questions of its own, both about our ability to measure what we really want to know and about the impact of so much measurement itself.

For school food service operators, participation is the "proof of the pudding," the final measure of how well they are doing. Chapter 5 looks at the reasons why children who have access to school meals frequently choose not to eat them, including not only issues of meal quality and price but also cafeteria conditions and scheduling and other factors that contribute to the "dining experience." Chapter 6 returns to hunger, the issue that drew me to school food in the first place, and tries to understand why some children in need cannot get meals at school. This necessitates explaining why some schools resist offering the programs, as well as understanding the ways in which the eligibility requirements for families interact with contemporary economic realities and the process by which eligibility is established and verified. Chapter 7 looks at the stigma conferred by the three-tier system and the "administrative absurdity" of maintaining this eligibility protocol. It explores the limits and potentials of the efforts that policy makers and schools have made to fix this broken system.

Chapter 8 looks at projects that are bubbling up around the country to improve the quality of school meals and increase effective access and considers the limits of such local action.

When I undertook this project, I assumed that by the time I finished, I would have a useful "answer" or prescription for school food programs, but fixing them is not as simple as I had imagined. By the time I was done, I had become convinced that a thorough overhaul, not just an incremental reform, is needed. The conclusion, "School Food at the Crossroads" poses a series of questions that I think citizens, policy makers, and school food professionals must confront if school food is ever to realize its full potential to promote the health, learning, and well-being of our children, and presents my own vision of a school food program that could accomplish its mission.

I believe that the challenge of fixing school food is urgent. For all my misgivings about linking school food reform to concerns about overweight, something that Dr. Terry Shintani said to me early in the course of this research keeps coming back to me. Dr. Shintani, a lawyer, physician, nutritionist, and author of *The Hawaii Diet* (1977) has had considerable success treating morbidly obese native Hawaiians by prescribing an eating plan based on the traditional foods of the Hawaiian culture. I interviewed him because I was looking into some Hawaiian-language immersion schools that were trying to integrate taro, the islands' ancient staple crop, into their school lunch programs and their curricula. After explaining that native Hawaiians have some genetic predisposition toward obesity and that poverty and discrimination have intensified the problem, he said something that changed the way I think about diet and health. "I think that what is happening to the native Hawaiians is an exaggeration of what is happening to everybody. . . . You have the human species eating whole, unprocessed food for millennia, and then in the last century or so, starting to eat sugar, white flour, refined oils, high-fat meats. And you don't expect anything to go wrong? That means that's a very poor understanding of what health really is." Eating habits, he declared, are at the root of most of our major health problems, and school food programs have the power to reinforce or to help change unhealthy and destructive eating patterns.[26]

I asked Dr. Shintani what school meals would look like in Hawaii if they followed the principles of the Hawaii Diet. "They would be mainly whole, unprocessed," he said. "They would have no deep-fried foods. . . . I'm not saying don't use any oils or sugars or white flour, but keep that to a minimum and focus on whole, unprocessed foods. And limit the animal products. Provide plant-based alternatives for those who want a vegetarian diet. Get all the sugar drinks out of the schools. They have no business being there. And base it on traditional foods from many cultures so that they learn the use of beans and brown rice and lentils and soy-based protein products. The school system," he concluded, "needs a lot of work, but if you can do it, you can make a lot of positive impact, because now you're teaching a generation. But you cannot base the school lunch program on what is the cheapest and what's the easiest to get them to eat. That is a recipe for obesity."

A decade ago, had I told friends that I was writing a book on school food, I can only imagine that I would have encountered stifled yawns or polite nods, quickly followed by attempts to change the subject. My colleagues in the anti-hunger community would have understood; they know that school food represents a central component of the nation's food assistance safety net, an essential bulwark against childhood hunger. And of course school food service professionals and public health nutritionists would have grasped the import. For most people, however, school food was just "there," taken for granted, a magnet for jokes and standard-issue grumbling. It appeared to merit the proverbial analogy to the weather: everybody complained about it but no one did anything about it. Today, however, people in many communities *are* trying to do something about it. As an article in *Family Circle* in 2006 put it, "In living rooms and lunch rooms, in meeting halls and school kitchens, there's a quiet revolution going on. . . . Parents are banding together to make sure kids eat healthy at school."[27] Marion Nestle, author of, among other books, *Food Politics* and *What to Eat,* has labeled this "a major national movement."[28]

This book is not so much a work *about* this quiet revolution as it is an attempt to empower it. In my initial conversations and interviews, early in this process, I was struck by how little many school food activists at the local level seemed to know about the National School Lunch and School Breakfast programs. These are the programs, after all, that provide the resources upon which the vast majority of local programs depend, and in the spirit of "he who pays the piper calls the tune," these are the programs whose rules constrain local food service operators. Thus I have tried to make the "big picture" of the national programs visible and comprehensible. Similarly, I have been impressed by the failure of public policies and reforms, including some of those initiated by USDA and some urged by activists, to reflect local realities "on the ground." Thus, I have also tried to make visible the "little picture" of the day-to-day lived experience of school meals as communicated to me by students and cafeteria personnel. I hope that these two approaches will combine to make a clearer picture of these vital programs and thus help the innovators and the reformers and the parents and the staff and the Congress members and the administrators to join forces to give our children the school food programs they need and deserve.

CHAPTER ONE

SCHOOL FOOD 101

My odyssey began in a kitchen, specifically, the kitchen of a high school cafeteria in a small city in a large northeastern state. I'll call it Any Town High School, or Any Town HS.[1] I arrived at the back door of the school's cafeteria at 7:00 A.M. on a cool October morning. The cafeteria manager looked at me quizzically when I introduced myself, then remembered: "Oh, yes, we have you this week." The district food service director had agreed to let me volunteer in the kitchen in order to observe the day-to-day realities of preparing and serving school food. In the school food hierarchy, the food service director is the boss, often reporting directly to the district superintendent, so the manager was stuck with me. She showed me where to stow my pocketbook and issued me a bright red apron while I vowed silently to make myself useful. I wanted them to be sorry, not glad, when I left at the end of the week.

FOOD PREP

The manager asked me what I wanted to do. I had decided not to hide my reason for being there, but not to carry on about it either. I wanted to fit in. I had invested in a pair of white uniform-style trousers and a white shirt and was relieved to learn that no hair net is required if your hair is short, as mine is, or confined. I explained that I was doing some research on school meals and just needed to get a feel for the work so that I would know what sorts of questions to ask when I interviewed food service workers. I told her that my experience in large-volume food production was limited to soup kitchens, and I needed to know what a typical work day was like in a school cafeteria.

She put me to work chopping celery for a tuna salad she was making: don surgical gloves, remove the leaves, put the stalks through the chopper, throw out the hearts because they are too small for the machine. The tuna salad was not for the students, however; it was for a catered lunch "down at the [school] bus garage." Catering school district and community events is one way that the Any Town food service department strives to break even. Every little bit helps. Catering, as the director had explained, is a way to get more use from the space and equipment, absorb any down time of staff or provide them with extra income through additional hours, and keep the food service department on the radar screen of district decision makers. They cater only school system–related events: school board meetings, awards dinners, faculty meetings, though some districts also prepare food for senior centers or child care programs.

When I finished the celery, the manager suggested that I go help Lila, the chief cook, who is in her seventies and has worked in Any Town HS food service for forty-one years. "Are you supposed to help me?" she asked skeptically, her tone betraying a decided lack of enthusiasm for the arrangement. I nodded, and she said that I could lay out pizza. You get a stack of trays and a stack of parchment paper, you put a piece of paper on a tray. The pizza, frozen, is in a box in segments composed of four triangular slices each, which need to be separated. She wants eight slices arranged in a circle at the top of the tray, with four pepperoni pieces added to each, and four slices across the bottom, separated but undecorated, a 2:1 ratio of pepperoni to plain. Once a tray is complete, it goes into a slot in a 6-foot-tall wheeled metal rolling rack, one tray in every other slot. I picked up speed as I went along, 12 trays of 12 slices = 144 slices. Pizza is an option every day on the high school menu; the middle school and elementary kids get it only when it is specifically on the official federally reimbursable school lunch menu. A single kitchen at Any Town HS prepares meals for the high school and for an elementary school in the same complex. The middle school prepares food for its own students and for an elementary school across town—called a "satellite" arrangement. Another elementary school has its own kitchen and cafeteria. Menus are planned centrally.

While I was disassembling and reassembling the pizza, Lila and her assistant, Laura, laid out hundreds of beef patties, also on parchment sheets. They said the beef was a USDA commodity that had been "sent out" for processing, in this case conversion to uniform frozen patties. Commodities are foods purchased by the federal government, sometimes in conjunction with price support operations, and donated to schools participating in the National School Lunch program. The option to have commodities processed externally and the more recent option to exchange the federal commodities for products already in the hands of the processors have gone a long way toward quieting the complaints of school food workers about federal commodity donations. These changes are welcome at Any Town HS, because maximum use of donated commodities is another essential component of the district's strategy for breaking even. Once Lila and Laura were done with the beef, they opened large white plastic bags of chicken nuggets and others of a reformulated potato product similar to Tater Tots (let's call them potato puffs), also a USDA commodity, and spread these out on parchment sheets on trays. Then we did pretzels; they come frozen raw in boxes. I laid them out (on a parchment sheet, of course), Laura brushed them with melted margarine, and I sprinkled on rock salt. Two boxes' worth (six trays) were laid out in this way, and another two trays were laid out but not brushed and salted; Laura explained that if they didn't need them and had to refreeze them they would freeze poorly if the salt had already been applied; they would add it later if there was demand for more pretzels. The pretzels are for sale in the a la carte line, another essential element in the break-even plan.

When we were done; I looked at the clock, feeling ready for lunch. It was only 9:15, but that is break time; I had a sausage-and-egg croissant left over from the a la carte items sold at breakfast. Lila had a chocolate chip cookie; she and Laura discussed their weekend, and she told us about gathering hickory nuts. It was a good year for nuts; none of us knew why. Black walnuts were also available, but they are very hard on your fingers, Lila said. Hickory nuts have to be cracked with a hammer. After the break, I helped make some sandwiches and set up the serving line, and then it *was* lunchtime.

LUNCHTIME

The first shift begins at 10:03, with four lunch periods of forty-five minutes each—generous by national standards, for the national mean is just over half an hour, and the most typical starting time, nationally, is 11:00 A.M.[2] I helped Rita on one of the two lines that served the official school lunch. Frankly, I don't see how she can do it on her own. Simultaneously, she has to serve the kids, manage the line behavior, and keep the line stocked. Serving is the simplest. That day we had hamburgers, cheeseburgers, plain and pepperoni pizza, and chicken nuggets, any of which could be served with potato puffs. The kids kept asking if the puffs were "free," meaning were they part of the lunch offered for free to eligible children, and she kept assuring them that they were—the published menu for the day had listed french fries, but the fryer was down, so potato puffs were a last minute substitution. Rolls went with the hamburgers, cheeseburgers, and chicken nuggets. The server, standing behind the steam table and wearing surgical gloves, uses scoops to measure out potato puffs and tongs to place the youngsters' choices on their hardened plastic tray-plates. Managing the line is an art. Rita, who works before and after lunch as a bus monitor, kept the kids in order— she did not allow any bad language and was diligent about ejecting any kids who were not in line to buy. She was brusque with them, but gracious about complying with requests—several times she had to stop completely to make a sandwich (tuna), an offering which was available but not prepared ahead, or to fetch a pretzel with cheese sauce from the neighboring a la carte line.

Keeping the hot foods stocked is the hardest part. All the while that we were serving, Laura and Lila were busy cooking additional trays of potato puffs, nuggets, pizza, and burgers. There are two ovens—one at 400 degrees and one at 350 degrees—and they have finite capacity. When food is removed from the oven, it goes to the warmer. Restocking the steam table involves going to the warmer, donning potholders, opening the warmer, which is awkwardly located in the doorway between two lines, removing an enormous tray of whatever, finding a place to balance it while you close the warmer, bringing the tray to the line, emptying its contents into the proper receptacle, and then finding a place for the tray—a place where no one is working or needs to work. If there is space by Belinda, the dishwasher, you can put the tray there, but you must cry out "hot" or "caliente" so she knows it's still hot. Some of my temporary colleagues demonstrated an admirable hip-swinging technique for closing the warmer door—the trickiest part of the process—but it looked downright dangerous to me. (The second line, overseen by Delia, was much closer to the warmer and had a row of counters behind it where reserve items could be stored within reach, making it easier to manage.)

After completing their hot food selection, students had a choice among fruit items—an orange or apple, a box of raisins, a cup of trail mix, or a cup of canned peaches—and they were offered several types of milk in half-pint cartons; then they moved on to a cashier. The cashiers have perhaps the most complex job in the cafeteria. Each lunch must be checked to see that it qualifies for reimbursement and then assigned to the free, reduced price, or full price category so the school can claim the correct amount of federal dollars.

As noted in the introduction, children whose family income falls below 130 percent of the federal poverty line qualify for free lunches; those whose family income is between 130 percent and 185 percent of the poverty line qualify for a reduced price lunch, for which Any Town HS charges $0.40. The rest pay what is called "full price," although these meals too are subsidized by the federal government and in some cases by the states. The cashier tells me that she knows all of the nearly five hundred children by sight and can look up their status on a master list if she is not sure. In order to protect the privacy of the children, she is not allowed to ask their status within earshot of other children. Some children purchase a prepaid 20-meal ticket for reduced or full price lunch, from which she must deduct each lunch consumed, so going through the line without paying does not necessarily mean that the child is eating free. Some pay cash on the spot. Some supplement the official reimbursable meal with items for sale at checkout, especially the freshly baked chocolate chip cookies, the aroma of which began driving me to distraction shortly after I arrived.

In order to be eligible for federal reimbursement, meals have to meet certain federal nutrition standards. Any Town HS uses the food-based approach to menu planning. A complete meal includes meat or a meat alternate such as cheese, beans, or peanut butter (i.e., a protein source); a grain product like bread, rice, or pasta; at least one serving of vegetables; a serving of fruit or a second vegetable; and a serving of milk. Under a policy called "offer versus serve," introduced in the late 1970s to reduce plate waste, a meal must contain at least three of the five components of the federal "meal pattern" in order to qualify for reimbursement. Partial reimbursement for a partial meal is not an option. Chicken nuggets (meat or meat equivalent) and french fries (vegetable) and milk constitute a reimbursable meal; so do a hamburger roll (grain product), french fries (vegetable), and a serving of canned peaches (fruit), though happily, I did not see anyone select that particular meal. Occasionally, the cashier sends a student back to get another item in order to make the meal qualify. Schools not using the food-based menu planning system may use one of several variants of "Nutrient Standard Menu Planning," in which a computer-based analysis checks menus for the requisite nutrients and fat content. In Nutrient Standard (or "NuMenu"), students may refuse up to two of the offered categories of items, but must include an entree. Under either plan, the cashier becomes both the enforcer and the crucial locus of accountability; it does not seem an exaggeration to say that the cashier has replaced the cook as the most important job in the cafeteria.

The a la carte line is on the other side of the cashier, more a window than a counter. Students there paid cash for their selections, which included all of the items we were serving in the federally reimbursable lunch, plus nachos with melted cheese sauce, pretzels (also served with melted cheese), ice cream, cookies, and a variety of beverages. The a la carte line was a constant hive of activity; it is often the longest of the cafeteria's three lines. If students happen to select a set of components that equals the official lunch, they are sold that meal, or that portion of their meal, at the appropriately subsidized price and counted as "participating" in the National School Lunch Program in the day's tally. It is important to the financial health of the operation to capture these meals, as they increase the "average daily participation" (or ADP) upon which commodity allocations are based.

In each 45-minute lunch period, after the line of students has dwindled, we keep an eye out for stragglers but also start getting ready for the next batch: refilling ketchup dispensers and mayonnaise and mustard dishes, checking on the supply of salad dressing, which is offered in big dispenser bottles with small cups for taking away. The kids use enormous quantities of ketchup! There is perpetual cleaning up. Not only the steam table itself, but also the shelf on which the students' trays rest and even the glass "sneeze guards" get wiped down. Any spare minute is devoted to some form of preparation for the next serving period. The last lunch period (from 12:31 to 1:16) is lighter than the others. As soon as the line has subsided, clean-up begins, although the line must remain open until the period is over. There is also lots of prepping for the next day—refilling various condiments, getting a head start on tomorrow's tasks. With another worker I bagged baby carrots for the next day's kindergartners. We were using the little sandwich bags that have a stitched-down fold at the top (not zip lock, not twist tie). The idea was to place six baby carrots in a bag, roll it up, then sort of flip it under the prepared flap. I never mastered this technique in a good fifty tries, all my advanced degrees irrelevant, but in the odd moments available among the immediate demands of the line, we bagged two boxes of carrots. We were ready!

I left at the end of the day—2:30 P.M.—completely exhausted. I hated to admit it, but the nonstop pace far exceeded my normal level of exertion. When I got home, I went directly to bed, still in my work clothes, and slept for two hours. I woke up perplexed. How could so much work at such a furious pace produce a meal that I found neither particularly appealing nor especially healthy? The appeal issue is obviously debatable. I do not fit the profile of the customer the program is trying to serve. In general, the students seemed satisfied with the food, though to me, it both smelled and looked greasy. I was not surprised when Lila told me her grandson, who attends the school, brings his lunch from home. The nutrition issue, however, goes far beyond the preferences of students to the question of the potential of the school lunch program to help improve health in general and reduce obesity and diabetes in particular.

There were healthy choices available at Any Town HS. A quiet young woman spent part of the morning preparing lovely fresh garden salads topped with grilled chicken. I was heartened by the inclusion of this healthy option until I spent the lunch period on Rita's line. I'm sure we went through at least seventy-five students before even one selected the salad. We had dispensed about three to students by the end of the day, and several faculty members bought them. The most popular lunch that first day appeared to be pizza with potato puffs, followed by chicken nuggets and potato puffs. I was impressed by the amount of effort and the easy, dependable cooperation among staff, and amazed by the pace, but I went home my first day disheartened that so much effort could produce food which falls so far from the nutrition goals that are increasingly urged on Americans.

BREAKFAST FIRST

Lunch is not the only meal prepared and served at Any Town HS. One of the reasons I selected the Any Town school system for my immersion course in school food was that it had recently begun an innovative breakfast-in-the-classroom program. The program makes use of a provision in the law that permits schools to serve meals free of charge to all children and obtain their federal reimbursements based on the school's ratio of meals served free, reduced price, and full price in a base year. The Any Town schools were offering breakfasts free to all children: universal free school breakfasts. I had had an opportunity to observe this program on my first visit to the school system, before arranging to volunteer there, and I had been very impressed. I watched kindergartners and first and second graders at an elementary school help their teachers unpack the plastic milk crates of breakfast foods and sit down with juice, milk, cereal, and a wrapped square of cheese. The cheese was necessary, the director explained, because the individual boxes of cereal were only one ounce, and the federal breakfast "meal pattern" specifies two ounces of grain/bread and/or meat/meat alternative. On days that a 2-ounce fortified pastry is served, no cheese square is included. The rooms were calm and quiet and the children appeared to relish the food. In one classroom of slightly older children, perhaps fourth grade, a child came to the door and said that the teacher was not there yet, but I saw that the children had unpacked and distributed the food and were eating, chatting, and doing homework.

I had seen films of universal free breakfast in the classroom, and I had read about it, but I had never actually visited such a classroom before, and I had come prepared for a certain amount of noise, mess, and disorder. It seemed a small price to pay to make sure that children got something nourishing to eat at the start of the school day. My expectations of noise and disorder proved to be unfounded. Advocates have been claiming for years that breakfast in the classroom produces a calm, nurturing launch to the school day, and in the case of Any Town Elementary School, at least on the day that I visited, their claims were born out.

Once I began working in the high school kitchen, I had a chance to take a closer look at the supply side of the operation. I went in early on my second day and helped Hillary prepare the breakfasts for distribution. This is essentially a process of counting and bagging. To pack the allocation for each classroom, tear a big clear plastic bag from the roll in the dispenser, turn it so that the seam is toward you, write the room number on it in magic marker, and consult the master list to see how many children are in that classroom. Put the designated number of items for that room in the bag, add a handful of napkins and a handful of straws—for those, Hillary said, "We don't count, we estimate." Tie up the bag and put it on the counter, organized by room number, grouped by grade. A bit later someone will add the bags to egg crates that have been packed with the requisite number of juices and milks, and load them onto a dolly to be wheeled to the elementary school which adjoins the high school.

The item for the day was minipancakes, six small round disks sealed in a wrapper. They are served without syrup or butter—the sweetener is built in and like almost everything in the breakfast program, they are designed to be eaten without utensils. "The kids don't like these. They won't eat them," Hillary told me.

"Can you tell the director not to order them?" I asked.

"We did it ourselves," she replied. "He isn't always around. We stopped them." Later the cafeteria manager told me that they had indeed stopped ordering them, but they still had commitments through October so they couldn't stop serving them until the beginning of November.

"What can you use instead?" I asked Hillary. "What do the kids like?"

"Cereal," she said. That's their favorite, but we can't do it every day."

"Is that a USDA regulation?"

"No, but I just don't have the time. If you do cereal, you have to do cheese squares, and that's double the counting, because the cereal is not enough ounces. I'm only one person."

Any Town uses a packaged, fortified pastry about four days per week. Shelf stability and individual serving packages are important in the choice of the pastry items. The food service director is pleased with the fortified products available; on the morning of my first visit, he showed me a "super donut" that was thawing out for use the next day: "Here, you can see how it says it's a good source, highly fortified with protein and everything else like that. You'll see the fat percentage is up, but it's the good fat that they're supposed to have, because 30 percent of all nutrient comes from fat." The USDA regulations actually specify that no *more* than 30 percent of calories should come from fat in a given week, a ceiling, not a goal, but I was there to learn, not to instruct. I bit my tongue. Some teachers have raised questions about the fat content, but the director says that every time a teacher or someone else reads the label and objects, "I say '30 percent of all nutrient comes from fat.'" He chants it, like a mantra. "You have to have the right fat and you should have 30 percent in your diet," he insists. A principal later told me that many of her faculty are members of Weight Watchers and initially judged the breakfast products from that perspective.

Another reason for the director's enthusiasm for the super donut and other fortified breakfast pastries was their extended shelf life. This surfaced in our discussion of how the meals are counted for reimbursement purposes. Unclaimed items like boxes of juice, cereal, or milk were to be returned to the kitchen for use another day. The pastries, however, are a different story. Each represents two of the required four components of a reimbursable breakfast, and under offer versus serve, a child must select a total of at least three for the meal to count. Because the pastries are individually wrapped and relatively shelf-stable, he explained, he could encourage teachers to keep them in the classroom. "This item here," he said, pointing to the super donut, "we don't want this back, because then it's not a qualified breakfast, so we want them to take it and have it or hopefully keep it and hold onto it. The share table could use it. A milk or a juice, if they don't take it, they still have the three components, but this equals two components." In other words, any pastry returned to the kitchen means that some child did not have a reimbursable meal; these must be counted and subtracted from the totals sent to the classroom in order to determine how many meals have been served, and thus the total federal reimbursement for the day.

Shelf stability is also a factor in the selection of milk products. Any Town schools now purchase a shelf-stable sweetened, fortified milk product that has 25 percent more protein and calcium than regular milk. The director said he would prefer to see the children drinking regular unsweetened reduced-fat milk, but

> it is a trade-off, we do make trades. . . . When I first started with the regular milk, even in the elementary, I was getting a couple hundred back. I went to chocolate milk. Because when I first started, I went total holistic, let's just have 2 percent white, every day of the week. Well, I was foolish. It didn't take. No matter how long I left it, I was throwing it out in the dumpster. Then I went to chocolate every day except cereal day. And put some white in there for those that still want white, and we found the ratio that worked. We dropped down to about a hundred returns out of about six hundred breakfasts going out. Then we went to shelf-stable milk, and we went down to days when we weren't getting any back, because they're sweet and there's the flavoring. With the shelf-stable milk, I don't have to throw it out, whereas before I was throwing it out. . . . Anything that's shelf-stable goes back into operation for the next day.

Initially, many teachers had expected that "breakfast in the classroom" would take away from needed instructional time. In order to check out teacher reaction, I visited the smaller elementary school, which I'll call Any Town Little School, where the program had begun with a pilot project a year earlier. The food service director chose that school because he knew the principal was concerned about the nutrition of her mostly low-income pupils, and because the school's relatively small size made it ideal for a pilot. If it failed, the monetary loss would be minimized. I observed the breakfast one morning, interviewed the principal, conducted an anonymous survey of the ten teachers who had homerooms with breakfast, and several weeks later, interviewed two teachers who agreed to talk with me. The results were mixed. The principal and most of the teachers surveyed believed that the program had been successful in increasing concentration and alertness during the morning hours and in reducing tardiness, morning visits to the nurse's office, and morning disciplinary actions. Nine of the ten teachers surveyed reported positive benefits of this sort. Interestingly, this included teachers who identified themselves on the questionnaire as having been "moderately opposed" or "neutral" toward the idea when it was introduced. Only the teacher who identified herself as having been "adamantly opposed" reported none of these benefits. As the director put it, when I asked him about teacher attitudes, "the fence sitters have all come over." The principal had figures to back up the claims of reduced disciplinary actions and fewer nurses visits. Nurses visits had declined, in fact, from more than fifty in September of the year before the program started to less than a dozen in September of the pilot year. Tardiness had been cut in half, and the principal, who recalls having been "inundated" by morning disciplinary referrals, now has almost none at all. Breakfast in the classroom seems to settle the children down and help them get along. Of the ten teachers who filled out my brief questionnaire, all but three became more positive about the program after it was actually implemented, and those three included one teacher who had been enthusiastic at the start and remained enthusiastic; only two expressed significant disappointment compared to their expectations.

The Any Town Little School teachers were unanimous, however, in their concern about the food. All ten respondents took time to fill in an open-ended question asking how the program could be improved. One suggested "faculty and student input into the breakfast selections," and two focused on the need for variety and the request for more hot items. All the rest asked for healthier food, either in general or with specific prescriptions; "breakfast should have more protein and less sugar and fat," or "more fruit and low-fat products" were typical comments. The other common complaint was about the temperature at which food arrived—the pancakes and pastries were often cold, even still partially frozen, and the juice was "always frozen solid." The overall image reflected in the questionnaires was one of considerable enthusiasm tempered by a general dislike for the menu.

My two interviews with teachers provided more detail—and more passion. While one teacher liked the fortified super donuts and similar items, the other characterized them as "starch on wheels." She taught older children, fifth and sixth grade, and she reported that her pupils remembered the substantial hot breakfasts that had been sold in the cafeteria (and offered free to those who were eligible) before the universal program came in: egg and ham on a roll, french toast, breakfast pizza, hot breakfasts.

> We get none of that now. We have no warmer for our food. The children are getting two loaves to three loaves of bread per week, . . . apple cinnamon bread or blueberry . . . . They get a donut hole or a very dry donut one day a week. And some weeks we do get cereal . . . and other weeks we don't. It's delivered to us with whatever kind of milk they choose for the day, so you may get chocolate milk with your cereal. The older kids, my kids, are totally incensed by this whole thing—they want white milk with their cereal, and they want a little bit of choice. There are kids that don't like Froot Loops, you know.

She said that the poor quality of the food had reached "the point now where it aggravates me. . . . I don't like to have something in my life every day that I don't approve of. You can't fool kids; they know what's going on, that this is a cheap shot. They're old enough to remember real hot breakfasts, and it's bothersome to them. It's like another promise not kept."

It happens that I had asked the director and the principal how they would change the breakfast program if money were not so tight. The aggravated teacher might have been glad to know that their wish list parallels her own. The director told me:

> Oh, then I could, if money wasn't an issue, there's many products, eggs on muffins that are all done, individually wrapped. Because it goes to the classroom, I do like everything to be wrap-sealed, vacuum sealed, for safety (and nutrition), for shelf life. There's a whole variety of products. We could serve fresh fruit daily because I wouldn't have to so much worry about the cost of it—you know, fresh fruit is a changing item daily, the cost of fruit. Juices, I could offer more variety of juices. We could possibly, with the right transport equipment, we could possibly send a variety of items, and the students could be choosing at the classroom, and then we take back everything so we wouldn't lose it.

MONEY VS. NUTRITION

In the breakfast program, as well as the lunch, the struggle to break even drives the menu. As a "severe need" district, Any Town was entitled to a government reimbursement of $1.58 for each free breakfast and $1.18 for each reduced price breakfast. As noted, however, the district simply offers the meals free to all children and then obtains reimbursements based on the proportions of meals served in the free, reduced price, and full price categories in the base year. Given the district's percentage of students eligible for free and reduced price meals, the director estimated that he needed to keep the per meal cost for breakfast down to $0.65 in order to break even. No wonder shelf-stable items that could be "recycled" were attractive, and staff time for extra preparation work is scarce.

My stint in the Any Town HS cafeteria left me a bit dazed and not a little troubled. Like the teachers at Any Town Little School, I was concerned about nutrition—about the healthiness of the foods served. I wasn't happy with the lunch menu. I'm not so much talking about the published menu, which appears to embody a fairly wide range of choices, but the de facto menu created by the practice of offering pizza as an alternative every day. I like pizza, and I think that a slice of pizza and a salad constitute a pretty healthy lunch. But pizza and potato puffs, the most frequently chosen lunch on my first day at the cafeteria? Or pizza and fries, a popular choice on my last day? A slice of pizza and a serving of french fries is a reimbursable lunch. The pizza satisfies the grain and protein components, and the fries are the vegetable. But from a common sense, everyday perspective, aren't potatoes too starchy to provide the needed balance? And don't fries, or even potato puffs, raise the fat content to an unacceptable level, especially since the pizza was "stuffed crust" pizza which carries extra fat in the cheese in its crust? Chicken nuggets and potato puffs didn't seem any better. The nuggets are coated with a bread-crumb-like surface, but technically, the nuggets must be served with a roll to provide the required serving of grains. So the resulting plate is monochromatic, often a signal of missing nutrients. I don't think one has to be caught up in a low carbohydrate mania to think that a lunch of breaded chicken nuggets, potatoes, and a roll is not nutritionally sound.

When I asked the food service director why he didn't pair the pizza with salad, he said, in essence, the students won't eat it. I expressed my concern about the potatoes, and he said "Potatoes have good nutrients; you have to take it, unfortunately, because in some cases, if you took out potatoes, the kids wouldn't get *any* nutrients." Over the course of the time I was there, we had a running conversation about what he saw as an imperative: the students are customers; you have to offer them what they will buy—and eat. If it sits on their trays or goes in the garbage, it delivers no nutrition at all. We had this conversation about sweetened cereals versus unsweetened in the breakfast program, and about french fries versus green vegetables in the federal lunch and chips versus fresh fruit on the a la carte line.

The director believed that students in a nearby upscale district would eat salads, but that most vegetables were a wasted effort at Any Town HS. "How your family eats is how your family eats," he declared. "If you don't eat that way at home, you're not going to eat that way at school, no matter how much we do." And what they are eating at home, he told me, is snack food and fast food. "Unfortunately, many kids don't eat vegetables at home. . . . The parents are bringing home McDonald's; they're not bringing home vegetables, because McDonald's doesn't really sell vegetables. Do you know when payday is, welfare check day?" he asked. He suggested that I go down to the local supermarket and stand by the register and look into the carts of families with children. Then I'd know what he was up against; he predicted that I'd be blown away by the percentage of "real pure crap food, low-end snacks." Now, I have a certain hostility to people who assess what is in other people's grocery carts—it comes from listening to food stamp program participants describe their feeling that people in checkout lines are always judging them, and generally by a double standard. Nevertheless, the exercise he recommended is one in which I suspect many of us have engaged since obesity and diabetes became public issues; I got his point.

It's not as if the Any Town food service director never tries to offer healthier foods. He told me a story that has remained lodged in my brain. "Recently, we got bottom round roast from the government. In one school, we made stew. In another school, we made pot roast, and in another school we made roast beef. . . . People wanted to know what pot roast was. They didn't touch the beef stew at all, even though it was delicious. It was homemade, from scratch. And the roast beef, even though it was cooked the same way as the pot roast, we put it on a sandwich and gave *au jus* to it. And that was the only one that was eaten, because they are accustomed to seeing roast beef out on the market, and it looked like an Arby's type sandwich. And unfortunately, that's reality." Still in pursuit of vegetables, I asked if there were many in the rejected stew. "Oh, it was unbelievably healthy. . . . Using the same pot roast recently, we made a homemade soup, a beef soup we made from scratch with local produce, we got it from the local farmers, we even had a student help make it as part of an enrichment program that he's working in with one of our employees. And it was tastier than any soup out there, any commercial soup you could buy, but yet it didn't go very well."

You would have to listen to my tape recording and hear the frustration and discouragement in his voice to get the full impact of this statement. I came away from that conversation with a strong sense that the nutritional well being of the school children of Any Town was being held hostage by an enormous catch-22. The director believed that the children were not eating fresh vegetables, whole grains, and other especially healthy foods at home, and he believed that they would not eat at school what they were not accustomed to from home. He may well have been right about what many students were eating at home, but I have seen enough instances of students from low-income communities enjoying salad bars to take issue with his assessments. Even if he was not correct in one or both of these beliefs, they shaped his actions and choices. As W.I. Thomas famously put the matter in 1928, in what came to be known as the Thomas Theorem, "If men define situations as real, they are real in their consequences."[3] That is, if school food service directors believe that children will not try unfamiliar foods at school, then menu planners will behave accordingly: the self-fulfilling prophecy. But there is more than ideology or pernicious belief at work here. There are structural problems built into the program that promote this outcome.

Even if the director wanted to impose more salads and vegetables on his charges, he probably couldn't under the current program rules. The offer versus serve approach, which is mandated by law for high schools and optional but in wide use in middle and elementary schools, means that students can always evade the veggies. On the Wednesday of my week at Any Town HS, when green beans were on the menu, I stood behind the counter and encouraged the students to try the beans. I smiled, I urged, I wheedled, and I estimate that I influenced the behavior of perhaps two students. At a more fundamental level, the a la carte line gives most students an alternative to the official lunch. Suppose the cafeteria were serving green salad and a stir fry with shrimp and vegetables as its sole choice. The a la carte line would provide all but the poorest students with a less healthy option. The impact of the a la carte line, however, goes far beyond providing students with an alternative on the days that they don't like the official lunch choices. It essentially puts the reimbursable lunch up against completely unregulated foods selected largely for their popularity with teenagers. A la carte sales are not subsidized by USDA, and they don't have to meet any federal nutrition standards other than avoiding the sale of a very short list of foods of minimal nutritional value, including gum, hard candies, sodas, and the like. To put it simply, the introduction of a la carte sales into school cafeterias has put the nutritionally regulated, federally subsidized official school lunch in competition with some of the least healthy food in America. With a la carte lines selling pizza and fries, is it any wonder that the official lunch offers pizza and fries?

So why continue the a la carte lines and other snack sales? Asking this question is an efficient way to identify yourself as an outsider among any group of school food service professionals. The Any Town director put it simply: "Without snacks, the lunch program couldn't survive; you couldn't break even." He gave me his numbers: "A couple of years ago, [the school board] raised the ceiling on what we could charge to $1.75. My lunches cost over $2.60 per meal when I figure out the cost. On a full-pay child, I'm getting $1.75 plus 27 or 28 cents from the government in per meal reimbursement, plus 14.9 cents per meal in commodities. So if you figure it out, it's not much over $2.00 for high schools." Where does he get the difference? "I have to generate that revenue through a la cartes. That's why it's a big issue, selling a la carte. We need to sell a la carte to be financially sound."

While the sales price for the official lunch is determined by the school board and subject to a variety of influences other than the need to break even, the a la carte line is a "free market." He can charge what the market will bear. Meanwhile, however, he needs to keep the free-lunch eligible students in the regular line. The federal reimbursement for a free lunch in a severe need district like Any Town in 2003, when the director gave me these figures, was $2.16 plus the 14.9 cents in commodities and a modest reimbursement from the state. If the food in the main line were completely different from the food in the a la carte line, however, then he would have a hard time maintaining participation in the official program even among students for whom it is free. So here is another catch-22 of major proportions. He cannot charge enough for the school lunch to cover the cost of producing it, so he must sell a la carte (and engage in catering when he can) to make up the difference. But if he sells a la carte, he sets up an informal standard with which the "official lunch" can be compared, and if there is too great a difference, he will lose participation in that program, defeating his fundamental purpose and eroding yet another crucial revenue stream. In short, the essentially unregulated a la carte service is calling the tune for the menu, and thus to a large extent the nutritional profile, of the National School Lunch Program.

Despite the similarities between the a la carte line and the "regular" lines, and despite the fact more students purchased full-price meals on the regular lines than were served free, the staff at Any Town HS are convinced that the fear of being labeled as poor deters many students eligible for free meals from obtaining them. On my second day at the school, when I realized that I really was superfluous on Delia's line, I decided to go out into the cafeteria dining area, which is not visible from the line itself, and see what school food at Any Town HS looked like from the other side. The cafeteria is a large rectangular room with long lines of rectangular tables set end to end with an aisle down the middle. Frankly, it reminded me of pictures of prison dining rooms that I have seen on television, but without the enforced silence of the penal setting. The first thing I noticed was the noise level—no wonder teachers dislike lunch duty! The furniture, the acoustics, the trays, and just the sheer number of energetic young people packed into the cafeteria created a decibel level that certainly discouraged conversation if not digestion. I asked one student what she thought of the lunch and received an unprintable reply. I asked what would make it better, and she said, "If they took half of the kids and put them somewhere else."

When I adjusted to the noise, however, I noticed a substantial number of students who were not eating anything at all. They did not have brown bags from home. They did not have trays or snack items. They were just sitting around, talking, with no food in sight. In fact, I later learned, only about 40 percent of the students in attendance actually took a reimbursable meal, very close to the national average for participation at the high school level; another several hundred bought a la carte items. I asked several students why they were not eating, and they replied that they were waiting for the lines to get shorter, but they did not get up and go to the serving area, even when the line virtually disappeared. One slim young man told me he was saving his lunch money. When I asked the cafeteria manager about this, she gave me a one word answer: "stigma." In Any Town, as elsewhere in America, it is not much of a problem at the elementary level, but it becomes a greater and greater concern as students grow older and more socially aware. As the director summarized the situation, "The older you get, no matter what it is, unless you have universal free, they don't want to take part in it because of that stigma."

I asked the director about the possibility of using an electronic swipe card system, a trend that has been getting a lot of attention in school food circles in recent years as a means of protecting student privacy. He told me that it came down to money. He estimated that a computer system and software would cost the district about $70,000, and as he said, he had other priorities for any money that could be found. The struggle to break even, to balance expenditures with revenues was pervasive in my conversations with the Any Town director. With money, he could offer more fresh fruit and more choice in the breakfast program. He could afford more staff time to count out cheese squares, so he could offer cereal more often. He could serve more chicken dinners prepared on site and more salads in the lunch program. He could expand the kitchen and add a pizza oven and make healthy pizzas on site as a colleague was doing in a more affluent district nearby. He could even permit staff members to work sufficient hours to qualify for benefits.

STAFF VIEWS

Because I have always been interested in work and in identifying the factors that contribute to job satisfaction, I welcomed every opportunity to talk with Any Town HS cafeteria workers about their jobs. The kitchen staff at the school were generally positive about working there, and turnover was very low. The pay was considered quite good for the area. The benefits were great, "Cadillac" as one long-time staffer put it, but most employees would never work enough hours to qualify for them. Jobs were carefully cut back and reconfigured to keep employees from qualifying for benefits, because there was no room in the budget to pay for them, and most employees seemed to accept this. Several had benefits through their spouses or at other jobs. They enjoyed each other's company well enough and seemed to feel they were fairly treated. Those who were parents were grateful for hours that were compatible with child-rearing, and most seemed to feel good about feeding kids. But no one talked about creativity, self-expression, or any other variant of the "joy of cooking."

The Any Town HS kitchen is not as deskilled as a McDonald's kitchen, but it is certainly no culinary school. Unless you want to count putting salt on the pretzels or topping the pizza with (pre-sliced) pepperoni, there was little combining of ingredients going on the days I was there, except for making sandwiches. There was a fair amount of opening cans and dishing out serving-size portions into plastic cups—as in canned pears—and there was a lot of laying out frozen foods on parchment sheets. Of course I wasn't there very long. The kitchen still has knives and pots, unlike some school kitchens, and clearly some "old-fashioned" fresh preparation takes place. In explaining why he didn't have all his USDA commodity chickens converted to nuggets, an option that many directors now exercise, the Any Town director mentioned that even though it is more labor intensive, he likes to have his staff cook a real chicken dinner now and then: "I can pay my staff a few extra hours, because you pay by the pound to have it processed, I can pay my staff a little extra to come up with a more Maryland Fried Chicken, which is not fried, but it's a special coating; there's a lot of production work to it, but it gives a different meal than always having nuggets."

No one complained about the minimal amount of actual cooking; what they did complain about was the lack of respect they experienced from teachers and other school staff. "We are the most under-appreciated group," one worker told me. "We work harder than anybody, but we only get noticed when something goes wrong." She saw it as symptomatic that for years, the cafeteria staff members were invited to the annual school district staff appreciation luncheon, but couldn't attend because they were all working, fixing the meal. Finally, the previous year, someone had come up with the idea of having an end-of-year appreciation dinner for the cafeteria staff at which the director and the members of the school board cooked. The sense of not being appreciated, of being seen as an interruption to the school day rather than an essential part of it, turned out to be one of the constant themes throughout my investigations, but I heard it first from the staff at Any Town HS.

I have traveled many miles and eaten many school meals since my stint in the Any Town HS kitchen. I have tasted better meals, and worse. I have seen easier working conditions, and harder. I have interviewed staff who expressed more passion for healthy school food, and less. But the fundamental images that I formed there have remained with me: great dedication, enormous effort, modest results. As to my efforts to make myself useful and earn the respect of my temporary coworkers, I'm afraid I'll never know. My stay at the kitchen was cut short by a family emergency, so I never got to say proper farewells, but I can tell you that I learned more in that week than in any other of my research. If you are reading this book because you hope to help improve the food in the cafeteria of your children's school, I'd encourage you to start by listening to the staff who are doing the work.

My volunteer work in the Any Town HS kitchen proved to be invaluable to my effort to learn about school meals—partly because I knew so little to begin with, and partly because the director and staff were so generous with their time in answering my questions. Nevertheless, I left with even more questions. Is the menu at Any Town typical? What *is* the nutritional profile of school meals in America? Is anyone still actually cooking in school kitchens? Are kids anywhere eating fresh vegetables? Is it true that children won't try new foods at school? What about the food temperature problems that plagued the breakfast program in Any Town; were they unusual? Were all cafeterias so noisy? Did all school food service directors have to struggle to make ends meet? And what about participation? Fewer than half the enrolled high school students at Any Town actually chose a reimbursable meal on any give day. Were such low participation rates typical, and if so, what explains them? Was stigma as important a factor as the Any Town staff believed?

CHAPTER TWO

FOOD FIGHTS

A Brief History

To an outsider, many of the rules, policies, and arrangements that the Any Town High School staff and other school food service professionals take for granted seem perplexing. Why does the United States Department of *Agriculture* (USDA) administer the program at the federal level? This is *school* food, after all. Don't we have a Department of Education? And given the long and fiercely defended tradition of state control of education, why are there *federal* nutrition standards when there are not, for example, federal textbook standards or teacher certification rules? And since there are federal standards, why are they enforced by *state* agencies? How are the federal reimbursement rates determined, and why is the program funded on a reimbursement basis at all? And since it is operated on a reimbursement basis, why does part of the federal support come as chicken nuggets and hamburger patties? Why does a monochromatic meal composed of a roll, a carton of milk, and an order of french fries qualify for reimbursement, while in most school districts, a stir fry of vegetables would not? Why do we have the three-tier eligibility structure that creates such an administrative burden for food service personnel and so much misery for the children intended to be its prime beneficiaries? To answer these questions and others, I turned first to the history of school food in America.

AN ACCIDENTAL PROGRAM

School meals began in the United States during the Progressive Era, roughly the period from 1890 until World War I. These early programs were purely local efforts, usually initiated by women's organizations or charitable groups outside the school system. As compulsory school attendance laws brought large numbers of very poor children into the elementary schools, educators and social reformers became convinced that they were too hungry to concentrate on their lessons. At the same time, the activists of the school hygiene movement became concerned about the nutritional quality and safety of foods sold to children by street vendors, concessionaires, and school janitors. They urged the establishment of lunchrooms under the direction of home economics teachers or dietitians that would provide safe, healthy meals and teach students the basics of the emerging science of nutrition. Together, the two groups of reformers were able to start school lunch programs in most of the nation's largest cities; often they succeeded in persuading the school board or municipal government to take over their operations. There was no movement for federal participation in such efforts, however. Schools were a local matter; federal involvement in school food would have to await the Great Depression of the 1930s.[1]

The onset of the Depression both intensified and called attention to the problems of hunger and malnutrition. With a third of the workforce unemployed, deprivation reached levels of severity unimaginable to most contemporary Americans. People spent down their savings, cashed in their insurance policies, exhausted their credit, scrounged for food in open air markets and even municipal dumps, and when they had used up all other resources, applied for relief. The relief apparatus, however, was quickly exhausted. Private charity, widely believed to be "the American way of relief," proved wholly unequal to the task. Municipal governments were the next line of defense, but they relied heavily on property taxes, property taxes relied heavily on rents, and people with no incomes could not pay rents. Tenants defaulted on their rents; landlords defaulted on their taxes. Municipalities went bankrupt. States teetered on the brink. People went hungry; children fainted in school.

In many communities, civic groups and PTAs started school lunch programs or expanded old ones. In New York City, teachers gave a portion of their salaries to fund such programs. In Chicago, the Board of

Education started a lunch program in about half the city's schools that relied on donated food and volunteer labor. A dozen states enacted legislation authorizing cities to use tax funds for school meals, and in some cases added state funds to help meet the cost. To many observers, as the historian Susan Levine reports, "school lunches appeared as a logical form of relief for the Depression's generation of hungry children."[2] Such local and state engagement, however, did not lead directly to federal assistance.

Ironically, it was surplus, not need, that prompted the federal government to get involved and that fundamentally shaped its role in school food. Huge surpluses of farm products had accumulated during the 1920s as farmers tried to compensate for falling prices by increasing production. By the time the Depression brought massive unemployment and desperate need to the industrial sector, the farm economy had been in shambles for a decade, and farmers were vociferously demanding help. The New Deal attempted to restore balance to agriculture by reducing production and removing surpluses from the market. In 1933, Secretary of Agriculture Henry Wallace undertook the slaughter of millions of immature pigs in an effort to forestall a price-depressing glut on the hog market. The results were a public relations disaster for the new administration. Stockyard pens built for big hogs could not contain the little pigs, and escaped piglets ran squealing down the streets of Chicago and Omaha. More troubling to the public, the smaller pigs could not be processed into meat with commercial equipment and were ground up into tankage, a sort of liquefied pig and, some reported, dumped into rivers and quarries. In the face of the public outcry over waste amid want, President Franklin Roosevelt ordered the secretary of agriculture and the Federal Emergency Relief administrator to set up a program to purchase farm surpluses and distribute them to the needy unemployed.[3] They hastily established an entity called the Federal Surplus Relief Corporation, chartered in the State of Delaware where the corporation laws were particularly flexible, to distribute surplus farm products through the State Emergency Relief Administrations.

When these distribution channels for surplus commodities were closed off by the abrupt termination of the emergency phase of federal relief in 1935, what was left of the program was transferred to USDA, which began donating some of the foods to schools. The relationship between school food and surplus farm products—and USDA—was cemented when Congress included a provision in the 1935 amendments to the Agricultural Adjustment Act, famous in food assistance circles as "Section 32." This provision established a permanent allocation of a portion of the nation's annual customs receipts for use in supporting farm prices and removing surpluses. The author of the provision saw it as a sort of recompense for the damage that had been done to the farm economy over the years by tariffs. Section 32 funds were thus regarded as "farmers' money," even though the surpluses they purchased largely went for school food and relief.[4] In keeping with its fundamental mission to expand the income of farmers and the market for their products, USDA's regulations governing the receipt of surplus commodities focused on making sure that the foods donated to schools would not reenter the market or displace other food sales. In order to receive the donations, schools had to agree that they would not sell or exchange the commodities or discontinue or curtail their normal food purchases. Lunch programs had to be operated on a nonprofit basis, and meals had to be provided free to children too poor to pay for them. The focus was on using the available foods, not on a balanced diet. The USDA staff who developed these regulations did not think they were setting up the parameters for a permanent national school food program. They had commodities; they needed a morally and politically acceptable outlet, and they established rules and procedures that reflected their farm income agenda. In fact, the regulations they established set the tone and structure for the program and have endured, in updated form, until the present.[5]

Meanwhile another federal agency with another sort of surplus also recognized the utility of school meals. In 1935, emergency relief was supplanted by work relief, and the creation of the Works Progress Administration (WPA) added a new actor to the school food mix. About one-sixth of the applicants accepted for work relief by the WPA were women, but the agency's typical sites, construction projects, were deemed inappropriate for females. Many unemployed women had previously worked in factories, but federal legislation prohibited the WPA from undertaking manufacturing projects that would compete with private industry. School lunch projects provided an ideal solution. There were schools in every community, the projects required very little capital investment, and women were assumed to have cooking skills. School lunch work projects were established in every state and gave useful work to more than sixty-four thousand persons; soon they were serving more than two million school lunches a day.[6] With the federal government contributing both free food and free labor, school lunch programs proliferated rapidly, especially at the end of the decade when the Surplus Marketing Administration of the Department of Agriculture hired an agent for each state to help in the establishment of new programs. By 1942, some ninety-five thousand schools were serving school lunch to more than six million children.[7]

War, however, changed everything. Labor went from surplus to scarcity almost overnight as the nation geared up for defense, and food surpluses disappeared as European purchasing agents arrived and the nation began feeding not only its own armies but those of its allies. The federal role in school lunch appeared doomed, though concerned women's organizations and child welfare advocates pointed out that with so many women in the labor force, children needed a good meal at school as much as ever. Further, a new emphasis on "defense nutrition," fostered by reports that large numbers of young men were failing draft physicals for reasons related to malnutrition in childhood, called attention to the importance of a well-fed citizenry.

When rationing of foodstuffs began to appear likely, the director of the Federal Security Agency asked the Committee on Food and Nutrition (later the Food and Nutrition Board) of the National Research Council to specify how much of various vitamins, minerals, and calories people actually needed to maintain health and productivity. The result was the development of the Recommended Dietary Allowances or RDAs, designed to make sure that workers and soldiers were sufficiently well fed to wage effective war.[8] Meanwhile, farm leaders, remembering the price collapse at the end of World War I, lobbied successfully for protections for agriculture. Congress passed the Steagall Act, committing the nation to support farm prices for two years after the end of hostilities, thus virtually guaranteeing that there would once again be large surpluses of food in federal hands at the end of the war. In an effort to make sure that school lunch programs would be there to help dispose of the surplus, advocates of school food succeeded in convincing Congress to provide a cash indemnity to reimburse schools for funds spent to procure foods locally. Thus, commodity donations and free labor were replaced during the war with a modest cash subsidy.

The War Food Administration (WFA), looking for a basis to determine which meals would qualify for the cash reimbursement, turned to the new RDAs to establish a standard. The Type A meal, which was designed by nutritionists to provide one-third to one-half the RDAs for children aged 10 to 12, had to include, at a minimum, a half pint of whole milk; two ounces of meat, poultry, or fish, or an equivalent amount of an alternate protein source such as beans, peanut butter, or eggs; six ounces of vegetables or fruit; a serving of bread; and two tea-

spoons of butter or fortified margarine.[9] Like the USDA rules designed
to protect farm interests in the donation of commodities, the WFA's meal
requirements turned out to be the basis for long-term public policy. The
Type A meal pattern endured until the late 1970s with only three minor
changes, and the meal patterns in use today still bear a strong resem-
blance to their wartime progenitor.

Despite the continuing federal support, however, many schools
dropped out of the program, unable to compete for labor with the high
wages paid in the defense industries and unwilling to commit their own
funds based on the uncertain hope of year-to-year appropriations. As
the war drew to a close, school food proponents began seeking a permanent program. Despite opposition from fiscal conservatives concerned
about the deficit and from Southern segregationists worried that federal assistance to the schools would prove to be the entering wedge for
school desegregation, champions of a federal lunch program won the
day by pointing out that Congress was already committed to remove
surpluses under the Steagall provisions. Without a school lunch program, the government would again face the difficult question of how
to dispose of them. It seemed foolish, they argued, to waste good food
when the nation's defense depended upon a healthy, well-fed citizenry.
An effort spearheaded by home economists and women's organizations
to locate federal management of the permanent program in the Bureau
of Education and to provide funds for nutrition education and training
was repulsed by those who saw the program as an extension of agricultural policy and were determined to protect its capacity to absorb
farm surpluses. The National School Lunch Act, passed in June 1946,
declared it to be the policy of Congress "as a measure of national security, to safeguard the health and well-being of the nation's children and
to encourage the domestic consumption of nutritious agricultural commodities and other food, by assisting the States, through grants-in-aid
and other means, in providing an adequate supply of food and other
facilities for the establishment, maintenance, operation and expansion
of nonprofit school lunch programs."[10]

The act provided for an appropriation to be distributed among the
states by a formula that took into account the number of school-aged
children in the state and the state's relative poverty. The funds were
to be used for an across-the-board subsidy for all meals served in the
program, what would later come to be known as the Section 4 subsidy.
Federal funds had to be matched by funds from within the state, including the fees that children paid for lunches, and the federal share was

scheduled to decline over time. Participating schools had to agree to feed needy children free or at a reduced price, to serve meals that met minimum nutritional requirements prescribed by the secretary of agriculture, to operate on a nonprofit basis, to maintain adequate records of all receipts and expenditures, and to utilize commodities declared by the secretary to be in abundant supply. Finally, in a effort to reassure Southern members of Congress that the Department of Agriculture would not be in a position to pressure schools to desegregate, funds were to be distributed within the states by a state agency, usually the State Department of Education, rather than directly by USDA to schools.[11]

President Truman signed the legislation on June 4, 1946, with the memorable comment that "no nation is any healthier than its children or more prosperous than its farmers."[12] The secretary of agriculture promptly adopted the Type A meal pattern as the standard for school meals, and the regulations designed to protect the farm income support functions were enshrined in law. Thus the National School Lunch Act incorporated most of the policies hastily cobbled together by USDA and War Food Administration staff.

Over time, the National School Lunch Act has come to have the air of rationality and deliberate policy-making that we often attribute to successful legislation after the fact, but on closer inspection, it appears to reflect a series of accidents. If the pig slaughter had not been so dramatic, if the chairman of the House Agriculture Committee had not seized on the connection between surpluses and relief and come up with Section 32, if the WPA had not been looking for jobs for women . . . one "accident" after another, setting the stage for the next. As the journalist Agnes Meyer of The Washington Post told the first National Conference of State School Lunch Officials when they gathered in Washington in 1946, "It is laughable to remember how we stumbled into the school lunch program. Surely God looks after our poor blundering democracy, and helps us do the right thing, even though for the wrong reasons."[13]

Once the National School Lunch Act was passed, school food policy entered a period of relative peace and quiet. Section 416 of the Agricultural Act of 1949 added another source of commodities, specifying that school lunch programs were among the first priorities to receive commodities procured by the Commodity Credit Corporation, but school food received little congressional attention in the 1950s. As the baby boom reached school age and new schools were constructed in new suburbs around the nation, many were built with kitchens and cafeterias, allowing these relatively affluent areas to take advantage of the NSLP.

Overall participation in the program doubled, rising from seven million in 1947 to fourteen million at the start of the sixties.[14] A special milk program was created by legislation in 1954, but otherwise, Congress left the popular program to develop on its own. Appropriations, however, failed to keep pace with either the expansion of the program or rising food prices; participating schools typically ran out of their federal apportionment in March or April. The average contribution per meal from the federal government dropped from 8.7 cents in 1947 to 4.4 cents in 1960, despite rises in the cost of food, labor, and transportation.[15] School food in the 1950s was definitely not an antipoverty program. In fact, the percentage of meals served free or at a reduced price to children deemed too poor to pay *dropped* in this period, from 17 percent in 1947 to less than 10 percent by 1960. According to the historian Susan Levine, the Department of Agriculture "largely ignored the School Lunch Act's provisions requiring participating schools to offer free lunches to children who could not afford to pay."[16] In short, in the rosy glow of presumed prosperity in the 1950s, no one was paying much attention to the capacity of the school lunch program to assist the poor.

Compared with these early years of relative stability, the subsequent decades have been marked by controversy and change. Roaming through this history, trying to figure out a way to embrace half a century in a single chapter, I was struck by the recurring metaphor of war: war on poverty, war on hunger, war on waste, war on spending, war on fat. In my own writing, I have generally tried to avoid this metaphor, despite its handiness, because I do not want to normalize or glorify what is almost always a disaster for human beings—and for other species as well. In the public policy discourse, however, references to war are ubiquitous. "The metaphor of war is ingrained in policy language" writes Deborah Stone. "If our government is at war, be it against poverty, or fraud or crime, then we are traitors if we do not support the cause. The symbol of war is an obvious tactic used by leaders to create support for their policies."[17] Each of these wars has mobilized public support, and each has resulted in both Congressional and administrative action that has changed school food. They provide a useful rubric for designating periods to help us keep track of a rich and fascinating history.[18]

WAR ON POVERTY

Lyndon Baines Johnson declared "unconditional war on poverty" in his first State of the Union address in January 1964, just two months after the assassination of President John F. Kennedy. The choice of language was neither accidental nor uncontested. The Bureau of the Budget had opposed the label, the historian Michael Katz reports, "because it raised unrealistic expectations about the amount of money available for the new program."[19] But Johnson later defended his choice: "The military image carried with it connotations of victories and defeats that could prove misleading. But I wanted to rally the nation, to sound a call to arms, which would stir people in the government, in private industry, and on the campuses to lend their talent to a massive effort to eliminate this evil."[20] He also needed to reinforce his image as a leader in his own right, not just the heir of the slain JFK. To this end he needed a project that "appealed to Kennedy's supporters but had not yet been publicly labeled a Kennedy effort."[21] A war on poverty was nearly ideal; not only did it have the sort of moral resonance that the times demanded, but substantial groundwork for such a war was already in place.

Food assistance had been an important, and early, part of the Kennedy administration's response to poverty. Kennedy, distressed by the deprivation he encountered in Appalachia while campaigning for the Democratic nomination in 1960, had promised immediate food aid as well as long-range economic development, and he made good on his promises. His first executive order, signed on inauguration day, expanded the list of commodities to be donated, both to impoverished families and to schools. A month later, in February 1961, he announced the first sites for pilot food stamp projects. And in his Message to Congress on Agriculture in March, he recommended the expansion of the school lunch program, urging increased funding for schools providing a high proportion of free lunches and a redesign of the formula for allocating school lunch funds among the states.[22]

With the backing of the administration, Congress in 1962 revamped the allocation formula and added a new Section 11 to the National School Lunch Act, which for the first time authorized funding to reimburse schools in impoverished areas for meals served free. Congressional action was hastened by the release of a USDA study showing that nine million, or just over one-fifth, of the nation's school children attended "lunchless schools." When the measure's sponsors sought to obtain an appropriation, however, they encountered major obstacles. On the one hand, the chairmen of the House and Senate Agricultural Appropriations Subcommittees, both long-serving Southern conservatives, did not want to use "farmers' money" for impoverished school children, especially black school children in inner city schools. Their power to thwart the intent of the legislation was a continuing legacy of Section 32.[23] On the other hand, neither USDA nor the state school lunch supervisors made much effort to secure such appropriations. As the policy analyst Gilbert Steiner has explained, "Expanding the lunch program turned out to be more complicated than it seemed." To begin with, more federal funds would do little to help schools that had no cafeterias or kitchens. Further, "state school lunch supervisors had come to understand the administrative aspects of the 1946 school lunch act, knew how to deal with the Department of Agriculture under the provisions of that act, and saw no special advantage but a good deal of potential trouble in changing the rules. When both House and Senate agricultural appropriations subcommittees regularly refused to earmark money for Section 11, no complaints were heard."[24] According to the political scientist Ardith Maney, "Section 11 remained unfunded for three years, even after the Johnson administration made poverty its chief domestic policy priority. . . . This same gap between authorization and appropriations would become a major stumbling block to the implementation of all the food aid programs adopted during the 1960s."[25] Perhaps if President Kennedy had lived, he might have intervened to secure funds for his school lunch agenda, but we shall never know.

Kennedy's assassination left the nation hungry for leadership. Looking backward, students of presidential action have concluded that Johnson's war metaphor was "brilliant political strategy" that "served as a unifying device, rallying the nation behind a moral challenge."[26] Perhaps that is why Senator Philip Hart was finally able to secure some funds for Section 11 Special Assistance by attaching a floor amendment (and thus bypassing the recalcitrant appropriations subcommittees) to the 1965 Agricultural Appropriations bill. By 1966, when the funds freed by Hart's amendment became available, poverty was a high-profile issue, both within the Johnson administration and in the larger society. It was not only the president's declaration nor the creation of the Office of Economic Opportunity (OEO) that publicized the issue. The civil rights movement had done much to call attention to the living conditions of impoverished African Americans, and newspaper and television reports, books, and magazine articles were raising the nation's consciousness about the "other America." People in many walks of life began to look at school food through an antipoverty lens. Educators now came forward to urge a breakfast program, arguing that school lunch came too late in the day for many poor children who arrived at school hungry, leaving them without energy and unable to concentrate in the crucial morning hours. And child development specialists pointed out that the most significant years in terms of nutrition were the earliest; children in preschools and day care centers needed food as much as or more than their school-age sisters and brothers. Education was a centerpiece of the human capital approach to poverty, and evidence was mounting that an inadequate diet could thwart the best designed enrichment project. Programs like Head Start and lunch and breakfast programs funded with money from Title 1 of the Elementary and Secondary Education Act (ESEA) were demonstrating that a good meal could invigorate poor children. This was the context in which the Johnson administration made plans for a new, more comprehensive approach to child nutrition.

When Johnson's staffers turned their attention to the impact of school food on poor people, they were disappointed with what they found. Internal memos pointed out the ways in which the Agriculture Department's commitment to the well-being of farmers worked against maximum use of the program to aid the poor. The new secretary of the Department of Health, Education and Welfare (HEW), Joseph Califano, urged the president to move child nutrition programs from USDA to HEW, but Secretary of Agriculture Orville Freeman lobbied hard to keep them in his department.[27] As Ardith Maney has explained, Freeman noted with unease the decline in rural population and expressed "fears that urban and liberal interests, once mobilized, might realize that their numbers in Congress would soon be enough to pass food stamp and food aid legislation on their own. If urban legislators did not have to bargain for rural support, this would leave the declining number of rural representatives in the House unable to enact the farm policy legislation that was of principal concern to them," that is, the commodity supports.[28] From the viewpoint of 2008, when Congress has once again passed a farm bill containing massive subsidies for basic commodities despite an increasingly articulate critique and an increasingly diverse opposition, Freeman's fears seem to have been exaggerated. Nonetheless, his decision to support food assistance *within* the Department of Agriculture and under the purview of the Agricultural Appropriations Subcommittees of the Congress has had a major long-term impact on food assistance, continuing and reinforcing the link to agriculture and agricultural politics that began with the little pigs.

The staffers charged with coming up with new legislation were primarily concerned with extending the scope of aid to hungry children. According to Ardith Maney, "presidential aides really had two objectives: (1) establishing legislative authority for a school breakfast program; and

(2) reorganizing and rationalizing the existing government-supported child feeding programs by extending them beyond the school setting" to day care and preschool programs and to summer recreation programs. In addition, they wanted more funding for special assistance for lunches served free. Once the Johnson administration began adding up the projected costs of this comprehensive approach, however, it quickly retreated. The cost of the war in Vietnam was escalating, and the Budget Bureau's prediction about limited funding for the war on poverty was proving true. Instead of adding new funding to cover the new initiatives, the Johnson administration proposed to "redirect" funding from the general Section 4 support for all lunches and from the Special Milk Program—thus, from middle-class families who could presumably afford to pay for their children's lunches—to new programs for poor children, the first in a long series of White House attempts to target school food to the poor.[29]

The formula proved to be a nonstarter. Congress would not accept a reduction in support for lunches served to children who were not poor. The administration could not even find a sponsor for its bill in the Senate. Hearings made clear the strength of Congressional opposition, and in the end, a compromise expanded child nutrition funding rather than redirecting it. The Child Nutrition Act of 1966 authorized schools to extend lunch program benefits to preschool programs operated by the schools. It also authorized a two-year pilot school breakfast program under which state educational agencies would select the schools for participation; the agencies were required to give priority to "schools drawing attendance from areas in which poor economic conditions exist and to those schools to which a substantial proportion of the children enrolled must travel long distances daily."[30] In a departure from previous law, which had limited USDA's contributions to the cost of food only, the secretary of agriculture was authorized to approve reimbursement of up to 80 percent of the costs of obtaining, preparing, and serving breakfasts. For the first time since 1947, funds were authorized for Section 5 of the National School Lunch Act, the nonfood assistance title that could be used for equipment. In order to assist states in expanding their lunch programs and developing school breakfast programs, and in response to testimony by state officials that they did not have the staff adequately to oversee the programs, the Child Nutrition Act of 1966 provided for federal money for state administrative expenses (which soon became known as SAEs). Finally, USDA won the territorial battle: the act specified that USDA was to be the administrative home for all federal child nutrition efforts, even those funded by the Office of Economic Opportunity. In the end, the war on poverty had achieved a modest reorientation of school food programs to include more poor children while reaffirming the programs' link to agriculture.

WAR ON HUNGER

It soon became clear that these minimal Congressional reforms were too little, too late. In the spring of 1967, hunger in America suddenly, dramatically became a public issue.[31] Hearings on the war on poverty took a Senate subcommittee to Mississippi, where the civil rights attorney Marian Wright convinced several senators to accompany her on a tour of the back roads of the Mississippi Delta. There they encountered poverty and hunger in their most desperate forms. "I didn't know we were going to be dealing with the situation of starving people and starving youngsters," the conservative Republican Senator George Murphy is reported to have said. Also among the senators was Robert Kennedy, the slain president's younger brother and a former attorney general, who had himself become a high-profile politician. In the spring of 1967, almost anything he did was of interest to the public, and his discovery of hunger in the Mississippi Delta was carried on the nightly news by television stations across the nation. Even people who had been involved in antipoverty action programs were shocked; they had imagined that somehow American agricultural abundance would protect the poor in America from severe food deprivation. Poverty was bad enough, but hunger amid the amber waves of grain, hunger in the "best fed nation on earth," hunger in the context of American abundance was not acceptable. Antipoverty activists seized the opportunity and undertook efforts to document the extent of hunger and poverty-related malnutrition and to investigate the performance of federal food assistance programs.[32] Among them was a coalition of women's organizations, the Committee on School Lunch Participation, which turned its attention to the fate of poor children in the National School Lunch Program.

The committee found that only about two million of the nation's nearly fifty million school children were receiving free or reduced price lunches: about a third of the estimated six million poor children of school age. The committee's report, entitled *Their Daily Bread*, released in April 1968, portrayed a program hampered at every point from meeting the needs of the nation's hungriest children. Many of the nation's poorest schools were old buildings in urban neighborhoods, built without kitchens or cafeterias, and unable to afford the equipment necessary to start a program. The National School Lunch Act had included a nonfood assistance component, Section 5, for equipment, but it had not been funded between 1947 and 1966. Even among schools equipped with cafeterias, however, many made little effort to find and assist children unable to purchase lunch.

Here the greatest design flaw in the 1946 legislation was revealed. The National School Lunch Act provided that lunches "shall be served without cost or at a reduced cost to children who are determined by local school authorities to be unable to pay the full cost of the lunch." Neither "reduced charge" nor "inability to pay" was given any legal or operational definition. Discretion was left to local schools to determine who would receive such meals. "Needy" was what the local principal or cafeteria manager or school board said it was, and the process for identifying hungry children in need of free or reduced price meals varied dramatically from place to place. As a Senate Select Committee report later explained,

> The lack of uniform national standards for determining the eligibility requirement for a free lunch created an inequitable situation. With no guidelines, local officials often were influenced by extraneous factors and community prejudices—e.g., the child's conduct or attendance record. Many administrators failed to connect hunger with lethargic or temperamental attitude on the part of the child. With varying guidelines, children from the same family attending separate schools were judged and fed by different standards. Hence a child might be "poor" in one school while his sister was considered not so "poor" in a different school just miles away. This lack of national standards denied many children the lunch that Congress had guaranteed them.[33]

It was not just the local discretion, however, that excluded so many children; it was local discretion in the context of a funding structure that gave schools no additional funds for serving free meals and, in many states, no funds with which to cover the costs except the amounts spent by "full price" children and the tiny federal contribution. Schools in affluent communities with few poor children could cover free meals from the proceeds of meals sold to paying customers. John Perryman, the executive director of the American School Food Service Association (ASFSA), called it the "bite tax"; every tenth bite, he asserted, went to support meals for poor children; it was the parents of the paying children who were really subsidizing the free meals.[34] Schools with few paying customers and large numbers of poor children simply couldn't afford to feed them all.

For its report, the Committee on School Lunch Participation conducted interviews with teachers, principals, cafeteria workers, and parents in communities around the nation. They found schools coping as best they could. In one school in Mississippi, more than four hundred poor, hungry children took turns eating one hundred lunches set aside for them. In a school in La Conner, Washington, the school lunch director reported that "children are given the opportunity to work one day for a free lunch the next day"; only 24 of the school's 459 children received free or reduced price lunches, despite a high proportion of needy families. Perhaps the most extreme report came from an elementary school principal in Mobile, Alabama, who reported that "lunches are rotated among the needy on a weekly basis; one thousand children need free lunches, but only 15 get them."[35] Some schools were able to use Elementary and Secondary Education Act funds to provide lunches for the first year after ESEA passed in 1965, but fairly quickly educators began to demand that those funds be made available for instruction. For schools in poor communities without ESEA assistance, the committee summarized its findings this way:

> It is when a large number of needy students attend a school that the system of providing free lunches for them collapses. It is in these schools that the stopgap measures noted in the above examples are employed—rotating the free lunches, or having the teacher buy the children lunch, or hoping the others will share, or having the children stand at the end of the line to see whether any food is left over. It is in these schools where the problem is so overwhelming that principals cannot cope with it, and the hungry children just sit and watch their classmates eat while they go hungry.[36]

Another major critique of all the nation's food assistance programs, *Hunger USA,* from the Citizens Board of Inquiry into Hunger and Malnutrition in the United States, gave only a brief overview of school food in deference to the near simultaneous publication of *Their Daily Bread*. In its succinct summary of problems, however, it concluded that "a majority of poor children are forced to pay the full price for school lunch or go without. The school lunch in fact operates for the benefit of the middle class."[37]

I often refer to *Their Daily Bread* and the other reports and documentaries produced by the extraordinary upsurge of anti-hunger advocacy that began in the late 1960s when I am talking with students about the potential impact of social research. Here are studies that made a difference. Of course, it was not just the studies themselves, with their moving revelations and insightful analyses; it was also the larger social movement for civil rights and economic opportunity, which fostered them. Martin Luther King, Jr., and much of the leadership of the civil rights movement had become increasingly convinced that there would be no true freedom for impoverished minorities until a real war on poverty was waged, and that the resources for such a struggle were being consumed by the war in Vietnam. In the months before King was murdered in April of 1968, he worked to organize a Poor People's Campaign that would bring thousands of poor people of all races to Washington, D.C., where he hoped that massive numbers and targeted civil disobedience would force the nation to confront the deeper evils of poverty and injustice. The Poor People's Campaign, now dedicated to honoring his memory, arrived in Washington in May 1968 carrying copies of *Hunger USA*. One of its best publicized demonstrations was at the Department of Agriculture. Resurrection City, where the demonstrators camped, was plagued by rain, conflict, and possibly mismanagement, and many of the goals of the campaign were not realized, but in regard to food assistance, the campaign had substantial impact.[38] Hunger proved to be one aspect of the poverty critique that mobilized the nation's sense of moral outrage. Why should Americans go hungry when there was obviously plenty of food?

In the context of wide public concern about hunger, a growing commitment to rights and entitlements, and an emerging alliance between the federal government and impoverished minority groups, Congress overhauled the funding structure of the school lunch and breakfast programs. In a series of bills, it established uniform national standards to define eligibility for both free and reduced price meals, and it coupled those standards with differential reimbursement rates.[39] That is, it required participating schools to offer free or reduced price meals to all children from households with incomes below federally defined standards and provided the funds to pay for them. Originally, there was a single cutoff, and the choice between free and reduced price was left to the schools, but in the spirit of ensuring the access so long denied, Congress soon established separate eligibility thresholds for the two categories and set ceilings on the amounts that could be charged for reduced price meals. It established the program on a basis called "performance funding": the federal government would provide full reimbursements for all qualifying meals served to eligible children—there was no cap on the funds that a state could receive. When rapid rises in food prices in the aftermath of the oil embargo of the early 1970s undermined the purchasing power of the reimbursements, Congress specified automatic semiannual adjustments based on food price inflation.[40] School meals became an entitlement for low-income children who attended schools that chose to offer the program. Other legislation established the School Breakfast Program on a permanent basis and made it available to all schools at local discretion. By the end of this process, in the mid-1970s, children from families with incomes below 125 percent of the federal poverty line were entitled to free meals, and those from families with incomes up to 195 percent were entitled to 20 cent lunches and 10 cent breakfasts. For the first time, schools had an incentive to identify children eligible to receive free meals, and participation in the program rose dramatically. Between 1967 and 1970, the number of children receiving free lunches doubled, and it continued to rise, nearly doubling again by 1973.[41]

The rapid increase in participation, and especially the need to find ways to get meals to children in aging inner-city schools without kitchens or lunchrooms, led to a major change in school food service: the practice of contracting out food service operations to private companies. Some USDA officials saw in the growing food service industry a way to bring new technologies to bear on the task of feeding schoolchildren. The idea of greater involvement for the private sector was welcome in the Nixon administration, which took office in 1969. The 1969 White House Conference on Food, Nutrition, and Health recommended that private sector food service management companies be contracted to provide food and management for school food programs in hard-to-serve areas. This was a recommendation that divided the school food community. The American School Food Service Association, composed of fifty thousand food service workers and managers, was staunchly opposed, but some anti-hunger advocates saw contracting out as a solution to the challenge of infrastructure. Jean Fairfax, for example, the chair of the Committee on School Lunch Participation, envisioned community-controlled corporations in low-income inner-city neighborhoods providing jobs and skills for neighborhood residents. Others saw such corporate involvement as a last resort in communities that could not afford to build and equip kitchens. In 1970, USDA issued regulations permitting school food authorities to contract with private companies to operate their school meal programs. The practice was slow to catch on; twenty-five years later, only about 6 percent of school districts had such contracts, but by 2005 the figure had reached 13 percent, and oddly, given the genesis of the idea, such contracts were more common in less poor areas than in high-poverty ones.[42]

School food programs were not the only federal response to the outrage engendered by the vivid discovery of hunger. In 1968, Congress established programs to feed children when school was not in session and to provide meals in child care settings—what eventually became the Child and Adult Care Food Program and the Summer Meals Program. The Special Supplemental Feeding Program for Women, Infants, and Children, commonly known as WIC, was established as a two-year pilot in 1972 and made permanent in 1974. The Food Stamp Program was dramatically expanded and liberalized. A program of nutrition assistance to the elderly was established. All in all, food assistance spending rose from about $1.25 billion in 1970 to $12.5 billion in 1980, a tenfold increase.[43]

Why did the war on hunger achieve so much more than the more official war on poverty? Some of the gains can be attributed to the skill and political astuteness of anti-hunger activists, but much of it reflects deeply held values. I believe that George McGovern was right when he wrote that "hunger exerts a special claim on the American conscience,"[44] that people were really outraged by the discovery of such severe food deprivation in what we fervently believed was the land of plenty. The suffering was needless, and it was causing lasting harm. But hunger is unique in another way, as well. It is at once a radical and a conservative issue: radical because it reveals the depth of the failings of the economic system, conservative because it can be ameliorated without seriously undermining that system. Because food assistance is "in kind," it evokes less anxiety that it will be misspent and less concern that it will deter work effort than do programs of income assistance.[45]

The discovery of hunger in America in the late 1960s changed the politics of food assistance in particular, and the politics of agriculture in general, in ways that have proven enduring. On the one hand, it gave rise to what social scientists call an "issue network," an interacting group of organizations devoted to a particular issue, in this case, hunger in America. This network, often referred to as the "hunger lobby," has persisted for four decades.[46] The Citizens' Board of Inquiry, the Physicians Task Force, and the Committee on School Lunch Participation that raised the alarums were ad hoc associations and were soon succeeded by more lasting organizations, staffed by attorneys, researchers, nutritionists, and organizers, that developed the specialized knowledge necessary to influence legislation and its implementation. The creation of the Senate Select Committee on Nutrition and Human Needs, co-chaired by Senators George McGovern and Bob Dole gave anti-hunger activists a

natural core of allies within Congress. This committee not only undertook a thorough review of domestic food assistance programs, but also
eventually turned its attention to broader issues of nutrition, developing a publication called *Dietary Goals for the United States,* a forerun-
ner to the *Dietary Guidelines for Americans* now published every five
years. Although it was limited by Congressional rules that prevent select
committees from introducing legislation and require them to seek reauthorization of their own existence every year, the Select Committee on
Nutrition and Human Needs is surely a success story in the annals of
such bodies. It endured for ten years, and during that time it managed
to keep hunger on the national agenda. Shortly after the committee was
created, the Nixon administration, which began its term of office with a
promise to "put an end to hunger in America itself for all time," established a unified agency within USDA, the Food and Nutrition Service
(FNS), to oversee all of the food assistance programs. Unfortunately,
when it came to school food, the Nixon White House did not live up
to its commitments, and child nutrition programs became an arena
in which a liberal Congress struggled with a conservative president.
Each Congressional expansion of child nutrition engendered a series
of administrative efforts to avoid or restrict the flow of benefits; often
these were followed by law suits filed by the Food Research and Action
Center (FRAC) and other advocates on behalf of hungry children. Even
after major legislative victories, advocates had to continue to wage war
on hunger.

WAR ON WASTE

However you measure it, the growth in school food that took place
in the late 1960s and early 1970s was massive. The number of participating schools rose from 74,900 in 1969 to 88,900 in 1975. Federal cash payments for school lunch rose from $203.8 million to nearly
$1.3 billion in the same period; total federal cost, including the school
breakfasts and special milk programs as well as the cost of federal commodities, rose from $582.5 million in 1969 to more than $1.9 billion in
1975. And the new bottom line, the number of participating children,
rose from an average daily participation (ADP) in 1969 of 19.4 million
to 24.9 million ADP in 1975. The only number that fell was the number
of paying children. As Susan Levine has summarized, "Put simply, as
the number of free meals soared, the number of paying children pre-
cipitously declined."[47] The free and reduced price categories combined,

which had accounted for only 15.1 percent of meals served in 1969, accounted for more than 40 percent of all meals by 1975.[48]

Perhaps it is not surprising that such rapid expansion generated a new round of challenges. As the decade progressed, attention turned to the interrelated issues of meal quality and waste, especially "plate waste," the food the children took but didn't eat. Meal quality had been a part of the critique of the late 1960s, but it was generally overwhelmed by the urgency of the concern about hunger and access. Once the access problem was substantially solved, however, and rapid expansion began, reports of inadequate and indeed inedible meals began to surface with increasing frequency.

Many of the loudest and most persistent complaints had to do with "meal packs"—the equivalent of TV dinners, produced in factories, frozen, shipped to school districts, sometimes hundreds of miles away, and held in freezers to be defrosted and reheated when they were needed. Meal packs were one answer to the challenge posed by old schools with no kitchens, though they were also adopted by some systems that had been feeding all or most of their children for a long while. The famed restaurant critic and food writer Mimi Sheraton described the meal packs she encountered in New York City, where they were one of four approaches in use in the city, employed in 434 of the city's elementary schools in 1976: "The standard items are tough, sodden hamburgers that are pasty with vegetable protein and usually bitingly salty; limply breaded fried chicken; gray, pulpy fish; damp grilled cheese sandwiches; sour, sticky pizza, usually on thick soda cracker bases; and salty hot dogs, often tinged with a gray-green pallor."

Sheraton arranged to have sample meals from several different suppliers tested at a laboratory and found about half of them to provide less than the two ounces of protein required. Another audit, by the state comptroller's office, found that the samples in seventeen of forty-seven meals it tested did not meet the basic requirements for six out of twelve required nutrients. After reporting the audit results, Sheraton continued: "If these packs often are short in nutrients and in protein weight, they are almost always unappetizing. The instant mashed potatoes are caked into the compartments like library paste, carrots are waterlogged, shriveled peas are often burned black, the corn kernels are almost empty, the string beans are brownish and the baked beans are mushy."

The meal packs were not the only sore spots. In general, Sheraton concluded that the meals prepared fresh on site in 528 schools with cooking kitchens were the best, followed by the "basic meal" of soup and a sandwich prepared in the Board of Education's central kitchen in Long Island City and trucked to 162 schools with no kitchens at all. Bulk frozen convenience foods, used in 119 of the city's junior and senior high schools, came in for criticism similar to the meal packs: "Fried chicken that is at once dry but greasy; curled up hamburgers; gray, soggy fish portions, and metallic-tasting meatballs are among the standard hot entrees." She also reported substantial quantities of food going directly into the trash.[49] Sheraton followed her review of New York City school meals with accounts of four other cities; in Milwaukee and New Orleans she found far more appetizing fare; in Chicago and Newark, New Jersey, she found the same four approaches used in New York with similar results: "good lunches when cooked on the premises, mediocre to poor lunches when comprised of meal packs and bulk convenience choices."[50]

Sheraton was not alone. Eight months later the *Chicago Tribune* ran a series based on ten weeks of sampling and laboratory testing of school meals in that city and its suburbs. Calling the meals a "Prescription for Malnutrition," the paper slammed the Department of Agriculture for relying on an outdated handbook of nutrient values. The series also focused on the amounts of food thrown away by children, including laboratory analyses of sample trays after children had finished, and concluded that waste in the program was massive. It estimated that as much as 49.6 tons of food had been thrown out in a single day, and that $19.5 million worth of school food was discarded annually in the State of Illinois. The *Tribune* story was picked up by *Newsweek* and led to hearings by state legislators; eventually USDA held a series of hearings around the nation. Like hunger a decade earlier, food waste in school meals had become a public issue.

Waste of food is an emotionally charged issue for many people, myself included. Many of us have been socialized to clean our plates, and the image of tons of food in the trash is disturbing at a visceral level, even when we tolerate other forms of waste with relative equanimity. In the early 1970s, the OPEC oil embargo had not only subjected Americans to long lines at the gas pumps; it had sent food prices rapidly upward and introduced, briefly at least, a period of environmental consciousness. The discovery of "massive food waste" in schools was reported to a nation experiencing heightened awareness of the limits of growth and the finite nature of some of our most important natural resources. It is not surprising, therefore, that these revelations of waste led to a declaration of "war on waste" and policy change at the federal level. Back in

1975, two years before the *Chicago Tribune* series, the House Committee on Education and Labor had proposed, and Congress had passed, an amendment to the School Lunch Act requiring high schools to permit students to decline two of the five elements of the Type A meal—"offer versus serve" or OVS for short. As long as the five required components were offered and students selected and were served at least three, including fluid milk, such meals would still qualify for reimbursement. The measure attracted little attention outside the school food service community; I could find no mention of it in the mainstream media. Once waste became a public issue, however, USDA and food service professionals pointed out that elementary school children threw away substantially more than their high school siblings. In 1977, OVS was made an option, at the discretion of the local school food authority, for middle schools and junior high schools and, in 1981, for elementary schools. In 1986, it was made an option for breakfast for schools at all grade levels—students had to accept three of the four components. By 2005, when the most recent national data were collected, OVS was in use in 78 percent of elementary schools and 93 percent of middle schools for both breakfast and lunch.

Many school food service professionals look back on the waste wars of the mid-1970s as the dawning of a new age in which a business model began to permeate school food. As Antonia Demas has explained, "more choices and variety were offered, food quality improved, varied portions were offered, and a view of the child as a customer to please rather than as a lucky recipient" was widely adopted.[51] The idea that children are customers to please may have a salutary impact on the school lunchroom, but OVS may also be seen as a retreat, both from adult responsibility and from a commitment to nutritional standards. As Josephine Martin, a former president of ASFSA, has pointed out, "It has been used in some places as a springboard to increase profit. If a student takes only three of the meal items, costs are reduced and profits generated as the school receives the same reimbursement rate for the meal regardless of the number of items taken. If the meal selected contains only three . . . items, the child's nutrition needs may not be met even though the meal was planned to provide one-third of the RDA."[52]

OVS was not the only policy change attributable to the focus on waste. The media revelations also brought attention to meal quality and triggered a series of studies by the General Accounting Office (the GAO, now called the Government Accountability Office), which repeatedly found sample meals falling short of the one-third of RDA nutrition requirements that formed the basis for the Type A meal pattern. Schools were complying with the meal pattern requirements, the GAO reported, but this did not result in meals that met the underlying nutritional standard. In 1979, USDA scrapped the old Type A meal and replaced it with what are technically called "school lunch meal patterns," which allowed smaller portions for younger children and introduced more variety and flexibility, especially into the starch and protein category—rice and other grains could be used instead of bread. The new patterns were still designed to provide one-third of RDAs.

Whether as a means of reducing waste or simply in an effort to maintain participation, there is no question that school food service became more responsive to children's preferences—and not just any preferences, but specifically the preferences for fast food items increasingly inculcated by advertising. It was in the 1970s that school food began the long march to its current heavy reliance on pizza, tacos, and chicken nuggets. A year after Mimi Sheraton published her critique of the meals offered in New York City schools, she turned her attention to those provided in Las Vegas, where a highly publicized fast food revolution was underway in the cafeteria. A local entrepreneur had offered to rescue the food service from huge deficits and declining participation by applying what he saw as the principles of the fast food sector: "sell better, fresher food . . . for less money." Len Frederick had negotiated nutritional fortification and other modifications with suppliers that enabled him to meet the USDA standards while offering "combo meals" and "super shakes" that appealed to the first fast food generation, and he reported a remarkable 90 percent participation rate. What's more, he had taken the system from a deep deficit to a substantial profit—in excess of $1 million, in about six years. Sheraton found the claims of participation inflated; students were reported as participating if they bought any part of a lunch. "In fact, the participation rate in Type A lunches is barely 45 percent," she reported; "many students were seen taking lunches such as two cinnamon buns and a Coke, four sugar cookies and a Sprite, two bags of french fries and a milk shake."[53] Nonetheless, the publicity surrounding the Las Vegas approach, and its sizable profits, caught the attention of food service professionals. Even schools that did not develop high-profile new formats began to include more and more fast food–type items in their menus and, significantly, to sell them on an a la carte basis.

The issue of foods sold in competition with the reimbursable meal, whether in vending machines or school stores outside the cafeteria or a la carte on the cafeteria line itself, was an old one in school food, predating federal involvement. In fact, as noted, many of the early school lunch pioneers were motivated by a concern about the "unwholesome sweets" being sold to students on or near school premises; school lunchrooms were developed precisely as a way to make sure that children had the option to purchase safe, clean, healthy food. Once the National School Lunch Act was passed, many nutrition advocates hoped that the USDA would regulate the sale of other foods in order to protect the school lunch, but USDA generally took a fairly permissive position, arguing that the "regulation of such matters lies within the province of the State Departments of Education and local school officials."[54] School food service personnel around the country expressed their frustration. Given the intense debate today over "competitive foods," it's interesting to consider this excerpt from an article in the December 1948 issue of *The School Director* by Florida State School Lunch Program Supervisor Thelma Flanagan. "Many school lunch programs in California, Maine, and Florida and in all the states between have the similar problem of 'the untouched plate' caused by 'in-between meal snacks.'"[55]

She goes on to quote an article from the *Atlanta Journal*:

> Small communities will dig down deep to spend thousands of dollars for a school lunchroom, PTA committees will labor over balanced menus, cooks will lend their best efforts to make food appetizing, and then defeat the whole purpose of the program by allowing the sale of candy, soft drinks and ice cream within the school.
>
> Ask any school lunchroom manager . . . what is her greatest single problem, and she will answer, "The untouched plate." And it makes her blood positively boil when she sees Johnny, who left a lunchroom meal of milk, apple salad, meat loaf and scalloped potatoes looking as if it had been examined and rejected by a disdainful mouse, barging down the hall at 12:45 with a soft drink in one hand and a candy bar in the other.[56]

School food service leaders attempted to get candy and soda sales removed from the premises and even to obtain zoning regulations that would ban commercial establishments from selling them within a few blocks of schools, but they met with limited success.

Congress had begun to involve itself in this aspect of child nutrition when school food came under increasing scrutiny in the 1960s. In 1970, amendments to the Child Nutrition Act of 1966 authorized USDA to ban the sale of competitive foods in or near cafeterias during mealtimes, but specifically permitted, as Marion Nestle has explained, "any food ever served as part of a school lunch to be sold at other times and places. This arcane distinction meant, for example, that cake could be sold but soft drinks could not." The restrictions kicked off a prolonged tug of war among competing interests that is still in progress today. Nestle continues: "As a result of these rules, soft drink companies lost revenue, but so did the schools. To protect the ongoing income they derived from sales of snack food, school officials joined soft drink companies in pressuring Congress to allow competitive foods to be sold at any time and place (again this meant in the cafeteria during lunch periods), provided that the proceeds went to the schools or to approved student organizations."[57] Further, they persuaded Congress to cancel USDA's authority to regulate competitive food sales, identifying state and local boards of education as the appropriate actors. This was the start of a fluctuating set of laws and regulations that over time changed the times and places that other foods could be sold, the nature of foods that could not be sold, and the locus of authority to regulate them.[58]

In the late 1970s, in the aftermath of the plate waste revelations, food service professionals pointed out that competitive foods played a major role in the problem. "We've declared war on waste," pronounced ASFSA president Josephine Martin. "One of the reasons children do not eat the food in the school lunch program is because of the foods served in competition with it. We have to get rid of foods that are nonnutritious."[59] In 1977 Congress restored the authority to regulate competitive food sales to USDA, and the agency, still grappling with the plate waste controversy and the resulting emphasis on the child-as-consumer, began developing rules. A draft, released for comment in 1978 elicited more than four thousand public comments. It was modest from a nutrition activist's perspective, restricting the sale of "foods of minimal nutritional value" (essentially some candy, soda, gum, and water ices) until after the end of the last lunch period, but it was too much regulation for the soda bottlers and the freedom-of-choice hardliners. USDA withdrew the proposed regulations and tried again the next year, this time defining "foods of minimal nutritional value" as foods that failed to provide at least 5 percent of the RDA for each of eight nutrients in a 100-calorie serving.[60]

It was an easy standard to meet; as one USDA staff member put it, "If a candy bar has only one nut in it, we feel it is above our minimal nutrient standards."[61] The new rule set no maximum levels for sugar, fat, or salt. It was quickly characterized by critics as "a total cave-in to the snack food industry" and "a disaster." They predicted that cakes and candies would simply be fortified, failing to deal with the underlying issue of spoiling students' appetites for healthy food. As the Columbia University nutritionist Joan Dye Gussow summarized, "If you are trying to sell a nutritionally sound lunch, you do not compete with yourself by offering other foods. After all, taxpayers are supporting a program to provide good food for their children and then they have the program undercut with the sale of food that brings profit to many outside groups. It seems ridiculous. The new rule is worse than the old one and fortification of these foods does not deal with the basic problem of having too high a consumption of salt, fat and sugar."[62] Despite criticism from both sides, including hundreds of letters objecting to the limitations on competitive foods that were later shown to be from employees of PepsiCo, USDA stayed the course and implemented the regulations the next year. Foods of "minimal nutritional value" could not be sold until after the end of the last lunch period, inside the cafeteria or elsewhere. Briefly, food service hoped for an end to "the untouched plate."

The soda bottlers, however, were nothing if not persistent; next they sued the government on the grounds that the regulations were "arbitrary, capricious, . . . and in excess of statutory jurisdiction." Although a district court sided with USDA, the bottlers won on appeal. In *National Soft Drink Association v. Block,* the circuit court held that the regulations were not arbitrary nor capricious, but that Congress had not actually given the secretary of agriculture the authority to regulate food sales except those in the cafeteria, during the meal periods.[63] The court found one exception, however: competitive foods that were not classified as "foods of minimal nutritional value" could be sold in the cafeteria during mealtimes if the proceeds went to approved school groups or to the food service itself. This is basically the regulation in force as I write, although the limitation on the allocation of revenues disappeared when USDA published revised rules in 1985.

WAR ON SPENDING: POOR FOOD FOR POOR KIDS

While health advocates and soda bottlers were arguing over competitive food regulations, another issue altogether was threatening both the quality of school food and the demographic profile of the program. During the 1970s, the American economy experienced a series of shocks, most notably a sharp rise in fuel prices accompanied by long lines at the gas pumps. By the late 1970s, the nation faced "stagflation," an economic slowdown coupled with inflation, that was widely blamed on mounting federal budget deficits. During the presidency of Jimmy Carter, school lunch participation rose dramatically as federal reimbursements for free and reduced price meals had their intended effects. More and more poor children were eating school lunch and breakfast, and the federal price tag was rising accordingly. Hoping to control spending without reducing benefits to poor children, the Carter administration in 1980 turned to the same solution that had appealed to Lyndon Johnson in 1966: it proposed reducing the federal subsidy for paid meals, which still constituted a majority of the lunches served in fiscal 1981. Congress, however, wanted to preserve the broad, middle-class character of the lunch program; it responded to the Carter administration proposals with across-the-board cuts to both the income-tested and the non-means-tested parts of the program. These cuts were substantial, totaling $400 million across the array of child nutrition programs, but they were mild compared to the fiscal shock that awaited school food in the next administration.

The election of Ronald Reagan in 1980 signaled the start of an all out assault on domestic social spending. A few years earlier the success of Proposition 13 in California, a ballot initiative that cut back property taxes and limited any future increase, had signaled a public mood often called the taxpayer rebellion. Charging that social programs were bloated, out of control, and prone to fraud and abuse, the new administration sought and won cuts in a whole host of programs serving poor and working-class families. In school food, however, the administration proposed to eliminate *all* federal subsidies for non-means-tested meals—those in the full price category—thus converting school meals into just the sort of welfare program it was elsewhere attacking. Reagan's budget director David Stockman declared the school food program "wasteful" because it subsidized meals for children from middle-class and upper-class families who could afford to pay, and he predicted that such families would continue to use the program, even if the broad Section 4 subsidy were eliminated. In response to ASFSA's projections that the program would be unsustainable without the general subsidies, he told a congressional committee, "All of these dire predictions are based on an assumption. I don't believe those assumptions have been verified. It seems to me middle- and upper-income students will stay in the program and that their families will be willing to put in 30 cents more a meal because it is still a good deal."[64] Congress refused to go along with the full changeover, but in an effort to find the financial savings that had been decreed by a congressional budget resolution, it authorized a substantial cut in the Section 4 subsidies, reducing the amount per meal by more than one-third, and it eliminated participation by most private schools, lowered subsidies and sharply raised allowable prices for reduced price meals, lowered the eligibility ceilings for reduced price meals, and increased the accountability and verification requirements, both for families applying for free meals and for food service departments. It terminated non-food assistance for equipment and reduced funding for nutrition education and training. All this was part of the infamous Omnibus Budget Reconciliation Act of 1981.

The results of these changes were just what school food service personnel, through their professional association, had predicted. Nearly 2,700 schools dropped out of the program, and as lunch prices jumped in schools across the nation, participation by full price students declined from 15.3 million in 1979 to 11.2 million in 1983. That is, the National School Lunch Program lost more than a quarter of its full price customers, much more than the loss that would have been expected due to the declining school enrollments of that period.[65] Students eligible for reduced price meals had seen their prices double—they also dropped out in substantial numbers. Even participation by students eligible to eat free dropped briefly, primarily because schools left the program.

In the long run, the most profound impact of these changes may have been to alter the image of the program, from a middle-class educational program to a welfare-oriented program for poor kids. In the immediate term, school food service directors found their bottom lines confronted with a very concrete quadruple whammy: fewer lunches sold, smaller reimbursements for each meal provided, a smaller commodity entitlement, and expensive new accounting requirements. To make matters worse, cuts in other federal assistance to schools made school systems highly resistant to picking up the slack. Declining enrollments put many school systems in a financial bind when it came to enrollment-based allocations, and the taxpayer revolt contributed to an unwillingness of politicians at the state and local levels to offer compensatory funds. School boards, confronted by wage demands from an increasingly unionized workforce, mounting pension costs, and a growing list of unfunded mandates (programs required but not subsidized) from the federal government, increasingly began requiring school food service directors to break even. "School food is a business and should operate like one" became the mantra in many systems.

It is not the eligibility cuts or the subsidy reductions that most adults of a certain age remember about the Reagan-Stockman assault on school food spending, however; it is the effort to save money by reducing nutrition standards and, most famously, counting ketchup as a vegetable. Lynn Parker, a nutritionist who headed the child nutrition program efforts of the Food Research and Action Center for years and is now directing a standing committee of the Institute of Medicine, was asked to serve on the panel charged with the task of revising the standards. Recently, she described this episode for me. "So I get on the task force, and the people who are there start talking about reducing the portion size, reducing the percentage of the RDA that school lunch and breakfast would have to meet, and then they started talking about ketchup as a vegetable, condiments as vegetables, crediting cookies as breads." The members of the task force, she recalled, "were so concerned that Stockman was going to cut their budgets and that they were going to have to continue to serve what was required in school lunch, that they were willing to give in to ideas that had no nutritional basis whatsoever, only an economic basis, because they were feeling that they had no alternative." They were probably also influenced by the plate waste discussions of the previous decade: all of the studies had shown that vegetables were the part of the meal most likely to be thrown away. When Parker realized that she would be outvoted, she and a fellow member convinced the task force to support a resolution explaining that the recommendations had an economic, not a nutritional basis. Meanwhile, FRAC worked with Representative Tony Hall to pass a resolution in the House of Representatives to the effect that "there should be no changes made in the school lunch program except those that had a sound nutritional basis." When USDA released the new regulations, advocates had the explanatory resolution which "said, bluntly that they had no sound nutritional basis" to back up their opposition. Activists and Congressional supporters of school food staged a lunch on the Capitol steps, showing just how meager a meal would be legal under the new regulations and capturing considerable media attention. The White House was embarrassed, sufficiently so that the official in charge of the program at USDA was transferred.[66] The ketchup regulations were withdrawn, but the episode remains—like Henry Wallace's little pigs—the way in which the Reagan administration's school lunch policy is remembered.

The Reagan administration continued to propose the elimination of the Section 4 subsidy every year from fiscal year 1983 to fiscal year 1988, but it had apparently reached the end of Congress's tolerance for cuts to the program. Republicans on the Senate Agriculture Committee wrote to the president's chief of staff, James Baker III, advising against any further efforts to eliminate the general subsidy, calling it "an option which is certain to fail."[67] Both houses agreed to a provision in the Balanced Budget and Emergency Deficit Control Act of 1985 that exempted school lunch and other child nutrition programs from a plan for automatic funding cuts triggered by deficits. Eligibility for all nonprofit private schools was restored by Congress in 1986.[68] A Reagan administration program, dubbed "New Federalism," that would have essentially turned child nutrition programs into a block grant to the states was handily rebuffed.[69]

In the meantime, however, the financial shortfall in school food triggered profound changes in the nation's school kitchens and cafeterias. All of the trends that had begun in the 1970s—the use of fast food items, the notion of the child as customer, the sale of competitive foods—were escalated by the financial crunch. Many school food service directors set aside their opposition to competitive foods and adopted an "if you can't beat 'em, join 'em" attitude. A la carte sales in many cafeterias were extended beyond the second servings that had traditionally been offered to include new fast food and snack items that would bring in profits and keep paying customers in the lunchroom. More and more schools began to resemble those that Mimi Sheraton had critiqued in Las Vegas. As Josephine Martin has described the impact:

> The uncertainty of funding combined with the cuts created turmoil in schools. A large number of schools dropped the NSLP. Many others, while maintaining the NSLP, expanded the a la carte offerings as a means of generating revenue to offset program cuts. In many of these schools, the NSLP was perceived as a welfare program where only poor children ate the NSLP meal. The a la carte program in many instances had the effect of being a food service in competition with the NSLP. The a la carte offerings were often based on student preferences without regard to the nutritional needs of students.[70]

A la carte was not the only trend that was escalated by the fiscal squeeze. Some school systems turned to private food service management companies in an effort to cope with the deficit. The use of private companies had been authorized by the Nixon administration in 1970, when they were touted as a strategy for dealing with the kitchenless schools that had hampered expansion of the programs into poor inner city neighborhoods, but use had not become widespread. In the 1980s, however, more and more local school food authorities, facing the cutback in federal funding, turned to such companies, which had a reputation for controlling labor costs. The increased demand for accountability also contributed to wider use of food service management companies, as these generally promised to maintain the records, handle the bookkeeping, and absorb the liability for any disallowed meals.

The threat of elimination of the Section 4 subsidy and the need to resist the use of block grants further activated the ASFSA, and with the initiation of an annual Legislative Action Conference, the organization's interactions with Congress became more frequent. Perhaps that is why the legislators finally listened to something that the food service directors had been saying for decades: that commodities were often difficult to handle and ill suited to the needs of school children and school kitchens, contributing to the waste problem. In the Commodity Distribution Reform Act of 1987, Congress set in motion a series of reforms in the commodity program that adjusted packaging and delivery to accommodate school realities and increased the options for processing.

By the end of the 1980s, school food seemed once again to be on an even keel; the threats of elimination of Section 4 support had abated, and block grants appeared to be off the table. When Senator Patrick Leahy, a long-term champion of child nutrition, became chair of the Senate Agriculture Committee in 1987, he initiated a series of improvements to school food and other child nutrition programs, winning bipartisan support for measures that expanded access, raised quality, and increased participation. ASFSA turned its attention from fighting defensive battles to envisioning a campaign for universal free school meals. As we shall see in greater detail in chapter 7, the mounting frustration of food service operators with the administrative burden occasioned by the new levels of accountability and verification imposed in the Reagan years had brought many to conclude that the three-tier eligibility system produced by the war on hunger was unworkable. After the election of Bill Clinton, they articulated what they called the "universal vision." Two things happened to derail the dream. The first was the declaration of war on fat. The second was a new outbreak of the war on spending.

WAR ON FAT

The opening skirmishes of the war on fat had taken place back in the 1980s, when two Washington-based consumer advocacy groups began to criticize the NSLP in general, and USDA-donated commodities in particular, for high fat content.

The backstory to what would become the war on fat calls to mind Franklin Roosevelt's little pigs. Price supports and farm technologies combined in the early 1980s to produce an enormous government inventory of surplus of dairy products. By the fall of 1981, cheese, butter, and nonfat dried milk were rolling into the nation's dairy storage facilities at the rate of twenty million pounds a week.[71] USDA began making large donations of dairy surpluses to schools. From 1981 until 1987, schools could order dairy products in unlimited quantities as "bonus commodities" that did not count against their allocations of entitlement commodities. Given that food service operations were adjusting to the Carter and Reagan budget cuts, it is not surprising that cheese became a mainstay on the school lunch menu. Midway through the decade, Congress took action to reduce the surplus; it lowered the price support levels for dairy products, and it offered dairy farmers cash to get out of the milk business. Under the "whole-herd buy-out," producers who chose to sell their entire herds for slaughter or for export could receive special payments. In order to minimize the potential adverse effects on beef, pork, and lamb producers, the legislation also required the secretary of agriculture to buy and distribute 400 million pounds of red meat. Schools, again, were a major recipient.[72] In 1987, schools were simultaneously helping to draw down the dairy inventory and eat up the beef surplus.

Meanwhile, concern about the role of fat in the American diet was on the rise. The old worries about vitamin and mineral deficiencies had given way to mounting anxiety about heart disease and diabetes, with overweight and diets high in saturated fats identified as the underlying cause. The *Dietary Guidelines for Americans,* first published in 1980 and revised every five years under the joint auspices of the Department of Health and Human Services and USDA, increasingly urged Americans to reduce their consumption of fats, especially saturated fats, as well as sodium and cholesterol. All that beef and cheese in the School Lunch Program made USDA look less than consistent, despite the efforts to improve commodities mandated by the 1987 act, which were slowly getting underway.

In the late 1980s, a Washington-based nonprofit consumer advocacy organization called attention to the discrepancy between USDA's dietary advice and its own programs. At the start of each school year, beginning in 1988 and for several years thereafter, Public Voice for Food and Health Policy issued a report critical of the nutritional profile, and especially the fat content, of school food.[73] These reports urged USDA to set limits on fat, sugar, and sodium in school meals. Ellen Haas, the media-savvy executive director of Public Voice succeeded in generating considerable newspaper coverage with these annual report cards, much to the distress of ASFSA, whose leadership wrote to Haas that they "were gravely concerned over the impact your Washington, D.C., press conference and other activities were having in undermining the confidence parents have in the school nutrition programs."[74] In 1991, the Center for Science in the Public Interest (CSPI) added its considerable influence to the cause. CSPI convened a citizens committee reminiscent of the ad hoc groups of the hunger wars; its members included cardiologists, nutritionists, pediatricians, educators, and school food service personnel, and they issued a "White Paper on School Lunch Nutrition," also urging USDA to set limits on fat, sugar, and sodium in school meals.

When the first of the Public Voice reports was issued, both the USDA and ASFSA responded by reaffirming their support for the *Dietary Guidelines for Americans,* with the explanation that, as the USDA spokesperson put it, "scientific evidence does not support setting absolute daily intake levels of sugar, fat or sodium for children. Nutrition strategies warranted for the general adult population may actually be harmful to children, particularly low-income children, during periods of growth and development."[75] The 1990 version of the *Dietary Guidelines,* however, established a standard of not more than 30 percent of calories from fat, and not more than 10 percent of calories from saturated fats for everyone except children under two. In other words, the scientific consensus now included the school-aged child in the population urged to limit fat calories to 30 percent. After the release of the 1990 *Guidelines,* Secretary of Agriculture Edwin Madigan initiated a large-scale research program called the School Nutrition Dietary Assessment (SNDA), and asked Mathematica Policy Research Inc., the research firm contracted to conduct the study, to measure school food against the standards set by the *Dietary Guidelines for Americans,* even though school meals at the time were not *required* to conform to the guidelines.

The results were disturbing. On average, school lunches were deriving not 30 but 38 percent of calories from fats, not 10 but 15 percent from saturated fats. The meals were also found to be high in sodium. Breakfasts were closer to meeting the goal for total fat—31 percent of calories—but they were considerably over the 10 percent threshold for saturated fats, with an average of 14 percent of calories from this source. Only 1 percent of schools were serving, on average, meals that complied with the dietary guidelines for percentage of calories from fat—1 percent! And only one single school in a sample of 544 served an average meal that complied with the guideline for saturated fat. Ominously, the SNDA study reported that there appeared to be a correlation between the percentage of calories from fat and the rate of student participation: those schools that served meals with less than 32 percent of energy derived from fat had participation rates 6–10 percent lower than schools with higher fat meals.[76] The report set off alarms both within and outside the Food and Consumer Service (FCS), the USDA agency in charge of administering the programs.

By the time the Mathematica research was complete, a new administration was in the White House, and the new head of the FCS was none other than the former Public Voice director, Ellen Haas. USDA released the findings at a press conference held at a school in southeast Washington, D.C. After eating a school lunch of fried chicken, green beans, salad, milk, and an apple, Secretary of Agriculture Mike Espy summed up the situation with a memorably mixed metaphor: "We can not continue to deep fry our children's health." Under Haas's leadership, USDA almost immediately began holding hearings and quickly commenced planning an effort to help schools reduce the fat and salt and increase the carbohydrates in their meals. While nutritionists in the FCS were urging lower-fat preparation methods, however, other branches of USDA were expressing concern about the economic impact of bringing school meals into compliance with the dietary guidelines. They estimated that purchases of cheese, beef, poultry, and potatoes would all decrease.[77] Needless to say, this roused the ire of the producers and processors of those products, but Congress acted anyway. By November of 1994, just a year after the SNDA report was issued, legislation requiring schools in the National School Lunch or School Breakfast programs to serve meals that complied with the *Dietary Guidelines* had passed both houses of Congress and been signed by the president: the Healthy Meals for Healthy Americans Act.

To assist school food authorities in meeting the new standards, USDA launched Team Nutrition, a program of technical assistance, financial support for training for school food service personnel, and resources for nutrition education in the schools. The reform effort, the School Meals Initiative for Healthy Children, or SMI for short, also included a program to improve the nutritional profile of the commodities donated to schools by the Department of Agriculture. In the process, USDA invited input from food service directors and, as a result, undertook what its authors dubbed a "Business Re-engineering Process" with regard to federal commodities. Among the many changes was a regulation that permitted schools to trade their commodities to processors for branded finished products. Rather than ship the raw materials to the schools and have the schools arrange for processing them—or ship them to the states for processing under state contracts—school systems could opt to have USDA ship them directly to commercial processors who would take them in payment for finished products ordered by the schools, a process called the commodity value pass through. (At last I understand how potato puffs became a commodity.)

Other aspects of the SMI proved more controversial and more acrimonious. The SMI changed the basis for menu planning, proposing a new approach based on computerized nutrient analyses, called Nutrient Standard Menu Planning (NSMP) or NuMenu, in lieu of the old, food based meal pattern. While USDA officials viewed the new menu planning system as a tool that would give school food authorities more flexibility in planning menus to meet the guidelines, many school food service directors saw it differently, and they mobilized through their professional association to resist the imposition of the new approach. The opposition to a required move to NSMP was partly practical. It would require computer hardware and computer skills that many food service directors simply didn't have. Some saw this as another unfunded mandate, predicting that there would be substantial costs associated with the new technology, particularly labor costs of entering recipes and menus into a computer database. Anti-hunger advocates, while supportive of the idea of improving meal quality, were deeply concerned that some schools that lacked computers or computer skills might simply drop out of the child nutrition programs, leaving impoverished children without access to free and reduced price meals. Some food service professionals simply resented what they perceived as high-handed micromanagement or felt ignored or excluded from decisions about an issue where their expertise should have been sought.

There were also those who feared that the use of nutrient-based planning might decrease rather than improve the quality of the resulting meals. As Dorothy Pannell, the author of a widely used food service management textbook, wrote in a special issue of *The American Journal of Clinical Nutrition* devoted to reporting and discussing the results of SNDA, "it is troubling to consider menus with fortification and enrichment taking care of many of the nutrients. Fruits and vegetables as a part of lunch at school could be something of the past."[78] The Washington-based lobby for fruit and vegetable producers, the Produce Marketing Association, was also concerned, fearing that schools would substitute fortified "super junk foods" for fruits and vegetables. Proponents of NSMP, on the other hand, believed that the new approach would increase the use of fruits and vegetables and whole grain, rice, and pasta items; one of the groups most in favor of the proposed change was the

Vegetarian Resource Center, which shared the view that the traditional NSLP meal patterns deterred the provision of vegetarian options and plant-based alternatives.

Some food service directors welcomed the system. In fact, the original experiments with computer-based menu planning had been done by food service directors on their own initiative, and some who had used the nutrient analysis system asked USDA for a rule that would permit them to substitute it for the food based approach. There is an enormous difference, however, between having the option to move to a new technology and being required to do so.[79]

The struggle over the menu planning component of the SMI was acrimonious, to put it mildly. The opposition of the ASFSA was intensified by what they perceived as an abrasive tone taken by Undersecretary Haas in her public statements about the program, both in her former role as director of Public Voice and in her new position at USDA. ASFSA's lobbying campaign was successful. The final legislation passed by Congress authorized school food authorities to choose any one of four approaches to menu planning. Two were variants of the old system of food based menu patterns: Food Based Menu Planning (FBMP), often called "traditional," and Enhanced Food Based Menu Planning (EFBMP). Two were variants of the new system preferred by USDA: Nutrient Standard Menu Planning (NSMP) and Assisted Nutrient Standard Menu Planning (ANSMP); the latter allowed for the menu planning to be done by a consultant, a state agency, or some other external source. When USDA issued a rule for implementing the Congressional legislation that appeared to some to circumvent the intent of Congress, Congress passed a bill granting schools the right to use "any reasonable approach" to menu planning.[80]

That piece of legislation, called the Healthy Meals for Healthy Children Act, was clearly a rebuke to Undersecretary Haas. According to the *Congressional Record,* "We are moving this bipartisan legislation because the USDA Food and Consumer Service under the direction of Ellen Haas is out of control. In the name of advancing good nutrition for children, the USDA is burying our schools in bureaucratic paperwork and regulatory micromanagement."[81] The undersecretary's criticism of commodities such as beef and cheese had won her enemies among commodity processors, enemies with powerful friends in Congress.[82] ASFSA also lobbied hard for the legislation, primarily because food service directors feared new costs associated with implementing the new approach to menu planning, but also because they were alienated by the undersecretary's public criticism of the quality of school meals. And finally, they resented what they saw as Haas's failure to act as a strong advocate for school food programs when a new outbreak of the war on spending threatened to undermine their federal entitlement status.

The election of an insurgent conservative majority in the House of Representatives in 1994 had put all advocates of child nutrition programs on the defensive. The conservatives' Contract with America called for, among many other things, converting child nutrition programs to block grants. As we have seen, this was not the first time—both President Ford and President Reagan had submitted similar legislation to the Congress—but this time, with the lower chamber in the hands of the aggressively antifederal conservatives led by Speaker of the House Newt Gingrich, and both chambers under Republican control, the threat seemed more real. The anti-hunger "issue network" and the school food service and school business organizations gathered their forces, but again they felt let down by Undersecretary Haas. As Laura Sims has written, "They felt she had taken personal ownership of the Team Nutrition project to such a degree that she had no time or interest in working with them to fend off the block-grant proposals."[83] That is, she was so busy waging the war on fat that she had no time or attention to give to resisting the war on spending.

In order to understand the intensity of the child nutrition community's opposition to block grants for child nutrition programs, it is useful to know a bit about what the implications of this would have been. As Peter Eisinger has explained, "As proposed, the block grants would have ended the entitlement to breakfast, lunch, summer food, and child care meals. Instead, states would have received a set amount of funding, which would not fluctuate to accommodate shifts in school or day care enrollment or economic changes, all of which change the demand for food assistance. Not only would the termination of open-ended entitlement funding end the stimulus to spending in times of recession, it would likely exacerbate interstate inequities as poor people clustered in some states." Eisinger goes on to point out that "none of these features is a necessary concomitant of the block grant form, although historically, capped funding has tended to accompany block grant designs, from the Community Development Block Grant of 1974 to the Reagan era education and health care block grants. However, state administrative flexibility is an inherent feature of block grants."[84] While the central concern of anti-hunger advocates was to protect the crucial victories of the war on hunger—the entitlement status and performance funding aspects of school food and other child nutrition programs—the memories of the failure of these programs to reach and serve so many needy children during the period of local autonomy also played a role. Anti-hunger activists have long seen the federal government as the guarantor of the rights of poor Americans; nobody in the child nutrition advocacy community wanted to go back to a situation in which eligibility levels or benefit amounts could be determined to suit state and local economic conditions—or local prejudices. In the end, the child nutrition community triumphed. Not only was the block grant proposal rejected, but Newt Gingrich is reported to have declared, ruefully, that he had been "school lunched."

By this point, the National School Lunch and School Breakfast programs had reached substantially their present form. Meanwhile, however, the day-to-day impacts of policy decisions made in the early and mid-1970s, the early 1980s, and the mid-1990s have ripened into an almost impenetrable thicket of regulations and procedures. Each "war" has left behind its own layer of rules and procedures. And while the wars that I have used to organize this history began in sequence, none of them has ever quite ended, so that by the beginning of the twenty-first century, school food is simultaneously tasked with alleviating poverty, ending hunger, reducing waste, controlling spending, and overcoming childhood obesity, along with its original goals of safeguarding the health and well-being of the nation's children and encouraging the domestic consumption of nutritious agricultural commodities. It's a tall order, to say the least.

CHAPTER THREE

PENNY WISE, POUND FOOLISH

What's Driving the Menu?

The menu that bothered me so much during my stint in the Any Town High School cafeteria—the pizza and potato puffs combination, as well as the various other relatively monochromatic offerings—turned out not to be idiosyncratic, not at all. The School Nutrition Association (SNA) conducts an annual survey of its members that asks, among other things, for the most popular item in each of several categories: entrees, vegetables, beverages, and dessert. The 2004 survey, the one that would have reflected the school year that I visited Any Town, reported that pizza was the favorite entree, for almost half (49.1 percent) of respondents, and it had been the best-selling entree every year since the polling began in 1998. The runner up was "chicken (typically chicken nuggets)" for 32.2 percent of respondents. Among vegetables, corn had the highest tally, 23.1 percent of respondents, and french fries were a close second with 21.3 percent. If, however, you add in "potatoes (type not specified)," the third place winner with 14.8 percent, the total for potatoes at 36.1 percent exceeds even the ever-popular corn. And that still doesn't include the mashed or whipped potatoes that were down in eighth place with 6.5 percent of respondents. With that added in, some form of potato was the favorite vegetable in 42.7 percent of reporting schools. Salads didn't even make it onto the list.[1]

Food service professionals are quick to point out that these foods are popular outside the school as well as in. I knew this from looking at national food sales data, but what really brought it home to me was a

84

story told by Virginia Webb, the director of the Education and Training Division at the National Food Service Management Institute, located at the University of Mississippi. Ms. Webb, a registered dietician and experienced food service professional, is also the sort of life-long learner who keeps going back to school. She told me that she had taken some graduate courses in the School of Education at the university, classes filled with teachers, principals, and superintendents, in which she was usually the only person from a food service background:

> And one night I was talking to . . . a superintendent and two teachers. And they really were kind of bad-mouthing their school food service. And saying, "All they serve are chicken nuggets and pizzas and hamburgers." And I just kind of stood there and took it in and let them talk and have their conversation. And when there was a little bit of a pause, I asked, "What do you feed your children?" And they got these looks on their faces. And they didn't have to say it, but I knew what they were feeding their kids at home.

Changing what people feed their children at home, however, strikes many observers as beyond the pale of public policy. The school lunch menu, on the other hand, seems like fair game. "The menu is the single most important factor in the success of a foodservice operation," declares an influential school food service management textbook.[2] It may also be the single most important target of criticism of school food. There are as many different reviews of the school food menu as there are reviewers, each representing a different set of food preferences or a different activist group. Animal rights groups want vegan options; parents of children with peanut allergies want peanut-free schools; members of various religious communities want menus—or at least options—that conform to their dietary laws. The most common critique, however, is dissatisfaction with the nutritional profile of the meals served.

Virg Bernero is a state senator in Michigan who has introduced legislation to curb junk food in school vending machines and a la carte sales. When I interviewed him, he had just visited a local high school in response to an e-mail from a constituent, and he had come to the realization that a la carte was not the only problem.

> And so I did go to the school, and it was appalling. It was worse than I'd even imagined, what I saw. I had thought that the main problem was the a la carte line, but maybe they go hand-in-hand. When I saw what was there, this popcorn chicken and the french fries and the pizza pocket, just garbage, I couldn't find anything to eat. . . . So I said, "Where's the vegetable?" I couldn't find any vegetable. They said, "Oh, the potato, the french fries." The number one vegetable in America. I finally found some broccoli. It was

broccoli to put on a baked potato. It was steamed to the point of no longer being green. It was more of a gray texture. . . . You need a spoon for this broccoli. You cannot eat this broccoli with a fork. That's not a vegetable . . . it's just mush.

Now I know everybody says school was better when I was in school, it was better when you were in school, because we walked to school, uphill, both ways. . . . But in fact, . . . the lunch program was better. Because we had a balanced meal. It wasn't always delicious, but some of it was. The shepherd's pie. It tended to be cooked on site. It wasn't all frozen garbage. It was cooked on site. It was actually pretty decent stuff. Some of that stuff was better than what a lot of people got at home. . . . You got your carrots-and-peas mixture. It was balanced. You got maybe a brownie or a cookie and applesauce. But you couldn't say, "Hey, hold the applesauce, hold the peas and carrots. I'll just take four brownies." That wasn't an option. They would laugh in your face. Mrs. Mack would never have tolerated it.

Bernero may not be noted for temperate language, but the central elements of his critique—the plethora of fast food items, the reliance on frozen and reheated foods, the scarcity of fresh vegetables and fruit, and the lack of balance introduced by the presence of a la carte options—are the criticisms I encountered most frequently, sometimes accompanied by fond memories of food freshly prepared on site and the lunch ladies who served it. "Pizza. Hot dogs. Chicken nuggets. The average school lunch menu in Maryland reads like a list of carnival fare," declares a recent report in Southern Maryland Online.[3] Tracy A. Fox, who is both a Bethesda, Maryland, parent and a well-known dietitian and school food activist, voices the concern: "Across the board, you still see a preponderance of fast-food-like items. . . . Districts will say their food is prepared in a healthy way, but if you look at the menu, it looks like a fast-food menu." Acknowledging her district's efforts to reduce fat and sodium and increase whole grains and fresh fruits, she still sees the heavy reliance on such items as a problem. By including so much fast food, the schools "are still confirming that these foods are OK to have." The students, she says "should be exposed to a wider variety."[4]

In many critiques, the menu for the official federally subsidized, reimbursable meal is confused with the a la carte options prevalent in school cafeterias. On the one hand, the USDA, the School Nutrition Association, and many of the anti-hunger advocacy groups are asserting that school meals conform to exacting nutrition standards. On the other, if you walk into the cafeteria, chips, pastries, and sweetened "juice drinks" abound. Mike Hendricks of the *Kansas City Star* recently pointed out that despite the new wellness regulations, schools . . . are still a long way from getting the junk-food monkey off their backs. . . . My youngest starts seventh grade this week. While cooling my heels in the registration line for an hour, I had ample time to study the "a la carte" lunch menu posted on the wall. Snickers bars, Milky Ways, ice cream and malt cups. This is wellness? . . . Junk food is all some kids eat for lunch nowadays. When they get to middle and high schools, they have choices beyond the standard school lunch. Chicken finger baskets, fries and pizza, not to mention all those sweets.[5]

Some parents are understandably confused. As the nutrition activist Margo Wootan told me,

I don't think when parents send their child to school, they tell them which line to buy their food out of. They don't say, "Don't buy it out of the a la carte line, because that's not healthy, that's not regulated. Buy it out of the reimbursable meal line." Parents don't even realize that there's a difference. . . . Parents picture lunch as it was when they went to school. Turkey cubes in gravy over rice with a vegetable, and a fruit, and a milk. And that's all that was in the cafeteria when I was a kid. And so the parents don't realize that their child might instead be using their lunch money to buy Flaming Cheetos and a Gatorade. They don't expect that that's even available.

Wootan's memories of school lunch as we knew it have many counterparts. As Donnis Badgett, the editor of the *Bryan–College Station Eagle* in Texas wrote, "When I was in public school back in the Pleistocene Epoch, we didn't have the option of pizza or burgers for lunch. If we had, you could bet your milk money we would've chosen them over the 'balanced' meals that ended up on our trays every day. If you'll recall, the lunchroom ladies in white dresses and hair nets ladled up our trays with bread, meat, veggies, fruit, dessert and such." Clearly there is an element of nostalgia here that may have little or nothing to do with nutrition. Badgett continued his recollections: "Take those big rolls, for instance, I don't think there's a better dinner roll in existence than those puffy, golden-brown rolls from a school cafeteria. The lunchroom ladies made them by the ton from scratch, and they were consistently good. I can still close my eyes and smell that warm, yeasty aroma. Of course they used bleached white flour in the dough, so now we know those cafeteria rolls weren't very good for you. But man, they tasted good."[6]

The "warm, yeasty aroma" of freshly baked breads is gone from many schools these days, along with any other smells derived from the actual cooking of food. Instead, as a reporter for a central California newspaper reported after a two-week tour of school cafeterias, "The majority of foods come fully cooked and frozen. Cafeteria crews simply place the food in the oven and set the timer."[7] Of course, the aromas of "scratch" cooking may still be pervading a central kitchen. School food "production systems" include "on site" kitchens, where the food is cooked, served, and eaten in the same school, "central kitchens" where food is prepared for distribution to all the schools in an entire system, and intermediate systems where food is prepared at a school with a large capacity kitchen for the students at that school and for transportation to several others nearby. When I started this research, I assumed that central kitchens and satellite systems were inherently inferior to food cooked on site; the closer to the child the meal was prepared, the better. I have learned, however, that there are many trade-offs. School systems that cannot afford to provide a cook for each school may be able to prepare excellent food in central kitchens and deliver it in bulk to satellite campuses. And on-site kitchens may be doing little or no cooking beyond defrosting and reheating frozen entrees. Central kitchens, as it turns out, are far more likely to make their own sauces, stews, baked goods, and salad dressings, and thus to control the use of preservatives, coloring agents, sodium, and other unwelcome components.

WHAT HAS HAPPENED TO SCHOOL FOOD?

What is driving the school food menu? Why has it become so full of defrost-and-reheat items and fast food clones? What has happened to the balanced meals and "warm yeasty aromas" fondly remembered by some observers of a certain age? The short answer is that school food reflects changes not only in school finances, the USDA commodities available, and a growing concern about food-borne illnesses, but changes in the wider society. Money seems to be the taproot for changes within the schools, so let us begin with the money story. For many inhabitants of the world of school food, the menu changes that attract so much negative attention are traceable to an upheaval in the program's financing in the early 1980s.

Lunch Money

Recall the deep cuts in Section 4 subsidies discussed in chapter 2, the war on spending that reduced resources amid the demand that school food "operate like a business." Faced with declining revenues and break-even ultimata, school food service operations did what any good business would do—they sought strategies to cut costs, and they tried to increase business. On the revenue side, following the massive exodus of full price students triggered by the reduction in subsidies, they sought ways to get the paying customers back into the cafeteria. Two strategies emerged: increased a la carte sales and adapting the menu to children's preferences. Many schools substantially expanded their a la carte operations, selling foods similar to those students were purchasing on the outside. In some systems, branded items—such as Domino's Pizza and Taco Bell tacos—were purchased in bulk and sold in the cafeteria in competition with the federal meal. A la carte items today are available in three-fourths of elementary schools and nine out of ten secondary schools, and school food service directors all over the country told me that they could not hope to break even without them. In some districts, a la carte sales are limited to items already on the menu, allowing a student to purchase an extra serving if the school meal is not sufficient to his appetite, but in most the emphasis is on fast foods and snack items.

Once the practice of offering kids' favorite foods as a la carte selections was established, it influenced the offerings in the reimbursable meals. School food service directors needed to keep participation in the federal program as high as possible in order to qualify for the maximum allowable commodities and to collect the reimbursements; if kid-friendly foods were available a la carte, they needed to offer them in the reimbursable meal as well. Further, if the kitchen and the supply system were set up to offer pizza and fries a la carte, there were savings to be achieved by incorporating them into the main-line menus.

On the cost side of the break-even equation, efforts to reduce labor costs had a similar impact on menus. Food service operators found that they could reduce the cost per meal by replacing the fresh preparation of food on site with bulk convenience foods. Such changes not only permitted schools to reduce total labor hours; they also allowed the substitution of less-skilled workers for employees with cooking skills. It is nearly two centuries since the English mathematician and mechanical engineer Charles Babbage pointed out that the true source of savings in Adam Smith's pin factory was not simply the division of the process into simple tasks in which various laborers specialized and thus developed great skill and speed, but also in the fact that cheaper labor could be used for those components of the work requiring less skill, and that lower wage groups—women and children—could be substituted for those processes not requiring manly strength. The same principle has been at work in school kitchens—as in other food service establishments—all across the country. People who have never heard of Charles

Babbage have realized that if the tasks to be performed require little skill, then people of limited skills can be hired to perform them, and that these people will earn—that is cost—less, not only because they have less skill, but also because they are more easily replaced, more interchangeable with other unskilled people. Thus they cannot successfully demand higher wages or other compensation in the form of benefits.

In school food service, the application of the Babbage principle has led to the decline in fresh preparation and in some cases, to the substitution of prepackaged industrially produced meals. Nancy May, the director of Child Nutrition in Healdsburg, California, described to me the system she found when she arrived there in the late 1990s: "The prepackaged meal companies supplied the big walk-in freezer, and they supplied the big oven. And so the food service employees, all they were doing was wheeling these stacks of prepackaged meals out of the freezer, wheeling them into the oven, and then wheeling them to the table." The system had taken hold in California, she said, "many years ago, when labor costs started to really increase. . . . At that time the prepackaged meal companies were starting to get real big," so they made "all these proposals to the school districts to serve prepackaged meals. You can cut your labor, and that became the bottom line, not kids, . . . not nutrition, . . . not the kids' well-being."

An alternate approach to restructuring the skill requirements to save money in school food service revolved around central kitchens. This is not to imply that central kitchens are a product of the fiscal crunch of the early 1980s. Indeed, several of the very earliest school feeding schemes in the United States employed them, famously the New England Kitchen through which Ellen Richards provided meals to the Boston Public Schools beginning in 1894. In the early 1970s, when the federal rules for reimbursement changed and school lunch programs were expanding rapidly, central kitchens were built in many cities that had large numbers of older schools without kitchens; they were an important part of the strategy for making sure poor children had the same access to school meals that middle-class children in the suburbs enjoyed. In the 1980s, however, many systems that had been cooking on site switched to central kitchens, driven by the same labor cost calculations that drove other schools to meal packs. One major food service management textbook estimates that "on average, an on-site preparation system can produce between 10 to 18 meals per labor hour, whereas the central kitchen can produce 100 to 160 meals per labor hour," but warns that "the labor hours and cost at the schools receiving the food must be considered when measuring . . . productivity and arriving at the cost of a lunch."[8] The Babbage principle applies here, too: highly skilled cooks can work in the central kitchen, while, as one study of school food production systems put it, "less skilled individuals may be hired at a lower wage to finish and serve the meals" at the satellite schools.[9]

Even the on-site kitchens, however, may be relying so heavily on frozen entrees that they have lost the "fresh prep" character altogether. As the School Nutrition Association's *Little Big Fact Book* summarizes: "many districts rely on *convenience* foods, in which the majority of menu items are received in nearly final form from food processors and manufacturers. The foodservice operation might buy bottled spaghetti sauce, frozen pizza, par-baked doughs or heat-and-serve entrees from vendors."[10] A South Dakota newspaper reporter on a tour of high school lunch rooms in the Sioux Falls area captured the flavor of this arrangement with a review of chicken patties: "The chicken patty burger is such a cafeteria staple that I'm convinced every person in the United States who wasn't home-schooled has eaten this mass of orangish-brown breading and white, peppery chicken. There has to be a huge, frozen warehouse of these patties somewhere in Ohio."[11] Like the use of meal packs and the reliance on central kitchens, the use of convenience foods reduces the skill requirements, and thus the costs. As one director put it, "the kinds of foods we are serving don't really require skilled culinary experience and talent. The kinds of things that kids want to eat now, you just pull it out of the freezer, pop it in the oven, and serve it. So that requires less skill, it requires less hours of labor."

A final approach to reducing costs has to do with fringe benefits. Many schools have redesigned work schedules to keep most employees from qualifying for health insurance or pensions. Known as "short hours" in the trade, such jobs also affect the skill level that prevails and even the receptivity to training. As former SNA president Donna Wittrock explained to me, "because we have so many of our positions that are short hour, we are not attracting a top-notch labor pool. We are attracting those that are just looking for a part-time job. They are probably not looking for career advancement." This is no small issue within the SNA, where there is real concern about who will replace the current generation of food service directors (and SNA leaders) as they reach retirement.

Although the budget cuts in the early 1980s were the biggest single shock to the financial foundations of school food, the fiscal squeeze is not just a piece of history that occurred a generation ago. It is the constant preoccupation of most food service directors. "What is the biggest challenge of your job?" I asked Mary Ann McCann, who runs an outstanding program in Taos, New Mexico. "Producing a meal that the kids will eat at a reasonable cost," she replied immediately.

> And salaries. And training. . . . We are trying to get salaries increased because they are underpaid, and I think, in most school districts, the food service is at the bottom of the salary scales, and there is no education required to be a cook. And I believe that there is as much required of them as there is an educational assistant, because, as I jokingly told our superintendent, "We are the only ones that can kill your kid." Because all it takes is one person not to practice safe and sanitary practices, and we can have an outbreak of food poisoning here.

She felt that money for training could make a big difference:

> There's a high level of expectation as far as what they are required to put out, and people complain that we have too much processed food, but where's the money to send these people to train, when everything has to come from our program? . . . Congress is going to have to put their money where their mouth is if they want good meals, where you have cooks that are trained to be cooks, instead of box cutters. I heard that on TV: one cook they interviewed said the only required piece of equipment she had was a box cutter—to take [food] out, heat it, and serve it.

I asked McCann what level of reimbursement would be enough. "If I were wishing . . . at least $3 a plate, because then you wouldn't have to have all the a la carte to help subsidize you."

McCann's operation serves 500,000 lunches a year. If she could spend another 50 cents a lunch, she calculated, she'd have an additional $250,000. I asked her what she would do with it—and her first priority would be getting rid of a la carte. "That would be wonderful for my program. I could die a happy woman, because I certainly wouldn't have to have my snack bar." Then, she would turn her attention to breakfast items: "One of the things we want to work on is producing a home-baked product for our breakfast in the classroom, because we buy burritos, we buy breakfast pizza, we buy muffins. And the muffins, to me are the worst because they are just nothing . . . they are just awful, hideous. But that's the only thing we can buy that meets the standard that the kids will eat. It's a school muffin," she said scornfully, and I found myself thinking about the individually wrapped, not quite thawed, quick-bread loaves that raised the ire of the teachers at the elementary school in Any Town. "But I would like to see a home-baked muffin that's got raisins or craisins or cranberries or something in it . . .

and have yogurt that we would do with our own fresh fruit." Coming back to earth, she summarized: "I want to see the kids eating meals that are home-cooked meals and not everything processed."

McCann's passion for reducing the reliance on processed food and finding healthier alternatives comes from her own experience as a cancer survivor.

> It was April 2000, and I was here in the cafeteria and I had started chemo. I had no hair. Just standing here in the cafeteria, and I saw this girl walk in with a 20-ounce bottle of pop and a bag of chips. And I said to myself, "This is done. We are not doing this anymore." Because all I could think of was my own daughters, who are at high risk . . . because of me. And if they are not drinking their milk and they are not eating fruits and vegetables, they are compromising their bone density and they are compromising their health. . . . It brought home to me that what we eat can affect us the rest of our lives. . . . There's nothing worse than compromising someone's health, and we do it every day in schools, because of the stuff that we allow to be sold.

In McCann's case, she knows firsthand how lucrative a la carte sales can be. Before her own diagnosis, she says, she resisted efforts to stop the sale of soda pop, "because at that time, all I could think about was budget, budget, budget. Money, money, money, because that was what I was brought in here to do, was to bring the program out of the red. And we did, we brought it out of the red . . . and for years we sold Coke and candy and potato chips, and we had a cash balance one year almost greater than the district did." After her diagnosis she got rid of the sodas, added salad bars to all of her schools—unlimited salad bars that have proved very popular—and worked to substitute home-cooked foods without additives for highly processed foods wherever possible.

McCann, of course, is not the only food service director to try to change the direction in which her school food menu has been evolving. "Throw a dart at a map," the New York Times columnist Lisa Belkin wrote last summer, "and you will find a school district scrambling to fill its students with things that are low fat and high fiber."[12] As Helen Mont-Ferguson, the food service director for the City of Boston, told a recent gathering of big-city school food service directors, "We are all beginning to see the importance of training people to cook fresh foods, use less processed foods. It's winding backwards from the direction we were going."[13] But it's not easy. Reformers, whether inside the system or outside, quickly encounter the legacy of the fiscal squeeze. As the old stoves wore out, they were replaced with convection ovens and "rethermalization" units suitable chiefly for reheating food produced elsewhere. As more freezer space was needed, pots and pans and knives and slicers were removed to make way. Or, if not removed, left to gather dust. "A lot of kitchens had slicers," one director told me; "they were just covered with plastic wrap, they hadn't used them in years." He found he had to train his staff in how to use a slicer as well as in basic knife skills, and not all were receptive to the new training and expectations. As the skilled cooks had retired, they had been replaced by less-skilled food service assistants, many of whom, like their young customers, are full-fledged citizens of the fast food nation. A panel member at a Child Nutrition Industry Conference I attended complained, "We have younger staff members who have eaten microwave meals all their lives and get their dinner at a drive-thru window. They don't know how to cook; they don't know how to operate the machinery. We're hiring them because they are breathing." Thus, even as the focus on obesity has subjected school kitchens to new scrutiny and to calls for the return of cooking from scratch, many school systems have found that they no longer have the skills or equipment to carry it out. "We . . . have to have foods that our cafeteria crews can make," a school nutrition specialist told the reporter from the Stockton Record who was looking into the nutritional state of school food. "We can't hire chefs. We hire people that are hard workers and friendly. We can't expect them to be qualified to prepare meals from scratch."[14]

Fear of Contamination

Skill levels and equipment are not the only factors constraining efforts to improve the menu. In our litigious society, fear of food-borne illness and the potential for a costly lawsuit also deter fresh preparation. Bertrand Weber came into school food service from a long career in the hospitality industry, managing top-rated hotels. His introduction to school food came when his son was diagnosed with type 1 diabetes. "I had to make sure that . . . the food that he ate matched the insulin that we gave him in the morning. The school didn't want to take the responsibility to assume that he had the correct amount of food and . . . at the time I could not get carb counts or anything from the school, so I spent the first three years of his school life in the cafeteria with him every single day." Weber didn't like what he saw of school food and tried with limited success to change it. When an opportunity came along to step in as food service director in a nearby district already committed to making changes, he applied for the job. I asked him to describe what he found.

What I saw was feeding kids [fast food] or duplicating what is in fast foods, to ensure that there was high participation, to ensure the program was financially successful. Complete absence of cooking. Everything was premade, right out of a box . . . fully cooked items. A staff that was very fearful the minute you mentioned fresh food because of the HACCP requirements [food safety regulations]. Very fearful of even touching fresh foods. It's a lot safer not to have to touch the food. That kind of guarantees that you won't have any lawsuits or problems or illness or any of those issues. And coming from the hotel industry, this didn't sit well with me. I fed thousands of people and we cooked using fresh foods. So why couldn't it be done in school?

The HACCP requirements to which Weber refers are the Hazard Analysis and Critical Control Point regulations, a food-safety proce-dure developed originally for the space program. The HACCP approach is comprehensive, but basically consists of identifying the points in the process of food receiving, storage, preparation, service, and cleanup at which contamination could occur or existing toxins could grow, and then developing preventive steps—the use of gloves, the control of temperature—and devising systems for monitoring and documenting important parameters at each point. In day-to-day practice, HACCP involves a lot of temperature taking in order to limit the time any food or ingredient spends in the "danger zone" between 41 degrees Fahrenheit and 135 degrees Fahrenheit—and then a lot of recording temperatures in logbooks to provide documentation. The Child Nutrition and WIC Reauthorization Act of 2004 required all school food authorities par-ticipating in the National School Lunch Program to have HACCP-based food safety programs in place by the end of the 2005–2006 school year, but many schools had been using or moving toward HACCP systems for some time. Both the SNA and the National Food Service Manage-ment Institute (NFSMI) offer HACCP training.

The issue of food-borne illness and the attendant problem of liability cropped up again and again in my interviews. I met Janet Gaffke, the food service director for Grayling, Michigan, at the enormous school food products exhibition at the heart of the SNA's Annual National Conference. I had just tasted some commodity hamburger, processed with Michigan (commodity) cherries to lend moisture, and shipped to the schools already cooked. I asked her if she purchased precooked burgers, and she said, in a resigned tone, "Yes, I do. The only time I buy raw hamburger patties now is when we have a cookout. And I really resisted that for a long time; I thought, well, I'm more of the philoso-phy of cooking from scratch, that sort of thing as much as we can, but there is an issue out there with food-borne illness that is kind of scary. I don't want to be the source of a child getting sick. So I've decided that we'll use precooked beef patties in our district." I asked her if it actually reduced the likelihood of food-borne illness or simply transferred the liability upstream, and I found her answer instructive. "I think it decreases the likelihood; I really do, because there is quality control in that plant." She exercises quality control at her schools as well, but she is not convinced that her staff has all the training they need to handle raw products safely. And even when she can control the temperatures and other components of safety within her school, she cannot be sure what has happened to meat en route to her loading dock.

Gaffke's concern about food-borne illness is justified. The Centers for Disease Control and Prevention (CDC) report approximately 76 million cases of food-borne illness in the United States each year; these typically lead to 325,000 hospitalizations and 5,000 deaths. The Outbreak Alert! database compiled by the Center for Science in the Public Interest (CSPI) has identified 11,000 cases associated with schools between 1990 and 2004, and Senator Richard Durbin cited nearly "100 reported outbreaks of food-borne illness in our schools between 1990 and 2000," when he introduced a Safe School Food Act in 2003.[15] A single "outbreak," of course, can involve many "cases." A successful lawsuit against a district can cause major financial damage; in 2001, a $4.5 million judgment against the Finley School District in Kennewick, Washington, totaled more than half the district's annual operating budget. In the wake of the judgment, the district switched to precooked beef, even though school and cafeteria administrators were convinced that the beef had not been the culprit: "With *E. coli,* people want to assume it's the meat," said the superintendent, who believes that shredded lettuce was a more likely carrier. The specific source was important to the case, because the school's liability was linked to its role as the site of cooking. "Product liability is at the manufacturer level, and the judge decided we were the manufacturer, because we cooked it," explained a spokesperson in the Finley case.[16]

Today, after high-profile recalls of spinach and green onions, a jury might be more willing to suspect produce. In fact, in 2004, produce surpassed meat as the identified source of outbreaks of *E. coli* 0157:H7, the serious and sometimes deadly variety of the bacteria.[17] Nevertheless, in the data accumulated in the CSPI Outbreak Alert! between 1990 and 2003, meat is far and away the largest single contributor, responsible for 31 percent of the outbreaks.[18] According to Dr. Robert Tauxe, head of the food-borne illness division at the Centers for Disease Control, "The new, highly industrialized way that we produce our food opened up new ecological homes for a number of bacteria, either on the farm, where animals might be together in much larger numbers than they used to be, or further down in the production chain."[19] The picturesque cows you see dotting green hillsides on a drive through the countryside are probably dairy cows; beef cattle in the United States are almost all fattened in enormous feedlots, the "CAFOs," or confined animal feeding operations. The same is true for hogs and poultry. In these cramped factory farms, crowding and constant exposure to manure allows pathogens to spread and new strains to mutate. Animals in feedlots are fed primarily on grains, not grasses; feed grains tend to produce highly acidic conditions inside their digestive tracts, and these acidic conditions allow some pathogens, including *E. coli* 0157:H7 to develop a tolerance for acidity that then enables them to survive the acid shock of the human digestive system.[20] CAFO operators routinely lace feeds with antibiotics, both to control the infections generated by confinement and grain-based diets and to promote rapid weight gain among animals. The result of these practices is a very high rate of pathogens in fecal matter and the evolution of new, antibiotic-resistant strains of bacteria.

Once the animals are trucked to the packing plants, the competitive pressure to keep the butchering lines moving as rapidly as possible sometimes results in contamination of meat when the contents of the digestive tract are inadvertently spilled or leaked. And because the meatpacking process often blends meat from many different animals, clean and healthy meat may be contaminated by dirty meat from another source. The resulting food-borne illnesses may prove difficult to treat because of the evolving resistance to antibiotics. All in all, buying precooked beef patties for the school lunch program does not seem like an overreaction. Several years ago, USDA became concerned enough about *E. coli* outbreaks traceable to commodity meats that it began offering schools irradiated meat as a means to reduce the likelihood of an outbreak, but this controversial solution did not sit well with many parents and educators.

Unfortunately for schools and households trying to increase vegetable consumption, *E. coli* 0157:H7 has migrated to the plant side of the menu. The most convincing explanations for this, however, go back to the way we raise our meat. CAFOs generate huge quantities of manure, which is generally stored, untreated, in large "lagoons." When heavy rains occur, some of the manure escapes, contaminating water supplies that may eventually be used to irrigate vegetables. Further, liquid manure is sold as a spray-on fertilizer, so the fields themselves may become contaminated. This is not the place for a primer on food contamination, but even this brief introduction is probably sufficient to explain why food service menu planners in the new millennium are far more concerned about food-borne illnesses than were their predecessors a generation ago. This mounting concern only adds to the pressure for more and more precooked items already resulting from the lack of funds to pay or train skilled cooks. Allergies, too, can drive food service operators toward items prepared elsewhere; they must avoid contamination not only from pathogens but also from allergens. Even food service directors who disapprove of packaged products report that they sometimes use them. "An Uncrustable, a peanut butter Uncrustable is an inappropriate sandwich," Kristy Obbink, who runs an innovative and health-oriented program in Portland, Oregon, told me. "We serve them because they are easy, they can be pulled out of the freezer and if there's nothing else the child will eat, we have a peanut butter Uncrustable. We don't want to make peanut butter and jelly sandwiches in our schools because of cross-contamination. I've been looking for somebody in the community to make me a peanut butter sandwich with natural peanut butter and jam that doesn't have high-fructose corn syrup on whole grain bread that has crust. A real sandwich has a crust."

WHAT HAS HAPPENED TO FOOD?

The question of money and the rise in food-borne illnesses are not the only changes in food that influence the school menu—or the only ones that influence our health. Indeed, changes in society at large—in food patterns, family patterns, and government regulations—are increasingly affecting school food.

Food Has Changed

A trend toward reliance on highly processed packaged foods is found throughout our society; so is a trend toward portable, hand-held items. Thus it should be no surprise to find these foods on the school menu. In the first place, the children like them, want them, are familiar with them. A group of food service directors in Vermont told me that they avoid foods that require forks because many elementary children don't know how to use them. When I mentioned to Donna Wittrock the amount of hand-held food I had seen in the schools I had visited, she replied,

"That's the way kids eat now. . . . That's the way families eat. Not sitting down with a knife and fork." Foods that do not require utensils save money: on the plastic forks and spoons (or combination "sporks") that are used in so many school systems, in the dishwashing costs (labor, electricity, water, soap) for those systems that still use metal flatware. Further, items purchased as single servings may reduce waste. As a California food service director explained to me, "A lot of the branded products are prewrapped [as single servings]. For instance, Tony's Pizza. Everybody knows Tony's Pizza . . . and it's wrapped. So instead of having to cook a whole pizza, in a pan, and cut it up, now it's prewrapped. You just have to put [a piece] in the warmer, and it's out." And finally, single-serving items save time on distribution as well as preparation—they keep the line moving, allowing more children to eat in the notoriously short and ever-shrinking lunch hour or allowing those who choose the school meal more time to consume it.

The growing American reliance on highly processed food is not some sort of inevitable, inexorable process driven by forces of nature. In many ways, it is an outcome of public policy. The farm subsidies created during the New Deal and revised in the period after World War II favored seven basic commodities. Among those are corn and soybeans, two ingredients essential to the kinds of long-lived processed goods that fill our grocery shelves. As Dan Imhoff has explained in his appeal to citizens to help overhaul the Farm Bill: "Federal policies send dangerous ripple effects throughout the food chain. It starts with corn and soybeans, storable crops that do double duty as both cattle feed and a source of processed sugars and hydrogenated fats. As Farm Bill subsidies have lowered prices of commodity crops over the past 30 years, the food industry has invested heavily in an infrastructure that turns cheap materials into highly profitable 'value-added' products."

High-fructose corn syrup (HFCS), which was not manufactured until the 1970s, has become a central staple of industrial food. "A liquid sweetener with six times the potency and far cheaper than cane sugar, HFCS can also be used to prolong shelf-life, resist freezer burn, create an oven-toasted effect, and other processing functions," Imhoff reports. And soybeans are almost as useful; they provide "a cheap and abundant source of added fats in the form of hydrogenated oils that have almost invisibly worked their way into the makeup of nearly every nonproduce item in the modern industrial diet."[21]

In short, crop subsidies make corn and soy exceptionally cheap, thus lowering the price and raising the profit margins on products in which they are primary ingredients, and their shelf-life-extending character-istics further increase the profit that can be derived. In a profit-driven system, it is no surprise that 51 percent of our calories come from such highly processed foods, nor that the grocery industry introduces thou-sands of new food items each year.[22] And given the huge role that these products play in our diets outside of school, it is no surprise that chil-dren bring a preference for these items into the cafeteria. As Donna Wittrock told me, "If the kids are not eating home-cooked meals at home, then they are not going to want those in school." I asked her if she would like to see school food evolve back in the direction of more "scratch" cooking, and her answer was immediate and forceful. "I don't think that what I want is the issue. The issue is we have to give kids what they are used to eating. We have to give them what they are famil-iar with. And we can't be the trendsetters and go back to home-cooked food if that's not what they are getting at home."

Families Have Changed

Of course, no one is force-feeding us products formulated from HFCS and soy isolates; no one has legislated reliance on microwaves. The phe-nomenal growth of the packaged and snack food industry both facili-tates and responds to the increasing pace of life in America. In 2003, Information Resources, Inc. (IRI) unveiled the findings of a study entitled "What Do Americans Really Eat?" to a group of more than six hun-dred industry professionals from the consumer packaged goods industry. According to a press release that accompanied the presentation, "Ready-to-eat snack products with strong convenience benefits are fulfilling the demand for snacks and meal replacements for on-the-go consumers." The release quotes the division president of worldwide innovation for IRI, Kim Feil: "These study findings directly support the unprecedented change the snacking industry is experiencing as consumers increase their pace of life." Commenting on an opportunity for manufacturers to "com-pletely redefine the American diet," Feil noted that "to a large degree, snacks and meals have become interchangeable." The press release drove home the point: "According to the study, snacking is ubiquitous and, in fact, is replacing meals to a large extent. . . . Speed and preparation ease are overwhelmingly rated as the top considerations in the food selection process. Portability and ease of consumption are also important."[23]

The IRI press release attributes this "fundamental shift in Americans' eating behavior" to "busy lifestyles," but we can be more specific than that. The average number of hours worked each week by American households has risen over the last several decades. Steven Greenhouse recently reported that annually a "husband and wife in the average middle-class household are, taken together, working 540 hours or three months more than such couples would have a quarter century ago, mainly because married women are working considerably longer hours than before."[24] Add in the vast array of organized activities—soccer and gymnastics, tutoring and knitting classes, play groups and community service—in which our overscheduled children are now participating, and reliance on snack foods, microwavable dinners, and quick-service (fast) restaurant food makes sense. And as such foods pervade the culture, they shape the expectations and preferences that children bring to school. Donna Wittrock told me that she had seen a great deal of change in the nearly three decades that she had been in school food service: "I think that as food trends change in America, they are going to change in school. As malls become the places where kids go to hang out, as the influx of fast food restaurants continues to escalate, as you've got two parents working and so the trends are to go and eat more meals outside the home, all this is going to impact on what kids want when they come to eat at school."

The pace of life and the increase in women's participation in the labor force are not the only changes in the school food customer base. Children today are far more likely to have money to spend, and are far more active as consumers, than children a generation or two ago. Particularly at the high school level, students often have their own funds. A recent survey found that 40 percent of teenagers have jobs, and 90 percent have weekly income of some sort.[25] A few years ago, Teenage Research Unlimited (TRU), which describes itself as "the nation's premier market-research firm focusing on the teen market" reported that teens ages 12–19 had spent $175 billion in 2003, an average of $103 per week apiece.[26] Children ages 4–12 spend around $40 billion a year.[27] The importance of the market represented by children and teenagers in America can be gauged from the enormous investment that companies make in advertising aimed at youngsters. The Institute of Medicine has reported that "food and beverage advertisers collectively spend $10 billion to $12 billion annually to reach children and youth."[28] Along with the push to lure paying customers back into the cafeteria with a la carte items and menu changes came an attitude shift: the perception of children as "customers." In some ways, this may be a welcome development, leading to improved attitudes and customer service. John Frombach, a former Pittsburgh-area school business director, told me he frequently reminded his cafeteria staff that "the kids have an option. And if they come in today, and you are nasty, mean, and surly, they are not going to come back tomorrow, and if our lunch counts drop, we might not need you tomorrow." In terms of the menu, however, the perception of children as customers can lead to an abdication of adult authority—the perception that the menu should consist totally of the children's favorites. Today's version of Mrs. Mack, the cafeteria director of whom Virg Bernero remembered "Mrs. Mack wouldn't have tolerated it," may be biting her tongue when a child opts for a pile of a la carte items.

Federal Policies Have Changed

Federal nutrition standards do, of course, limit the selections that children can make with the taxpayers' help in the reimbursable meal. Uncle Sam, like Mrs. Mack, will not allow a student to "hold the applesauce, I'll just have four brownies," not in the official meal. But the combination of children with their own money and a la carte and vending options means that many children elude the nutritionally crafted meals prepared for them. The nutrition standards are a big topic in school food at the moment—big enough to warrant their own chapter, which follows. For this chapter's effort to identify the factors that drive the menu, suffice it to say that school food departments must not only offer foods that children like and that have been prepared safely at a remarkably low cost, they must do so within two sets of federal nutrition guidelines: the old set, dating from World War II, specifying that lunches meet a third and breakfasts a quarter of the Recommended Dietary Allowances (now officially the DRIs, Dietary Reference Intakes, but still referred to almost universally as the RDAs), and a second set establishing ceilings on the percentage of calories that can come from fats and from saturated fats, the product of the war on fat discussed in chapter 2. Either of these sets of standards is easy enough to meet by itself, but the combination poses many challenges. Most school districts use a set of federal "meal plans" designed to supply the requisite amounts of various nutrients. Failure to comply with the requirements can result in meals being "disallowed"—not reimbursed—so the pressure to comply is significant and constant. In the effort to make sure that they are meeting federal guidelines, many schools have turned to precisely the prepackaged, highly processed foods about which critics complain, in part because many of these foods come complete with a

"Child Nutrition (CN) Label" specifying the parts of the meal plan that they supply. As a fact sheet on the USDA website explains,

> A CN label statement clearly identifies the contribution of a product toward the meal pattern requirements. It protects a school from exaggerated claims about a product.
>
> A CN label provides a warranty against audit claims, if used according to the manufacturer's directions.

That is, if state-level reviewers find a school's burrito has less than the two ounces of meat or meat alternate specified in the meal plan, it is the manufacturer, not the food service department, that is responsible and must pay for any meals that are disallowed for federal reimbursement.

Complying with federal nutrition requirements is not the only federal specification that complicates the procurement process or constrains the choices of food service directors. The commodity donations that were the original raison d'être for federal participation in school meals continue to play an important role, supplying about one-fifth of the food on the plates of participating students. Commodities are very important to the bottom line of most school districts, but in order to maximize the fiscal impact, food service directors need to choose commodities with care. To begin with. there are two basic types of commodities, entitlement commodities and "bonus" commodities. The entitlement commodities are by far the greater component. Schools are entitled to a specific dollar amount of these, depending on the number of reimbursable lunches served the previous year—lunches in all three categories, free, reduced price, and full price.[29] They can allocate these dollars by choosing from a roster prepared by their state's administering agency, usually the state's Department of Education, in turn drawn from a list offered by USDA. Some states offer all of the USDA possibilities; some do not. Most states survey participating districts for their preferences before deciding what to offer in any given year. Some permit districts to order directly from USDA through the new Electronic Commodity Ordering System (ECOS), although this is a feasible option only for systems large enough to receive entire truckloads.

In choosing from the list, savvy directors try to weigh delivery and processing costs and compare prices with alternative sources. As a result, many districts choose high-value items like meat and cheese from the commodity list, preferring to procure vegetables and produce more locally. They pay the same delivery charge for a case of high-value products or a case of lower-value items, so it makes sense to get their higher-cost supplies as commodities when they can. One result is that observers outside the school food system perceive the federal offerings as driving the menu toward high-fat entrees. An article in the progressive magazine *Mother Jones,* for example, summarized the situation this way: "The trouble is, most of the commodities provided to schools are meat and dairy products, often laden with saturated fat." *Mother Jones* went on to quote a nutritionist who had worked with schools to the effect that the program was "basically . . . a welfare program for suppliers of commodities. . . . It's a price support program for agricultural producers, and the schools are simply a way to get rid of the items that have been purchased."[30]

A closer look suggests that such charges are an oversimplification, with both a grain of truth and considerable distortion. The bonus dairy and beef donations of the 1980s conformed to this image, but USDA currently offers more than 180 commodity products including more than 30 fruit products and 40 vegetable products, although meat and cheese are indeed the most heavily ordered. School food service directors argue that they do not buy more meat and cheese than they otherwise would because they are available as commodities; these choices simply free up more money for other purchases. In the context of the concern about obesity, many commodity specifications have been changed—for example, canned fruit packed in juice instead of syrup, leaner meats, and part skim cheeses. Ground beef available through the program averages 85 percent lean, for example, as compared with 70 percent lean (and thus 30 percent fat) in the fast food industry.[31]

The purchase of fresh fruits and vegetables for schools has also expanded significantly, both through the inclusion of a limited number of fresh fruits and vegetables on the regular commodity roster and through a special arrangement with the Department of Defense called DOD-Fresh. As a report by the Food Research and Action Center explains, "The reason that the regular school lunch commodity program does not offer a variety of fresh fruits and vegetables is that its ordering, purchasing, storage and transportation methods generally lend themselves to shelf-stable products, and not fragile perishables." As national concern about children's diets mounted, however, and the demand for fresh fruits and vegetables grew in the 1990s, USDA turned to the procurement and supply system of the Department of Defense (DOD). Military bases, federal prisons, and veterans hospitals relied upon a nationwide system of purchase and distribution that had proven very successful in delivering high quality produce at reasonable prices, and the closing of some military bases had left the system with excess capacity. A pilot project, begun in 1994, to use the DOD system to purchase on behalf of schools was quickly judged a success, and the approach expanded rapidly. In the 2002 Farm Bill, Congress included $50 million over five years for continuation and growth of the program, and renewed this funding level in the 2008 Farm Bill. At present, there are nearly nine hundred fresh fruits and vegetables available through DOD Fresh. In addition to using their commodity entitlement funds for fresh fruits and vegetables through this program, school districts can also use their cash reimbursements and students' lunch payments.[32]

Even with USDA's growing responsiveness to nutritional concerns, however, it is still clearly the case that the department must consider agricultural market conditions as well as schools' preferences when planning its commodity offerings. Only about a third of its funds—the proportion varies from year to year—for commodity purchases come from Section 6 of the National School Lunch Act and are not tied in any way to market conditions. As a USDA white paper explains, "Since Section 6 funds are not required to be spent on direct intervention in agricultural markets, USDA has greater flexibility in the type of products it can buy with these funds. Purchases are made to provide nutritious foods and accommodate school preferences for the types of foods purchased."[33] The other two-thirds come from Section 32 (and sometimes from Section 416 of the Agricultural Act of 1949) and must be used support the farm sector.[34] Given the mix of Section 6 and Section 32 commodities, the wide variety of foods offered, the increased availability of fruits and vegetables, and the participation of both state agencies and local districts in choosing what actually arrives at the district's warehouse or school loading dock, and given that commodities generally account for no more than 20 percent of the food in any given system, it is difficult to see how they can be held responsible for the percentage of fat calories in the menu.

School districts, furthermore, don't always take advantage of the healthier USDA products. A careful assessment of orders placed by California districts, conducted on behalf of California Food Policy Advocates, found that lean meats constituted a larger proportion of the meats offered by the federal agency than they did of the meats actually ordered by California districts. Similarly, while whole grain products represented 19 percent of the grain and grain product category offered by USDA, they were only 5 percent of the grain and grain products ordered through the commodity system by California schools.[35] This does not mean that California schools were not ordering whole grains and lean meats from other sources, but rather that the commodity program cannot be faulted for failure to offer such products if it is the schools that are not selecting them.

The perspective offered by the *Mother Jones* article appears to be quite widely held, however. In part, this simply reflects a lag—commodities are clearly healthier now than they were a decade ago, and the federal commodity distribution program is far more responsive to the needs of schools. But it also reflects the enormous complexity of the system, the less than transparent way in which commodities have been selected for inclusion in the program, and the accurate perception that USDA's loyalties have been divided. For many years, food service representatives were decidedly critical of the system. "The most prevalent complaint," wrote Penny McLaren in 2000 in a review of opinions in the food service community, is that the commodity system "provides farm support first, foodservice support second."[36] A more sophisticated critique raises questions about *which* farmers USDA supports—large-scale agribusiness versus local farmers struggling to stay in business; producers of grains and legumes for feedlots and exports or producers of fruits and vegetables. Farm to school activists and other advocates of a "buy local" approach to provisioning have been critical of ways in which the commodity program has worked against local procurement in schools, though recent innovations have made it easier to buy locally.

The bonus commodities constitute a much smaller component of the system, in recent years between 1 percent and 18 percent of the total funds spent on commodity purchase for child nutrition programs. Funds are set aside from Section 32 for purchases to relieve "rapidly developing market surpluses." Yet these are probably the purchases most likely to give the commodity system a bad name. In the first place, they are unpredictable, and food service directors do complain—not usually about nutritional qualities but about the difficulty of incorporating unexpected items into menus. They are not required to take them, but with budgets tight, most cannot afford to reject a gift, even a gift of prunes. And because they are designed to support farm incomes by purchasing surpluses, they are also more prone to charges of favoritism. I've heard food service directors and child nutrition advocates quip that you could tell who was in the White House by looking at the bonus commodity roster: canned fruits, dried fruits, and raisins during the Reagan era; peanuts and peanut butter under Carter.

There was a time when federal commodities helped to promote "scratch" cooking in the schools, because they were generally basic ingredients. In Norwalk, Connecticut, the head cook looked back with a bit of nostalgia: "When the government had a lot more commodities available to us, we used to do actual whole pizzas from scratch: make the dough, roll it out, make the sauce from scratch, shred the cheese, do the whole production of pizza. . . . We used to do our own dinner rolls." As consumption patterns changed, however, and staff cooking skills declined, preparing whole foods from scratch became more and more problematic for school food service departments, and food service directors waged a long battle with Congress and USDA to "modernize" commodities.

First there were changes in federal regulations that made it easier to process—or rather to contract for the processing of—federal commodities; then further changes made it legal to exchange the commodities for commercial products that contained the same ingredients. As a result, schools can now arrange to receive a portion of their peanut butter, cheese, and/or soy allotments as Smuckers Uncrustables, and their chicken as Perdue fully cooked, CN-labeled "snackatizer Breaded Spicy Ckn Breast Chunks, Formed." Food service directors worrying about the preferences of their "customers" welcome both branded items that are already familiar to children through advertising and CN-label products that take the guesswork out of complying with nutrition standards. Don't comfort yourself, however, with the notion that these prepackaged branded items are just a handy version of the homely sandwich. The Uncrustables Cheese sandwich provides half the daily allowance for saturated fat and more than two-fifths the daily allowance for sodium. It lists fifty-one ingredients on its label—fifty-one! The availability of such highly processed products from the commodity donation program clearly pushes the menu toward the "carnival fare" that is troubling to many observers.[37]

There is a sort of self-reinforcing circle here; as more directors opt for the processed products, fewer states order the raw ingredients, and eventually, the whole foods necessary for local on-site preparation cease to be available. Together with the fickleness of the bonus commodities, this can pose a real challenge for local operators. John Frombach explained to me why he was having to reevaluate his reliance on "home" baking in his district:

We have our own nighttime baking operation. Now I'm having to examine that because of the cost. At one time, we were getting a lot of donated flour and butter, the different ingredients, and so on. We're not getting that anymore. I'm right now facing that issue, to determine the financial feasibility to continue the nighttime baking operation. . . . We had everything there to do the baking, and now we're just not getting it. And I have to look at the cost of purchasing all those raw materials versus just having it baked. And there's nothing better than our homemade dinner rolls, I mean, they're so wonderful. We make our own hoagie rolls; we make our own pizza shells.

Marketing Has Changed

Federal commodities, as noted, are only about a fifth of the overall food source for schools. I no longer remember how I imagined that schools were supplied before I began this journey. Certainly I knew that they didn't go to the local supermarket to shop for their ingredients, but the whole complicated chain from farmer or manufacturer to school cafeteria was something of a black box to me. It turns out that food makes several stops along the way. Most typically, it goes from a farmer to a processor, who turns it into a "product": canned tomatoes or tomato sauce or frozen pizzas. The product may then be promoted, either by a "direct manufacturer's representative," who represents only the products of a single manufacturer, or by a "broker," who represents the products of several noncompeting manufacturers. The broker or manufacturer's representative tries to get the product into the warehouses of distributors, either directly, by persuading distributors to carry it, or indirectly, by persuading the distributor's customers to ask for it. Distributors play a crucial but often largely invisible role in the food system. These are firms with warehouses and trucks that store selected products and deliver them to schools (or other food service customers such as hospitals, restaurants, and corporate dining rooms). School districts contract with one or more distributors from whom they order most of the foods—and often paper and plastic goods as well—that they use.

Effectively, distributors are the gatekeepers of the food system. When I met Janet Gaffke at the SNA conference, she told me that her small district was in a purchasing group with several other districts and some health care facilities, called Hospital Purchasing Service. Hospital Purchasing Service goes out to bid every year and has for many years awarded its contract to a distributor called Gordon Foods. Gaffke was pleased to see that Gordon Foods was represented at the conference, not only marketing its own services as a regional distributor in the upper

Midwest, but also "talking with brokers who are on the floor at the exhibits and looking at new products." If she saw a new product that she wanted, I asked her, could she speak to Gordon and expect them to order it? "No guarantee," she replied, "because there'd have to be a lot of people who had enough volume interest for them to use a slot. They have so many thousand slots that they can use, because they're limited by their warehousing space, and they also have criteria; they have to turn so much product in a month's period of time and that sort of thing." A survey of the industry in 2004 showed that on average, each distributor stocks 7,862 items (or slots) per branch warehouse.[38]

A distributor will generally assign a distributor sales representative, or DSR, to each account, who becomes the primary contact for the operator (i.e., the school food service person in charge of menu planning or ordering). Brokers and direct manufacturer's representatives also interact frequently with other school food service personnel. According to a helpful guide to the industry published in the SNA magazine, "Brokers will learn how each district or co-op bids, when new items can be added to the bid and the procedures for showing new items to the district or to co-op members." Sometimes, "a broker, direct manufacturer representative [DMR] or regional manufacturer representative may accompany a DSR during sales calls. These are often referred to as 'Ride With's,' which means that someone representing the manufacturer is riding along with the DSR for the day, in order to meet customers and introduce new items. Their goal will be to sell new items and/or to train a new representative about the product line that is being featured."[39] I cannot help but imagine this as a giant game board with different colored pieces representing the various players, all moving around, trying to sell products to food service operators, or maybe a real-life game like television's *The Amazing Race,* with DSRs and DMRs and brokers driving around the countryside showing new products and offering "promotions." School food is big business, and despite the fond memories of ladies with hairnets, food service directors wield considerable market power.

That market power helps to explain the promotions and the parties and the various means by which processors and manufacturers and distributors court food service directors. The most intense version I observed was the exhibit hall at the SNA's Annual National Conference. There were acres of displays, and each one offered some inducement to drop by—a food sample here, a nutrition education poster there, an invitation to a party at another. I came home with an enormous tote bag full of trinkets. Trinkets aside, however, I couldn't help thinking, as I stood in the Any Town High School kitchen one day when an equipment company representative visited, that it must be refreshing, even seductive, for cafeteria managers and food service personnel to be sought after, pursued, and treated with deference, because they get so little respect within many educational bureaucracies. Among the factors driving the menu, I would have to add the personal relationships that develop between the sales representatives and the food service menu planners.

SYNERGY

There is a certain mutually reinforcing character to the factors driving the school menu toward carnival fare. Jack Kloppenburg and Neva Hassanein have provided an elegant summary:

> Across the United States, the great majority of public school food services are constituted as stand-alone financial units that are uncoupled from the revenue-based allocation of funds to the educational function of schools. School food services must almost always pay for themselves. These semi-privatized structural conditions produce a race to the bottom in which food quality continuously degenerates as food services, in an effort to retain student customers, are forced to mimic commercial fast food competitors even as they try to cut costs while embracing USDA commodity foods and pre-packaged meal items that are (literally) assembled rather than cooked.[40]

Fortunately, there is now a growing chorus of voices calling for a move in the opposite direction, toward fresher, healthier meals, greater reliance on plant-based foods, purchasing practices that strengthen local and regional economies, school food that helps students to understand where their food comes from and teaches them healthy habits. As noted in the introduction, the farm-to-school movement, various vegetarian activist groups, animal welfare proponents, and advocates representing not only the anti-hunger and public health communities but also environmentalists and a host of other constituencies have turned their attention to the school food menu. We will discuss examples of these endeavors, along with efforts to make school food more truly accessible to the students who need it most, in chapter 8. Meanwhile, we need to take a closer look at the controversies surrounding the nutrition standards that govern school food.

CHAPTER FOUR

HOW NUTRITIOUS ARE SCHOOL MEALS?

"All school lunches have to be delicious and nutritious. It's a law," declares May, a character in Barbara Parks's *Junie B., First Grader: Boss of Lunch.*[1] May, the quintessential tattletale, is not a particularly appealing character in this series aimed at children ages four to eight, but she is right about the law—at least as far as nutrition is concerned. Specifically, the law has said that in order to qualify for federal reimbursements, school lunches must supply one-third and school breakfasts one-quarter of the Recommended Dietary Allowances (RDAs) for calories, protein, vitamin A, vitamin C, calcium, and iron. They are required to do this without exceeding the proportion of fat recommended by the *Dietary Guidelines for Americans:* no more than 30 percent of calories from fat of any type and no more than 10 percent from saturated fats.[2] In addition, schools are urged to lower cholesterol and sodium and increase fiber in accordance with the recommendations of the dietary guidelines. States can set their own targets for these components, but there are as yet no federal standards written into the school lunch or breakfast regulations, though a committee convened by the Institute of Medicine is currently reviewing the nutrition regulations.

STANDARDS: FOR BETTER AND FOR WORSE

Most of the nutritionists with whom I've talked regard the current standards as minimal and relatively easily satisfied. For food service operations on limited budgets, however, they can be a challenge. It took a trip to the Mississippi Delta to raise my consciousness about just what compliance entails. I went there because I wanted to see what had become of school meals in the county that made hunger a national issue in the late 1960s—the county where Bobby Kennedy discovered near starvation in America. I found the school food programs flourishing, particularly in schools that use Provisions 2 or 3 to serve all children free meals, like the Ray Brooks School in the small town of Benoit.[3] Typically, on any given school day, all but one or two of the children eat the meals that are carefully planned and cheerfully served by a kitchen staff under the direction of Patsy James. Shortly before my visit, however, the Mississippi Department of Education had reviewed her meals and found them wanting . . . in calories! The school has 313 children in attendance, pre-K through 12, and for her high school students, her meals do not supply the requisite one-third of the RDA for calories. An energetic, good-humored woman who came into school food service from a background as a church hostess, Ms. James loves her job, wants to do it well, and certainly wants to give her high school students, almost all of whom are from poor families, every calorie to which they are entitled. What are her options? She probably cannot afford to increase the size of her entree, but even if she could, entrees are often the primary source of fat. A bigger burger might push her over the 30 percent limit. If she had more money, she would happily offer another serving of fruit or vegetables, but she has stretched her federal reimbursements as far as she can, and more local money as a supplement is not on the horizon in decidedly poor Benoit, one of the poorest townships in the famously poor Mississippi Delta. Perhaps USDA will come to her rescue with an offering of low-fat but calorie-dense "bonus" commodities. Bonus commodities may be free, but they are not something she can plan on. They are offered, as we have seen, only when the Agriculture Department or the Commodity Credit Corporation decides to remove a surplus from the market.

What advice did the state reviewers offer? In 2005, in what I sometimes think of as the Year of the Obese Child, in Mississippi, the state with the highest obesity rate and the second highest diabetes rate in the nation, the School Meals Initiative reviewers from the state Department of Education suggested that she offer more desserts. Specifically, they recommended a low-fat pudding that would add calories without adding fat. Caught between calorie minimums and fat ceilings, more sugar appeared to be the most affordable fix. The children don't need it, especially if they are making use of the soda machine located just outside the cafeteria door, but it is the least expensive way to bring the meals into compliance.

The School Meals Initiative for Healthy Children or SMI for short, is the name given to the federal government's efforts to improve the nutritional profile of school food. In keeping with the long-term division of labor in school food programs, the Food and Nutrition Service (FNS) of USDA sets the standards, but the responsibility for monitoring and enforcement rests with the state agencies (SAs), usually the state Department of Education, but in several states, the state Department of Agriculture. SAs are required to review the menus and meals of at least one school in every school food authority (SFA) every five years. A school food authority is legally defined as "the governing body which is responsible for the administration of one or more schools and which has legal authority to operate a breakfast and lunch program therein,"[4] most commonly a school district food service office. This is why reviewers from the Mississippi Department of Education were checking up on the nutrients in Patsy James's lunches.

School food service directors, SMI reviewers, and other insiders to the world of school food take calorie minimums for granted. But to people looking in from the outside, they come as a surprise. "Don't you mean *maximums?*" asked a friend to whom I described James's predicament. Many of us have experience with trying to reduce the role that fat plays in our diets, but we are generally trying to cut back on overall calories as well. The task of lowering fats while maintaining a floor under calories is daunting to say the least. Patsy James's situation is not idiosyncratic. Once I was alerted to the challenge of the fat ceilings vs. calorie floor conundrum, I found it nearly everywhere I went. As one director of a large district in the Southeast explained, "You've got issues of trying to reduce the fat and meet the calories, so what you're doing is you're perhaps adding sugar. Some people may add a fruit cobbler, which would be good. There are some dessert items that might work in there in trying to boost the calories. You could also increase portion sizes, so we've gone to half a cup of fruits and vegetables, a two-ounce roll, a bigger roll, and in secondary school, eight ounces of juice. Now all of those are cost issues." I talked to SMI reviewers in several states; all told me that the combination of inadequate total calories and excessive fat calories was common, and that they often recommended a sweetened gelatin salad or dessert.

Sodium levels are another challenge for menu planners. Many states have set ceilings or targets. New York State SMI reviewer Sandy Sheedy told me that when schools are high on fats but low on calories, if they want to avoid adding sugar, they might try to add more bread. "Most often what they are going to try to increase is a bread item. And most often the bread item is a white bread item and what is going to happen in that case is then your sodium is going to go way high." New York has set a target for lunch of 1,500 milligrams of sodium, which Sheedy explained to me was itself very high—nearly twice the 800 milligrams that would be one-third of the daily maximum recommended by the National Research Council, the organization that sets the RDAs (and also a part of the National Academies of Science). Nevertheless, few schools were meeting it: "I can't tell you how many schools, at this point, have low calories, high fat, high sat [saturated] fat, and the sodium over 1,500. So it's really hard because white grains equal sodium; they are really sodium laden. . . . An ounce of potato chips has less sodium than a slice of white bread." Ms. Sheedy meant "I can't tell you how many" in the colloquial sense: there were a lot. But it was also true in the literal sense. She couldn't tell how many of the schools reviewed by her office had failed to comply with assorted standards, because New York, like many states, does not have the resources to aggregate the data from its SMI compliance reviews. A director and a staff of four have 1,300 SFAs to review each year.

Some states, however, do aggregate their data. New Jersey, for example, was kind enough to send me a summary of the percentage of schools found to be in compliance with nutrient standards in the 2003–2004 school year. Protein at lunch was the only standard met by all schools reviewed. Other scores ranged from a high of 98 percent for protein at breakfast to a low of 5 percent for sodium at lunch. Less than half of the lunches reviewed were meeting the calorie minimums, and only a little over a third—36 percent—were below the fat ceiling. Saturated fat at lunch was particularly a problem; less than a quarter of the schools reviewed in that year met the standard, though they did better at breakfast, when 45 percent complied. In general, at either meal, the great majority of the schools met the standards for protein, calcium, iron, vitamin A, vitamin C and cholesterol, while most did not meet the goals for fiber, saturated fat, fat, sodium, or calories. Patsy James's lunches are looking better all the time; if New Jersey's results were typical, the meals at the Ray Brooks School might prove to be among the most compliant in the nation.

SMI reviews, however, are not a good basis for assessing the overall state of school nutrition. They are not at all random; in fact, since their basic purpose is to help schools achieve compliance with the regulations, states might be expected to select those schools in which they anticipate encountering difficulties and shortfalls. Why invest limited resources in schools that can probably get along fine without help? In order to make reliable generalizations about the overall state of school meals, we need a randomly selected sample. Fortunately for our purposes here, the federal government has commissioned just such scientifically designed investigations.

THE SCHOOL NUTRITION DIETARY ASSESSMENTS

The largest effort to compare actual meals and menus with the federal standards is a series of studies funded by USDA and carried out by major private sector research organizations, known as the School Nutrition Dietary Assessments (SNDAs). The original SNDA, which I'll call SNDA-I, was completed by Mathematica Policy Research, Inc., using data collected in 1991–92 and released in 1993. SNDA-II was conducted by Abt Associates, Inc., using data collected during the 1998–99 school year; the report was released in 2001. SNDA-III was again conducted by Mathematica, with data collected during the 2004–2005 school year, and the report released late in the autumn of 2007. These studies involved nutrient analysis of menus for a target week submitted by a randomly selected sample of schools participating in the National School Lunch and School Breakfast programs, surveys of school food service personnel, interviews with state school food agency directors, and, in the case of SNDA-I and SNDA-III, 24-hour food recall studies of food intakes by samples of students from the schools surveyed.

Before looking at the results of these three studies, some background on their policy and political context is in order. Although such studies sometimes seem to generate little interest beyond the research community, the SNDA series has a more dramatic history, since, as we have seen in chapter 2, it has been inextricably intertwined with the war on fat and subsequent efforts to overhaul menu planning and improve school meal quality. For the first half century of federally supported school meals, schools did not have to prove that they were meeting the RDA targets, only that they were following the meal pattern that was designed to meet them. Large national surveys in the early 1980s and the early 1990s showed that with rare exceptions schools were in fact meeting and often exceeding the RDA requirements.[5] SNDA-I, however, with its findings of very high percentages of calories from fat and general poor showing with reference to the Dietary Guidelines, was a wake-up call. The regulations that grew out of it, the same rules that added the ceilings on the percentages of calories from fat and saturated fats, now specified that schools had to meet the actual nutrient standards as well as the menu plans. As one school food service director described the change to me: "We've always had regulations. They just keep getting stricter and stricter. When I started, [it was] food-based; you just had to have your five components, your milk, your fruit, your vegetable, your meat and bread. And that was easy. Then they added calories, you've got to have calories. . . . But now, you got to have calories, and total fat, and A, C, calcium." The regulations promulgated in the mid-1990s shifted the basic orientation of the standards away from foods and toward nutrients. And this was also the effect, of course, of moving to Nutrient Standard Menu Planning (NSMP), the change described in chapter 2 that sparked the feud between Ellen Haas and the American School Food Service Association.

Whether because of the acrimony, or simply because of the inherent obstacles such as a lack of computer equipment and expertise, or because of skepticism about the impact on children's diets, uptake of the nutrient standard approach to menu planning has been slow. USDA hired the Gallup Organization to trace the implementation of SMI; by the end of the third study year, the 1999–2000 school year, only about a quarter of school districts were using one of the two nutrient-based options. Of the districts using a food-based system, some reported that they were working toward implementation of the nutrient-based approach or that they intended to do so. Significantly, the proportion indicating that they did not intend to adopt a nutrient-based approach rose over the three years of the study from about 50 percent in 1997–98 to around 64 percent in 1999–2000. By 2005 when the SNDA-III data were collected, a decade after conversion to the new approach was proposed, 30 percent of schools, and only around 20 percent of SFAs were using NSMP.[6]

If USDA had been able to wait for the results of its own research, it might have anticipated the concerns of food service directors and crafted a program that more fully addressed them. The agency had initiated an investigation, called the Nutrient Standard Menu Planning Demonstration, in the summer of 1993, to study both the impact and the process of conversion to NSMP. According to the evaluation, "Compared to pre-NSMP menus, NSMP lunch menus included more . . . skim milk and flavored lowfat milk; fresh fruit; raw vegetables and salads; extra bread and grain choices; pasta-based entrees; rice; and desserts. NSMP lunch menus also included *less* . . . whole milk; french fries and similar potato products; entrees that tend to be high in fat, such as breaded meat, poultry and fish, burgers, nachos, and hot dogs; and snack chips."[7] These results seemed to support the predictions of the NSMP optimists, but the study was very limited in scope. A real test would have to await the results of SNDA-II.

Given the poor performance in meeting the Dietary Guidelines reported by SNDA-I, it is not surprising that the results of SNDA-II were awaited with both high hopes and considerable anxiety by USDA, school food service professionals, and other concerned observers. The data were collected when the SMI was only two years old, so no one knew whether there would be measurable impact. Fat, unsurprisingly, was the major focus of attention. There was both good news and bad news in the report. On the one hand, as the Government Accountability Office explained to Congress, the assessment "reported a significant trend toward lower total fat levels in school lunches from nearly 38 percent of total lunch calories in 1991–92 down to about 34 percent in 1998–99."[8] If you have ever tried to reduce the proportion of fat in your own diet, you will recognize that this was no small accomplishment. On the other hand, the figure was still substantially above the required 30 percent standard, and the great majority—more than three-quarters—of public elementary and secondary schools had still not managed to conform to this fat guideline. In fact, only 18 percent of elementary schools and 21 percent of secondary schools made the grade, a significant improvement over SNDA-I, but still far from the goal. For saturated fat the mean for all schools was 12 percent of calories, or 20 percent above the standard. Breakfasts fared better; the mean percentage of calories from total fat was 27.1 percent, well under the 30 percent limit, and the percentage from saturated fat was 10.2 percent, just over the 10 percent ceiling. In both breakfast and lunch, the improvement in compliance with the fat ceilings was achieved without sacrifice of other targeted nutrients, with the exception of calories, which were low in secondary school lunches—30 percent rather than 33 percent of the RDA—and in breakfasts at both the elementary and secondary levels.[9]

SNDA-II, as noted, took place quite soon after the inauguration of the SMI. Many observers, therefore, looked forward to SNDA-III as perhaps a more realistic test of the new approaches. By the time SNDA-III data were collected, commodities had been reformulated to offer lower-fat meats and cheeses, products incorporating whole grains, and fruits packed in juice rather than syrup, and these reformulated commodities had been available long enough for school districts to get used to ordering them. Milk regulations had been changed to emphasize low-fat varieties, and both menus and preparation procedures had been revised. Substantial training and technical assistance on lower-fat preparation techniques had been provided. Many new tools were available for schools to use in the front lines of the war on fat. I, for one, waited for SNDA-III with great interest.

When SNDA-III finally arrived in November 2007, however, it reported exactly the same percentage of calories from total fat in school food as had SNDA-II: 34 percent. Saturated fat showed a slight improvement, from 12 percent of calories down to 11 percent. Further, SNDA-III found that roughly the same proportion of schools, 20 percent, offered and served lunches that met the total fat standard. There was some noticeable improvement in the percentage of schools that met the saturated fat standard: it more than doubled in elementary schools, from 15 percent to 34 percent, and almost doubled in secondary schools, from 13 percent to 24 percent. Whether you see this as good news (the proportion of schools meeting the saturated fat standard roughly doubled) or bad news (nearly two-thirds of elementary schools and three-quarters of high schools are still not meeting the standard) depends on your expectations and your point of view. Breakfast again performed better on the fat front: 85 percent of schools met the standard for total fats at breakfast, and 78 percent met the standard for saturated fats, but again, most schools fell short of the required number of calories.[10] That there was so little change in the total fat performance between SNDA-II and SNDA-III suggests that most of the readily achievable gains in compliance had already been garnered by the time of SNDA-II. It certainly does not augur well for a future of steadily declining proportions of fat calories. Perhaps this is why there was remarkably little publicity attendant upon the release of SNDA-III. No secretary of agriculture eating lunch in a public school in the District of Columbia, no headlines in the major papers. As a colleague bluntly put it, "They buried it."

OFFER VERSUS SERVE

If you were in the habit of reading pronouncements from the School Nutrition Association, these figures might surprise you. SNA routinely claims that the great majority of American schools offer healthy choices that meet the guidelines. The key here is in the terms *offer* and *choices*. When SNDA-III talks about lunches offered and served, it is talking about the average lunch offered and the average lunch served. The SNA, on the other hand, is talking about giving students the opportunity to select a lunch that meets the guidelines. Any Town High School, for example, offered its wonderful fresh salad; the fact that so few students chose it does not change the fact that it was offered. A little over a third of elementary schools had offered such low-fat menu options that met the guidelines in the early 1990s; SNDA-II reported that 82 percent did so. For secondary schools, 91 percent offered options for a complete, reimbursable meal that derived no more than 30 percent of calories from fat—up from 71 percent in SNDA-I.[11] SNDA-III showed continued improvement: 93 percent of elementary schools and 86 percent of secondary schools offered students the opportunity to select a low-fat lunch on a typical day.[12] Understandably, these lower-fat options also tended to be lower in calories compared to the RDA standard. The SNDA-II report tried to be helpful: "The calorie content of the lowest-fat lunches could be increased by adding additional servings of fruit, vegetables or breads, or by adding a low-fat, high-carbohydrate dessert choice (e.g., gelatin, animal crackers, fruit dessert, low-fat baked good)."[13] Like the SMI reviewers who analyzed Patsy James's menus in Mississippi, the research team that conducted SNDA-II saw sugar as an option for boosting calories. Calorie minimums remained problematic for SNDA-III as well; only 71 percent of schools offered the minimum requirement for energy, and only half actually served it.[14]

The gap between what students are offered and what they are served is due in part to the offer versus serve (OVS) reform begun in the 1970s and expanded in the 1990s in response to studies of plate waste. The OVS regulations were intended to reduce the quantities of food ending up in the trash cans. High schools are required to implement this option, and elementary and middle schools may do so at the discretion of the local school food authority. Most do: USDA reported that nearly 90 percent of elementary schools were using this approach by the 1997–98 school year.[15] Once the new menu planning systems were introduced, the OVS rules had to be adjusted to fit them. The rules vary slightly by menu-planning method, but the gist of the matter is that students may refuse some of the offered items without making the meal ineligible for reimbursement. Thus students in systems using food-based menu planning can get by with just three of the five offered components; a hot dog (meat), a bun (grain), and milk would be a reimbursable lunch. So would a serving of french fries (our favorite vegetable), a carton of milk, and either the hot dog or the bun by itself. Students in systems using either of the nutrient-based systems (NSMP or Assisted Nutrient Standard Menu Planning, ANSMP) must select at least two of the USDA meal components, including an entree, and may decline up to two.

Even with OVS, there is a certain amount of plate waste. SNDA-I reported as follows:

> The use of OVS slightly reduces the chances that a student will select each meal component. Waste is somewhat lower in OVS schools, however, which offsets the reduction in the proportion selecting each component. The net effect is that nutrient intake is unaffected. Students in OVS schools are less likely to select milk than students in non-OVS schools but also less likely to waste it. Overall NSLP participants waste about 12 percent of the calories in the food they are served.[16]

The 12 percent figure has become widely accepted. It's worth a closer look, however, since it seems a lot lower than the prevailing impression. "You know that half the food that is on those kids' trays ends up in the garbage," one SMI reviewer told me, and she spends a great deal of time in school lunchrooms. The 12 percent figure came from dietary recall interviews conducted with a randomly selected sample of about 3,350 students in grades 1–12 as part of SNDA-I. Dietary recall involves remembering what you have eaten in a period just past and is obviously subject to errors—primarily omissions and inaccurate estimates of quantity. In the SNDA study, trained interviewers prompted students with lists of commonly consumed foods and comparison figures to help them estimate the amounts involved; they were not left to recall unaided, on their own. For example, they were asked if they ate "all, most, about half, just tried it, or none" of the serving that they took. Researchers believe that children generally report more accurately than adults, who have been known to distort what they recall and what they report. (That half a chocolate bar I ate with my breakfast wasn't typical, so why report it; in the interests of science, I won't mention it so as not to distort the research results.)

Even with children, however, dietary recall seems a fragile basis for an estimate of food waste. A few years ago, the Committee on Appropriations of the House of Representatives asked USDA's Economic Research Service to review the literature on plate waste in school nutrition programs and make suggestions for reducing such loss. In addition to dietary recall, USDA found three other methods in use: visual estimates by trained observers, visual estimates by school food service personnel, and physical measurement of waste. A study conducted by Abt Associates Inc. in the early 1990s used visual estimates. Trained observers made on-site observations of twelve children at each of sixty schools in twenty school food service authorities over five consecutive days. The study found that middle and high school students consumed almost 90 percent of what they took, while elementary school students consumed only about 75 percent of what they were served.[17] A related approach was taken by the United States General Accounting Office in 1996 when it surveyed cafeteria managers to ascertain their perceptions of plate waste by children in the NSLP. Of those who responded and provided an opinion, 55 percent perceived plate waste as "little or no problem," while 22 percent saw it as "some problem" and 23 percent reported it to be at least a "moderate problem." Cafeteria managers reported that the amount wasted varied with the type of food. Average estimates were 42 percent for cooked vegetables; 30 percent for raw vegetables and salad, 22 percent for fresh fruits, but only 11 percent for milk.[18]

Perhaps the most accurate way to measure plate waste is to weigh it, but this is clearly a demanding job. In order to calculate a percentage of food wasted, the food must be weighed before students eat, and then the plate waste must be weighed—for each student—after the meal is concluded. As noted in the Economic Research Service report to Congress, "The primary advantage of this method is that it can provide detailed and accurate plate waste information. Disadvantages are that it is costly and time consuming, requires space to hold the trays until the food is weighed, and is impractical for samples of over 50–100 children."[19] Consequently, very few studies of this type have been done in school food settings. A Montana weight-based study conducted in nine elementary schools in 1997 found that 25 to 30 percent of calories and nutrients were wasted, and that vegetables were the food item with the largest waste: 42 percent—interestingly, the same figure reported by the GAO's cafeteria managers.[20] The most consistent finding across all of the studies reviewed for the report to Congress was that younger children tended to waste more than older children.

I gained some insight into this after standing beside the garbage pail at an elementary school in Santa Fe, New Mexico, and watching what seemed to me distressing quantities of food being thrown away. I asked the cafeteria manager about it, and she told me that the portions were just too big for the younger children. When I asked about serving smaller portions to the lower grades, she explained that the law required them to serve portions adequate to meet the needs of the older children, and that although the option existed to customize smaller portions for the lower grades, she did not have time between the various lunch shifts to convert.

It would be too complicated, both in terms of menu planning and in terms of accounting, to offer two or more different sizes of servings.

All of this is not to say that the school food programs don't have a positive impact on children's nutrition. Here is how USDA recently summarized the available research: "The findings consistently suggest that NSLP participants consume more milk and vegetables at lunch and fewer sweets, sweetened beverages and snack foods than nonparticipants." The higher vegetable consumption, the report continues "may be due to higher consumption of french fries and other potato-based items." Looking at individual nutrients, especially those that are "underconsumed," the report indicated that middle school participants "were more likely to have usual adequate daily intakes of vitamin A and magnesium than nonparticipants" and that high school participants "were more likely than nonparticipants to have adequate usual daily intakes of vitamin A, vitamin C, vitamin B6, folate, thiamin, iron and phosphorus." On the other side of the ledger, NSLP participants were even more likely than their nonparticipating peers to exceed recommended sodium levels.[21]

COMPETITIVE FOODS

If a nutrient profile of the food served in the National School Lunch and School Breakfast programs leaves something to be desired, it is probably outstanding when compared to the nutrient profile of the other foods available on campus—the so-called competitive foods. Competitive foods vary more from school to school, and precisely because they are not governed by federal standards (except for the absurdly frail prohibition on food of minimal nutritional value in the cafeteria during meal times), it is difficult to generalize about them. SNDA-III has provided some data, but before turning to it, let me summarize what we already knew from smaller studies.

In the first place, we know that competitive foods are ubiquitous; the GAO reported that in the 2003–2004 school year when it conducted a survey, nearly nine out of ten schools sold competitive foods to children, and over the previous five years, the availability of competitive foods had increased. The GAO study identified three "venues" or means of delivery of competitive foods: the sale of a la carte items in the cafeteria, vending machines, and school stores or snack bars.[22] Ninety-nine percent of high schools, 97 percent of middle schools, and 83 percent of elementary schools had one or more of such venues.[23] There is great variation among schools—and even among parts of the country—as to the role of competitive foods in the school and in the child's consumption. In some, these venues are providing just an occasional snack or beverage, supplementing rather than replacing the school meal or the food brought from home. In others, a la carte and vending may be major food sources. A California survey found that 70 percent of all food sales in the responding districts were a la carte items. Nor is this just a California phenomenon. A study of three schools in the Northeast by Mathematica Policy Research, Inc., designed to test methods of assessing competitive foods, found similar percentages of food sales to be from the competitive venues.

Competitive food sales are revenue driven. That is, as we have seen, school food service operations sell them in an effort to break even, and principals, PTAs, and student organizations sell them to raise money for school activities. Patterns vary widely, but the most common is for funds from a la carte items sold in the cafeteria to accrue to the food service operation, while those from vending machines and school stores go to principals' discretionary funds or to the parent or student organizations who sponsor and staff a school store. Obviously, sales from dedicated fundraisers, bake sales, candy sales, and the like go to the sponsoring organization.

The GAO survey found it more difficult to generalize about the types of food available. Competitive foods can include nutritious options such as fruits, milk, vegetables, and salad, and less nutritious items such as chips, soda, and candy. In general, a la carte lines were likely to include more nutritious items than vending machines. The Institute of Medicine, however, after reviewing a number of local studies, was willing to assert that

> available data show that competitive foods are often high in energy density (often high fat or high sugar) and low in nutrient density. . . . Although fruits and vegetables are generally available—they are sold in the a la carte areas of 68 percent of elementary schools, 74 percent of middle schools, and 90 percent of secondary schools—energy dense foods tend to comprise the majority of competitive foods offered for sale. For example, at . . .
> 20 Minnesota high schools . . . , chips, cookies, pastry, candy and ice cream accounted for 51.1 percent of all a la carte foods offered, while fruits and vegetables were at 4.5 percent, and salads 0.2 percent.[24]

These findings will come as no surprise to most concerned parents. It may be worthwhile to establish a national profile of the foods being sold to our children in competition with the school lunch and breakfast programs, but parents who have taken a look at the offerings in their own children's schools are already aware of the preponderance of junk food.

The impact of competitive foods on the nutrition of children is not limited to the negative consequences of ingesting too much fat, salt, and sugar. These snacks displace foods with the vitamins and minerals young bodies need. And it's not only a problem for some youngsters who choose a plate of nachos and a Little Debbie snack pastry instead of the reimbursable meal; competitive foods also affect what children select and what they actually consume when they do participate in the federal lunch program. That is, these foods may aggravate the problems associated with OVS and plate waste. Why choose an unfamiliar green vegetable if I know that I can get a Snickers from the candy machine if I'm still hungry after lunch? Why drink milk, which may be regarded by my peers as "uncool" or "lame," if I can get a Gatorade from the machine outside the door? Two recent studies have shown that fruit and vegetable consumption was lower among students at middle schools where a la carte items were available than at matched middle schools where there were no a la carte choices.[25] Another study used weighed plate waste data to determine the nutrients consumed at lunch by two groups of children at each of three schools; one group chose only the reimbursable meal, and the other chose both the reimbursable meal and competitive a la carte items. The students who bought additional items from the a la carte offering chose less food for their reimbursable meal, and wasted more of what they selected. The net effect was to replace milk and vegetables with sweetened sports drinks and snack foods.[26]

With these studies as background, the SNDA-III data, the first to present a national picture based on a randomly selected sample, actually came as a bit of a relief. The picture is not good, but it is not quite as bad as I had imagined. On the good news side of the ledger, nearly half of the 82 percent of schools that offered a la carte items in the cafeteria during lunch offered only milk, and among elementary schools that offered a la carte items at lunch, nearly three-fifths offered only milk. On the other hand, between 35 and 42 percent of schools offered baked goods, frozen desserts, and snack items. More than three-fifths of middle schools and more than three-quarters of high schools offered entrees on an a la carte basis; the most popular were pizza, hamburgers, cheeseburgers, and breaded chicken patties. In the vending machines, nearly as many schools offered water or 100 percent juice as offered beverages with added sugar and/or caffeine.

TWIXT CUP AND LIP

There is much more to be said about competitive foods, and efforts at the state and local levels to develop and impose standards will be explored in chapter 8. What interests me here is their net effect on the nutritional quality of food at school and their implications for the menu planning protocols and standards with which the official reimbursable meals must comply. The conflicting requirements that I encountered in my visit to Patsy James's lunchroom started me thinking about the standards and the measurement process, which to an outsider, may appear patently absurd. There is many a slip twixt cup and lip, as the old adage goes, and in school meals, there is so much slippage between the ideal and the real, between the aggregate and the individual, as to render the entire complex structure of nutrition standards an exercise in futility. Let me explain.

First there are the RDAs. They are allowances set high enough to meet the needs of most healthy people in the population. Although, as noted, the official term has now changed to Dietary Reference Intakes or DRIs, for most school food menu planners, as for most consumers and product labelers, the operant concept is still the RDA, which was clearly defined by the National Research Council in 1974: "The Recommended Dietary Allowances are the levels of intake of essential nutrients considered, in the judgment of the Food and Nutrition board on the basis of available scientific knowledge, to be adequate to meet the known nutritional needs of practically all healthy persons."[27]

Clearly, then, these levels will be set high for substantial numbers of people in any age or sex category. For vitamins and minerals this is not a problem; there is no such thing as too much vitamin A or vitamin C—at least not at the levels we are discussing—but calories are a different matter. The calorie minimum that is sufficient to meet the needs of half of the members of an age or sex group will be, by definition, high for the other half. Calorie minimums for school meals necessarily blend the needs of widely divergent children. The RDA tables can vary recommendations by sex and activity level, but the school food service must have a single target for each age or grade group. It cannot offer boys one lunch and girls another, nor measure students' height before deciding what calorie count to target. A meal that is way too much for one eleven-year-old may be way too little for another, but school lunch menus are reviewed and judged based on averages. As a New York State SMI reviewer told me, "What it does is look at the average meal for the average child on an average day, but it never would talk to me about how my child is eating." I am not suggesting that school food service meal planners or researchers should undertake such individualized assessments. I am only pointing out that like most measures designed for large populations, the standards will be a poor fit for significant numbers of children.

The requirement that school lunches supply a third of the RDAs has been around so long that it generally goes without question. No one that I interviewed in the course of this study suggested that it be revisited—at least no one from what might be broadly defined as the "school food community": school food service personnel, anti-hunger activists, public health advocates. But somewhere in our calculus, don't we need to take into account the extent to which snacking has become a norm? The one-third requirement was first established in 1941, when people typically ate three meals per day. Now researchers tell us that most of us eat several more in the form of between-meal snacks. Patsy James's meals were deficient by only a few dozen calories; meanwhile, her school is one of the lucky ones selected for the federal fresh fruit and vegetable pilot that distributes free fruit or vegetable snacks to children in participating schools. In all probability, the calories from the fruits and vegetables would compensate for any shortfall in her lunches, but she cannot count those calories in her totals. In the case of such federally regulated, subsidized, and institutionalized snacks, of course, a simple change in the regulations could fix that problem, but the fruit and vegetable program is quite small.[28] Most of the snacking that contributes to children's calorie totals is of the informal or unauthorized variety, not something upon which you can plan.

The other side of the calorie conundrum is the percentage of calories derived from fat. The 30 percent limit on fat is the target that school menu planners find most difficult to meet if they are meeting the calorie minimums and is thus the source of what one group of researchers has called "the fat-sugar see-saw in school lunches."[29] But how certain are we of its validity? It was certainly the prevailing wisdom in the late 1980s and early 1990s, but then the low-carb mania took over, reminding us that sugars consumed and not burned off are turned into fat for storage on the body. All carbohydrates are not equal, and neither are all fats. Eliminating trans fats may be as important to long-term health as reducing the fat proportion to any specific number, although most health professionals agree that lower is better than higher. The recent release of findings from the Women's Health Initiative suggested two challenges to the guidelines now governing school meals. The report showed more modest reductions in disease than had been anticipated for the low-fat diet group as compared with the "normal diet" group, and it showed that even women who were voluntary participants in a study, committed to its goals, supported by intensive counseling at the outset and maintenance sessions thereafter, were unable to meet the target of 20 percent of calories from fat, and six years into the study, were averaging 29 percent from fat. By the eighth year, reported one of the principal investigators, the average intake of fat calories may have increased further.[30] That is to say, it is apparently really difficult, at least in our culture, to maintain a regimen of 30 percent or less of calories from fat. I am not proposing to substitute my best guesses for those of nutrition scientists and medical professionals, but if I were a school food menu planner, I think I'd find myself looking at the 30 percent fat target with some suspicion if not hostility. In fact, the latest Dietary Guidelines, from 2005, recommend keeping total fat to between 25 and 35 percent of calories for children, but for the time being, at least, school food menu planners are stuck with the 30 percent ceiling because the regulations specify adherence to SMI standards based on the 2000 Guidelines, and new regulations based on the 2005 Guidelines have been delayed.

The story of this delay is itself indicative of the morass that standard setting has become. The 2005 Dietary Guidelines for Americans (DGAs) contain recommendations to increase consumption of fiber, whole grains, and fruits and vegetables, and to reduce sodium, cholesterol, and trans fats. In the Child Nutrition and WIC Reauthorization Act of 2004, Congress directed USDA to update school meal planning guidelines by June 2006 to "reflect" these new recommendations. While USDA has issued advice on interim steps state agencies can encourage school food authorities to take, it has apparently found the task of actually agreeing on new regulations more complicated than expected. An excerpt from the FNS memo to regional offices and state agencies gives a flavor of the situation:

> Following the release of the 2005 DGAs, USDA assembled an internal working group of experienced nutritionists and program administrators to examine ways to implement the 2005 DGAs into the school meal programs, within group feeding limitations and cost restrictions, in preparation for beginning the rulemaking process. Given the complexity of issues uncovered during this process, USDA decided to contract with the Institute of Medicine (IOM) to convene a panel of experts from diverse specialties

in child nutrition. This expert panel will provide USDA with recommendations to update the meal patterns and nutrition requirements for both the NSLP and the SBP. Once a cooperative agreement is signed, USDA estimates that it may take IOM from 18 to 24 months to provide the Department with these recommendations. USDA will then engage in the formal rulemaking process to promulgate a proposed rule that incorporates the IOM recommendations to the fullest extent practicable.[31]

As the policy analyst David Beller has observed, "Nearly six months after the new guidelines were suppose to be completed, the USDA announced the task was too complicated, and they would need to contract the job to another federal agency. Now, the Institute of Medicine will lead the process, and insiders say they don't expect any improvements to be implemented until 2012. That's six years late."[32] By that time, presumably, there will be a new set of DGAs, and there will certainly have been another Child Nutrition Reauthorization. Something is wrong when advice intended to be followed by "average Americans" requires years to translate into new regulations. It is not clear whether the new regulations will change the fat-calorie ceilings, since Congress did not specifically mandate such a change, but since the underlying legislation requires the secretary of agriculture to set standards based on up-to-date nutritional knowledge, it seems probable.

Let's suppose, just for the sake of argument, that the older, stricter target is eventually proven correct and government was justified in pushing school food service to reduce fat to 30 percent. The school food menu planning process is still subject to many forms of error. The evaluators who conducted the Nutrient Standard Menu Planning Demonstration found errors to be ubiquitous, reporting that

> all SFAs made errors in their nutrient analyses. The most common errors were omission of a planned menu item [from the analysis] and inaccurate serving projections. In a weekly analysis, about half of the SFAs omitted five or more menu items. Condiments, including salad dressing, tartar sauce, mayonnaise and other high-fat items were the most frequent omissions. Major menu items omitted from an analysis were generally alternative entree choices (e.g., salad bars, other specialty bars, or sandwiches) or one or more types of milk. In general, such omissions were made consistently in each daily analysis.[33]

Another source of error in the process is the information supplied by manufacturers and vendors for products. NSMP is based on the assumption that each time a new product is added to school meals, its nutrient information will be added to the local database. USDA was responsible for providing an initial database for the most commonly used products, the National Nutrition Database–Child Nutrition Programs (NND-CNP), but as the evaluators noted, "Another problem . . . was the poor response USDA received from food manufacturers contacted to supply nutrient information for the NND-CNP. Very few manufacturers responded to the request, and much of the data submitted was found to be incomplete, inaccurate, or otherwise questionable."[34] If large national manufacturers gave inadequate and sometimes inaccurate information to USDA, imagine the possibilities for error and misinformation when a small local food service operation is requesting the nutrient data on a local specialty. As the evaluators wrote of the NSMP demonstration, "Several respondents who were particularly knowledgeable about nutrition and dietary data analysis expressed concerns about the accuracy of the nutrition data supplied by vendors and, in some cases, included in the . . . data base. A related concern is that many SFA directors are not able to detect errors in nutrient values provided by vendors because of their lack of experience with nutrition data."[35] All of this reminds me of the acronym in common use when I was a graduate student first exploring the uses of the computer: GIGO. It stood for Garbage In, Garbage Out and was intended to warn us that the computer could not compensate for errors made in data collection, coding, or entry. By now I suspect that any errors in the original NND-CNP have been remedied, but new foods are introduced in the United States at the rate of thousands per year, so the potential for error is perpetual.

The impact of this particular set of errors applies most fully, of course, to the 30 percent of school districts that use nutrient-based approaches to menu planning, but one has to assume that it may also apply to the nutrient analyses that followers of the food-based approach are urged to perform and the reviews conducted by SMI reviewers.

What happens when these carefully if imperfectly planned menus reach the cafeteria? Offer versus serve means that students don't have to take all of the components. This in and of itself could easily render both the calorie minimums and the fat calorie ceilings inoperable in the case of any particular child. In the food-based system, the child may skip the entree altogether. If the lunch as planned is at or close to the specified ceiling, but the student foregoes the calorie-dense "center of the plate" item, she is likely to fall through the calorie floor, and if she takes the burger but skips the bun, her percentage of calories from fat will rise. I am a lifetime member of the clean-plate club, and I have a profound aversion to waste of food, so I'm not calling for an end to OVS or student choice. I'm trying to point out that this is one more slip twixt cup and lip—one more reason to question the entire enterprise of applying such detailed and exact standards to menu planning. And finally, of course, my aversion to plate waste doesn't keep it from happening, so there is another deterioration in the effectiveness or applicability of the standards to the actual meals consumed. Even if the 12 percent figure is accurate, a 12 percent deviation would certainly change the likelihood of achieving any of the standards when the margins of safety are small. You can afford to be 12 percent off your protein or vitamin C target because the typical meal supplies considerably more than the requirement, but where the values are closer to the targets, 12 percent is plenty to undermine the process. And, as all studies have reported, children are not equal opportunity food wasters; salads and other vegetables, raw or cooked, were the most likely to be dumped in virtually every study.

Finally, we must try to factor in the impact of those competitive foods. I wouldn't be concerned if a child skipping the entree was a few calories too low—most of us eat too much anyway. But if she is skipping the fish sticks and substituting a sticky cinnamon bun, well, it makes the entire exercise feel a bit futile. To me it seems patently absurd to hold the official federal meal to standards that actual menu planners clearly find difficult to meet, while permitting other foods to be sold in or near the cafeteria which meet virtually no standards whatsoever. The possibility of regulating competitive foods is currently a hot-button item in the world of school food, and as we shall see in chapter 8, states and localities have taken the lead in establishing stricter standards. One result of the proliferation of state and local codes, of course, is that the snack food industry is now far more open to federal regulation, hoping for uniform standards in place of the variety of state and local rules. As I write, Senator Tom Harkin of Iowa, Chair of the Senate Agriculture committee and a tireless campaigner for regulation of competitive foods, has just reintroduced the Child Nutrition Promotion and School Lunch Protection Act to give the secretary of agriculture the power to regulate all foods sold at schools that participate in the National School Lunch and School Breakfast programs, and Representative Lynn Woolsey has introduced a companion measure in the House. This measure came close to passage in 2008. In the long-overdue effort to regulate what is offered to children in competition with the federal meals, however, let us not obscure the problems with the standards applied to those meals themselves. The more complex and precise the nutrient standards become, the greater the possibility for menus to be found out of compliance.

Among the consequences of this nutrient-driven approach is an increasing reliance on manufactured products and meals. Sitting in Industry Boot Camp, a seminar offered by the School Nutrition Association to firms interested in doing business with school food service operations, I asked a representative of the manufacturer of a food product—not one I would like to see in my own family's lunch—whether he preferred dealing with schools on the NSMP or those using the food-based system. "Oh, Nutrient Standard," he replied. "No contest. When they tell us they are on NSMP, I know we're in the door." As food manufacturers have caught on to the implications of the current regulations and the new menu planning technologies, they have begun to fortify and tweak products, just as the Produce Marketing Association and the other NSMP pessimists predicted they would, creating "food" that makes it easier for menu planners to meet the guidelines. And now that the schools using food-based menu planning also have to meet specific nutrition targets, compliance has created a whole new market. As Nancy May, the Healdsburg, California, food service director, described the situation to me, "There are these huge shows of products, trade shows, full of things that I would never want to serve to kids, because they may be compliant, but they are not food. My opinion . . . [I] just don't believe that's what we should be doing with all our resources. But it's being done, and it's big business, the business of feeding kids . . . and we see the results of that attitude everywhere. Our kids are not healthy."

USDA has made compliance easier for food service personnel, as we have seen in chapter 3, by offering the CN label that specifies precisely what portions of the menu plan a given product meets, and many companies have provided the information and guarantees needed to obtain such labels. But while such products make compliance, and therefore a successful SMI review, more likely, they often make it more difficult for schools to teach children anything about healthy eating. What does a carefully crafted, low-fat Hot Pocket teach a child about eating a healthy variety of foods? From a nutrition education standpoint, I think the emphasis on specific quantities of particular nutrients is not only of questionable value but is downright destructive. And this is not the only downside of our current approach to designing and assessing school meals. The social science concept of "opportunity cost" is relevant here. What else could USDA and all the state agencies and the thousands of SFAs be doing with the energy and effort they are currently putting into complying with these standards?

Years ago, the sociologist Amitai Etzioni warned that measurement can lead to the overproduction of the measurable (as compared with the not-so-measurable) outputs or products of human endeavor. He was talking about the desire of organizations to measure their efficiency and effectiveness, and he was concerned about those situations in which some products or desired outputs are more readily measurable than others. "Frequent measuring," he wrote, "tends to encourage over-production of highly measurable items and neglect of the less measurable ones." He used an example from education that now seems quaint: "High schools which measure the quality of their curricula by the number of students who pass the Regents Examinations (stressing here one component of effectiveness) find that some teachers neglect the character-development of their students to drill them for the tests."[36] I thought about this tendency of measurement to introduce distortion when I started noticing all of the things that the nutrient analysis is *not* designed to quantify. We have already noted that there are as yet no federal school food standards for sodium, cholesterol, or added sugars. But there are many other concerns, expressed by parents and health professionals, that are also excluded from the measurement apparatus and thus from the consideration of many hard-pressed school food service directors. What about the toxic burden from pesticides and fertilizers used in the production of the preponderance of fruits and vegetables served in schools that are not organically grown? What about hormones in the milk and the meat? What about the unknown consequences of ingesting genetically modified organisms (GMOs)? And even more basic, what about the taste of the food?

CHAPTER FIVE

THE MISSING MILLIONS

Problems of Participation

Expecting controversy, I took a seat at the very back of the enormous ballroom in the Austin, Texas, Hilton Hotel, a vantage point from which I could observe the audience as well as the speakers. The School Nutrition Association's Child Nutrition Industry Conference was in full swing. The overall theme for this gathering of upper-level school food service staff, school business officials, and representatives of the food industry was "Managing the Forces of Change," and the morning's opening plenary had been devoted to the childhood obesity epidemic. The afternoon's session was billed as a "Town Hall on Commercialization and Its Effects on School-Aged Children." For more than a year I had been receiving e-mail from activist organizations committed to reducing the role of brands and marketing in the lives of our children; I had followed with keen interest a growing societal concern, both in the United States and in Europe, about advertising aimed at young children in general and advertising in the schools in particular. The Institute of Medicine of the National Academies of Science had recently undertaken a study called "Food Marketing to Children and Youth," and legislation to regulate such food marketing had been introduced into Congress. I imagined that this was creating lively debate among school food service professionals, and I expected some sparks to fly. Perhaps if I had read the fine print on the program, I would have been better prepared for what actually transpired: "This session will feature interactive panel discussions designed to stimulate your thought process. You will learn innovative approaches to environmental design enhancements, program branding and points of service that will help you apply commercialization strategies in a positive way."[1]

In other words, this was a how-to session on branding and marketing. I listened with a blend of admiration and incredulity as successful food service directors explained their recipes for increasing student participation in the National School Lunch and School Breakfast programs and selling more food a la carte. "Branding" your school cafeteria was recommended: find a theme, a logo, a mascot, a color scheme that will appeal to your customers. Use focus groups if you need to, but get to know the students, their tastes, preferences, and preoccupations. And once you have chosen your brand identity, "put it everywhere." Put it on the wall in colorful graphics and on banners over the lines. Print it on plates, cups, trays, tray liners, napkins, and food wrappers; emblazon it on employee shirts, hats, and aprons. Stencil it onto the serving equipment. Put it on the school district's website and print up mouse pads, pencils, pens, book covers . . . the possibilities are endless. One school had had success with a computer theme: cafe.com. Their fruit and salad area was called "Anti-Virus," their snack foods were called "Quick Bytes," and the trash cans were called "downloads." Another had built its theme around the school's armadillo mascots and was considering investing in a pair of armadillo costumes so that Pete and Penny could make live appearances. Special theme days were recommended, complete with employee accouterments: leaf through the pages of *School Foodservice and Nutrition,* and you can see school food staff people dressed in leis and flowered headdresses for a Hawaiian theme month or in a banana costume to promote fruit and vegetable consumption, or you can read about the red-and-white striped hats worn by staff serving green eggs and ham at a Wisconsin school in celebration of Dr. Seuss Day.[2] Other suggestions include contests, posters, giveaways, taste tests, celebrity endorsements, you name it: the full panoply of American marketing has been brought to bear on the challenge of raising participation.

Participation, usually referred to as ADP (for average daily participation), is the Holy Grail of school food service personnel. It is the goal that they pursue and the standard they use to evaluate themselves—and each other—and it's easy to see why. In the first place, a high participation rate is a vote of confidence, evidence that students are enjoying the food, a testimony to the skill of the menu planner and the cooks alike. It is "the proof of the pudding." As one director told me when I asked about the rewards of her job, "Kids. The satisfaction . . . when kids run through a line and you're standing there and they're happy with what they got and they're actually eating it. I have a staff member who runs our dish room at our elementary school, and she loves to report to me how much garbage there was or there was not. When she comes and says 'Boy, they really ate that item today,' or whatever, when we try something new, it's fun, it's exciting."

Participation is the sine qua non for achievement of any of the program's goals. "If they don't eat it, it doesn't do them any good," as the director at Any Town High School was fond of asserting. The meals cannot prevent hunger or enhance health or educate future consumers—or even provide an acceptable outlet for farm surpluses—if children do not eat them.

The participation rate has an enormous effect on the operation's bottom line, the measure that school cafeterias share with most of the rest of American society. As participation in the official federally subsidized meal rises, the chances of breaking even increase. You have to buy more food to feed more children, of course, but food does not account for the major per-meal expenditure—that honor goes to labor and administration. As one school food service director from Michigan explained to me when I asked why more participation would lower her cost per meal, "because my salary is still the same. So the more numbers you have to spread it over, then that takes your cost down per meal. Certain things are stable; they are going to cost you, no matter what. My salary and benefits would be one." Utility bills are another; the cost of fuel used in actual cooking may go up if more food is cooked, but the cost of lighting and heating the cafeteria will remain the same, no matter how many children are using it. The incentive for a school food service director who likes her job is very concrete and very personal: if participation falls too low, school boards may decide to withdraw from the program or to contract out its operation to a private company—or they may simply replace the food service director.

If increasing participation in the reimbursable meal is the mantra, however, increasing a la carte sales can be equally attractive, even more attractive, from a revenue perspective. The prices that school food operations can charge for a reimbursable meal are generally set by the school board and may bear no relation to the cost of actually producing the meal, but the a la carte prices can be whatever the market will bear. The situation is complex, however, because not all a la carte revenues accrue to school food service. In general, as I have noted, the sales of items on the cafeteria line or at windows or kiosks located in the cafeteria are part of the food service, but revenues from vending machines may go to the school administration, and a school store or snack shop located outside the cafeteria may be run by the school administration or even by a student organization. No wonder school food service directors sometimes sound a bit schizophrenic when talking about a la carte. Many have made an art of inducing students to buy both the reimbursable meal and additional a la carte items. The reimbursable meal entitles the school to the reimbursement and increases the commodities allocation for the subsequent year, and the a la carte items help to balance the budget. Unfortunately, however, as we have also seen, the addition of a la carte items also tends to reduce the nutritional value of the meal that is actually consumed.

From the food service point of view, then, the more participation in the official meal, the better. From the student's viewpoint, however, the calculations are more complex. Some children who need the meals and are eligible to receive them free or at sharply reduced prices do not complete the application and certification process, and some who may be in real need are technically ineligible, issues we shall explore in depth in the next chapter. These students are effectively excluded, as are all students who attend schools that do not offer the program. But what about students in participating schools who have the funds to purchase the meals or who have successfully completed the certification process? What do we know about their participation? Overall, the most recent federal study (the School Nutrition Dietary Assessment-III or SNDA-III) found that on a typical day, 62 percent of students attending participating schools eat a school lunch: almost three-quarters of elementary school students, three-fifths of middle school students, and somewhat over two-fifths of high school students. Boys were considerably more likely than girls to participate at the middle and high school levels. Almost four-fifths of students whose parents reported that they received free or reduced price meals participated (78.8 percent) while just under half (49.6 percent) of those whose parents reported that they did not receive free or reduced price meals bought the lunch.[3]

From a program evaluation standpoint, there is both good news and bad news in these figures. Overall, participation has increased since a similar analysis was conducted for SNDA-I using data collected in 1992, from 56 percent to 62 percent. It has increased similarly among males and females and at all school levels, and similarly among those certified for free and reduced price meals and those paying "full price," rising from about 75 percent of those certified for free and reduced price in 1992 to 78.8 percent in 2005 when the SNDA-III data were collected, and from about 45 percent of those not certified to 49.6 percent.[4] If you view school meals as a possible tool to improve children's diets and food habits, then these increases in participation seem like good tidings; the movement is in the right direction. An overall increase of 6 percent over thirteen years, however, is just under a half a percent a year. Given the government's fairly substantial investment in efforts to improve meal quality through the School Meals Initiative for Healthy Children (SMI), and given the equally vigorous efforts of many school food service operators to boost participation through marketing and branding, the pace of increase seems very modest. An entire cohort of kindergartners passes through school in thirteen years; at this rate, it would take another whole cohort from kindergarten through grade 12 to bring overall participation above two-thirds of students. Participation by high school girls is particularly low—only 38.2 percent participated—but high school participation in general is low: only about a third of high school students who do not receive free and reduced price lunches participated on the target day.[5] Of particular concern is that a third of high school students who, by parent report, do receive free or reduced price meals, did not participate on the data collection day. In high schools, there is a long way to go to reach the potential of this program.

School Breakfast Program participation follows the same general pattern seen in school lunch, though at a much lower level. That is, participation declines with age and school level, is higher for males than females, and is higher for students who receive free and reduced price meals (by parent report) than for students who do not—more than four times as high. Breakfast, as we have seen, used to be available only in schools in poor neighborhoods and in schools to which students must travel substantial distances. Advocates have waged a long battle to make breakfast available in more schools (see chapter 6), and as more affluent schools have been added, the overall participation rate among students who attend schools that offer the program has declined, from 19 percent in 1992 to 17.7 percent in 2005. Only 7.2 percent of students who do not receive free and reduced price meals purchase a full price breakfast.[6]

DECISIONS

Almost every school I visited publishes a menu, sends it home with the children, prints it in the newspaper, and/or posts it on a website. And every morning in homes across America, students and parents check the menu attached to the refrigerator door or tacked up on the bulletin board to decide whether or not to buy school lunch that day. This decision, however, involves much more than the student's preferences and the school's menu; it is the product of a complex web of factors. An algorithm that would predict participation would have to take into account both the characteristics of the meal and the setting in which it is offered on the one hand, and the resources and alternatives available to the student on the other. Does the student have a lunch period? Is it long enough to get through the lines? Does it occur at a time of day when the student is ready for lunch? Is the student eligible for a free or reduced price meal? If so, has the application been submitted and the certification completed? Does the student fear ridicule or rejection from peers? If the student is not certified to receive free meals, does he have the money, or does the school permit charging meals? Does she like the food? Does she perceive it as a good value? Are friends eating the school meal? Does he have positive interactions with the school food service staff? Is the cafeteria clean and comfortable? Does the student find the noise level tolerable? Does she believe the cafeteria is safe?

What are her alternatives? Did she bring a lunch from home? Was there food at home to bring? Did she or her parents have the time to pack a meal? Does she like the food she brought from home? Are there a la carte items available in the cafeteria? Are there vending machines in the cafeteria or nearby? Is there a snack shack, school store, or alternate food source on campus? Is the campus "closed" or "open"—that is, are students permitted to leave during their lunch periods? About 25 percent of high schools in the United States maintain open campuses; a larger number extend this privilege to seniors. If going out for lunch is an option, how is the weather? Does the student have other, more pressing business to attend to during the lunch period? And if he prefers to go out, does he have sufficient funds?

Amid all this welter of factors in students' decisions about school lunch, however, studies of nonparticipation and related studies of student satisfaction have all boiled down to the same basic few: the quality and variety of the food, the time available for meals, the cafeteria environment, the price, the availability and attractiveness of alternatives, and the stigma attached to free and reduced price lunches and to school food in general. The problem of stigma will be discussed in chapters 6 and 7. Here let us look at the remaining factors that explain the "missing millions" of students who do not eat school meals.

FOOD FACTORS

There was nothing desirable that could compel me to go to lunch: the food was terribly unhealthy, and the lunch rooms were loud and noisy. A meal generally consisted of greasy food: pizza, hot dog, hamburger, and fries. There were no fruits and vegetables that I can recall.
University of Pennsylvania student,
describing high school lunch in New Jersey

The literature on school food participation and nonparticipation is not as extensive as I had expected, and much of it is quite old, but the finding that taste appeal is a central concern is consistent. A study conducted in Cincinnati and published in 1995 involved a detailed survey of the attitudes and beliefs that affected participation among 1,804 randomly selected high school students. The study found that many students judged the food quality as poor, that participating students were more likely to perceive the quality as fair or good than were nonparticipating students, and that nearly two-thirds said they would participate more often if the quality improved.[7]

Quality is intimately interwoven with palatability and students' preferences. A large national study conducted for USDA in the early 1990s reported that "most parents believe that school lunches are convenient, economical, and nutritious, but fewer reported that their children like the lunches. Both parents and students cited students' dislike of the food as the most common reason for not getting the school lunch."[8] In fact, when researchers asked students who had not eaten school lunch on the day of the survey to identify the primary reason why not, 42 percent chose "do not like the food."[9] Of course, quality is an elusive concept. Focus groups, however, have provided some useful insight into what both students and parents mean by poor quality. "You should have a chapter called 'It's Nasty,'" a Southern California anti-hunger advocate told me. "It comes up every time; that's all the kids say, 'It's nasty.'" To clarify the meaning of "nasty," he passed along a report prepared for California Food Policy Advocates by the research firm of Lake Snell Perry and Associates. The firm had been hired to conduct focus group research on the School Breakfast Program with both participating and nonparticipating middle school students and their parents, but the group facilitators found that they couldn't restrict the conversation to breakfast. Very quickly, it expanded to include lunch. The groups were conducted in Bakersfield and Los Angeles in 2004. The researchers' summary of food quality issues is revealing.

We heard several complaints about food quality. As several students put it, "It's nasty." Some students say the food is sometimes served cold or is partially frozen or uncooked in the middle. As one participating female LA student explains, "They should also defrost their food. It is pretty much frozen." Others say that the food is burnt or overcooked. The food being "greasy" was also a very commonly voiced complaint. Some complain that the food served is not fresh; one Bakersfield student reported having been served milk that was past its expiration date. We also heard some complaints about food choices. Some students say there are not enough options or complain that they serve the same things all the time.[10]

When I read this, it sounded so familiar that at first I thought I might have seen it before or heard it presented, but that seemed unlikely since the report had only recently become available. Then I remembered. A decade earlier, another research firm, based three thousand miles across the continent in Cambridge, Massachusetts, had also conducted focus groups with parents and students, eligible nonapplicants and eligible nonparticipants, to find out why students entitled to free or reduced price meals were not eating them. Abt Associates, Inc., ran twenty-four focus groups, six apiece at four different sites around the nation, and their summary of students' concerns about the quality of the food included: "poor taste, cold or undercooked, overcooked, too greasy, unfamiliar seasonings, and unappealing presentation," and noted that students wanted more variety and choices.[11]

In order to obtain more recent assessments, I asked students at five different colleges or universities to write down "school food memories" for me. I asked them to describe briefly the school and then their experiences with school food. What is most striking about the responses in these five pools is their enormous convergence and the extent to which they express the same complaints identified by the focus groups. There were differences, of course. Students at Hunter College in New York and Gustavus Adolphus in Minnesota were less likely than the other groups to complain about a lack of vegetarian options. Climate makes a difference: California schools are often built without a large indoor seating area; students purchase their food from snack shacks or kiosks and eat outdoors. New York and California students were far more likely than Rhode Island or Minnesota students to report leaving school to eat at fast food restaurants or convenience stores, and California students were far more likely to mention using cars to do so. The Minnesota students were, on the whole, more satisfied and more likely to report having eaten school food than any of the other groups. This is neither a sufficiently representative sample nor a sufficiently structured exercise to warrant a quantitative analysis, but on the other hand, I learned a great deal by reading through these accounts. So many students claimed that they had "never" or "seldom" eaten the reimbursable meal that, taken together, they shed considerable light on the nonparticipation phenomenon.

Among those who did participate, temperature problems were common. "There were times that I had to stay inside to eat; I would dread the fact that I needed to eat that food. The food would come out too cold or too hot. Even sometimes it would look like it was not cooked through." This, from a New York City student, echoes what advocates from the Food Justice Center told me about the most common school food complaints in LA: "Food is served cold; beverages that should be cold are warm. Raw meat, that's a big one . . . raw meat, frozen meat, moldy meat." Another New York City student reported that frozen lunch meat ended his participation in the program. "Since you couldn't just get french fries I would usually get a sandwich. Tuna fish, ham and cheese, things like that. I usually ate this until one day I bit into the sandwich and the meat was frozen; it had ice on it. After that day I never ate school lunch though I did purchase chips or cake from the stand in the lunch room." A Gustavus Adolphus student recalled that "the cafeteria was small with many students; sometimes the food ran out and you ended up with unheated food."

The ubiquitous temperature complaints reflect both the persistent realities of large-scale feeding operations—who has not been dissatisfied with the temperature of a meal in an airport or a workplace cafeteria?—and the specific conditions of contemporary school food. In 1973, John Hess observed in the New York Times that an applicant for a job with the Stouffers chain "was told that they didn't need any cooks, only 'thawer-outers.'"[12] As we have seen, food service operations of all sorts rely heavily on "defrost and reheat" approaches and have done so for decades. Burgers that have been cooked by the supplier and then frozen may not taste very good, but they move the liability out of the school district and onto the manufacturer. Further, aging buildings and rising enrollments have accelerated a move to central kitchens, and these, in turn, contribute to temperature issues.

"Rethermalization," or "retherm" for short, is the term that food service industry spokespersons use to refer to the reheating process, and they claim that the technology has become more sophisticated and more important to schools: "The increased popularity of retherm equipment among child nutrition professionals is not due solely to equipment advances. With more districts opting to go the route of central kitchens—either large-scale production facilities or schools with prep kitchens that satellite meals to other sites—the equipment needed at individual serving sites changes dramatically. These sites need equipment that can reheat and/or hold food at appropriate temperatures after it has been delivered and before it is to be served."[13]

That is the "ideal"; the reality, as Francesca de La Rosa, a Los Angeles advocate for healthy food, explained to me, can be far less appealing: "If we don't have full-service kitchens and we are getting all these meals coming in, you may not even have time to warm them up. . . . Our cafeteria workers . . . complain all the time: 'How do you expect us to get the food ready for a 10:30 nutrition recess break and we just got the food fifteen minutes before and we have twelve hundred to get out and ready?' "

Grease was a central complaint when Abt conducted its focus groups in 1994, and it remained a common complaint when I collected memories a decade later. According to my students: "High school lunch was gross . . . everything was loaded with grease." "Mostly greasy cheeseburgers, french fries, and canned green beans." "We would try to avoid school food like the plague. The chili dogs looked like unnamable garbage. The french fries were always too salty and too greasy." "The chicken was usually an odd color and very fatty. The ground taco beef had so much oil in it that it looked like soup." "All I remember about Junior High School is the worst meal. That was the Sloppy Joe, all that nasty oil." "Almost everything was soaked in oil and grease." "Greasy! Fatty! Pricey!" "The cafeteria food was adequate," recalled one more balanced assessment, but even he/she then noted, "it usually contained some sort of greasy, carbohydrate filled dish such as chalupas or french fries."

Grease and temperature are food preparation issues, but as we saw in chapter 3, an even more common complaint among my students—and among advocates and observers of many persuasions—is the menu itself. The brown baggers tended to be the most critical among the students. "The cafeteria food was edible, but I wouldn't call it good," wrote one nutrition-conscious California student. "The a la carte items consisted of baked potatoes with all the toppings, greasy frozen pizza, and Chinese chicken salad. . . . The snack bar consisted of hamburgers, pizza, fries, ice cream, and candy. There was really nothing of any nutritional value to choose from at all. I made sure to always pack my own lunch, because I could never find anything healthy enough to eat." For my students who rejected school food on nutritional grounds, the operant word was "junk," and most of them made little distinction between the reimbursable meal and the a la carte selections. "In a word, junk. Big cafeteria with several different 'stands'—one for sandwiches, one for pizza, one for nachos, etc., one for burgers and fries, and one for buying chips and candy. Vending machines for soda and soda-like juice were abundant. At the time I was a vegetarian, and there were very few options available for me. . . . Everything seemed heavily processed and not very healthy." Not surprisingly, vegetarians were particularly critical of the menu; a brown bagger summarized the school food situation on his rural high school campus: "No vegetarian options besides iceberg salads and baked potatoes. Students primarily spent money on snacks, vending machine foods, sugar beverages, or corporate pizzas or burritos provided through the school. Vending machines (owned by Pepsi) littered the entire campus, and I would say that 75 percent of the cafeteria lunches consisted of low quality, pre-prepared, super-processed frozen foods. Yuk!" A Rhode Island student who described her suburban community as "more affluent than poor" wrote, "I hardly ever bought school lunches because I didn't want to eat fries or pizza or chicken burgers or hamburgers every day. I always brought a lunch including turkey on wheat, yogurt, etc. I just didn't want to spend money on junk." A New York City student recalled, "I stopped eating the school lunch because it was unhealthy, not very good, and it was all junk food." Another student from Rhode Island also tried the school food but stopped: "I ate school lunch because it was new to me freshman year. Starting sophomore year, the lunches became boring and I started bringing my lunch from home, mainly because the supposedly healthy school lunches were in reality junk."

"Junk," of course, is in the eye of the beholder. When the Abt Associates' researchers conducted their focus groups in 1994, they reported a considerable divergence between parents and students as to what constituted good food. "Of note is that the concept of quality had different meanings to parents and students. Where parents perceive quality to mean nutritious, well-prepared or tasteful, or better cuts of meat or fresher vegetables, students often perceive quality in terms of their preference for fast-food items."[14] A number of the student comments I received bore out this statement. If one subset of students fails to choose school meals because they do not perceive them as nutritious, another group wants precisely the "junk" that the first group rejects. "We probably all wanted to eat the unhealthy french fries, etc.," recalled a young woman, remembering middle school, "but our parents wouldn't let us or give us the money to buy it." A University of California, Santa Cruz student recalled that she hated the lunches her mother packed for her because "we didn't really eat processed foods, and I wanted to have chips and cheetos and sodas and other junk food." More commonly, however, students looking back from the viewpoint of college were critical of their classmates' choices. A student from Bangor, Maine, summed it up this way: "I brought my lunch throughout high school but watched my friends and others eat ice cream, chips, pizza, and soda or drinks very similar to soda. There were chicken nuggets, pizza, and the classic 'hot lunch,' but most of the shelves were filled with junk or what I consider junk." Another student, from Long Island, New York, reported that "some kids ate pizza and Tater Tots every day." A few students recalled their own choices with chagrin: "We ate primarily candy, doughnuts, and other pastries as well as extraordinarily sodium-filled, salty food," wrote a UC Santa Cruz student, who described her school as urban and predominantly African American. "All the food was trash; the standard was probably the healthiest. I ate mostly candy, pizza, and cinnamon rolls," recalled another of my Santa Cruz students.

With a diet like that, one might expect a few upset stomachs, but students tended to blame their bellyaches on the cafeteria, not on their own choices. "I only ate school lunch about two times," recalled a Hunter College student who attended high school in Brooklyn: "Both times I came home with a stomachache. After that, I never ate school lunch again. I do remember always buying cookies and pretzels in the cafeteria. The cookies were chocolate chip, and they were cooked in the oven and sold right away. They were still warm when I would buy them. They tasted really good, too. The whole school loved those cookies. They would melt in your mouth. I would also buy chips and soda in the vending machines. That's about all I ever ate in high school."

Of course some students had had more specific negative experiences with school meals: "I would never eat school lunch at my high school because it smelled putrid, and I had bad experiences with school lunch in elementary school. . . . Sometimes when I'd get school lunch it would be almost completely inedible. Once I found disgusting cartilage that was carelessly left on the chicken. Another time I found a piece of scotch tape on the fried chicken. I would highly recommend not eating school lunch. The food is not real, and strikes me as being unhealthy and even unsafe for children to eat." Another student told of finding broken glass in his pizza, and one was sure that school food had given him a "virus." The Abt study reported that some parents were afraid to let their children eat the school food: "My kids got sick from the food. It is not cooked well, especially the hamburger."[15]

I am not in any position to investigate these claims; what is clear is that if students believe that school food will make them ill, they are unlikely to participate. Recall the "Thomas Theorem," invoked in chapter 1 for the Any Town food service director's beliefs about children's willingness to eat vegetables: "If men define situations as real, they are real in their consequences." I have thought of it again and again as I have traveled through the world of school food. It applies to contamination as well as to nutrition. If students or their parents believe that school food is unhealthy, they will act accordingly. This does not mean that there are not real issues of both nutrition and contamination, but a rumor of contamination can be nearly as troublesome as a documented case, and schools, as small closed worlds, are natural rumor mills. One of my students wrote about the impact of such a rumor in his high school: "One day a group of guys said they saw roaches in the kitchen. Then the story changed to mice being seen, and the hamburgers started being called 'ratburger.' Some people didn't care and went on eating it, but others were like me and stopped eating. Because of that experience, I still don't eat ground beef from any where, not even fast food."

A rumor spread from student to student is one thing; an exposé on national television is another. Not long after I began this research, I watched such a report; it didn't make me feel much like eating in school cafeterias. In the last few years, both NBC's Dateline and ABC's Prime-time Live have taken cameras into school kitchens and cafeterias and reported on a variety of egregious violations: rodent and roach infestation, mold growing on food in a walk-in refrigerator, food held at the wrong temperature, and yes, a cooler where a glass light bulb protector had shattered and sprinkled broken glass around. Combined with news about meat and produce contamination, downer cows and toxic spinach, such reports create anxiety among students and parents, but how safe are school meals?

The Centers for Disease Control and Prevention (CDC) keep track of food-borne illnesses, both in the general population and in schools. Two sets of numbers result, the number of "outbreaks" and the number of "cases." An outbreak is "an incident in which two or more persons experience a similar illness after ingestion of a common food."[16] An outbreak may thus involve as few as two cases—i.e., individuals who become sick—or many more, hundreds and sometimes thousands of individuals. The CDC records show that between 1990 and 1999, there were 195 outbreaks of food-borne illness in schools, affecting some 12,733 children. CDC did not then distinguish in its records whether the source of a school-based outbreak was a food prepared by school food service personnel, food brought from home, or food sold elsewhere on campus. The General Accounting Office (GAO), in 2003, surveyed state health officials about the largest outbreaks—fifty-nine school outbreaks each involving fifty or more cases that had occurred in the 1990s. They found that forty of the fifty-nine outbreaks, or about two-thirds, were derived from school meals and cited "inadequate cooking, improper food storage and handling, poor food worker hygiene, sick workers preparing food, and improper hot holding and cooling of foods" as the practices within schools that were believed to have contributed to the outbreaks. Six of the outbreaks were caused by foods that were contaminated before delivery, and in two outbreaks, state health officials believed that both prior contamination and practices within schools were to blame.[17] During the 1990s, 52.5 billion breakfasts and lunches were served by the National School Lunch and School Breakfast programs; if two-thirds of the 12,733 school based cases were derived from school meals, or 8,531, this represents less than one case in every six million meals served. It is a fairly reassuring statistic, though that is small comfort if your child is sickened by a school meal. The odds of any given school meal being safe are really, really high, or were in the 1990s.

Unfortunately the trend data is less reassuring. After trying to adjust for changes in CDC collection procedures and more frequent reporting due to heightened public awareness, the GAO in 2002 calculated that the number of school based outbreaks in the 1990s had increased by an average of 10 percent a year, while the number of students participating in the school food programs increased by 12 percent over the decade, or a bit more than 1 percent per year.[18] The increase in school-based outbreaks paralleled the increase in outbreaks in the general population. The explanations for these increases probably lie in the changes in the way in which food, particularly meat, is produced in the United States—the same reliance on factory farms and grain-fed animals discussed in chapter 3—and grave limitations on the federal government's food safety inspection apparatus. Even the GAO, an agency dedicated to precision and certainly cautious in its testimony, told Congress it believed that "to make substantial improvements in the safety of school meals will require, in part, addressing the overarching problems that affect the nation's federal food safety system as a whole."[19] The diffusion of responsibility among disparate agencies, underfunding, an inadequate number of inspectors, and the inability to require a recall in most situations are among the "overarching problems" identified by critics.

"Even one outbreak of one child sick from foodborne illness is too many," declares the School Nutrition Association.[20] Despite this recognition that food safety is a problem much larger than the school food programs, there is widespread consensus that children are particularly vulnerable to food-borne pathogens—more likely than adults to get sick from a given level of contamination and more likely to suffer serious damage to health because of such an illness. Therefore the 2004 Child Nutrition Reauthorization required that schools participating in the national programs institute the federal HACCP (Hazards Analysis and Critical Control Points) procedures and that schools be inspected at least twice yearly by local health authorities and display the results of their inspections. Each new regulation, of course, creates the possibility for new forms of failure, so perhaps it should not have been a surprise when the Center for Science in the Public Interest (CSPI) issued "Making the Grade: An Analysis of Food Safety in School Cafeterias" at the beginning of 2007. In sum, the Center found what it called "risky food-safety gaps, including outdated food codes and insufficient inspections."[21] The SNA rose to the defense of its members, pointing out that school food service departments were being held accountable for factors over which they had no control, including the state legislature's choice of a food code and the availability of sufficient inspectors to conduct two inspections annually. "Failing a school cafeteria because a health inspector could not visit twice per year—even if the one visit resulted in a score of 100—is misleading to the public and irresponsible."[22] My point is not to take sides in this controversy, but to return to the Thomas Theorem: if reports convince students and parents that their health is at risk, then they will act accordingly; each new exposé or critical report deters participation.

By the time they reached the college classroom and wrote down their school lunch memories for me, some students were ready to take a more tempered look at school food. "In general, though, I didn't think the food was as terrible as most people say it is," recalled a New York City student. Another, who had described an aversion to the school meal, went on to assert: "Now that I look back at my behavior in those years, I would say that it definitely was exaggerated, not only by me but collectively by the student body. Those very meals, extremely cheap I might add, got me through the day, uplifted my emotional . . . state, . . . overall, not too bad." A third looked back a bit wistfully: "I kind of miss those days of free lunch. Now being in college, you have to pay for lunch. In High School, if you were hungry or not, there would always be food waiting for you. In college, you have to look for it when you're hungry."

For high school students, it is primarily their own perceptions and attitudes that are reported, though a few attributed their nonparticipation to their parents' preferences or beliefs. For elementary school students, however, parents' beliefs are crucial. In two papers published in 2001 and 2002, researchers reported the results of focus groups conducted with parents of elementary school children in two schools in Mississippi, designed to determine both what their primary concerns were and how important these factors were to them. They found that parents cared about nutrition and about whether or not their children liked the food, and believed that these concerns were important. They reported that participation in the lunch was convenient for them but did not feel strongly that such convenience was important. In addition, parents expressed concern that they would not know how much or what their children actually ate if they ate the school lunch; they believed they had more control if they sent a lunch from home. Finally, leading in to the next factor on our list, more than a third of parents believed that their children would not have enough time to eat if they went through the lunch line, and almost all the parents—93 percent—believed that this was an important concern.[23]

TIME TROUBLES

Our lunch period was 20 minutes long. I usually only got drinks or snacks from the cafeteria or french fries. I never ate any of the meat or prepared meals. . . . Most people usually got the fries, ice cream, drinks, or chips. A main problem was that standing in line for the "real food" took too long. By the time a person paid and got a seat, lunch was just about over.

University of Rhode Island student, recalling high school lunch in the suburbs of Providence, R.I.

The Mississippi elementary school parents' concern about time to eat was reflected in virtually every other study I found. The Abt study was designed to learn why eligible parents did not apply for free school meals and why students whose applications had been approved did not participate. The study found that conditions varied among the four sites and among schools within each site, but in general, lack of adequate time to eat was a significant deterrent to participation. "The time they have to eat is a big problem," asserted one of the Abt study parents. "They end up dumping it." Another reported that "my child finally suggested to me that she bring her lunch because she's a slow eater and she wasn't getting enough time." Of course, it is not just the length of the lunch period in absolute terms, but the total lunch period minus the time spent waiting in line. "If you arrive late to the lunchroom, the lines are so long that there's not enough time to eat and visit with your friends," said one of the Abt study students. Another concurred: "You're hungry and your stomach is growling, so you make for the snack lines to get something to eat quickly. And when you're hungry you can't concentrate in class and you fall asleep." And another: "It gets too crowded in the cafeteria, the lines are too long. All the best food is gone by the time you get to it. All you get is the leftovers." The researchers summarized what they heard as follows: "Long lines often drive students to the a la carte lines so they can assuage their hunger more quickly, have more time to socialize with their friends, and be assured of the availability of the foods they like."[24] The Cincinnati study also found insufficient time to be a major reason for nonparticipation. "The majority of students surveyed reported the lunch period as being too short (82%) and the wait in the food lines too long (65%)."[25]

My students had the same complaint: such long lines, so little time. "Sometimes, the kids who bought school lunch wouldn't even have time to eat because they had had to stand in line for the whole period. Also, our school was overcrowded so some students had to eat their lunch standing up," recalled a Hunter College student who had a "measly 20-minute lunch period." Even longer lunch periods did not necessarily solve the problem. According to another Hunter student, "from what I remember of school lunch, it was not bad. The food was very good. But the fact that you had to make a huge line to get it was not very pleasant. In my school you had to have your lunch ticket, which sometimes got lost, and the staff people wouldn't give you the food without it. I think that the cafeteria was so small that you wouldn't be able to sit when you got your lunch. . . . By the time you got the lunch, the time was over." "We did not have enough time to eat," recalled a UC Santa Cruz student; "the lunch thing was so disorganized that it took 30 minutes to get lunch since the lines were so long, and people would just all push and shove to get in line. There was never a straight line. When we got to the stand, the good food was already gone." "The lines were ridiculous," wrote her classmate. "You had to get out of class early to eat on time, otherwise standing in line took half to three-quarters of the lunch period. . . . There was enough time to eat only if you didn't buy lunch." Another Santa Cruz student concurred: "In high school I did not buy lunch once. The food was not worth it to me. There were always long lines, and I didn't want to spend my money and half of the lunch period trying to get food."

The School Nutrition Association reports that lunch periods have been getting shorter. Their survey shows a decrease in the average length of elementary school lunch from 29.7 minutes in 2003 to 23.7 in 2005; middle schools saw a drop from 29.7 to 24.6 minutes in the same period, and high schools went from 31.8 minutes to 26.7, averages which include the time allowed to get from classroom to cafeteria and back.[26] The SNA recommends a minimum of thirty minutes, pointing to the likelihood of poor digestion if students are rushed in consuming their food.[27] Nutritionists generally express concern that brief lunch periods promote poor eating habits. A director of school food service in Missouri linked the short lunch period to the obesity epidemic when she explained to a reporter, "If you consume your food too quickly, your body doesn't have time enough to tell you when you are full."[28] And dieticians also point out that children tend to eat their meals in reverse order, sweets first, vegetables later. A longer lunch period, as the Wichita journalist Cara Kumari explains, gives them more time "to get to the healthy foods on their tray."[29]

Nutrition issues are not the only time concerns. As a California food service director explained to me, "not only do we serve the food, but meal time is supposed to be community time." Short lunch periods, she complained, mean that youngsters are herded out to make room for the next group without any time to relax. "That's not how you socialize. How do you teach them the etiquette of a meal? You don't, because they're just shoveling and running." In Massachusetts, a state legislator became so concerned about the impact of abbreviated lunches that she proposed a law mandating a minimum thirty-minute lunch period in the state's public schools. In response, school administrators pointed out that their hands were tied by the need to comply with state and federal school requirements. They felt pressured by the accountability required by No Child Left Behind and caught between the state's mandated minimum of nine hundred hours of instructional time and the limitations of days and hours in the teachers union contracts.[30]

Some schools have tried to deal with the lunch crunch by starting lunch service earlier in the day. The 2000 School Health Policies and Programs Study reported that lunch starts before 11 A.M. in over a quarter of the nation's schools.[31] The late 1980s and the 1990s saw the "baby boom echo" reach school age, with associated pressure on school facilities of all sorts. A task force convened by the California Department of Education summarized the situation this way in a report on best practices for facilities:

> All too often in older schools, cafeterias were designed for the number of students occupying the site at the time of initial construction. However, as the student populations grew and relocatable classrooms were added to the campus, the cafeteria facilities typically remained the original size. To accommodate increased student population, schools must sometimes provide three or four different lunch periods. This schedule means that some students will have their lunch period either very early or late in the day. This solution is not ideal for maintaining consistent blood sugar levels, which is important for students' academic focus and concentration.[32]

It is not ideal for encouraging participation or healthy eating, either. A recent study of high schools in Pennsylvania found that almost a quarter of them reported a lunch period that begins at 10:30 a.m. or earlier, and that the early start times were associated with higher rates of a la carte purchases. The study's authors hypothesized that students with early lunch periods were stocking up on items to be eaten later in the day, but it seems equally likely that some students are just not ready for a full scale lunch at 10:30 in the morning and chose an a la carte snack instead.[33] Certainly very few are ready for lunch at 8:59 a.m., the earliest lunch period I encountered. Students scheduled for this first lunch period at Richmond Hill High School in Queens, New York, must somehow still get through the day until school is dismissed just before 3:30 p.m. The school, originally built for about 1,800 students now houses a student body of more than 3,600.[34]

Lunch scheduling is generally done by the school administration, not the school food service staff, and it reflects a variety of factors, including the priority, or lack thereof, that administrators place on school food. The seating capacity of the lunchroom and the number of students to be fed must be taken into account. So must the overall bell schedule—students' lunch periods must coordinate with the other periods of the school day, and lunches are typically either a full period or a half period. If classes are 45 minutes in length, then lunch will often be only 22.5 minutes. The shortest lunch that I encountered was only 18 minutes—probably a 55-minute class period split into thirds, though 15-minute lunch periods (followed by another 15 minutes for recess) were reported in a number of communities in the Boston area. It is not impossible to eat in that time; a series of stopwatch studies found that students actually spend an average of between seven and ten minutes consuming food, but additional time was needed for standing in line, carrying food to the eating area, socializing with friends, and bussing trays. Combining the results of several studies using the stopwatch methodology, Martha Conklin and her associates reported that the average total time in the cafeteria for the eighteen schools included in the study was twenty minutes for elementary and middle schools and twenty-four minutes for high schools, including the time spent waiting in line to obtain food.[35] Thus it is not surprising that another study found that brown baggers spent more time eating than youngsters consuming school lunches.[36]

Ironically, schools with open campuses tend to have longer lunch periods—the students who leave need time to get to their destinations and back, so the students left behind have more time to relax and socialize. And the lines they face are shorter, of course, since many of their classmates are eating elsewhere. Many school food service directors and cafeteria managers expressed frustration with open campus policies that put them in competition with teens' favorite restaurants and convenience stores, but some were philosophical. As Deb Neal explained, her cafeterias in Lansing, Michigan, couldn't possibly accommodate all the students in the senior high schools: "Even though we have a low participation at our high schools, our cafeterias are busy for the entire hour of lunch. We could never accommodate an entire population. Our largest high school is almost seventeen hundred students and our smallest is about eleven hundred. And we could never, never accommodate that entire population in any given hour of the day. There would need to be some major changes. If we closed the campus, we would have to stagger lunch schedules. That's all there is to it."

THE CAFETERIA ENVIRONMENT

The cafeteria was usually packed to capacity—a sea of bodies with barely any room to sit. You'd have to shout at the top of your lungs to have a conversation, and at least once every week we were treated to a new fight that would break out. . . . A noisy, greasy, one-of-a kind experience.

**Hunter College student, recalling school lunch
at a parochial school in Queens (New York City)**

Ambiance, as any restaurateur will tell you, is an important part of the dining experience. Light, noise, crowding, temperature, cleanliness, decor, furnishings—they are all part of what makes a meal pleasant, or not so pleasant. I don't think I realized how many American school lunchrooms were in basements until I visited schools in Sweden and noticed the natural light from large windows and the thriving plants. Of course some American school cafeterias are lovely—decorated with murals or student artwork, clean and comfortable. I remember one in Hawaii, windows on three sides and the fourth a large display of photographs of students planting and harvesting the islands' traditional taro crop. With 98,000 schools in the country, you can probably find an example to illustrate any claim. For some students, however, cafeteria conditions can be a deterrent to participation. As one of my students recalled her high school experience in Brooklyn,

> I would like to start off saying that I never ate lunch in high school or any school for that matter. . . . It would be hard for me to describe the food and its taste because I never ate in the lunch room, but I can tell you of the feeling I got when I entered the dreaded cafeteria. . . . I guess it was a combination of factors that lead to my disgust of school food. The huge room or floor, being in the basement, was this faded lime green, green being a color I hate. Then there was the smell of bleach and disinfectant mixed with french fries, cold chicken patties, and what was supposed to be a salad. Not to forget that everyone on the line could breathe, sneeze, cough, spit, etc., all over your food just waiting to pay. Also the countless stories of finding little "surprises" in your food, like a hair or some other thing.

The odor is a particularly popular target of student complaint: "What I remember most about high school lunch is the horrible smell that was always present in the cafeteria. Even though I graduated two years ago, I can still remember that smell. It was somehow a cross between dirty gym clothes and frying oil."

Cafeteria cleanliness undoubtedly varies from school to school. Several thousand students surveyed in fourteen suburban middle schools in six states on their perceptions of school food tended to agree with statements that "the food serving lines are clean," "spills and trash in the dining area are cleaned quickly," and "tables in the dining area are clean." They were considerably more likely to agree with those positive assessments than with positive evaluations of the appearance and quality of the food, or a statement about sufficient time to eat.[37] Students from large city schools, on the other hand, frequently complain about the appearance of the cafeteria, and their assertions are often supported by adult observers. A graduate social work student involved in a project to increase school meal participation described to me what she had seen in visits to half a dozen of New York City's high schools: "Overall, a lot of these cafeterias seem like they are in the basement, not a lot of light. They are old, dirty, they just don't seem like they are very well cared for, especially throughout the lunch period itself." She went on to explain that conflicts between the custodial staff and the school food service employees, referred to by the new name of the city's school food service department, "SchoolFood," complicated the task of keeping the cafeteria clean during the succession of lunch periods:

> Technically, it's SchoolFood who wipes off the tables, and it's the custodians that clean the floors, but there's not always the people power to keep up with it, and that ends up meaning that SchoolFood . . . just wipes up the crumbs and spills and technically, they don't have to physically remove trays. I think, it's a little odd. And there seems to always be this friction between SchoolFood and custodians about cleaning, particularly. . . . So you have the SchoolFood who wipes off the table and . . . pushes off the milk carton, and it spills onto the floor, and so then they've got a milk spill, but then the custodial staff has to come around and clean that up, . . . and . . . because they also had to cut back on their custodial staff, I believe that they clean the school every other day. So that would mean that mopping the floors—I'm sure they sweep, but mopping the floors every other day. . . . I found the floors to be really gross. But you know, I mean, not every school has really disgusting cafeterias.

It is not surprising that crowding too was a common complaint; the same demographic factors that contribute to the need to schedule multiple short lunch periods result in crowded conditions. "Overcrowded, noisy, long bathroom lines, smelly and sometimes unsanitary are the words that come to mind that best describe my lunch room," wrote one of my students. "There were always long lines and a small crowded lunchroom overflowing with teenagers," commented another. A Polish foreign exchange student who had attended high school for a year in Tennessee recalls his surprise at the lunch situation: "I was shocked by the fact that everyone ate at the same time. It seemed pointless to me to get all the students to one big warehouse at the same time while they could also easily be divided in groups. . . . The cafeteria was huge, noisy, and quite unpleasant."

Overcrowding, of course, contributes to noise. Sometimes adults, reacting to the noise level, have tried to impose rules of silence. A recent silent lunch controversy in a parochial school in Providence, Rhode

Island, generated several days of press coverage, with the principal explaining that the silence rule—silence for the first ten minutes—was imposed as a safety measure after a student's choking went undetected amid the noise.[38] Administrators have developed a variety of systems for dealing with excessive noise; that beautiful elementary cafeteria in Hawaii was run by a cafeteria manager who monitored every meal. When noise reached a troublesome level, she gave a hand signal, followed if need be by an announcement from the microphone, and students simultaneously lowered their voices and waved their hands to attract the attention of their schoolmates. In about a minute, the lunchroom went from uproar to a congenial hum, with the cafeteria manager reminding students to "use our lunch voices." Some schools have installed large lights patterned after traffic signals and attached to decibel monitoring equipment. Green light indicates an acceptable level, yellow means noise that is approaching an unacceptable level, and red is a signal to stop talking and lower the overall volume. In at least one school the device is in the shape of a large ear, and occasionally students have been known to shout in concert to make the ear turn red on purpose. Such high spirits notwithstanding, these are schools that have made a commitment to maintaining the cafeteria as a space in which social interaction is possible. The crucial factor seems to be the school's culture—the expectations of civility—and the assignment of adults to monitor and enforce noise limits.

Crowding and noise go hand in hand, of course, but so can noise and sanitary protections. Many school cafeterias are walled with ceramic tiles that are relatively easy to wipe clean but that tend to echo and magnify sound. Others were originally designed for other purposes—auditoriums or gymnasiums. In general, however, noise seems to be less an issue for students than it is for adults. Noise levels above eighty decibels can cause permanent damage to hearing. In one study in Lubbock, Texas, in which researchers measured average decibel levels ranging from 70.3 to 79.3, most students disagreed with the statement "There is too much noise in the cafeteria during lunch time."[39] In another study of satisfaction with school meals, students tended to agree with the statement that the "noise level in the dining area is ok"—in fact, they agreed with that statement, on average, more strongly than with any other indicator of satisfaction.[40] SNDA-III found that 44.6 percent of students thought the cafeteria was too noisy, while 53.9 percent thought it was "about right."[41]

PRICE

They offered deli sandwiches, burgers, fries, pizza, and entree salads every day. And they had two entrees that changed every day, from turkey dinners to pasta to calzones. All the lunches came with salad, fruit, and milk as well. I bought lunch a few times a week because it cost something like $2 or $2.50, so I couldn't afford it every day.

**University of Rhode Island student, recalling
high school lunch in suburban Rhode Island**

Much of the early research on school food participation found that price was a significant factor, and for years, school food service directors have used the rule of thumb that for every 5 cents they raise the price, they will lose one percentage point of participation. Food service personnel told me that participation generally recovers eventually after a price increase, but it takes a while, and they lose money in the interim. Both the original SNDA-I in the early 1990s and SNDA-III, released at the end of 2007, found a relationship between price and participation that essentially supports this idea, though with less elasticity than the directors had assumed.[42] These studies were not looking at price increases, but rather at the relationship between price and participation in a large sample. When other factors are held constant, the higher the price, the lower the participation among those students not certified for free and reduced price meals. In both of these studies, however, conducted more than a decade apart, the cost of meals seemed to be a factor of limited importance in explaining overall nonparticipation. Only 7.5 percent of those who did not eat school lunch on the target day reported "monetary reasons" in SNDA-III, and in SNDA-I, 7 percent gave "too expensive" as a reason for not participating on the interview day.[43]

Nonetheless, some of my students were deterred by price considerations. "Everything . . . was ridiculously overpriced, like [at] a theme park. . . . I always ate a sandwich or lunch (leftover dinner) from home. If I ate at the cafeteria it was 'cause I had a craving for (overpriced) nachos or forgot my lunch," wrote a California student from an affluent suburb. "My mom refused to pay $2.50 a lunch/kid (2) so we made our own or went hungry," reported a University of Rhode Island student who had attended high school in Connecticut. A Minnesota student with four siblings wrote that he liked the food, but "I only had hot lunch once a week because my family couldn't afford to feed 5 children from the school." At least as frequent were students who reported price as a positive factor in their choices: "I ate school lunch every day; I ate it because it was cheaper than going to fast food and less time-consuming than making a lunch." In the next chapter, we will look more closely at the problem of students who are priced out of the lunch program.

ALTERNATIVES

Our school food consisted of a hot lunch line, an a la carte line, and an open campus (with many surrounding fast food restaurants—McDonald's, Taco Bell, etc.). School food never appealed to me. I ate it infrequently due to the high prices as well as the unhealthy food available. I always found it humorous when they would sell a huge slab of pizza with grease dripping off the corners, with a "mandatory" side of "healthy" corn. I always knew that I could make a much healthier lunch at home and "brown bag" it.

**Gustavus Adolphus student,
recalling school lunch in Wisconsin**

Bringing a lunch from home is always an option; this does not vary from school to school or district to district, though it does seem to have varied over time. In the first SNDA study, 18 percent of the students had brought a lunch from home and another 4 percent reported eating at home. SNDA-III did not report the data in this form, but among the 38 percent who did not participate in the NSLP on the target day, 28 percent gave "brought lunch from home" as a reason. This would suggest less brown bagging, since 28 percent of 38 percent is just over 10.5 percent. A decline in brown bagging won't surprise anyone who keeps an eye on the statistics on the average number of hours worked by American households, which has been going up, or the overall percentage of meals prepared at home, which has been going down. Although a small study has found school meals to be nutritionally superior to lunches brought from home, it is not the brown baggers who worry health experts.[44]

The two major alternatives to school meals that do vary from school to school and that do worry health advocates are a la carte or vending machine items and the option of leaving the campus. Both are widespread, and both are contested turf. Efforts to eliminate or limit these alternatives come up against opposition, both from students and from those who benefit from selling them food.

In secondary schools with open campuses, students may choose to eat out, no matter how good the school food is, or how much of a bargain, simply for the pleasure of escaping the campus or in order to impress peers. As one New York City college student who had attended a private high school in Tulsa, Oklahoma, wrote: "My senior year in high school I was allowed to go off campus. I still didn't eat very much. Usually my friends and I were so happy to get away we'd buy sodas and drive around smoking cigarettes, screaming our favorite song of the moment. Lunch was not a time for food, but an opportunity to escape and relish the fact that I wasn't sitting in a classroom being bored out of my mind."

Overall, only about 11 percent of schools have a general open-campus policy, but about 25 percent of high schools permit some or all students to leave during the lunch period. If my students' accounts are any indication, however, we should not assume that leaving campus is limited to those who have permission to do so. "Only seniors were given free use of the outside world during the school day," recalled a New York City student; "when I had free period or lunch with the senior class, I would often just sneak out with them." "Many students cut class and some had connections with the security guards who let them out for an hour," complained another who wanted to leave school but couldn't. I might have thought this was an idiosyncrasy of New York if I had not noted that in the Cincinnati study cited above, 41 percent of the students reported leaving to eat off campus, despite the fact that all high schools in the district had a closed-campus policy.

How much impact does an open-campus policy have on participation rates? It is difficult to say. School food service personnel believe that it is substantial: "We have a fairly good participation rate at our elementary and middle school level, and of course high school is very low participation, because of the open campus situation," one Midwestern director explained. It seems common sense that an open campus would reduce participation. The research, however, is less clear. SNDA-III found that predicted participation rates were lower in schools with open-campus policies than in schools with closed campuses, but the difference was not statistically significant. I was surprised, but when I looked more closely, I realized that the variable was defined as an either/or situation—the school had an open campus or did not. For the individual student, however, the unit of participation, this is not so; students in some schools that had open campus policies were eligible to leave only if they were seniors.[45] It also makes sense that open campuses reduce participation in a la carte more than they reduce participation in the reimbursable meal. That is, a student with money in her pocket may be choosing between fast food on campus or fast food off. For a food service director whose eye is on the bottom line, the off-campus option represents unwelcome competition, but it may not show up in an analysis focused on uptake of the official meal.

Competitive foods on campus are much more widely available than open-campus policies. SNDA-III found results very similar to the GAO study results reported in chapter 4. All high schools, 97 percent of middle schools, and 80 percent of elementary schools had some competitive food source available to students. Overall, just over half of schools reported vending machines available to students: 98 percent of high schools, 87 percent of middle schools, and 26.5 percent of elementary schools.[46] In many schools, however, these machines are supposed to be turned off during the lunch period, and in some they actually are shut down. School stores and snack bars are another venue for competitive foods; about one-third of high schools, two-fifths of middle schools, and one-fifth of elementary schools have at least one other competitive food source on campus. By far the most common source of competitive food, however, was the sale of a la carte items in the cafeteria; overall, three-fifths of schools offered a la carte at breakfast, and more than four-fifths did so at lunch. Such tabulations overstate the issue, however, since more than two-fifths of the schools selling a la carte at lunch offered milk as the only item.[47]

SNDA-III found a pattern for the availability of competitive foods very similar to that reported for open-campus policies: participation was lower in schools where competitive foods were offered during mealtimes, but again, the difference was not regarded as statistically significant. School food service personnel don't see it that way. If they operate the a la carte service themselves, they tend to characterize it as an "add on" to the main meal, but if the principal or a student club offers a snack shack or controls the vending, it is seen as a factor limiting participation in the reimbursable meal. A high school nutrition program manager in Georgia told a reporter that when her school's vending machine area was temporarily locked off after a break-in, "our lunch count went up 200 meals per day.... The vending machines really hurt us a lot."[48] My guess is that the SNDA-III result that is so counterintuitive—that participation is not (statistically) significantly influenced by the availability of competitive foods—has to do with the definition of the variable "competitive foods offered during mealtimes." If this variable includes those schools that offered only milk, for example, the limited impact on participation in the reimbursable meal begins to make sense.

One thing that is clear about competitive foods is that under some circumstances they stigmatize the reimbursable meal. "There was a student lunch line and a snack bar," wrote a student from Minnesota; "the 'cool' kids ate from the snack bar and the others ate from the line." Or, as another student at the same college put it, "School lunch was for the kids who couldn't afford to eat from the a la carte line, who were on the free-lunch program." In 2001, USDA summarized this issue for Congress: "Since only children with money can purchase competitive foods, children may perceive that school meals are primarily for poor children rather than nutrition programs for all children. Because of this perception, the willingness of low-income children to accept free or reduced price meals and non-needy children to purchase school meals may be reduced."[49]

For me, stigma is the most troubling of the factors that deter participation in school meals. Stigma simultaneously prevents some students from eating, devalues the meal for those who do consume it—free, reduced, or fully paid—and imposes a burden of shame on students who opt to exercise their right to free or reduced price food. The stigma, of course, derives from the three-tier system of eligibility. Chapter 7 explores that system and the administrative burden that it imposes. First, however, we must look at the issue of hunger and the factors that contribute to a situation in which millions of low-income children don't even get the chance to turn up their noses at school food.

CHAPTER SIX

HUNGER IN THE CLASSROOM

Problems of Access

The prevention of hunger is the most widely agreed upon goal of school food programs, and school meals make a crucial difference in the lives of literally millions of American children every school day. I asked Dr. Suzanne Hallings, the superintendent of schools in Benoit, Mississippi, the school district where Patsy James serves lunch and breakfast, what she saw as the role of school food in the overall educational experience of Benoit students. "For our students," she replied, "I think it is very important." She went on to explain why:

> I think many of them do not have food at home that is readily accessible. We know that for many of them that's a good reason to get up and come to school in the morning, because there's going to be breakfast. . . . I think that our children suffer when we have holidays and breaks because those two meals that they have during the week are not there for them. And that's not all of our children, but a lot of our children are growing up in homes where that's just not happening, and nobody is really taking the responsibility to make sure that food is there.

Unemployment was very high in Benoit, she said, and some families were just getting by on food stamps and whatever they could scrape together. In the absence of any full-service grocery store, food was actually quite expensive.

It's not just in very poor communities like Benoit that hunger is a problem. I returned to my own former high school, Francis C. Hammond, now a middle school, in the affluent suburbs of Washington, D.C., where I talked with Dr. Becky Domokos-Bays, the school food service director in Alexandria, Virginia, and with Lena Purifoy, her cafeteria manager; both are veterans of long service in school food. There was an extended weekend coming, and they predicted that breakfast participation would be up the following Monday. "Not only that, you can tell the hungry kids when they come through a line, how they behave. They are not misbehaving, but they are just . . . it's almost like they are grabbing the food," commented Dr. Bays. "They want to eat right away," broke in Ms. Purifoy. "They do," responded Dr. Bays, "and they will start eating in line, that kind of thing."

The Monday morning post-vacation phenomenon is widely observed and commented on in school food circles. The Sarasota Herald-Tribune described the principal of Charlotte County's poorest school: "Eunice Wiley worries each time a school vacation rolls around: 'Who's going to feed my children?' Wiley . . . also worries on weekends, and with good reason: the breakfast line in the school's cafeteria is longest on Mondays."[1] Those of us who live comfortable lives far from the preoccupation with survival may forget, but those who work daily with poor and hungry people will remind us if we give them a chance. I still remember a comment made to me a decade ago by the director of the Harry Chapin Foodbank of Southwest Florida when I was working on research for an earlier book. "You listen to a child," Hawley Botchford said,

> ask "Are you looking forward to Christmas?" and they get this funny look. Okay, no, they're not going to get presents because the mothers can't afford it—it's the end of the month. All holidays come at the end of the month. What do we have at the end of the month? No food stamps! There's no school lunches, there's nothing to do. . . . Now these kids, they didn't ask to be in this situation. . . . That child still has a potential, and we're denying that child the ability to achieve his or her potential by lack of nutrition while we are throwing it away in the dumpsters daily. To me, that is a sin.[2]

Advocates and concerned school personnel have worked hard to make sure that all children have access to school meals, but there are still too many children in need who do not get them. They attend schools that do not offer the programs, or they cannot afford the meal but are not certified to receive it free, or their pride and fear of ridicule prevent them from taking advantage of a meal for which they are certified. When the system fails them, they go hungry. The director of the Vermont Campaign to End Childhood Hunger told me about his own experiences with hunger as a teenager in New York City:

Because my father made too much money and we didn't qualify for free meals, I didn't eat, because I didn't have any money and that's how it was. . . . In high school, the first two years of high school, I remember what hunger meant. And it's hard to describe the pain, it's always there. And my grades were barely passing. And then the third year, I lied on the application. My father made—I remember he was five bucks over the limit. So we lied. And I got free meals, and I went from being a C student to an A student and then graduated with honors the last two years of high school. How much of that is attributable to food versus I had grown up at that point, I don't know. But obviously having food in your stomach does help.

HUNGER AND LEARNING

The effort to fuel learning by reducing hunger among the nation's schoolchildren has been a constant amidst the shifting aims of school food programs. The movement for "school feeding" emerged in the United States in the context of compulsory school attendance. By 1900, thirty-two states and the District of Columbia had laws requiring school attendance for children in certain age groups. Compulsory attendance was inextricably intertwined with efforts to end child labor, and enforcement of the attendance laws brought into the public schools many very poor children who had formerly worked doing piecework or "homework" in tenements or laboring on farms. As their numbers increased, educators discovered the simple reality that has become the mantra of child nutrition programs: a hungry child cannot learn. Robert Hunter put the matter powerfully in his 1904 classic, *Poverty,* widely credited with raising the consciousness of the Progressive Era about the extent and severity of destitution. "It is utter folly, from the point of view of learning," Hunter declared, "to have a compulsory school law which compels children, in that weak physical and mental state which results from poverty, to drag themselves to school and to sit at their desks, day in and day out, for several years, learning little or nothing."[3] He urged the schools to feed the children and the municipalities to provide them with the resources to do so. His call to action was amplified two years later when John Spargo released *The Bitter Cry of the Children.* The work of Hunter and Spargo brought national attention to widely scattered local efforts to provide meals for poor children at school.

School food programs were not without controversy. Some opponents argued that providing meals at school would undermine the family and rob the workingman of the incentive to exert himself to provide for his children. Others, as a contemporary observer summarized, complained that lunch programs "led to pauperizing, to relieving women of maternal responsibility, to creating wrong values and in many instances to promoting wastefulness and disorder."[4] Some, influenced by the Social Darwinism of the era, argued that feeding the children would sap their moral vitality. "If you attempt to take hardship and suffering out of their lives by smoothing the pathway of life for these children," a New York City school principal told John Spargo, "you weaken their character, and by so doing, you sin against the children themselves and, through them, against society."[5] Others, including the traditional charity organization societies, favored the provision of meals as a charitable endeavor, but did not believe it should be undertaken at public expense. They worried about fostering "dependency." "Who hesitates to take advantage of the State?" a member of the Ohio Board of State Charities is reported to have asked. The New York Times opined that "anything that enables the family provider to shift his burdens upon the State tends directly to State Socialism."[6]

Proponents of school feeding made a case that will sound familiar to contemporary child nutrition advocates. As Robert Hunter put it,

> the poverty of any family is likely to be most serious at the very time when the children most need nurture, when they are most dependent, and when they are obtaining the only education which they are ever to receive. Guidance and supervision of the parents are impossible because they must work; the nurture is insufficient because there are too many hungry mouths to feed; learning is difficult because hungry stomachs and languid bodies and thin blood are not able to feed the brain. . . . This curse which poverty lays upon innocent children is an awful one, for it means that they may not grow, that they may not learn, and therefore that they may not be strong enough mentally or physically to overcome the cause of it all—poverty.[7]

The core of Hunter's argument—that hunger interferes with learning and healthy development and thus perpetuates the cycle of poverty— remains the central argument of anti-hunger activists a century later. In the interim, developments in both medicine and social science have enhanced our capacity to study and document the impact of deprivation. As the science has piled up to support Hunter's claims, we have become more specific—we say "iron deficiency" instead of "thin blood"—and we have extended his argument to consider the impact on others in the classroom. Not only do rumbling stomachs distract children from their lessons, not only does fasting interfere with concentration, not only does inadequate nourishment make a child vulnerable to infection and thus to missing school, but poorly fed children are more likely to be disruptive in the classroom. Children who are "hangry," made irritable or angry from hunger, interfere with their classmates' studies as well as their own.

The more the research accumulates and the more we recognize the profound interconnectedness of body and mind, the more important access to school meals appears. A recent synthesis of studies of the impact of hunger on learning prepared by J. Larry Brown and his colleagues as part of an effort to estimate the societal costs of hunger made the point:

> When faced with insufficient dietary intake, the human body engages in a form of triage by directing limited energy to be used for its most important functions. Chief among these is maintaining critical organ function. If enough dietary energy remains after allocation to key bodily organs, the second priority is body health, which in children means normal height and weight gain. The final priority, depending on the availability of energy, is the individual's interaction with the social environment—playing with peers, interacting with parents and siblings, and awareness and participation in school. Hungry children haven't the capacity for normal learning and play; while their bodies are in the classroom they lack the dietary fuel required to engage meaningfully with those around them.[8]

And those around them respond in kind. Sharman Apt Russell has described the process in her remarkable book *Hunger: An Unnatural History*:

> The development of the human mind is not just an interior process. When children who must conserve energy withdraw from the world, the world withdraws from them. Mothers become less responsive to their less responsive infants. Bonding and emotional attachment may be affected. The malnourished child sits later, crawls later, and walks later. He is less interested in exploring his environment. He doesn't play as much. He is smaller and seen by adults as younger than he is. They expect less of him. They talk to him less. In school, he is less social and active. He is less motivated. His teachers are less interested in him.[9]

The result of this energy deprivation can be long-term: a deterioration of cognitive function or missing out on crucial lessons can have lasting impact on the child's life course and development. As Russell puts it, "Scientists now think that any extended malnutrition in childhood will affect a child's mental ability in some way. It will change who he or she is in the world."[10] Brown and his colleagues note, "Hungry children do less well on tests of mental ability and school performance, and are more likely to fail, to be held back, and drop out." Large national studies of household food insecurity, they report, have found that children from food-insecure families are more likely than others to miss school, to be suspended, and to repeat a grade. And, like Robert Hunter a century ago, these observers point out that the consequences will frustrate the ability of education to end the cycle of poverty: "In their adult years, children so affected will face greater likelihood of limited employability, lessened workforce productivity, and poorer judgment and job performance," leading to "a more limited lifetime earning potential."[11]

COUNTING HUNGRY CHILDREN

Perhaps I don't have to convince you that hunger in the classroom interferes with the ability of children to learn and schools to carry out their vital functions. There really has not been much significant debate on this point for at least the last several decades. There are few voices today arguing that hunger builds character in children, though that line of reasoning continues to be heard with regard to their parents. There has been debate, however, and there continues to be debate, over just how many children—and adults for that matter—are hungry.

The debate over counting the hungry—or as the federal government prefers to call them, the "less food secure"—leads as it always does to the issue of definition. As Deborah Stone has pointed out, "Counting always involves deliberate decisions about counting as. . . . Counting must begin with categorization, which in turn means deciding whether to include or exclude. We categorize by selecting important characteristics and asking whether the object to be classified is substantially like other objects in the category. Categorization thus involves the establishment of boundaries in the form of rules or criteria that tell whether something belongs or not. . . . Only after categorizing does mere tallying come into play. . . . Every number is a political claim about 'where to draw the line.' "[12]

The difficulty in establishing the boundaries of our category has its origins in our language. "Hunger is a country we enter every day, like a commuter across a friendly border," writes Russell.[13] It is a normal part of our experience and an essential aspect of our functioning as organisms. Without hunger, and its opposite, satiety, we would not know when to eat or when to stop. "Hunger is the best seasoning" goes the saying.[14] It contributes to our pleasure in eating. Not all hunger is a problem to be solved. But some hunger, hunger that is prolonged and/or severe and involuntary is a problem for us all. How hungry does someone have to be and for how long before it becomes a matter of concern to public policy?

What do we really mean when we talk about hungry children? Some children are clearly in this category; they do not get enough food for healthy growth and activity. This may be a temporary episode. School cafeteria managers in schools in poor communities describe the rush for Monday morning breakfast among children who have not had enough to eat over the weekend. Some of these are children who experience the shortfall of calories frequently enough or long enough that they suffer "undernutrition," a prolonged or chronic deprivation of sufficient food energy for normal development. Some children, on the other hand, get enough energy, but lack specific needed nutrients—iron or magnesium or certain vitamins. Some of them may in fact get too much energy and may be overweight. "Deprivation can cause overeating," Russell notes. "When we skip a meal or go hungry for a day, the body gets alarmed— and then overcompensates."[15] These children are more accurately characterized as "malnourished" than hungry, but they are certainly among the children we have in mind when we speak of hungry children.

What about a child who has filled up on soda and donuts on the way to school? She may not be "hungry" if we use the term in the every-day sense of the annoying sensation by which the body signals its need for more fuel, and if this is a rare or occasional behavior, and she eats healthy meals most of the time, she may not be malnourished either. Nevertheless, her food intake can be a problem for the school if rapidly fluctuating blood sugar levels interfere with her mastery of the multi-plication table.

The boundary issues in establishing our category are further complicated by the fact that it matters to us why someone doesn't eat well. The affluent suburban cheerleader who passes up lunch in an effort to achieve a model's slim figure may indeed be "hungry" all afternoon, and she may space out in algebra as a result, but she probably won't be counted among the hungry. In part, this is because her pursuit of the ideal of thinness is perceived as voluntary; in part it is because she is not poor, and when we talk about hunger and counting the hungry, we are generally talking about poverty. But that leaves us in the anoma-lous situation in which the child who brings a lunch of Ring Dings and a sweetened drink to school because he has only a dollar and cannot afford anything more is "hungry," while the child who has cash to spare but picks up the same combo at the corner store, just because he likes it, is not.

Social scientists call the categorization that allows us to move beyond all these pesky hypotheticals an operational definition. This concept was memorably explained to me by a professor in graduate school as "a definition that allows me to know one when I see one," that is, a definition that allows me to sort actual real life cases, to put them into the category in question or leave them out. Think about a triage nurse or an emergency room doctor trying to determine whether or not a patient is "oriented." She docs not interview the patient at length about his sense of awareness, alertness, and connection to the world around him; she runs down a checklist: what is your name, what year is this, who is the president of the United States, and (the one that terrifies me) now count backward from 100 by sevens. Clinicians have decided that those who can answer those questions accurately are "oriented" and those who cannot are "disoriented." Establishing an operational definition of hunger, however simple it may sound, has proven quite difficult.[16]

Anti-hunger activists and government officials sparred over the operational definition of hunger for years, with the Reagan administration memorably asserting that there was no reliable way to count the hungry, and advocates pointing to the lengthening lines at soup kitchens and pantries as behavioral evidence. Gradually, however, through much hard work and research, a consensus emerged that the incidence and prevalence of hunger could be reliably measured by using a survey instrument designed to elicit specific behaviors and experiences associated with household food shortages. It is probably a triumph for the science of measurement, but it is also something of a writer's nightmare; there just is no simple way to describe it. Since 1995, the USDA has monitored the "food security" of U.S. households through an annual survey conducted by the Census Bureau. The annual Household Food Security Survey is based on data collected in December of every year and consists of eighteen scaled items that concern increasingly severe conditions, ranging from whether the respondent worried that food would run out through situations in which adults cut back their food intake to whether a child in the household has gone without food for an entire day. A household is classified as "food insecure" if it reports at least three of the eighteen conditions. (Thus the operational definition of "food insecurity" is a score of 3 or higher on the 18-item scale.) Within the "food insecure" category are two subcategories that used to be called "food insecure with hunger" and "food insecure without hunger," but in 2007 USDA announced that the term hunger would no longer be used. Despite an outcry from advocates and derision from editorial writers across the nation, the new language has become official. USDA now designates the households in the most severe category "households with very low food security," and households that once would have been classified as "food insecure without hunger" as "households with low food security."[17]

The most recent survey, with data collected in December 2007 and released in November 2008, found that more than 36.2 million Americans lived in households that were food insecure, almost one in eight, and 11.9 million lived in households with "very low food security," formerly known as hunger. Among the nation's 73.5 million children under eighteen, more than 12.4 million, or nearly 17 percent, lived in households with low food security, and 3.7 million lived in households with very low food security. "Children in most food-insecure households—even in most households with very low food security—were protected from reductions in food intake" according to the USDA report, but the survey is designed to detect households in which even children suffer reduced food intake, and in 2007, more than 690,000 children lived in such households, which the agency labels "households characterized by very low food security among children," its most severe designation. As noted in the introduction, the number of children living in such households rose by more than 60 percent between 2006 and 2007.[18]

Of course, these figures don't really answer our question of how many children are hungry, because, as Deborah Stone said, "every number is a political claim about 'where to draw the line.'" In general, people and organizations who see hunger as a serious problem and want the government to direct more resources toward its prevention and alleviation use the larger number—the food insecure, including both those with low food security and those with very low food security—as a proxy for hunger, while people who believe that the problem has been exaggerated and that few people in America go hungry use the smaller number, including only those with very low food security. I am in the first group; I have been impressed by extensive research that shows that the prevalence of a whole series of hardships that I would not want to face, including running out of food, eating at a soup kitchen, and being evicted for nonpayment of rent, are common in households with incomes up to 200 percent of the poverty line—a pool of households that is more comparable to the "food insecure" than those with "very low food security." Further, as the 18-question "food security core module" has gained in respect and authority, it has been used in a host of other studies, and these studies generally suggest that it is the larger group about whom we should be concerned. For example, children who live in food-insecure households, both low and very low, are sick more frequently, miss school more often, and do less well in school than those from food-secure households.[19]

It won't surprise you to learn that families with incomes below the poverty line are more likely to be food insecure than their more affluent peers. Among households with children, 43.7 percent of those with incomes below the federal poverty level were food insecure, and nearly as high a rate, 41.5 percent, of households with incomes below 130 percent of the federal poverty line, the cutoff for eligibility for free school meals, were food insecure. And more than a third—35.4 percent—of households with children and incomes below 185 percent of the federal poverty line, the cutoff for eligibility for reduced price school meals, were food insecure.[20] These figures probably understate the need; they do not include any children living in homeless shelters or institutions, because they are based on a Census Bureau survey of households.

In public programs like the National School Lunch Program, definitions turn into rules governing access to benefits: eligibility thresholds. The National School Lunch Act passed in 1946 provided that lunches "shall be served without cost or at a reduced cost to children who are determined by local school authorities to be unable to pay the full cost of the lunch." But since no extra moneys for reimbursement of meals served free were provided, this proved to be a recipe for exclusion. Most poor children did not receive free or even reduced price meals under this system. As we have seen, in the late 1960s, Congress reacted to revelations of severe hunger and malnutrition in the United States by setting uniform national eligibility thresholds for both free and reduced price lunches. Currently American schoolchildren from households with incomes below 130 percent of the federal poverty line ($27,560 for a family of four in 2008) are entitled to free meals, and those from households with incomes below 185 percent of official poverty ($39,220 for a family of four in 2008) are entitled to lunches that may cost no more than $0.40 and breakfasts that may not exceed $0.30—if they attend a school that chooses to participate in the programs. Unfortunately for hungry children, however, not all schools do choose to participate.

INSTITUTIONAL PARTICIPATION

All children in American schools are "eligible" to participate in the school lunch and breakfast programs, but not all students have access to them. "Institutional participation" is the term given to the phenomenon that determines access at the most basic level. Schools are not required to participate in the NSLP—at least they are not required to do so by the federal government, though they may be required to do so by state law.[21] This is not an oversight. From the very beginning of federal participation in school meals, the federal role has been conceptualized as "aiding" local schools that wanted to offer meals. Fear that the Department of Agriculture or other federal agencies would use the school food subsidy as a means to "control" or "exert pressure on" local schools was the source of considerable opposition to the passage of the National School Lunch Act. States rights enthusiasts were worried about everything from control of the curriculum to a federal assault on school segregation. Supporters of the act hastened to clarify. "It is not a program that is Federal; it is an effort on the part of the Federal government to cooperate with and further and intensify this great humanitarian movement that is designed to make strong, vigorous, healthy red-blooded Americans."[22] Nevertheless, a title that would have provided for funds to the Federal Education Agency to distribute to the states for nutrition education and training, a title that opponents said would lead to federal control of schools, had to be stricken from the bill before it could be passed.

In the decades since 1946, the federal role has certainly grown, but the fundamental initiative remains with the local school board. So even though school food is regarded as an entitlement, some children cannot participate because they attend schools that choose not to offer the program. The overwhelming majority, 92 percent, of public schools do offer the National School Lunch Program, as do between 20 and 25 percent of private schools. USDA estimates that more than nine-tenths of American schoolchildren attend schools that offer the NSLP. On the one hand, the figure for participation by public schools is impressive— but on the other hand, approximately seven thousand public schools do not offer the NSLP.

I encountered one such school in the course of my travels, the Leland and Gray Union High School in Townsend, Vermont. There were about 435 students attending this school, and I visited at lunchtime to observe the food service operated without reimbursements, or supervision, from USDA by a local husband-and-wife team. They were what school hygiene activists of the Progressive Era would have called "concessionaires": the space was provided by the school; the equipment was owned by the caterers. Most of the food was prepared off site and warmed up (or chilled) at the school. The food was similar to what I had seen and eaten at NSLP schools—better than some, not as good as others. The variety was good, and the prices were comparable to what I have seen in NSLP schools, perhaps a tad higher, but not to the point of being burdensome. The school itself had just the sort of busy, engaged atmosphere, with student art on the walls and evidence of student activity everywhere, that makes one hopeful about the future. Nevertheless, I left the school with a big problem: the situation of poor families who would be entitled to free or reduced price meals if Leland and Gray participated in the federal program.

The school has its own version of a free lunch program, which the principals of the middle and high schools described in a joint letter to the Brattleboro Reformer: "Each fall a letter is mailed to all families informing parents of our policy. Any family that requests assistance receives free lunches. We take parents at their word without requiring any evidence or federal forms. Free-lunch students eat a nutritious and healthful lunch at no cost to their families or the taxpayers. These meals are provided by the generosity of . . . Leland and Gray's contracted food service providers."[23] Using census data, Vermont anti-hunger advocates had calculated that about 130 of Leland and Gray's 435 students had incomes that would make them eligible for free or reduced price lunches in the USDA program; in 2006, 17 were actually getting free meals through the district's charitable approach. Dorigen Keeney, a staff member with the Vermont Campaign to End Childhood Hunger, suggested to a reporter that families did not take advantage of the free lunch because they were embarrassed. Interestingly, the school principal has the same explanation, but delivered with a different inflection. In a phone conversation, the middle school principal, Steven John, told me that when families find out that "there are no federal dollars falling from the sky," he senses an attitude change; people don't feel that the program is their right, and they are reluctant to ask. He contrasted this with a situation in which people feel that "it's a federal pie, and I'm going to get my piece of it." The old controversies from a century ago still crop up; the principal's remarks remind me of the early 1900s Ohio charity leader quoted above: "Who hesitates to take advantage of the State?" When the concessionaires whose meals I observed retired a year or so after my visit, the new contractor quickly brought in the National School Lunch Program.

I'm glad I had a chance to see Leland and Gray while it was a non-NSLP school, because my visit shed considerable light on an otherwise nearly invisible issue. In fact, I'll never know how typical it was, because there is no systematic study of schools that don't participate in the NSLP. USDA doesn't collect such data, a result, I suppose, of the local initiative principle described above. There may be state studies, but I have not found them. There is, however, a study of schools that withdrew from the NSLP, school lunch dropouts we might call them, between July 1989 and February 1993, which provides some helpful information. The first thing to note is that private schools were overrepresented among the dropouts, and most of the private schools that left were fairly small elementary schools. In general, small schools were the rule; nearly two-thirds of the withdrawing schools had fewer than five hundred students—like Leland and Gray. Among public schools, however, secondary schools (like Leland and Gray) were more likely to leave the program than elementary schools. And more than two-thirds of the schools that withdrew continued to offer food services of some sort, primarily full cafeteria service. A little over half of the schools indicated that they made some provision for students who had been receiving free lunches, and about a quarter did so for students who had been using the reduced price option.[24] With the exception of small elementary schools, the school lunch dropouts had served a relatively small portion of their meals free or at a reduced price—about 15 percent for the two categories combined. While withdrawals from the National School Lunch Program did not leave large numbers of children without food, they undoubtedly caused hardships for some families, and deprivation for some children.

The federal government is not the only stakeholder in the school lunch arena that seems to pay little attention to nonparticipating schools: for the most part, the national anti-hunger advocacy organizations don't either, although state and local groups sometimes do. The Vermont Campaign to End Childhood Hunger, the organization that pointed out how many Leland and Gray students were missing out on free or reduced price meals to which they would be entitled if the school participated in the federal program, is part of a remarkable nationwide network of anti-hunger organizations. Some, like the Vermont group, are organized at the state level. Others are organized at the local level—most large cities and a fair number of smaller communities and rural counties have some sort of coalition against hunger, hunger task force, hunger action network, or the like. Some are multi-issue groups—organizations dedicated to ending hunger and homelessness or even broader peace and justice groups. Some see hunger as part of a larger set of food system issues. Some are associations of emergency food providers. At the core of this diffuse network is a set of national organizations, most of them based in Washington, D.C., that function as lobbyists on hunger-related legislation, conduct research, and supply leadership, information, and tools to the state and local groups.

This network, sometimes collectively dubbed the "hunger lobby," is in part a legacy of the war on hunger in the late 1960s and the exciting period of public policy reform that followed it. In the first phase of anti-hunger activism, the hunger lobby paid considerable attention to the issue of institutional participation. In the immediate aftermath of the findings of *Their Daily Bread,* extending the school lunch program was a top priority, and in early 1970, the Senate demanded that each state's plan of child nutrition operations describe how it would use program funds to include every school in the state, even those with no kitchen facilities, by September 1972. The Department of Agriculture reacted strongly against any such mandate and successfully convinced the House to remove any specification of a deadline and to soften the language, changing the requirement that the state lunch program plan "shall include" every school to the requirement that states "extend" their lunch programs to all schools. As the Citizens' Board noted in a follow up report, "Local freedom to reject federally financed food for the poor was vigorously defended."[25] Once the new federal reimbursement plans were in effect, however, the number of schools participating grew steadily, reaching a peak of 90,800 in 1979, about 85 percent of all schools. The emphasis among anti-hunger activists seems then to have switched to protecting the privacy of children who received free and reduced price lunches in participating schools and challenging practices, such as issuing applications only in English, that appeared likely to deter families from making use of the program.

The 1980 and 1981 cuts in school food funding—the same cuts that escalated reliance on a la carte sales—engaged advocates with the issue once again, as several thousand schools dropped out of the program, and participation declined for the first time since 1946. Though the Reagan administration tried to portray the cuts as targeting scarce resources more effectively to the children who needed them most, advocates were quick to point out that many poor children attended the schools that were driven from the program. A year after the cuts, the *New York Times* reported that fully one-third of the students who had stopped participating were from low-income families.[26] Congress did respond to the outcry raised by anti-hunger advocates and school food professionals, passing legislation protecting child nutrition programs from automatic cuts triggered by budget shortfalls and gradually undoing some of the Reagan cuts, such as the exclusion of private schools.[27] As schools and cafeterias adapted to the new regime, anti-hunger advocates now turned their attention to the other school food program: breakfast. Without the constant vigilance of the hunger lobby, the percentage of all schools participating in the lunch program has gradually declined from 85 percent in 1979 to about 76 percent today, and the percentage of public schools participating, while higher, has also lost significant ground in recent years, declining from 97.6 percent in 1989 to 91.2 percent in fiscal 2004.[28] Meanwhile, however, the percentage of schools offering the breakfast program has steadily grown.

CHAMPIONS OF BREAKFAST

Nothing illustrates the cooperation between the national-level advocacy organizations and the myriad state and local groups better than the decades-long campaign to make school breakfast accessible and available. The School Breakfast Program was established as a pilot project by the Child Nutrition Act of 1966 and converted to a permanent basis in 1975. The original legislation gave state education agencies the authority to select schools to participate, specifying that they give priority to schools in areas of high economic need and schools to which children traveled long distances by bus. A product of the War on Poverty, the School Breakfast Program has always been viewed as primarily a program for poor children, despite valiant efforts by many of its supporters to point out that affluent children also suffered if they skipped breakfast. Only recently, with the spread of "universal breakfast in the classroom," the program that I saw in action at Any Town Little School, has it begun to lose its poverty-program profile.

The decision about whether or not to offer breakfast in any particular school is made by the local school food authority, generally the school board, with very strong and often decisive input from principals and superintendents and sometimes from food service directors. Opposition has sometimes been philosophical—administrators who believe that children should eat at home with their parents or that providing another meal at school is asking too much of schools (the "where will it stop?" argument). Often it is practical. Schools must adjust bus schedules or risk having children late to class. The custodial bill may rise, and schools in cold climates may have to open the school earlier in the day, thus incurring additional heating costs. When the program was new and few educators had firsthand experience with it, such obstacles could be made to seem insurmountable. As school breakfast has become more common, however, and evidence showing its positive effects on everything from attendance to test scores has mounted, the arguments have become more financial in nature. Can the breakfast program support itself?

Once performance funding was established in the early 1970s, breakfast became a target of opportunity for hunger activists. For some, breakfast at school is primarily an income support: one more expense that impoverished families don't need to squeeze out of an overstretched budget. Years ago, the economist Sar Levitan characterized the hunger lobby as a group of people and organizations who saw food programs as a means of "getting more for the poor by raising the cry of 'hunger in America.'"[29] I have always thought it was an apt characterization of my own participation in anti-hunger advocacy and of the participation of many advocates whom I know. Most would prefer to see an income distribution that would permit all Americans to have incomes sufficient to purchase an adequate diet. Realism, however, is a defining characteristic of anti-hunger activism, and the evidence is substantial that food programs have done a better job of securing resources for poor people than have means-tested income support programs, with the possible exception of the Earned Income Tax Credit.

For many anti-hunger advocates, however, a different kind of realism contributes to support for expanding access to school breakfast. Study after study has shown that our mothers were right: breakfast is the most important meal of the day from a health perspective. In the first place, breakfast provides much needed energy and nutrients after the overnight fast, the most prolonged that most of us experience. Second, breakfast tends to contain a favorable ratio of needed micronutrients—vitamins and minerals—to energy measured in calories. And third, people who skip breakfast are more likely to snack on unhealthy foods. All in all, it is no surprise that recent studies have shown that eating breakfast promotes weight control and overall diet quality.[30] Many aspects of American life, however, have undermined the habit of eating breakfast—more parents working, longer work days, the dramatic increase in nontraditional hours, and increased reliance on school buses—and analyses of the Nationwide Food Consumption Surveys and the Continuing Survey of Food Intakes by Individuals have shown a significant decline in breakfast consumption between 1965 and 1991.[31] Analyses of more recent data, while smaller in scale, support the idea that Americans in general, and American children in particular, are not taking my mother's advice about three squares: a study of more than 1,500 adolescents in

2001, for example, found just 69 percent of eighth graders eat at least three meals per day; overall, 20 percent of adolescents in the study said they ate just two meals (not counting snacks), with breakfast the most frequently missed meal.[32] Missing breakfast is certainly not confined to low income students. As Representative Lynn Woolsey, a longtime champion of the School Breakfast Program told a symposium sponsored by the USDA:

> School breakfast programs are too often categorized as just another form of welfare, but we know that, in this society, if a person is lucky enough to have two parents, both of them are usually working.
>
> That is the norm these days. That means that breakfast programs are vitally important because working families are commuting. They are leaving the house. They might have food available for their children, but the children don't always sit down and eat it. They want to get on to school.
>
> I've talked to more professional people than you can imagine who say to me, "You know, I would be so glad if I knew my child had had breakfast this morning. It's there, but I don't think they ate it." So we need to look at breakfast programs as a learning tool just as we look at a book, or a pencil or a computer. . . . Breakfast ensures that all our children are ready to learn.[33]

These two fundamental arguments—the antipoverty argument that school breakfast helps poor families get by on limited incomes and the health argument that children of all income groups are increasingly likely to show up at school without breakfast—plus studies showing that school breakfasts are often nutritionally superior to the breakfasts eaten by children outside of schools (including, of course, the donut and soda breakfast picked up at the corner store) have generated a substantial momentum for expanding the breakfast program.[34] Add to this the growing realization by food service directors that a bigger breakfast program can help their bottom lines, and there is real energy behind the movement to serve more breakfasts. Efforts to draw more students into the program by improving the food, marketing the program, and/or changing the location or form or time in which it is offered (e.g., Grab 'N' Go Breakfast, Breakfast on the Bus, Breakfast in the Classroom, Second-Chance Breakfast) will be discussed along with other innovations in chapter 8, but the issue of basic access—whether a school offers the program—belongs here with our discussion of institutional participation.

The Food Research and Action Center (FRAC), the oldest of the national anti-hunger advocacy organizations, has led the campaign to make breakfast available. Beginning in 1991, the organization began issuing an annual School Breakfast Scorecard. The scorecard calculates, for each state and for the nation as a whole, a ratio of the number of low-income children (i.e., those eligible for free or reduced price meals) participating in School Breakfast for every 100 who eat a free or reduced price lunch. When the scorecard campaign began, the ratio, nationally, was less than a third: 31.5 low-income children were eating breakfast for every 100 eating lunch. By 2007, the total number of free and reduced price breakfasts served daily to low-income children was 8.1 million, up from 3.7 million in 1991, and the number of such breakfasts served for every 100 free or reduced price lunches was 45.3.[35] It is in the state-by-state figures, however, that the genius of the scorecard lies, because the comparison empowers advocates working at the state level to lobby for state legislation mandating that breakfast be offered, for state financial contributions, and for outreach and promotional activities. To aid them, FRAC reports the number of federal dollars that the state is forgoing, compared with the amount they would receive if the state met a target of 60 percent of the low-income students who participate in lunch also eating breakfast. Thus in 2007, the scorecard reported that the biggest loser, California, left more than $90.2 million of federal money lying on the breakfast table.[36]

Each year, when the scorecard comes out, my Google School Breakfast alert is flooded with stories of advocates addressing governors, state legislatures, and state boards of education with strategies for improving the state's performance. Wisconsin can serve as an example. It had the lowest participation ratio in 2006, with only 29.3 percent of its free and reduced price lunch eaters consuming a school breakfast. That was the second year in a row that Wisconsin had occupied last place, and the results of the earlier revelation are probably reflected in the fact that it was also the state that saw the greatest percentage rise in its score (from 26.5 percent to 29.3 percent, a growth rate of 14.2 percent). By 2007, its breakfast participation score had grown another 25 percent, and the state had escaped last place to rank forty-sixth, with a ratio of 35.7. Wisconsin advocates have been working hard. At the state level, a partnership was formed between the Family Living Programs of the University of Wisconsin Extension and the Department of Public Instruction's School Nutrition Team. In Milwaukee, the state's largest school district joined with the Milwaukee Hunger Task Force to test the use of Provision 2 to offer breakfast free to all students in six pilot schools. When participation in pilot schools that served the free breakfast in the classroom doubled, Milwaukee went on to implement that approach in most elementary schools, which alone raised the statewide numbers by 16 percent.[37]

The biggest barrier to participation, of course, is failure of a school to offer the program. Overall, nationally, there has been great progress; after all, the program started as a pilot in only a few schools. By 1991, the year the Scorecard was begun, just under half of the schools that offered the National School Lunch Program also offered the School Breakfast Program; by 2007, 84.8 percent did so, with an increase of 2.5 percent, or 2,100 schools, in the last year alone.[38] Sixteen states offered breakfast in at least 95 percent of their schools, with South Carolina and Arkansas, where breakfast is served in more schools than is lunch, leading the way with 100.1 percent of NSLP schools offering SBP. The Scorecard concludes with a listing of "School Breakfast Legislation by State," including mandates requiring some or all schools to participate, state funding including funding for universal free projects, reporting requirements, scheduling requirements, and outreach requirements. The 2006 report highlighted New Mexico, which had appropriated money to allow eighty schools that were identified as failing to make adequate yearly progress under No Child Left Behind to offer a free breakfast in the classroom to all children during the second half of the school year. The program was successful enough to be expanded to 129 elementary schools for the next school year. As a result, New Mexico achieved a 10.4 percent increase in total student participation and an increase of almost 5 points in its ratio of low-income breakfasts to lunches.[39] By 2007, New Mexico had the highest ratio, with 61.1 students eating a free or reduced price breakfast for every 100 eating a free or reduced price lunch, the first state to exceed the new 60 percent target set by the Food Research and Action Center. State action can make a big difference in access to breakfast, a phenomenon that will be explored further in chapter 8.

Once the issue of institutional participation is resolved, once a school is offering breakfast and lunch, the barriers to participation shift to the level of the family and its interaction with the school.

OBSTACLES TO STUDENT PARTICIPATION

Attending a school that offers the program is the most basic form of access, but institutional participation does not guarantee that individual children will have effective access to the program. Between the hungry child and the meal, there are four major barriers: application, certification, verification, and the price of the meal. Picture a child who is hungry at school. His mom has no food to fix him a lunch to carry and no money for him to buy the school lunch. He is poor: income-eligible for a free lunch. What can be standing between him and that lunch?

Application

First, his mother may not have applied for the free lunch. The letter containing the application form may have been misdelivered, or the school system may have tried to save on postage by sending the application forms home with the children, and his may be languishing in the bottom of his backpack. Possibly his mother is not sufficiently literate to read the letter or complete the form or finds it too daunting. "The form is incredibly intimidating," declared a parent at a school budget committee hearing in San Francisco. "It asks for all sorts of financial information. It's phrased in very intimidating language."[40] The mother may know she earns a little above the poverty level and mistakenly believe that the poverty line is the eligibility cutoff. School business officials report that this misperception is common,[41] and research on eligible nonparticipants in the early 1990s found that an inaccurate belief that they were not eligible was the most common reason given by parents for not applying. If the mother is an immigrant, even though she is here legally, she may fear that information will be turned over to the immigration authorities. (It won't be, but she may believe it will.) We might categorize these explanations as inadvertent non-application: mistakes, misinformation, and misunderstandings.

On the other hand, her decision not to fill out the form, not to apply, may be informed and intentional. In her community, there may be a stigma attached to parents whose children eat free lunch and/or breakfast. When Abt Associates conducted its study of eligible nonparticipants in the school lunch program, the researchers discovered that stigma was a bigger issue at the application phase than at the consumption phase and a larger issue for parents than for students. "If my kids were starving," commented one focus group participant, "I'd send them up here to get it, but as long as we can find some way to pay it, well, they're not going to be taking a handout." "The way I look at both the breakfast and lunch program," said a focus group member at another site, "for some kids, that's all they get. Some parents are so neglectful that the kids have to fend for themselves. Some kids are fortunate enough to have parents who take care of them but for others, if it weren't for the school meal program, they wouldn't eat." In a third site, the Abt researchers summarized their findings this way: "parents refer to the 'shame' in taking the free lunch and not being able to feed their children. Furthermore, they feel strongly that it is their responsibility to feed their children, not the schools." Only at a site in which the great majority of children were eligible did parents not see stigma as a barrier to application: "It's so popular. . . . More people get it than don't. Now everybody gets it, so it's nothing to be ashamed of."[42]

Back to our hypothetical mother. Maybe her income is sufficient for herself and her own children, the people who are normally and legally in her household, so she didn't apply because she figured she was not entitled. But her sister's preschool children are staying with her while her sister is hiding out from an abusive husband, and she doesn't want to tell the school about the sister's children for fear that word will get back to her brother-in-law or that the child welfare authorities will remove the children because of overcrowding, so she keeps mum about extra mouths to feed in her household, even though their presence would in fact make her own children eligible. You can use your imagination to make up your own story here about why someone who is income eligible would decide not to apply.

Certification

Then there is the possibility that she has applied and the school has made an error in processing her application. Besides the chance that the school has simply lost the application—or that the completed application is lost in the child's backpack—a processing clerk may have counted the household size wrong; failure to count the child in question because the parent had not listed him was common in one study. Or the parent may have failed to sign the application. Or perhaps the child was not eligible in August or September when the forms came home, but in the interim, the mother has given birth to another child, raising the household size and thus the eligibility threshold, but hasn't thought to report this to the school. Or maybe the household size has remained the same but the income has fallen: the mother's hours at her job have since been cut back or her husband's employer has moved to Mexico; she now lacks the money to provide lunch but does not realize that she can reapply at any time in the year. Recent research has shown that "income volatility" (as the economists label the month-to-month and week-to-week fluctuations in income that make planning so difficult for poor families) is a major factor in shifting eligibility, and that changes in hours worked and changes in the share of adults earning are its major causes.[43]

Verification

Another possibility is that the family was eligible in August when the mother applied, but since her income was close to the cutoff, and thus in the "error-prone" category, she was selected as part of the random sample of 3 percent of such error-prone applications to be subject to verification. The school food authority has sent her a letter asking her to bring documentation of her income and household size to the school. Here the whole cycle starts again. Perhaps she did not receive the verification letter or did not understand it or misplaced it. Maybe she is a babysitter or a cleaning lady, paid in cash, and cannot get documentation of her earnings from her employer. Remember Nannygate? Or perhaps she comes from a culture that dreads authority and is afraid to submit her pay stubs. Or maybe she doesn't keep old pay stubs or cannot find them, and by the time she gets the verification letter, her income has risen, and she is no longer eligible. If she had her old stubs and could document that she was telling the truth about her income when she applied, the eligibility thus established would endure for the school year (and until the certification process the next year), but if she cannot supply those old stubs, she may be found ineligible. Or maybe she is too disorganized and distracted and overwhelmed—or too depressed—to comply with the verification request. Procrastination or the complex schedule of her two jobs may interfere with her getting to the school. Or maybe, heaven forfend, she does not care enough to gather the documentation and take it down to the school.

For whatever reason, 50 percent of parents to whom documentation letters were sent in a 2002 study failed to respond, and their children's benefits were terminated.[44] "Common sense" suggested to many observers that these were cheaters who had lied on their applications and could not document the incomes they had reported, but follow-up interviews conducted by researchers from Mathematica, Inc., found that of those originally approved for free meals who failed to respond to a verification request, 51 percent were still eligible for free meals and another 26 percent were eligible for reduced price meals. Less than 25 percent were not eligible for either. Among those who had been approved for reduced price meals, 23 percent were eligible for that benefit, and another 31 percent were eligible for free meals—that is, a larger benefit than the one for which they had originally been approved. In sum, the great majority of nonresponders were eligible for either free or reduced price meals.[45] And among those who were not eligible, in some cases their erroneous eligibility certification had been a product of the school's arithmetic, not their own. If the parents report a weekly income, schools must multiply by a "conversion factor" of 4.3 to determine the monthly amount, but it has been a common error for school personnel to multiply by 4, thus understating the monthly income even though the parent reported the weekly income accurately.

Between the mistakes and the misunderstandings and the miscalculations on the one hand and the rational decisions (however misguided) on the other, recent studies have shown that 31 percent, nearly one-third, of eligible children in the districts studied were not certified for the free meals to which they are entitled. Of those children about a quarter were mistakenly certified for reduced price meals instead, but three-quarters—23 percent of the overall group of eligible children—were not certified for either benefit.[46]

Price

Now let us suppose that the child in question is eligible for the reduced price meal, and certified to receive it, and has complied with an income-verification request. That doesn't mean that he can actually afford the meal. In the last decade or so, we have learned a great deal about the actual expenses of low-income families. The Self-Sufficiency Standards for various metropolitan areas and assorted counties in at least thirty-six states provide us with a basis for calculating just how tight such budgets can be.[47] Figures are derived from real world data. Housing cost, for example, is set at the Fair Market Rent calculated by the Department of Housing and Urban Development and is set at the fortieth percentile of actual rents for an area determined by the decennial census, the American Housing Survey, and random-digit dialing telephone surveys for updating; the housing cost figure also includes electricity and heat, but not telephone, which is included under "miscellaneous."

Let us look at a hypothetical student who lives with his mother and a preschool-age sibling in Pike County, on the edge of the Pocono Mountains in northeastern Pennsylvania. Suppose that the mother's income is $30,504 a year, just under the national cutoff of $30,710 for eligibility for reduced price meals for a family of three in 2006. She would have a monthly income of $2,542 before taxes. In Pennsylvania, she would have paid $458 of that for Social Security and federal and state income taxes, leaving her with $2,084. Eventually she will qualify for an Earned Income Tax Credit of $52 per month, a child care tax credit of $65, and a child tax credit of $167, raising her after-tax income back up to $2,368. (Of course, she won't actually be able to collect the tax credits until she files her taxes.) She pays $850 per month for rent, leaving her with $1,518. If she spends $496 on food, the USDA Low Cost Food Plan figure for her family size, that leaves her with $1,022. Child care for the preschooler will take another $380, leaving her $642. Transportation costs in her county, which has no public transportation to speak of, are estimated at $244 a month. (Again, this would be in 2006; the dramatic fluctuations in gas prices since then have only added to the stress on low-income families.) This takes her down to $398. She needs $319 for health care—her premiums on an employer-sponsored health insurance policy with family coverage (plus copayments for doctors' visits)—leaving her $79 for everything else. The self-sufficiency standard, however, calls for $229 for "miscellaneous," which it defines as "all other essentials including clothing, shoes, paper products, diapers, nonprescription medicines, cleaning products, household items, personal hygiene items and telephone service. It does not allow for recreation, entertainment, savings, or debt repayment." This would also have to cover school supplies or a birthday present or a get-well card for a sick friend. What about something to put in the offering plate in church? What about a newspaper or a magazine? What about an occasional movie or fees for the soccer team that our student wants to join? And this family doesn't have $229 for "miscellaneous"; they are already $150 short of that for the month.[48] Thus there may well not be the $2.00 a week or $8.66 a month charged in Pike County for the reduced price lunch, even though it is such a bargain. Rationally, of course, the mother would be better off forgoing something else—taking the $8.66 out of the food budget and prepaying the lunch bill with it—but sometimes life isn't like that. Children eligible for reduced price meals show up at schools across America every day without the money they need to buy the lunch.

School food service personnel, through the School Nutrition Association, have proposed eliminating the reduced price category, serving meals free to all children from households under 185 percent of the federal poverty level. Two arguments fuel the campaign for the elimination of reduced price, known as ERP for short. In the first place, as school food service directors and cafeteria managers report, too many poor children assigned to the reduced price category simply don't have the money. Participation by reduced price students drops toward the end of each month, suggesting that students lack the $0.30 or $0.40 a meal just when they probably need those meals the most. As one SNA member wrote to Nebraska Senator Chuck Hagel, "While 40 cents may not seem like a lot of money, I have had families in Lincoln calling me [as the] Director of Nutrition Services and saying they can't afford the 40 cents. . . . The 40 cents reduced meal hurts the working poor. When they are out of money these kids don't eat."[49] And second, they point out, a great many of the errors reported in the various error rate research projects stemmed from the misassignment of students between the two benefit categories. ERP would reduce paperwork, simplify applications, and reduce error rates all at once. In the 2004 Child Nutrition Reauthorization, Congress authorized an ERP pilot in five states to test the impact of the elimination of the category, but, in a process reminiscent of the child nutrition politics of the 1960s, no funds were appropriated for it. Calling on Congress to fund the measure, SNA reported that food service directors tell of parents bouncing $2.00 and $3.00 checks intended to pay for reduced-price meals, and the Military Impacted Schools Association pointed out that many military personnel miss the income requirement for a free meal and have difficulty affording the reduced price.[50] SNA estimated that a million children across the nation are eligible for reduced price meals but are not participating.

ERP makes sense from the hands-on common sense viewpoint of the school cafeteria, but from a social policy point of view, there are questions that must be raised. When a means-tested program has a unitary benefit structure, people are either eligible or they are not. There is nothing in between. One dollar over the income threshold, and you lose the entire benefit. This may be efficient, but to many people, it seems unfair, and it often generates resentment among those who experience a "near miss." That is one reason that so many means-tested programs have graduated benefits. In a program like SNAP (the Supplemental Nutrition Assistance Program, or food stamps), benefits are gradually reduced as the income of participants nears the eligibility threshold, until a "minimum benefit" is reached. At the minimum benefit, there is still what policy analysts call a "notch problem"—an area where those who qualify for the minimum benefit will actually end up better off than others who just missed being eligible for the program. In SNAP, however, the minimum benefit has been so low—it was stuck at $10 per month for three decades—that people who fail to qualify are not missing much.

Technically, in school meals, there are three levels of benefit: free, reduced price, and so-called full price. As we have seen, full price meals are still a "benefit" because they are subsidized by federal government by the combination of a modest cash reimbursement—$0.24 per meal for the coming year—and commodity donations worth, currently, $0.2075 for every lunch served the previous year. In some states there is an additional state allocation that brings the total closer to $0.50 per lunch. The language that we use, however, and the program procedures combine to obscure this universal minimum benefit. Because they do not have to apply for it and they cannot see it, many parents do not even know that they are receiving this subsidy. To them, the minimum benefit appears to be the reduced price meal. Schools can charge what they want for a reduced price meal up to a maximum of $0.40 for lunch and $0.30 for breakfast. Because the federal subsidy for reduced price is set at $0.40 and $0.30 less than the reimbursement for the free meals, most schools do charge the legal ceiling price. Thus a family that just misses the eligibility cutoff for free meals gets a substantial consolation prize of reduced price meals.

The actual value of this benefit to families can be calculated by looking at the federal reimbursement rate, but for families on tight budgets, it probably makes more sense to calculate it by looking at the prices charged for the so-called full price meals. These vary significantly from community to community. Suppose you have three children in high school in a town where the high school lunch sells for $1.90, the national average for the 2006–2007 school year. If you miss the cutoff for reduced price meals, you are looking at an annual outlay of $1,026, presuming your children have perfect attendance for an 180-day school year and eat lunch but not breakfast at school. If you qualify for reduced price, you'll only have to pay $216. This is already a very substantial "notch" problem; the perceived minimum benefit would be worth $810 per year to our hypothetical family with three children in high school. This figure is large enough to shed some light on the anxiety about underreporting of income. If the reduced price category is eliminated, the notch will be even bigger, the cost of the full price meals times the number of children and the number of days they want to eat the school lunch. Although we can point out that all the meals are subsidized, the experience of the family will be that they either qualify for free lunches or they need to find more than $40 per month for each child. In schools where payments are in cash only, this often depends on whether mom can find $2.00 per child on any given morning. In systems where parents can prepay by putting money on account, the totals will be even more visible.

As noted, from an administrative point of view, it definitely makes sense to get rid of the reduced price category. There will be less paperwork for schools and fewer errors, and the savings thus achieved could be used to reduce the price of lunch charged to all students or to improve the quality. We would all be better off. But if this argument holds for eliminating the reduced-price option, it holds even more strongly for getting rid of the entire means test. If we found a way to make school lunch free for all, a regular part of the school day, we could do away with all of the applications and certifications and verifications. We would save the labor costs and the printing costs and the postage, and we would not need to invest in elaborate computer systems to accurately assign each meal to its proper category. We would reduce the errors and eliminate the incentive to cheat. As we shall see in the next chapter, this has been the solution most often proposed by school food service professionals.

A further argument for getting rid of the means test comes from a closer look at the eligibility thresholds themselves. Once an eligibility threshold is established, it seems to take on a life of its own. We may discuss raising it or lowering it, but we quickly lose sight of the fact that it is a blunt instrument, really only an average figure, suitable for classifying large data sets—for looking at census data and figuring out whether the poverty rate is higher or lower than it was two years ago, say—but not very accurate for determining if a particular family is in need of whatever benefit or service we are discussing. Let us suppose that the intent of the free/reduced price/full price system is to make sure that children can afford to eat the school meals that are offered to them. The basic Section 4 subsidy in combination with the donated commodities is intended to make the meal affordable for most children, and the Section 11 reimbursements are intended to make sure that the meals reach children for whom the subsidized full price is too high. Makes sense.

In reality, however, the full price meals will be within the reach of some children who are classified eligible for reduced price or even free meals on the basis of cash income, while they will be too expensive for some whose incomes are over that line. This is what I mean when I say that price is the final obstacle to participation, and there are three primary reasons for this distortion. In the first place, the prices that school charge for "full price" meals vary significantly, even dramatically, from community to community, but the eligibility threshold is uniform. So if your income is just over the reduced price cut off in Hawaii, where meals are heavily subsidized by the state government and run about $1.00 per lunch, the cost may be manageable. But if you are ten dollars over in Nantucket, Massachusetts, where lunches run $4.00, you probably cannot afford the meals.

Second, the cost of living, as we well know, varies substantially from location to location. So a family of three with an income of $32,000 in one community may be doing fine, while a family with the same configuration, a mom and two kids, say, and the same income in another community may be in real need. Some communities have much higher heating costs; some have higher food or housing costs. Local and regional variation make inflexible income thresholds very clumsy and often inaccurate bases for determining need.

Third, even within a particular town or school district, a single threshold may exclude some who are in real need while including others who are not. If my income is below the national eligibility threshold, but I live rent-free in the parsonage, I may not really need the reduced price meals, though the help is probably welcome. On the other hand, if I am diabetic and have to purchase expensive sugar-free foods or must provide members of my household with a gluten-free diet or other medically prescribed specialties, I may be in real need even though my income is over the threshold. If I am paying off college loans, I may have less money available for food than the eligibility thresholds assume. (Recall that debt repayment was excluded from the list of miscellaneous "essentials.") If my job requires expensive uniforms, I may not have as much money as you think. If my family of four consists of a working mother and three high-school-aged children, I will not have to pay for child care while I work, though I may have to work overtime to feed three teenagers. But if my family of four has one school-aged child, one toddler, and one infant, well, the school-aged child may need a free lunch because so much of my income goes to pay for day care.

In fully means-tested programs like SNAP, there are "deductions" from income that help to adjust for these regional and individual realities. Thus households that live in areas with high fuel costs are more likely to qualify for the "excess shelter cost deduction"; some child care expenses are deductible; and documented work expenses were deductible until the administrative burden of processing such deductions and the evidence needed to support them became such a nightmare that they were rolled into a "standard deduction." But schools were never set up to administer such means tests, and school food has never had "deductions" or similar adjustments to income. As Robert Greenstein pointed out to Congress in his testimony concerning errors in verification, even agencies that employ armies of "income maintenance clerks" and "eligibility specialists" are unable to deal with month-to-month fluctuations in income. Means testing is serious business. When it is not done well, serious inequities result. The more closely I look at the means test in school food, the more strongly I feel that means tests just don't belong in public schools. There is too much at stake to take the risk of not feeding children who need the food, and the means test introduces invidious distinctions where they do not belong.

Whether the problem is with application, certification, verification, or price, the end result for too many children is the same: hunger in the classroom. And even when the system functions as intended and needy children are certified to receive free meals, they may be deterred by stigma or fear of rejections by their peers. The next chapter explores both the social-psychological and the administrative consequences of the three-tier system.

CHAPTER SEVEN

FREE, REDUCED PRICE, PAID

Unintended Consequences

The problems inherent in a one-size-fits-all eligibility threshold and the myriad opportunities for error in the means-testing process are not the only problems with the three-tier eligibility structure for school food. In fact, they are not even the biggest difficulty. The biggest problem is the stigma that comes from being different, from being marked as poor, from being unable to pay in a culture that places excessive value on being able to pay and a school food subculture that increasingly views children as "customers." Let us begin then by looking at how this stigma undermines the program.

STIGMA

Depending on what type of money your parents made, you would either receive lunch for free or be charged. At lunch time, many students would chastise others for receiving free lunch. If you received lunch free it symbolized poor, unwealthy.

Hunter College student, recalling high school lunch

Sherry Carrigan is the Director of Industry Relations for the School Nutrition Association, and thus more involved with the suppliers than the distribution end of school food service, but she captured the heart of the matter when I asked her about the stigma issue:

Well, I think in terms of self-esteem . . . for children, you know, to have to be different and get a reduced price meal. I don't know how they handle it in every cafeteria, but just the idea that they're not like the person next to them, through no fault of their own. Kids shouldn't have to suffer that feeling of being inadequate—"Oh, there's something wrong with me because my mom can't afford to buy lunch." So what kids will do rather than go through that humiliation—they'll probably elect not to participate at all, and not eat. . . . They shouldn't have to go through that.

School food service directors seem to agree that stigma is not a problem in elementary schools—at least not in the lower grades. "I don't think that it is an issue in the elementary," commented Deb Neal, the director of school food services in Lansing, Michigan. "A lot of times kids will just spout it right out, 'I'm free!' They are a lot more innocent in the elementary. And I don't really think it's a huge problem in our middle school. But I do believe it is a problem in the high schools." Michelle Tingling Clemmons, who worked as a child nutrition advocate and later ran the Washington, D.C., school food service operation, agrees about the youngest children but sees an earlier onset for awareness: "A lot of food service people will tell you this, when the kids are little nobody cares. In fact, the kids will say, 'I eat free.' And younger kids will say, 'I wish I ate free.' It's not until they hit about third grade or so that they start feeling funny about it." Mary Ann McCann, the school food service director for Taos, New Mexico, believes that the stigma starts when an alternative to the reimbursable meal becomes available. "I don't think they understand the stigma at the elementary. They only start seeing the stigma when they would go to middle school, because there was an alternative choice to a meal." By high school, and probably by middle school in most communities, however, the stigma is obvious. As one Hunter College student put it, "Students in my school understood the concept that if your parents' annual salary met certain requirements, you would be eligible for free lunch."

The stigma generated by the eligibility system reduces participation at two different steps of the school food process. First, as discussed in the previous chapter, it deters some families from applying for the meals, and second, once applications are submitted and approved, it deters some children from taking part. In some cases, the two combine: parents choose not to apply because their children expect to be ridiculed and decline to participate. "My son asked me not to apply because other students made fun of him," reported a parent in the Abt study. "You start telling your parents not to apply when you enter high school," suggested a student in the same study; "you say you just won't eat it."[1] In other families, however, it is the parents' feelings that shape the decision. One Washington-based anti-hunger advocate told me that she felt a special relationship to kids in need of school food because of her experiences growing up:

> I started out as a child who was raised by a single mother who was always struggling to get by. So making sure that we had enough food was always a struggle . . . but my mother would never ever apply for free meals. And so I didn't eat all the way through high school because she couldn't afford to buy meals and we needed to apply for free meals. . . . So I know what it's like to have to go to the lunchroom and not have anything to buy a lunch with. And to have to sit at a table with your friends and say, 'No, I'm not hungry' or 'I had a big breakfast' or 'School gets out at 2:00; I'll just eat when I get home' or 'I'm too nervous.' You just make up stories about why you're not eating.

She said she didn't realize what was driving her mother's refusal to apply until, as an adult, she had an argument with her mother over the use of WIC benefits: "And I was oblivious to it until that moment, but it was a pride issue and 'we don't accept help from the government.' "

Even when families do successfully enroll their children, the other aspect of stigma can frustrate the intent of the program in two opposite but complementary ways—by deterring children from eating or by inflicting shame on those who do so. "You keep it to yourself if you get it for free. So many people are embarrassed to tell others that they get their lunch free. It's embarrassing because the people who are on it are the ones who don't have that much money," declared a student in the Abt study. "Some kids look down on people who don't have money and think they're worthless," commented another. And a third observed, "Even if some kids are eligible, they may not want to take it because they think they're just too cool, or others may not want to be seen with those who do take it because they want to fit in."[2] As the president of the student body at Balboa High School in San Francisco told a reporter, lunchtime "is the best time to impress your peers," and getting caught with a subsidized meal "lowers your status."[3]

Anyone who has spent time with adolescents knows how concerned they are about how they are viewed by their peers. Murray Milner has recently shed considerable light on this phenomenon through his fascinating ethnographic study of status hierarchies in American high schools. In *Freaks, Geeks, and Cool Kids: American Teenagers, Schools, and the Culture of Consumption,* he argues that the structured separation of high school students from meaningful work and significant political participation exaggerates the importance of the one form of power they can exercise: status. Explaining that the primary sources of teen prestige are associations with fellow teenagers, conformity to group norms, and the ability to separate themselves from others through putdowns and petty cruelties, he points to the particular significance of lunch. "Why are adolescents so concerned about who 'goes out with' whom and who eats with whom? It is because they intuitively know that who you associate with intimately has a big effect on your status. In all societies food and sexuality are key symbols of intimacy. Where status is important, people try to avoid eating with or marrying inferiors— as executive dining rooms, upper-middle class dinner parties, debutante balls, and the marriage and eating restrictions of the Indian caste system all indicate."[4]

Milner goes on to point out that "in some respects, whom you eat with has even more importance than dating because this occurs every day." He quotes a student from Northern Virginia who recalled that there had been, in his high school, "a great deal of concern as to what the lunch arrangements would be. As freshmen, people scurried around the lunch room, searching desperately for friends to sit with, so that they would not have to suffer the ultimate embarrassment of eating alone or sitting at an uncool table." Another student, from Boulder, Colorado, reported, "Eating alone wasn't cool, and [since my school had] three different lunch periods, I couldn't always find a friend who I'd want to eat with. . . . And when I sat with friends in the cafeteria I always felt that my level of coolness was being judged by the respective status of each individual I was with."[5] In the context of this constant ranking, and thus the search for bases upon which to rank people, a system that ties access to lunch to a public declaration of poverty seems almost cruel. Of course, the declaration is not supposed to be public, but as we shall see, efforts to protect the privacy of students eating free and reduced price meals have been only partially successful.

Negotiating the narrows of the adolescent passage is a tricky business. One of my Hunter students recalled vividly how the school lunch line played into this process, even in a school where most students were eligible for free meals:

In high school, it just wasn't cool to eat school lunch. It was the low quality of the meals. Everything was canned, processed, or heated and reheated.
Those few times that I did eat it, I probably had no money to purchase
snacks from the vending machines that sold name brand "junk food." If
you ate [the lunch], you were made fun of. Even just to stand on the line
was embarrassing. That is when you don't have a sense of who you are. But
as my senior year grew nearer and I had a strong sense of who I was, it was
no longer embarrassing. It was actually more economical to eat it.

This student attributed the lack of coolness to the quality of the cafeteria food, and there is probably an element of truth to that in some
schools. A reverse process, however, also seems to be at work. The food
is disparaged precisely because the poor kids, the kids who are not cool,
eat it. The stigma that originally attached to the students who received
free meals clings to the food itself. "Most of my high school friends were
too proud to eat lunch in school, which was considered welfare food,"
recalled another Hunter student. In large city systems, even where the
great majority of students eat free, the disdain seems to be imported
from the larger culture. As a Los Angeles activist explained to me: "I
would say more than half of the students that I talk to, who qualify for
the program, who have the tickets in their hands, in their possession, do
not go into the cafeteria generally. Obviously because the food is bad, it
tastes bad. But they know that because they have a ticket, because they
have to be part of this program, it's poor people's food, it's county food,
and 'I don't want nothing to do with it.' . . . That's the perception that
they are feeling. That's the stigma." A cafeteria manager in New York
City expressed similar frustration: "We use the same vendors as the outside stores, and students think that the food tastes different because it
is school food, not realizing that it is the same food that they buy at
the store, take home to their houses. It's the same food, but it's just that
stigma that because it's school food, it's not good."

According to Marilyn Hurt, the food service supervisor for La Crosse,
Wisconsin, and a former SNA president, the national food service organization has tried to address this negative image. "One of the things we do
in SNA is make certain that the program doesn't continue to be so stigma-
tized. So we really work at telling a story, that this is a program for all children, and that all children need good nutrition, regardless of their family's
income. . . . And we also know that if children of means eat in the program
because it's good, then children without those same means will eat in the
program." But children of means, especially high school students, are less
likely to eat in the program if there are enticing alternatives.

ADDING A LA CARTE

The expansion of a la carte sales, especially where they take place in separate lines, has intensified the stigma problem. "There was the cafeteria line, mostly filled with Hispanic kids with lunch tickets. Then there was the food area adjacent, and that sold cookies, bagels, sodas, brand name . . . expensive items, Pizza Hut and Subway," recalled one of my University of California, Santa Cruz students. "Those who were provided with lunch . . . were the only ones who actually ate the school food," wrote another. "There was also a separate door for them to go to, to receive their lunch, and they had to eat in the cafeteria because the school dishes and trays were not allowed outside. The system for free or reduced lunches made the students who received them stand out, it divided the high school." Students with money gravitate toward the a la carte line where they can indulge their taste for pizza and fries unconstrained by federal nutrition standards, and very quickly, the rumor spreads that only the "poor kids" eat the federal meal. Then, in a classic display of the self-fulfilling prophecy, affluent students, especially at the high school level, avoid the regular line, worried that someone might think they are getting a free meal. "The cafeteria was for the poor kids. The food there was gross. Kids who did not eat in the cafeteria were embarrassed to go into it during lunch for fear that others would think they were getting free or discount lunch." And then, to complete the vicious circle, students who do qualify for the free and reduced price meal begin to shun the reimbursable line as well; "I was eligible for free, but I was embarrassed and annoyed my mom for pizza money," wrote another of my UC Santa Cruz students, recalling school lunch in her middle school.

It is not an accident that many of the accounts of lunchtime segregation come from my interactions with students in California. Many schools in that state were built without the sorts of cafeterias that would be familiar to Easterners, but rather with large metal-gated dispensing windows that open onto outdoor eating areas, the sort of arrangement that you might find at a ballpark. Students line up at the hot dog window or the pizza window or the burrito stand; the reimbursable meal may be dispensed from one or two of these windows, or it may be in a separate location with an attached indoor seating area. "The area where the standard school lunch was served, where almost only free-lunch students ate, was pretty far away from where most everyone else ate and bought food," recalled one California student. And another: "The cafeteria was composed of two parts, inside and outside. The inside served hot tray lunches while the outside served chips, coke, candy, pizza. . . . It was easy to see who received free or reduced lunch because they went 'inside' the building."

Separate lines, however, appear all around the country. I asked students at universities in the Northeast and the Midwest, as well as California, to record their school lunch memories for me. The association of the reimbursable meal with poverty and its separation from the a la carte food sources cropped up in all these places. As one New York City student who had attended high school in Brooklyn put it, "only the poor or socially inadequate stood on that lunch line. The majority of students got by on eating overpriced vending machine snacks." A student at Gustavus Adolphus College in Minnesota, who had attended high school in Montana, explained: "It was easy to tell who was eating the free meal because they were the only ones eating in the cafeteria. The high school cafeteria was in the basement and no one wanted to eat there. The 'cool' kids ate upstairs in the entrance to the school or outside." A student at the University of Rhode Island recalled lunch at Portsmouth High School: "Lunch was segregated. There was one place for a la carte menu such as soda, pizza, snacks, and candy bars. The other side was for the federal school lunch program and anyone using the free or reduced lunch."

When I suggest that this situation results in segregation, I am not using the term lightly. Because race and class are so closely linked in many schools, a separation between paying customers on an a la carte line and students receiving free and reduced price meals in another quickly translates into racial separation. "Our campus was big and split by the upper level and lower level. The kitchen was on the lower level and you could only get the free or reduced lunch on the lower level. My school was very segregated in that white kids ate upstairs and Mexicans ate downstairs. I was eligible for free lunch but chose not to get it, because I was embarrassed," recalled a student who had attended high school in the city of Santa Cruz. Another, from the San Francisco suburbs, described her high school of fifteen hundred students: "It was located in the suburbs but not far from downtown Richmond from whence came the 'ghetto' children, . . . mostly nonwhite students. These kids were the ones who ate the free lunches." A community worker who attended school in New Rochelle, New York, painted a similar picture: "New Rochelle High School has one cafeteria that is divided into two floors. The top floor has the 'café,' which does not take school lunch vouchers. It serves bagels, juices, cookies, and a few hot food and snack items like hot pretzels. The bottom cafeteria serves hot lunch and accepts school lunch vouchers. . . . As a result of how the school divided . . . , the bottom cafeteria . . . was composed of predominantly African American and Latin American students. Consequently, the upstairs eating area was predominantly white."

Separation into groups is a reality in virtually any heterogeneous high school campus, with or without a la carte lines. The existence of separate "competitive food" options reinforces the segregation; it doesn't create it. In a society theoretically committed to multiculturalism and diversity, however, such separation raises troubling questions. It may have positive functions, as Beverly Daniel Tatum suggests in her provocatively titled book, *Why Are All the Black Kids Sitting Together in the Cafeteria?* Adolescence is a crucial, and delicate, phase in the essential process of identity formation, Tatum argues, and minority youth benefit from surrounding themselves with friends who share their minority status without the baggage of negative stereotypes so often found among their nonminority peers.[6] Adding a class-based stigma to this mix, however, can hardly be a recipe for positive identity formation. Minority students sitting together by choice is one thing; minority students eating together because they are poor and are channeled into a separate line is another.

Open campuses further aggravate the situation. The kids with money leave, the kids without stay behind. "There was no cafeteria, and there was open campus, so everyone left and went out to lunch or went home for lunch, or bought food at the snack shack except for those on the school lunch program. They lined up outside the office to get their bag lunches . . . (mostly Mexican from farming immigrant families)." Students who participated in a focus group in a suburban school in the Southwest, a school with a clear division between haves and have-nots, described the open campus situation this way: "Students that go out [to eat]—they're part of the in crowd. They're smart, they dress well, and they have lots of friends. The kids that stay in [to eat]—well, they can be from a bad environment or get into trouble, like selling drugs, or they can be studious and want to stay in and study, or they may stay in because they don't have anybody to go out with."[7] The Lansing, Michigan, school food service counts on a significant number of high school students leaving campus. The cafeterias do not have the capacity to serve them all, and the stigma makes sure that those who can leave do. According to the director,

There is the stigma that the only kids that go to the cafeteria are the free kids. And I think that is partly because we are still working with old buildings. It's not a real inviting place. It's not a real hip, cool, happening place for kids to be. It doesn't look like McDonald's, it doesn't look like an Arby's or a Wendy's. It looks institutional. And until we can move into something that looks a little more commercial, like a food court environment, I think we are going to continue to have that. Because kids feel that the only ones who use the cafeteria are the free kids.

The relationship between a la carte and open-campus options and stigma is a two-way street. The availability of the a la carte and off-campus options makes the main line "uncool," and the "uncoolness" of the main line drives students to the a la carte counter or away from campus altogether. The situation deters some eligible students from taking advantage of the meals for which they are certified, imposes a "self-esteem tax" or a "coolness penalty" on others, and deters middle-income youngsters from participating in the main line, depriving them of the financial, nutritional, and educational benefits that Congress intended them to have. It is a lose-lose-lose situation.

AN ADMINISTRATIVE ABSURDITY

The problem of stigma is inextricably intertwined with the administrative burden imposed on schools by the means test. As we saw in chapter 6, the eligibility formula is cumbersome to administer, and in fact, the efforts of schools to protect the privacy of children and reduce the stigma associated with the program have made the process even more cumbersome. Congress did not set out to stigmatize the needy child—nor the meal—but the three-tier structure created by the reforms of the 1970s had many unintended consequences. Along with national eligibility standards and enhanced federal reimbursements for free and reduced price meals came a substantial menu of new tasks for school food administrators. First, they had to distribute applications and collect the completed forms. If they sent the forms by mail, they incurred postal charges. If they tried to send forms home with children, they risked failing to reach substantial numbers of parents. Then they had to devise systems for identifying each child at the register, collecting the right amount of money, and assigning the meal to its proper category, all supposedly without identifying the recipients of free or reduced price meals to their peers. Then they had to establish procedures for the timely reporting of documented claims to state education departments.

No wonder the director of the American School Food Service Association told a Senate committee in 1971 that "the economic means test is an administrative absurdity." Senator Hubert Humphrey agreed that the new requirements posed special difficulties: "In a sense, we—the Congress—are putting the school official in an impossible position. First, we say to school officials that some children are going to be treated differently than others (in this case, a free lunch to needy children); and then we tell the school official that under no circumstances, however, should he let the children know that he is doing what we tell him to do. Now children are a lot smarter than that."[8] Needless to say, such requirements generated considerable hostility among administrators, many of whom saw means testing as inimical to the school's unifying function in the community, and among school food personnel, who complained that they were being turned "from bean cookers into bean counters."

When the Citizens' Board of Inquiry, author of the original *Hunger USA* exposé, went back to look at food programs in 1972, it found substantial problems associated with the new free and reduced price guarantees: "The determination of inability to pay, which should have been governed by a one-page or less affidavit form, supplied by the department, has mushroomed into a tangle of 13 separate income blocks in Iowa; requires costly notarization in Texas; probes into parental employment status in California; demands proof of special needs in Mobile, Alabama; requires lists of places where the family spends its money in Minatare, Nebraska; and puts into general use a three-factored income scale . . . calculated to confuse even the veteran tax-table decipherer." Turning to the issue of recipients' privacy, the advocates found separate lines, differently colored or figured tickets, designated tables, and other violations, and they found schools that gave less food to free-lunch recipients, denied them dessert, or used the threat of withholding food as a means of discipline. Lamenting the Agriculture Department's "refusal to cross state lines and energetically enforce standards," the review blamed the program's failure to reach close to a million impoverished children on a combination of "budgetary concerns . . . [and] jurisdictional proprieties."[9] In 1975, Congress specifically outlawed separate lines and differently colored tickets, and these practices were replaced by what one careful observer called "less obvious but more administratively cumbersome systems for keeping track of which children were participating in various segments of the program,"[10] thus aggravating the difficulties experienced by school principals and superintendents.

Nevertheless, with urging from national and local advocates and growing sophistication among school food service personnel and school administrators, schools developed considerable skill in the art of what came to be called "counting and claiming," keeping the required records of participation in various categories. Both total participation and the percentage of meals served free or at a reduced price crept upward throughout the 1970s, reaching 27 million ADP (average daily participation) by 1979. Rising participation, of course, meant rising costs, and the reforms of the late 1960s and early 1970s had fundamentally altered the relationship between the federal government on the one hand and the states and localities on the other, shifting a larger share of school food costs to the federal government.

Escalating costs have a tendency to set off alarms of their own. Just as anti-hunger advocates and school food service personnel were celebrating the success of their efforts to expand access and include more children from impoverished families, other observers were launching a crusade to cut federal expenditures and root out "fraud and abuse" in the lunch and breakfast programs. The same budget reconciliation acts that reduced federal subsidies and drove millions of paying customers out of the programs, thus intensifying stigma, triggering the rush to labor-saving fast food, and escalating the sale of a la carte items, now complicated the already daunting administrative challenge by adding new paperwork requirements. Specifically, the Omnibus Budget Reconciliation Act of 1981 required applicants for free and reduced price meals to provide additional documentation, including social security numbers, and for the first time, it required schools to verify a percentage of applications. Although many observers would probably disagree with me, I think this may have been the most significant—and damaging—element of a watershed piece of legislation. By increasing documentation requirements and mandating verification, Congress increased the number of points at which errors could be made and signaled to school food service personnel and USDA administrators alike a new atmosphere of suspicion. From here on out, a "burden of proof" rested upon families to demonstrate their eligibility, on schools to verify the accuracy of their certifications, and on school food authorities to prove their claims for reimbursement. Federal oversight of state agencies would be increased, and states would be required to more closely monitor local school food authorities. I think of it as the dawning of the Age of "Accountability."

It is not surprising that the spending growth that preceded the funding cuts had also led to increased scrutiny of claims for reimbursement.

Beginning in the mid-1970s, USDA experimented with a whole series of review procedures aimed at reducing inaccuracies in counting and claiming. The list of systems proposed and sometimes implemented reads like alphabet soup. There was the MTA (Management and Technical Assistance) review system proposed in 1975, and the PARS (Program Administrative Review System) suggested in 1978. There was the AIMS (Assessment, Improvement, and Monitoring System) proposed in 1979 and put into practice in 1980. Then there was the SPAM (Strategic Planning and Management) system initiated in 1987, and Accuclaim introduced in 1988, followed in the same year by CNFRI (Child Nutrition Federal Review Initiative), which later changed its name to Federal Accountability Review Initiative. In 1989 there was the FRS (Federal Review System), which was announced while USDA was still trying to comply with the negotiated oversight rules to incorporate public comments into the regulations for implementing Accuclaim. In the fall of the same year, the 1989 Child Nutrition and WIC Reauthorization Act included provisions directing USDA to develop a unified system for state and federal reviews of programs, launching the process that culminated in the CRE, or Coordinated Review Effort, that is now in place. Before the CRE rule-making process was completed, however, USDA announced MELLRS, (Management Evaluation Local Level Review System), which included a 102-page document for use in reviewing local programs.

The long list of acronyms might be comical if it did not represent so much costly effort by so many people. Each time the system changed, state reviewers and local program directors had to learn a whole new vocabulary and devise a new set of forms and reports. As a leading school food service management textbook observed, after compiling the five-page "Selected Chronology: USDA Review Initiatives in the School Nutrition Programs, 1975–1998," a "review of the chronology indicates to the reader the frequency of changes in program operations that may be experienced solely as a result of the external review or audit function."[11] Or, as ASFSA explained to Senator Patrick Leahy's staff in 1992, in an effort to delay implementation of the CRE regulations, which it perceived as inadequately developed and tested,

> over the past thirteen years, state and local program personnel have been
> subjected to numerous systems of accountability prescribed by USDA.
> Because of inadequate development, testing and refinement of such systems,
> they have all too soon been replaced by new systems. This has caused a
> high level of frustration for those reviewers who use standards that are con-
> stantly subject to change and for those local personnel trying to prepare for

a review against unclear standards. This has caused state and local personnel to be less than effective in all areas of program management because of the resources necessary to retrofit to each new accountability system.[12]

The errors that such systems are designed to detect—and punish and thus deter—are divided into two main classes: certification errors, including errors in the application, certification, and verification process, and non-certification errors, including cashier error and several forms of aggregation and reporting error. For example, a non-certification error occurs when a cashier misinterprets offer versus serve and counts a meal as reimbursable when it is not. Although non-certification errors account for substantial erroneous payments—about 48 percent of the total in the most recent study—certification errors have generally received most of the attention.[13] The problems discussed in the previous chapter—the various errors, miscalculations, and so forth that result in eligible children not being certified for free and reduced price meals—have their mirror image: some students are certified for benefits who are not actually eligible. Parents can misreport their incomes, accidentally or on purpose. Mistakes in converting weekly or bi-weekly amounts to monthly amounts are common; as noted, office personnel sometimes multiply weekly incomes by 4 instead of the requisite 4.3 to obtain monthly figures. Confusion about the meaning of "income" is also frequent. If you ask most lower-wage workers how much they make, they will tell you how much they are paid per hour or how much they take home per week, but school food eligibility is based on monthly gross income before withholding. Until the most recent Child Nutrition Reauthorization in 2004, households receiving free or reduced price meals were required to report to their child's school any change in income in excess of $50 per month or any change in household composition, and schools were supposed to adjust certification accordingly. Thus, a household that was eligible when the application was filled out in August could easily have been no longer eligible, or eligible for reduced price instead of free, by the time the verification process took place in December. A very substantial portion of the errors reported in verification studies before 2005 were due to unreported changes in income. Even when verification detected errors and changed the child's certification category—from free to reduced price or from reduced price to paid—the information was not always communicated effectively to the cashier or the processing staff. Thus some ineligible children continue to consume free or reduced price meals even though their certification for the benefit has been terminated.

When you stop and think about it, program designers face a challenging task. As an "Issue Brief" from Mathematica, Inc., put it, "Like other means-tested programs, the NSLP must balance three competing objectives—ensuring that approved children are income eligible, maintaining easy access for eligible children, and keeping administrative costs to reasonable levels (for both schools and families)."[14] The rub is that each of these objectives can be achieved, as it turns out, only at the sacrifice of some portion of the other two. Which risk do we prefer to take? The risk that ineligible children are being certified to receive free meals, or the risk that eligible children are not being certified? And how much time, energy, and money are we willing to devote to either or both of these goals? How much is it worth to us to make sure no eligible child is left behind by the lunch wagon? To make sure that no ineligible child eats free?

USDA has been concerned about these issues for quite some time. It began commissioning studies and pilot projects in the 1980s, shortly after Congress imposed the verification requirement as part of the Omnibus Budget Reconciliation Act. With only 3 percent of approved applications subject to verification in most districts, and even fewer in districts that chose to use a "focused sample" of "error prone" applications (those reporting incomes within $100 of one of the thresholds), the primary purpose of verification was not so much to catch a limited number of inaccurate applications as it was to deter applicants from intentionally misrepresenting their incomes.[15] Studies have consistently shown, however, that verification has limited efficacy as a deterrent to cheating, but substantial impact as a barrier to participation by eligible children. The problem is twofold: first, eligible households are apparently just as likely to shy away from the possibility of income verification as are ineligible households. Second, because school food authorities are required to terminate the benefits of any child whose parents fail to respond to a verification request and because study after study has shown that most such families are in fact eligible, substantial numbers of eligible children lose their benefits each time a verification request is sent out. Furthermore, children who are erroneously certified for free meals when they are in fact eligible for reduced price lose the entire benefit if their parents fail to respond to a verification request in a timely manner. In some cases, parents reapply and children can resume eating the free and reduced price meals, but schools have had limited capacity to follow up with parents who fail to respond, so many parents never reestablish their children's eligibility.

These concerns might have remained largely the precinct of Washington bureaucrats and research contractors had not politics intervened. In 1999, the Office of Analysis, Nutrition, and Evaluation of the Food and Nutrition Service conducted an analysis of data from the Census Bureau's Current Population Survey, comparing the numbers of school-aged children in households with incomes within the free and reduced price eligibility range with administrative data on the numbers of children certified to receive such meals. The report showed that the number of children certified to receive free meals substantially exceeded the number that the Census Bureau estimated to be in households in the appropriate income range—by more than 25 percent! This provoked considerable discussion and concern within USDA. Early in 2003, as Child Nutrition Reauthorization approached and the Bush administration prepared to release its fiscal year 2004 budget, the Office of Management and Budget made the comparison study public and announced that it was "seriously considering" requiring all applicants to submit pay stubs or other evidence of income in support of their applications. Charging massive "overcertification" in the National School Lunch and School Breakfast Programs, the administration began looking for remedies to "preserve program integrity."[16]

The overcertification challenge galvanized anti-hunger advocates and their allies in Congress. It was very nearly a textbook case of competing claims, with administration spokespersons and conservative pundits talking about fraud and abuse and anti-hunger activists pointing to the mounting evidence that many more eligible than ineligible children would lose benefits. Estimates derived from the accumulated research ran as high as six eligible children cut off or prevented from applying for each ineligible recipient identified. With dynamic leadership from the Food Research and Action Center, child nutrition advocates mobilized under the banner of "First, Do No Harm" to resist administration proposals to require the submission of documentation with every application; the administration countered with a plan for "enhanced verification," requiring schools to verify 15 percent rather than 3 percent of applications. School food service personnel joined in to point out that the additional paperwork could swamp the program and would certainly raise costs. As the president of the American School Food Service Association succinctly put the matter to a committee of the House of Representatives, "the greater the regulatory burden on the program, the greater the cost to produce a meal."[17]

The Center on Budget and Policy Priorities turned its remarkable analytical capacities to the data that formed the original basis for the charge, and quickly pointed out that a comparison of the two data sets—administrative data on certifications and census data on household poverty—was inherently flawed. In the first place, the two data sets did not cover the same time periods—the census data were more recent and captured a period of economic upturn when in fact fewer children were probably eligible than had been certified the previous year. Far more important, however, in explaining the discrepancy was the fact that school meal applications are certified on the basis of monthly income, while the Current Population Reports collect annual income data. Research over the last several decades had revealed that poverty is a highly dynamic condition in the United States, with households moving in and out of "spells" of poverty as work hours increase or are reduced and members enter and exit the household. More children are likely to be eligible in any given month, they argued, than to have annual incomes that fall below any particular threshold. Using an alternate Census Bureau data set, the Survey of Income and Program Participation, the director of the Institute for Research on Poverty at the University of Wisconsin was able to show that 2.8 million more children had family incomes below 130 percent of the poverty line in August or September 1988 than had annual incomes below that cutoff in calendar 1999, a number that would account for nearly all of the "overage."[18]

The overcertification threat turned out to be a cloud with a silver lining. By mobilizing more accurate data and the testimony of school food service personnel and school business officials and by calling attention to the research accumulating in the Office of Analysis, Nutrition, and Evaluation and the Economic Research Service, anti-hunger advocates were able to educate Congress about the downside of monthly income reporting requirements in the school food program and raise consciousness about the need to streamline the eligibility determination process. As the founder and director of the Center on Budget and Policy Priorities Bob Greenstein explained to the Senate Agriculture Committee, errors in certification could stem from intentional or accidental misreporting of income or household size by applicants, from administrative processing errors by schools, or from changes in household income or size that occurred between application and verification. School food was not the only program, he reported, to have difficulty coping with the shifting incomes of the poor.

Increasingly, major means-tested benefit programs are moving to make children eligible for benefits for 12-month periods, rather than trying to track month-to-month fluctuations in the incomes of low income families. . . . Medicaid, S-CHIP, and the food stamps program—which employ tens of thousands of caseworkers and incur administrative costs of some billions of dollars a year—have taken these steps because they have found they simply are not able to keep up with households' monthly income fluctuations. If these programs, with their much larger infrastructures and bureaucracies, cannot track such income fluctuations, it should come as no surprise that the school lunch program—which has no comparable bureaucracy—cannot do so either.[19]

Both the advocates and the USDA Food and Nutrition Service urged Congress to revise the program to make a child's eligibility last for the entire school year, while permitting families to apply at any point in the year if their income dropped. In addition, they asked Congress to mandate direct certification in all districts, a process by which children in households receiving Temporary Assistance for Needy Families, food stamps, or benefits from the Food Distribution Program on Indian Reservations are automatically certified for free meals based on information provided directly to the schools by the agencies that administer those programs. Direct certification had been an option since 1991, and studies showed that it reduced errors and lessened the administrative burden on both families and schools, since no application and no verification would be needed. And that is just what Congress did, along with a host of other provisions, making Child Nutrition Reauthorization 2004 a victory for poor families and their advocates.

It would be a mistake, however, to picture the reauthorization battles as USDA versus advocates. The department was concerned about over-certification and program integrity, but it was also concerned about preserving access for eligible children and about avoiding a major increase in the paperwork burden or in the program cost. Nor were advocates insensitive to the program integrity issue. It would be more accurate, I think, to picture USDA, Congress, food service personnel, and the advocacy community as struggling with the inherent trade-offs among these four concerns, with somewhat different priorities. Congress needed to keep the costs down; USDA needed to ensure an acceptable level of program integrity; the School Nutrition Association needed to restrain the growth of paperwork and reporting; and anti-hunger advocates needed to protect access for eligible children without increasing the stigma attached to participating in the programs.

THE SEARCH FOR SOLUTIONS

The overcertification controversy brought public attention to these trade-offs, but in fact the process of searching for solutions to the twin challenges of stigma and the paperwork burden has been going on for years. As Marshall Matz, the Washington counsel for the School Nutrition Association explained to me, the effort to relieve the administrative burden is a question of priorities.

> At the local level, there are only so many people running these programs, . . . there are only so many hours in the day. How do you want them spending their time? Is it chasing income documentation, or is it working on meal quality and nutrition? I think you've got to get out of one to solve the other. . . . If you want school meals to be a part of education, it has to function like an education program, which means no means-testing. Means testing is the guts of the problem here. I think to focus all the time and attention on nutrition, to be able to have the ability to do that, which I think is so important, you have got to figure out how to take this program out of being means-tested.

Probably the most obvious solution is the idea of universal free school meals: free for all. Simply make lunch a regular part of the school day and serve it without charge to all children in attendance, on a par with free bus transportation or free textbooks.

The Road Not Taken

Universal free school meals (or "universal" as it is generally known in the trade) is not a new idea. This goal was urged at the very first National School Lunch Conference hosted by USDA in October 1946. Agnes Meyer, chair of the National Committee for Support of the Public Schools told the gathering that "the present form of the school lunch movement is only the beginning. . . . What we must aim at is a gradual evolution toward a free hot midday meal for every child."[20] The universal approach was advocated for years by the long-term executive director of the American School Food Service Association, John Perryman, who in retirement told an interviewer that not securing universal free meals was his greatest disappointment. "I was a devotee of the idea of a universal school lunch program and I'm still convinced it makes a great deal of sense. But I think the enormous, complicated structure of legislation that we have now is unfortunate and really doesn't make any sense at all. This mechanism by which a program is reimbursed is cumbersome, it's awkward, it's a tremendous administrative nightmare."[21] Universal was set as a long-term goal both by the Committee on School Lunch Participation in *Their Daily Bread* and by the Citizen's Board of Inquiry in *Hunger USA*. It was recommended by the Panel on Large-Scale Meal Delivery Systems at the 1969 White House Conference on Food, Nutrition and Health, and it was urged by the famed anthropologist Margaret Mead in the opening hearings of the Senate Select Committee on Nutrition and Human Needs. Asked by Chairman George McGovern if she would support such a program, she replied "Yes, definitely. It is very foolish to talk about integration and democracy in our schools and then provide a school system where we stigmatize some of the children in that school as the children of parents who are unable to provide for them, and especially in terms of food . . . the fact that someone cannot provide it for his children is very stigmatizing."[22] Legislation proposing universal was introduced in 1971 by Senator Hubert Humphrey and had the support of House Education and Labor Committee chair Carl Perkins and Senate Select Committee chair George McGovern. Congressman George Miller introduced universal legislation in 1992 and again in 1993, for which he secured the support of forty cosponsors. And I found that universal remains the most common response of the people "on the ground," the food service directors and cafeteria workers whom I interviewed, when I asked them to describe their ideal program.

For most of the school food service personnel to whom I talked, support for universal is a reaction to the day-to-day realities of operating the program. "Well, nationally, I would like to have everyone on a lunch, free. Then you don't have to worry about all these papers, filling out forms," a cafeteria manager from Eden, North Carolina, told me. "If I had unlimited resources, I agree with a lot of other food service directors, that I would like to see universal lunch," said Deb Neal of Lansing, Michigan. "Universal breakfast and universal lunch. So that we don't have to worry about whether the child is free or reduced or paid. Whether mom and dad can pay for lunch or not. It's just part of the school day." "Free lunches, that would be my dream," declared a Vermont food service director; "let us worry about portion size, fresh fruits and vegetables, good milk, ethics." "Philosophically, it's the right thing to do, . . . taking that stigma of free and reduced out of the way and giving them a lunch every day," declared Mary Kate Harrison, director of child nutrition for Florida's Hillsborough County.

Frank Harris, who recently retired from the Norwalk, Connecticut, public schools after thirty-nine years as food service director, has made universal his special crusade. In part, this reflects his frustration with the amount of time consumed by the three-tier system and the related need to protect privacy.

> Now, the way it's set up now, we try everything in our power to protect the anonymity of all kids, free, reduced, paid. Many kids do not take advantage of it because they feel they are singled out. . . . And all the rules and regulations that we now get from the Department of Agriculture that we have to conform to, that we have to watch the computer and watch the fax machine and watch the letters and the rules and regulations, [without those] we could do what we do best, which is to prepare and provide nutritional meals, instead of interpreting all the rules and regulations. It really makes no sense.

Harris, who came to the United States in the early 1940s as a refugee from Nazi persecution, sees universal as a solution to these problems, but also as an expression of democracy: "I have always said, it's right. It is morally right. Intellectually, it's wise to do it. Every child is the same. They've got to go to school. They get their school books, they get their transportation, they get their meal. . . . Kids got to go to school. Let's once and for all educate them and if you educate them you've got to feed them. A hungry child can't learn. Simple and plain." As Nancy May, the food service director at Healdsburg Unified School District in California's wine country put it, "To be able to just feed kids would be great. It would help with the accounting and the dividing by eligibility category and all the paperwork that goes with that. And to be able to just provide all kids a good meal that everyone at school can sit together and eat, the same good food, made right there at their school, I think would be a great thing."

Despite the near unanimity of school food service personnel and the consistent efforts of the School Nutrition Association, universal remains the road not taken. The last serious effort to start a national discussion of the option was an effort by the then-ASFSA in 1992. In statements on behalf of its "Universal Vision," ASFSA stressed not only the desired reduction of administrative burden and the potential "to eliminate the identification of low-income students as well as the welfare stigma of the program," but also the capacity of a universal program to "integrate school nutrition into the total educational process" and to "use the school nutrition program as a laboratory for nutrition education."[23] ASFSA's work led to a Senate resolution requiring USDA to report to Congress on universal-type programs and a House bill introduced by Congressman George Miller proposing to give every school the option of providing universal lunch and breakfast by the year 2000. In a statement on the introduction of his bill, Congressman Miller declared:

> The current school nutrition program is at a major crossroads. Since 1980, we have seen a very disturbing trend with regard to school nutrition programs. In the last decade, federal subsidies for school nutrition programs have been reduced; bonus USDA commodities have essentially vanished; the administrative complexity and cost of administering the school nutrition program has increased dramatically; and indirect cost assessments made by local school administrators are draining the financial resources of the school food service authorities. . . . In the last decade, we have treated the National School Lunch and Breakfast Programs as a welfare program, emphasizing the income of the child participating in the program. We are hampering the administration of the program with more and more paperwork trying to document the income of the children's families.

As a result, he reported, schools were dropping out of the program, and a USDA study showed four million children eligible for free and reduced price meals who were not participating.

Miller's remarks near the close of his speech to the House proved predictive: "I fully appreciate, Mr. Speaker, that there will be those who say this is a great idea but it is one we cannot afford given the size of our deficit."[24] The hopes for conversion to a universal program were indeed dashed on the shoals of the federal budget deficit. Even the anti-hunger advocacy community was not of a single mind; a memo circulated by the Center on Budget and Policy Priorities opposed the measure on the grounds that the benefits of the new expenditure would go largely to families with average incomes of about $50,000 per year. After identifying a long list of pressing, unmet needs among low-income Americans, it concluded, "Enacting a universal school program in the current fiscal atmosphere would mean placing a universal lunch program that primarily benefits middle-income children, most of whom are not undernourished, ahead of many of these other needs."[25] Instead, the Center's memo suggested the possibility of enacting legislation to permit all schools to use procedures then being tested in four pilot communities, procedures that allowed schools to feed all children free of charge, though federal reimbursements would be provided based on percentages of children eligible for each level of reimbursement, established by surveys of income data. Congressman Miller's bill never made it to the floor.

Provisions 2 and 3: Alternatives

Meanwhile, however, an option for just such a localized universal program already existed, and had for more than a decade. In 1977 Congress had amended the special assistance component of the National School Lunch Act, Section 11, to establish two alternative approaches to eligibility and counting and claiming, referred to as Provisions 1 and 2, intended to reduce the paperwork burden. Provision 1 was available only to schools in which at least 80 percent of children were eligible for free or reduced price meals. It simply allowed such schools to collect applications every other year instead of every year. It did not require schools that chose to implement it to feed all children free of charge, and it did not eliminate the counting and claiming process of assigning meals to the correct category. Provision 2, however, was a kind of temporary universal program. It authorized schools to collect applications and certify eligibility only once every three years, provided they offered meals free to all children. It took a while for USDA to create regulations for this approach, but it has been available since 1980. Under Provision 2, schools can collect information on the number of meals served in each category during a "base year," and then receive reimbursements proportional to that distribution in subsequent years. Local school food service or other non-federal funds must make up the difference between the cost of feeding all children and the total federal reimbursement. It eliminates not only the application certification and verification requirements in the non-base years, but also the necessity to assign each meal served to the proper category.[26]

The approach has been amended several times, changing the length of the authorized period and of an allowable extension. At present, the program allows schools to use the base year proportions for four years (including the base year) and to obtain a renewal for a second four years if it can show that "the income level of the school's population remains stable." Thus schools can avoid the onerous application collection and verification procedures for a full seven years after the base year—long enough, state reviewers point out, to forget all they ever knew about how to conduct such procedures efficiently and effectively. Another universal-type alternative, Provision 3 was added in 1995; it allows schools that feed all children free to opt for the same actual amount of federal reimbursement that they received in the base year, adjusted only for enrollment change and inflation. The most recent Child Nutrition Reauthorization amended Provisions 2 and 3 so that entire districts, and not just individual schools, could claim Provision 2 or 3 status.

These provisions have worked well in many communities, and advocates have invested considerable time and energy in encouraging schools and districts to adopt the approach, but there are problems. As suggested above, by the time schools exhaust their extensions and renewals and have to collect the forms again, both parents and school administrators are out of the habit, and the return rate on forms is often quite low. Audits then often reveal very high rates of error, and in New York State, at least, the result has been that many schools have been barred from using the approach for the next several years after a disappointing review. The situation is further complicated by the fact that many of the schools most likely to benefit from Provisions 2 or 3, schools with high percentages of children eligible for free or reduced price meals, find they must continue to collect the application forms because these are needed to establish eligibility for federal Title I (antipoverty) funding or for purposes related to No Child Left Behind. Finally, some districts have rejected Provisions 2 and 3 because they introduce confusion when only some schools in the district are participating, and children from a single family attend several different schools. Parents can be forgiven for being confused if their elementary school children attend a school where meals are free for all, while their youngsters in middle school are expected to pay or to submit applications and go through the application and certification process.

Provision 2 has been something of a sleeper: very few schools made use of the provision until quite recently. A full decade after it became available, it was in use in less than one half of one percent of schools.[27] The provision was buried in the regulations and poorly publicized. By the time school food service operations became aware of it, in the midst of Reagan era budget cuts, they had their hands full coping with new documentation requirements, funding cutbacks, and the loss of customers. Nevertheless, the problem of the administrative burden continued— and grew—and Congress remained interested in reducing the paperwork demands associated with school meals. The Child Nutrition and WIC Reauthorization Act of 1989 required the secretary of agriculture to carry out pilot projects to test alternatives to annual application and daily meal counts, the pilots to which the Center on Budget and Policy Priorities memo referred.

The Philadelphia Story

One of the most interesting approaches to emerge from these pilots was developed by the Philadelphia schools, which contracted with a Temple University demographer to calculate eligibility based on welfare and food stamp records, and supplemented that with a survey. Based on the demographic profile that emerged, Philadelphia chose to offer meals free of charge to all students in 144 of its 272 schools. Thus, in Philadelphia, not only was the counting and claiming process simplified, but the entire application process—including distribution, retrieval, and review of applications, the certification of applicants, and the verification of a sample of applications—was avoided in the schools designated to use the alternate approach. Based on an estimate that schools spent an average of fifteen minutes to process each application—that is, "to distribute, collect, transport, review, enter information into a computer file and file the application" and to verify a sample of applications on file—researchers reported that Philadelphia saved 20,480 hours of staff time, "over 10 staff years—about 1 staff year for every 14 schools in the pilot program."[28] Time was also saved by simplification of the process of meal counting, estimated at an hour and a half per school day in each of the 144 participating schools in Philadelphia, or nearly another 20 years of staff time. Some of the saved time was reallocated to other activities; some resulted in an actual decrease in labor costs. In addition, Philadelphia saved money on printing (applications and tickets) and money handling—no need to hire the Brinks truck. Overall, despite the cost of the initial social-demographic survey, Philadelphia saved $0.19 per meal. Participation went up 18 percent overall, and rose dramatically in the high schools, where the percentage of students opting for the reimbursable meal rose 186 percent! Clearly the Philadelphia story was a great success.[29]

Unfortunately for the ongoing effort to reduce stigma and administrative burden, the required reports of the Philadelphia experiment were released just as Congress was undergoing the changes brought about by the conservative triumph in the 1994 congressional elections. Extending school food programs was not an element of the Contract with America. In fact, the Contract called for converting child nutrition funding to block grants, diverting the energies of anti-hunger advocates and school nutrition professionals to the preservation of the federal entitlement status of the school lunch and breakfast programs. By the time that challenge had subsided (see chapter 2), the results of the first School Nutrition Dietary Assessment were out, and both Congress and the School Nutrition Association turned their attention to the fight over school meal menu planning options and the effort to upgrade the nutrition profile of the meals. The war on fat upstaged the war on paperwork.

Direct Certification

A less dramatic approach to reducing the paperwork burden, direct certification of eligible children from welfare and food stamp records, was tested in Columbus, Ohio, and in the State of Maine as part of the set of pilot projects that included the Philadelphia experiment.[30] Children whose families received welfare benefits or food stamps, or participated in the Food Distribution Program on Indian Reservations were "categorically eligible" for free school meals. In direct certification, the traditional application and certification process remained in place, but was supplemented by computer matching and other data sharing between the state departments that administered food stamps and welfare benefits and the school food authorities. Both test areas experienced significant increases in participation during the pilot, and in Columbus, where baseline data on application processing time had been collected, substantial time savings could be documented.

These pilot projects proved to be just the first in a long series of pilot projects, studies, investigations, and demonstrations, all aimed at finding and testing ways to reduce the administrative burden and social consequences of the three-tier system. The direct certification experiments in the initial pilots led to a much larger study of direct certification, undertaken in 1995 and released by USDA in 2000. This, in turn, led to extensive studies of the possibilities of computer matching, one of the direct certification modalities. Advocates for the poor were not universally enthusiastic about computer matching, however. Some pointed out that the process violated the privacy of food stamp and welfare program recipients by notifying school officials which families were receiving public assistance. They preferred an approach in which the welfare department or food stamp office would notify recipient families that they were automatically eligible for free school meals, and that instead of filling out the application, they could simply submit a copy of their notification letter or case number. This gave parents the option of protecting their privacy, but it thwarted one of the fundamental goals of direct certification, establishing eligibility for children whose parents for whatever reason (pride, privacy, distraction, disorganization, procrastination, illiteracy, fear of the immigration authorities, orneriness) failed to return the application.

Despite these objections, the computer-matching pilots were widely regarded as a success. Because the families of computer-matched directly certified children do not have to submit applications, the practice reduces the paperwork burden for both families and schools. In some communities, where large numbers of children are directly certified, the savings can be substantial. The same reauthorization legislation that rebuffed the overcertification forces also mandated a gradual nationwide implementation of direct certification—in districts with an enrollment of more than 25,000 students by 2006–2007, in districts with 10,000–24,999 pupils by 2007–2008, and in all districts by the 2008–2009 school year.

Meanwhile, a development in another area of federal policy has given principals and superintendents a strong incentive to identify all of those children who are eligible for free or reduced price meals, whether directly certifiable or not. Compensatory and Title I funds flow to school districts based on the number of "economically disadvantaged" children in the district, and eligibility for free and reduced price meals is now an official definition of "economic disadvantage." Under the No Child Left Behind Act, even more federal funds are at stake. Students qualify for special Supplemental Educational Services (SES) like tutoring if their incomes are under the reduced price cutoff, and schools with large numbers of SES-eligible children can receive additional funds to provide such services to all their pupils. So, while the paperwork burden has been reduced by direct certification, the stakes have risen. Principals have come up with all sorts of devices and incentives to induce parents to fill out the forms: rallies, billboards, letters, competitions, and lotteries. In Houston, the names of parents completing applications were entered into a drawing for a television and other prizes donated by local businesses or purchased from the food services budget. The New York City school food services persuaded the New York Jets to donate an all-expense-paid trip to the Pro Bowl in Hawaii for use as a grand prize in a lottery that could only be entered by returning the forms. Some principals have taken the challenge too much to heart: in 2005 The New York Times reported that the principal of a Manhattan high school had been removed for "urging parents to falsify income information on school lunch forms, apparently to increase government aid to the school"; he had sent out a letter to parents in which he suggested, "The lower you estimate your income, the better for the school budget."[31]

Technology to the Rescue?

Direct certification, at least in its computer matching incarnation, is made possible by modern computer technology—the rapid electronic matching of identification numbers. And that is not the only form of digital technology that is changing the face of school food. Technology offers what many perceive as a solution to the problems associated with the three-tier eligibility system. Beginning in the 1980s and escalating through the 1990s, schools began adopting computerized point-of-sale (or POS) systems that permitted students to use a swipe card, a personal identification number (PIN), or more recently, a biometric—finger image or retinal scan—to check out at the end of the cafeteria line. Such systems generally allow parents to prepay for meals, establishing an account that can be drawn down; more recent iterations allow parents to pay online via credit card. In either case, they eliminate the need for lunch money and the problems that have traditionally been caused by lost lunch money, pilfered lunch money, lunch money extracted by playground bullies, and lunch money misspent at the corner store or snack shop on the way to school. POS systems were supposed to address both the administrative burden and the stigma problems associated with the three-tier eligibility system. On the administrative side, each meal would be electronically assigned to the appropriate reimbursement category, eliminating the need for counting tickets or similar tasks at the end of the day, reducing errors and inaccuracies, and generating automatic reports. Faster line speeds are another selling point, since long, slow lines are widely recognized to deter some children from participating. Although some school systems found their cafeteria workers initially resistant to the change to the new technology, most reported that front line staff came around when they realized how much tedious labor the system would eliminate. A Long Island school board member who wrote an account of the computerization process in her school district's food service operations for the American School Board Journal reported that cafeteria staff who started out tearful or hostile—"If they make me touch that computer, I'll quit"—quickly converted once the benefits became clear: "They were thrilled when they learned that they no longer had to produce handwritten cashiers' reports."[32]

Overall, POS computerization has been a resounding success, and as the word has spread and the software options have multiplied, the rate of adoption has accelerated. Currently just over 50 percent of school districts responding to an SNA survey reported using automated payment systems; another 4 percent had firm plans to implement the system, and an additional 11 percent had the matter under consideration. As with any new system, there were glitches and problems. Lost swipe cards have been common among elementary school children, as have forgotten passwords, slowing down the line as cashiers must stop to look up a child's account number on a roster or database. If a child makes a mistake in entering a PIN, a child later in line may be told that she has already eaten. "Sharing" of cards created problems until software manufacturers began adding the child's picture to the screen that pops up when the card is swiped; now the cashier can easily check to make sure that the right child is using the card or PIN, though, again, this can bring the line to a halt as an administrator is called to deal with an instance of juvenile identity theft. Software designers have also added food allergies and birthday alerts to their systems, and newer designs permit parents to bar or limit certain items.

Biometrics is the newest new thing in point-of-sale automation, and finger imaging is the most common form. "Students never forget their fingers," commented one early adopter.[33] The goal of speeding up the line, however, can fall prey to other problems. Sometimes the scanner fails to read the student information, and then cashiers will have to enter it manually. Cuts on the finger will interfere with reading. And some observers note that the scanner can be unsanitary.[34] The biggest barrier, however, has probably been parental discomfort with the idea of fingerprinting schoolchildren, and concern about larger scale, adult-style identity theft. Advocates of the system explain that the computer does not store an image of the child's fingerprint, but rather creates a numerical code based on data points extracted from the finger image, but many parents still find the prospect unsettling. The Taunton, Massachusetts, School Committee recently abandoned plans to implement a biometric system after parents launched a "Ban the Scan" campaign in which they were supported by the American Civil Liberties Union of Massachusetts.[35]

Regardless of the particular form chosen—swipe card, PIN, or biometric device—POS technology can eliminate stigma only if it also eliminates cash. As long as some students have an opportunity to flash their cash, and especially where they do so in separate a la carte lines, the stigma-reducing impact will be limited. As one state reviewer for the School Meals Initiative for Healthy Children explained to me, "My daughter who is in high school now, I could never send in a check and have her prepay. That would be so humiliating to her because she says, 'When you do that, they are going to think I'm poor and that I'm getting my lunch for free. I need to have money in my hand; I need to pay.'" Cashless systems do exist, systems in which prepayment is the only option, but these also pose problems. What happens when a student reaches the end of the line, lunch already selected and on the tray, and discovers that the balance in her account is not sufficient to cover the lunch she has chosen? The school cannot now sell the food to another student; if she is not permitted to pay the difference in cash, both the child and the school suffer. There are technological solutions to this, as well. I read about one school in which students who need to increase their balances can deposit cash in their accounts, with instantaneous updating of their balances, at kiosks like reverse ATM machines located in the cafeteria and at several areas around the school.

All of this equipment, and the software to operate it, costs money, of course, but the biggest problem with prepay POS systems is probably the child whose parent has neither deposited sufficient funds nor provided cash. A reverse ATM kiosk won't solve the problem if the child does not have the money and her account has insufficient funds. Called "low balance" or "charging policy," this is the newest major headache in the ongoing saga of problems associated with paying for lunch. What happens when that child reaches the cashier? The issue first came to my attention when my Google School Lunch alert directed me to a news story from North Port, Florida. School food was in the news in North Port, not because of new healthy menu items or the elimination of vending machines, but because a cafeteria worker confiscated a tray from a six-year-old boy whose account was out of money and dumped the contents into the garbage, giving the child a peanut butter and jelly sandwich instead. "Brutal school policy upsets child" read the headline on a feature story, complete with a picture of the cherubic child doing his homework.[36] "School food payment policy a form of bullying," opined the North Port Sun; numerous letters to the editor followed, and the incident became a hot topic in the paper's online "Soundoff" column. Readers complained about the humiliation of the child, about the waste of food, about the irresponsibility of parents who allow their children's accounts to languish in the red, and about the failure to use technology effectively to avoid such incidents. The school food service apologized and clarified that the confiscation and the substitution of a sandwich were school board policy, but that the tray should not have been dumped in view of the child. "We do throw the lunch away because we cannot give it to other children," the food service supervisor explained, "but staff is instructed not to throw it out in front of children."

After the North Port incident raised my consciousness, I found the problem nearly everywhere I looked. I asked "Tootsie," a cafeteria manager from Eden, North Carolina, how she handled this. "They're still allowed a lunch. You cannot turn them down," she replied. Her computer generates low-balance letters, and when a new check comes in, it is applied against any charged lunches. If no check arrives, "we try to get it. If we don't, then a lot of time, I will pay . . . , personally. We have a lot of children. Sometimes they just absolutely cannot afford it. And some of them will not fill out the lunch forms, and circumstances that I know about or something, sometimes I will put the money in. And if we find money in the cafeteria, we have a little container that we keep it in; then if they need money, we just apply it to that." In many school systems, however, the amounts in question are too large to be handled by change found on the cafeteria floor or the generosity of cafeteria staff. One Florida food service director told me that children in her district annually charged about $2.2 million dollars worth of meals. "And in 70 percent of those charges, 65–70 percent, we get it back; parents will pay it back . . . but we're still left with a balance of $675,000, and we're writing that off, and I'm tired of it. . . . We have got to do something. . . . Never do we want to embarrass a child, and we don't want to get the child in the middle, but there's got to be some consequences, . . . and if you don't pay your bill after five meals, you are going to get a cheese sandwich, and you are going to get something different. This has been a real volatile issue in our district, and we're really working toward changing it."

Despite her hopes, the "alternate meal" as it is often called, does in fact put the child in the middle. As one outraged California children's advocate asserted, the "stigma sandwich" punishes the child for the parent's failure and uses children to collect their parents' debts. (In some schools, the peanut butter sandwich has had to be abandoned as the "alternate meal" because children liked it too much—and thus it lost its punitive quality.) A further challenge arises because federal law says that children eligible for free and reduced price meals cannot be denied a meal because of "lost tickets," where "the term 'ticket' refers to any and all forms of exchange used in the schools' or institutions' food service collection systems including daily, weekly or monthly paper tickets, cards, coins or tokens" unless the student has been permitted to use replacement tickets for at least three meals, and parents have been notified in writing that no further replacement tickets will be issued.[37] States may have additional requirements. In California, for example, schools are required to provide at least one meal daily to all free or reduced price eligible students who seek them—as one California food service director put it to me, "We have to feed 'em." Thus schools in California are legally required to feed those children eligible for reduced price meals, even if their accounts are in the red, while they are not legally bound to feed "full price" children, but they are legally obligated to avoid overtly identifying free and reduced price children.

Have parents suddenly become less reliable and responsible than they were two decades ago? I suspect that the issue arises in part from the point-of-sale technology itself. Back when lunch money came in cash, I imagine that many a cashier let the child without funds go by and simply didn't count the lunch at all. Once the lunch is made and served, it has little impact on the lunchroom's bottom line. Or perhaps she counted it as a reduced price lunch or a free lunch and hoped the discrepancy would not be noticed. With an old-fashioned cash register, such lenience was possible, and who would be the wiser? With the point-of-sale device, however, neither the child nor the cashier may be aware of the shortfall until the lunch is already entered into the computer. The technology eliminates the "wiggle room," a good thing, perhaps, from a "program integrity" standpoint, but not such a good thing if what you are trying to do is make sure that no child goes unfed.

It is probably also the case that back when parents needed to scrounge up the cost of the day's lunch before sending junior off to school in the morning, they knew when they didn't have it, and sent a bagged lunch along. In the era of prepaid meals, however, parents may get fairly substantially into debt before they realize it—especially if junior has been spending money at the a la carte line. The check that mom thought would last the month may be spent by the third week—or sooner if the child has treated friends to extras. The Technology-to-the-Rescue camp has responded with online systems that allow parents to monitor exactly what their children are purchasing and even to block certain items or amounts. This too is controversial, with some arguing that such systems "empower parents" to play their vital role in the child's developing nutrition habits and others arguing that such "big brother" technology deprives the child of the opportunity to become a responsible consumer. Further, it requires parents to have access to a computer and some online savvy; computer use may be widespread but it is not universal.

The more closely I look at the realities of trying to feed children at school, the more strongly I feel that lunch should simply be a part of the school day: free for all. There is, of course, no such thing as a free lunch, but the choice of how we pay for it is ours to make. The conclusion will present my arguments for a universal approach. Short of a universal free policy, however, schools must try their best to protect the privacy of students, manage the paperwork, accurately account for the meals served, lure the customers into the cafeteria, and serve meals that comply with the federal nutrition standards. At the same time parents and activists around the country are organizing to seek better, healthier, tastier food, and to increase access. Their efforts are the topic of the next chapter.

CHAPTER EIGHT

LOCAL HEROES

Fixing School Food at the Community Level

The road that leads up the Maunawili Valley on the windward side of the Island of Oahu is rutted and uneven. When the truck had bounced along for a mile or so, my host, Mark Paikuli-Stride, stopped to open a forest gate and say a brief blessing. The valley, he told me, was sacred. In that almost mystical setting, it was easy to absorb his reverence for the fertile land and clean water that are needed to produce taro, the most traditional of Hawaii's traditional crops. Paikuli-Stride is both a taro farmer and the executive director of the Aloha 'Aina (which means "love of the land") Health Center. In a clearing at the top of the valley, he has been restoring ancient taro beds with the help of children from the Kailua Charter School, a Hawaiian-language immersion school, along with some of their teachers and another Kailua parent, the curriculum development specialist Kekai Irwin. Here the younger children clamber around barefoot in the water and the mud, planting the corms that will grow into new taro plants, while the older ones help to rebuild the embankments and containment walls needed to regulate the flow of water. Children plant the taro and harvest it and learn the time-consuming process that produces po'i from the roots, and how to cook the leaves and stems. At the same time, they learn about the *ahupua'a,* the wedge-shaped ecosystem that follows the falling water from the mountain heights to the sea; this is the basis of the traditional Hawaiian resource management system that fed the native population for centuries before the missionaries, and then the container ships, arrived. The school's lunch and snack programs try to serve po'i at least twice a week, but not all of it comes from Paikuli-Stride's gardens, which can not yet produce enough; some they purchase at Costco.

In the Hawaiian creation story, the cosmic parents' first offspring is stillborn and deformed. When the grieving parents bury the rootlike creature, the taro plant rises from his grave. Their second child is born healthy and becomes the progenitor of the human race. Thus the taro plant is the older brother of humanity. The two brothers are linked in an enduring symbiosis. If we take care of the taro by taking care of the land, the taro will take care of us. I had come to Hawaii to see how some Hawaiian schools are incorporating taro—kalo in the written version of the Hawaiian language, which has neither a t nor an r—into their curricula and their school lunch programs. The effort reflects both a concern about healthy eating and a desire to preserve and transmit traditional culture. For Paikuli-Stride, the two are one and the same:

> For us, it's a privilege to be on the land, and we really want to see this land fulfill what it was meant to do. . . . We have some kids come up here who have never been in a stream before, don't even know how the taro plant is grown, never been in the mountains; it's amazing to see how detached the kids are from that. And when they are detached from that, then they don't know where their health and their vitality come from. So, we're trying to help the kids make that connection back to what sustains us on this earth, the fertility in the land, us taking care of the land in the proper ways.

Paikuli-Stride and Irwin met because they both have children attending the Kailua School. As parents concerned about the quality of school meals and the messages those meals communicate to children, the two have a great deal of company. All across the country, parents, concerned food service staff, and community activists of various persuasions are trying to "fix school lunch." They are working to improve the health profile and palatability of the meals, to increase the likelihood that children will actually choose and consume the healthier offerings, to expand access to school meals, especially breakfast, and to harness the potential of school food procurement to benefit the local economy, preserve nearby farming, and as in the Kailua Charter School, conserve a culture. Indeed, some observers have characterized the ubiquitous local initiatives to improve the quality of school food as a "quiet revolution."[1] There is not space here for a comprehensive accounting of these programs. That is another book, and I hope that someone will write it. A brief overview with some concrete examples, however, can help us understand both the potential contributions and the limitations of local action in the broader scheme of school food reform. Keeping in mind that motivations for engagement are complex and mixed, let us look in turn at each of the three primary goals articulated by school food reformers: health, sustainability, and inclusion.

HEALTH

There are three aspects to making school food healthier: the quality of the reimbursable meals, the health issues of competitive food, and the receptiveness of the children.

Improving the Quality of School Meals

People have been trying to improve the quality of school food from a health standpoint for a long time. As we saw in chapter 2, a number of national organizations became alarmed at the fat content of school food and, beginning in the latter part of the 1980s, took USDA to task; their exposés led to the School Nutrition Dietary Assessment and eventually prompted Congress to require school meals to comply with the Dietary Guidelines for Americans. The School Meals Initiative for Healthy Children, or SMI for short, embodies USDA's efforts to help local school food authorities achieve this goal.

In my travels, many school food service directors and workers described to me their efforts to meet the new standards, which can be summarized as reduce fat, salt, and sugar and increase fruits and vegetables and whole grains. "In my district we don't even own any deep fat fryers. . . . We don't serve fries," a child nutrition director from northern Michigan told me. "We serve other potatoes. We serve Tater Tots, and we serve potato wedges that we bake in the oven and we serve a lot of mashed potatoes. The product we're using is very tasty; it's got one gram of fat in a half cup serving. . . . That is the way we have gone about trying to offer kids what they would like to have but do it in a healthier way through our preparation methods." The substitution of lower fat versions—reduced-fat cheese on the pizzas, baked fries instead of deep-fat-fried, baked tortilla and potato chips instead of fried versions, low-fat instead of whole milk—was the most common approach I encountered in individual school districts.

The addition of a salad bar is another response to dietary concerns that has received a lot of attention, though the School Nutrition Dietary

Assessment of 2007 (SNDA-III for short) reported that salad bars were available every day in only 13 percent of elementary schools and 18 percent of secondary schools.[2] Furthermore, not all salad bars are created equal. The idea for a "farmers' market salad bar" was pioneered by Robert Gottlieb, a professor of urban planning, when he became concerned about the quality of fruits and vegetables offered to his children and others in the schools of Santa Monica, California. He urged the procurement of fresh, local produce from local farmers markets, and after some logistical adjustments, a pilot salad bar was deemed a success when participation rose. The project was then expanded to every school in the district.[3] The same thing happened when the concept was replicated further north in Davis, where the Crunch Lunch Salad Bar became famous among advocates of fresh, local food because researchers photographed the meals that elementary school students selected, demonstrating that they did in fact choose a healthy balance. Some observers speculated that such a program could thrive only where many students came from relatively affluent homes and had already been exposed to a wide variety of fresh produce, but when assistant food service director Tracie Thomas brought the concept to Compton, California, where poverty rates are exceedingly high and the student body is overwhelmingly African American, another myth was vanquished. The students in Compton made the salad bar a huge success; offered a choice, more students chose the salad bar than the hot entree.[4]

Some school systems have undertaken fairly complete and dramatic overhauls of their cafeteria fare, involving not only healthier foods but also fresh preparation on site to make the food more palatable. The transformation at the Berkeley Unified School District (BUSD) has attracted considerable attention, in part because of the high profile Edible Schoolyard developed by Alice Waters, in part because the director of nutritional services is herself a well-known chef and author.[5] Chef Ann Cooper recently summarized her work with BUSD for an interviewer from a popular blog site: "I have 90 employees in 17 locations. We are doing about 7,000 meals a day. It is really a huge undertaking because in just two years we have gone from typical school food—all highly processed, all frozen, all prepackaged—to salad bars in every school, everything made from scratch, almost no processed foods at all, hormone and anti-biotic free, trans fat and high fructose and corn syrup free, and all the grain products are whole grain."[6] Bertrand Weber became fairly famous in school food circles for creating a similar transformation of the food in the schools of Hopkins, Minnesota. I asked

Weber if he encountered resistance from his staff and how he dealt with it, and he explained his process to me: "We had a lot of brainstorming sessions . . . within the food service staff and looked at all the statistics on childhood obesity, childhood diabetes, on cardiovascular disease . . . and the trend of basically serving fast food in school." In short, he "made a case with my staff that we needed to make a change, and solicited their ideas." He asked them to think back to what was served when they were in school.

> And that kind of opened up the conversation, "Oh, yes, I remember, we used to have hamburger and gravy and they used to do hot dish." Being from the Midwest, hot dish [casserole] is the thing. . . . Once we agreed that we would move towards scratch cooking, our goal was to have two meals per month that were scratch. The staff actually got quite excited and were reminiscing about what they used to do, and they came up with ideas and we moved to four meals per month. By the spring of that year, we were up to about 60 percent scratch. It moved rather quickly.

Weber acknowledges that the new menus required more effort from the staff, and not everyone was converted; "We had some that left—probably about 20–25 percent—because they did not want to conform. And part of that group were the nonbelievers, the 'kids won't eat it; don't even try' group."

Nancy May, who led a total transformation of the meals served in Healdsburg, California, from prefabricated heat-and-serve meal packs to extensive fresh preparation on site, reported a similar process of involving her staff. May had found the staff really demoralized when she first arrived at Healdsburg: "All they were doing was wheeling these stacks of prepackaged meals out of the freezer, wheeling them into the oven, and then wheeling them to the table, . . . and these were women who are professional food service people." Many of the women, she told me, "had been in food service for many, many years, raised their families, cooked, worked with kids. They had contributions to make, and there was really no place to make those contributions, given the existing context."

When May began the journey back to fresh preparation and cooking on site, she said, she encountered "a bit of hand on hips and the like," but that very quickly, staff rose to the occasion, because "it really spoke to who these women are. So the morale already started to pick up because they are part of something that they believe in and that's good." With the students, the "customers," May felt she had to proceed slowly. She calls the transition from the previous regime a "weaning process," in which she substituted healthier items one at a time, adding a salad to the burrito plate and then substituting a homemade burrito for the familiar frozen packaged item. "So it was a slow process to raise their awareness. And that weaning process really worked. Our participation started to grow."

Participation again. The efforts to reduce fat, salt, and sugar and increase whole grains and fruits and vegetables all take place in the context of the children's preferences and tolerances—and the need for fiscal success. When I asked Mary Kate Harrison, the child nutrition director for Hillsborough County (Tampa), Florida, about adding more fruit and vegetables to comply with the increased number of servings recommended by the latest Dietary Guidelines for Americans, she replied quickly, "It's certainly a cost issue, and it's certainly another issue. We can increase the amount that we're serving, but will the kids take them? I think there's a real balancing act here. You need to find those things the kids will eat. . . . If cost were not an issue, I think there would be lots of things that we would love to introduce to our children and . . . be able to truly use it more as a nutrition ed lab. But the cost, the reality of it is that cost is an issue, so we have to do the best we can within our cost parameters." As a recent research and trend summary released by USDA's Economic Research Service put it, "schools already face a 'trilemma' involving the meal's nutrition, student participation, and program cost. Improving the nutritional content of school meals may raise program costs, especially if it includes the necessary changes in food purchases, preparation, and marketing to prevent lower participation or higher plate waste."[7]

It's one thing to transform school food in a relatively affluent, relatively small system like Hopkins, Minnesota, or Healdsburg, California. It is another proposition altogether to change the systems in large cities like New York, Chicago, and Los Angeles, but that is precisely where change must take place if the goal is to reach a majority of children with healthier meals and healthier habits. There are nearly fifteen thousand school districts in the United States, but the hundred largest districts, less than 1 percent of the total number, account for almost 25 percent of the nation's school children. Further, these hundred largest districts serve nearly 40 percent of the nation's minority school children and have a disproportionate share of low-income students, the two demographics most severely impacted by rising rates of diabetes and other diet-related illness.[8] This is what makes the efforts now underway in the nation's largest school systems so important.

Again there is not room here for even a small portion of the relevant activities. Fortunately, the internet has changed the writer's job, from telling it all to pointing readers in the right direction. You can find out a great deal about these efforts with a few clicks of your mouse. Check out the Healthy Schools Campaign, based in Chicago but targeting all of Illinois; the campaign works on healthier school environments, including school cleaning products and construction practices as well as improved meals. Or take a look at what has been happening in LA. The board of the Los Angeles Unified School District passed an obesity prevention motion in 2003 that established standards for competitive foods and directed the superintendent to upgrade cafeteria meals with an emphasis on fresh fruits and vegetables; recently the district followed New York City's lead and appointed an executive chef to try to make the healthier meals more appealing and palatable.[9]

New York City has the country's largest school system, with 1.1 million students enrolled, and is the nation's second largest food buyer; only the Department of Defense has a larger food procurement operation. When Joel Klein became chancellor, he brought in a team of advisors to look at every aspect of the school system's notorious bureaucracy, under the rubric of the Children First Initiative. The business development consultant Stephanie Sarka ended up with the school food portfolio, and she envisioned a "top to toe" turnaround. The system was "hemorrhaging money," she recalls, due to a widespread failure of parents to return applications for free and reduced price meals, and meal quality and appeal fell far short of the ideal. Sarka envisioned and initiated a plan to "make school food cool" by the use of modern marketing techniques: a logo and a tag line ("Feed Your Mind"), colorful signs and attractive displays, an overhaul of the management and accountability structure, a new, catchier name for the Office of School Food and Nutrition Services (SchoolFood)—and better food. A food service director, David Berkowitz, was brought in from the private sector, and an executive chef, Jorge Collazo, was hired to revamp menus.

Meanwhile, the nutrition advocate Toni Liquori undertook a thorough review of nutrient standards and other issues related to the supply of foods to the New York City system. Her recommendations were incorporated into a change agenda that also included a partnership, called "School Food Plus," between nonprofit organizations and SchoolFood and a focus on integrating menus with nutrition education. The Cookshop program that she had pioneered in an earlier collaboration between a New York City nonprofit and selected schools became the basis both for teaching children about food and for increasing the use of whole unprocessed foods in the school menu. New recipes were developed to incorporate ten plant foods that can be grown in the region, and these became the basis for enhanced menus and classroom lessons in a set of schools, designated School Food Plus schools. Only some of the city's schools still had full cooking kitchens, and the School Food Plus project began in fifteen schools and was gradually expanded to sixty-some, with another thirty or so receiving the special recipes on a satellite basis. At the same time, with the leadership of Chef Jorge and his "regional chefs," healthier items and menus began to appear throughout the system.

The progress of school food reform in New York is both a beacon and a cautionary tale. The system uses no artificial colors or flavorings, no trans fats, and fewer and fewer products containing high-fructose corn syrup. There is clearly more whole and fresh food in the system, and the use of the new recipes exceeded expectations. New York Harvest for New York Kids and other farm to cafeteria proponents have managed to get New York apples and carrots into the schools on a regular basis, as well as pears and peaches when they are available, and a yogurt is produced by an upstate dairy without high-fructose corn syrup to meet the specifications of Chef Jorge. It is progress, but it is not transformation. For one thing, evaluations report that the children often do not eat the new healthier recipe items.[10] And then there are questions of scale, which in New York City are mind-boggling. The Cookshop classroom lessons are currently reaching about seven thousand children in three hundred classrooms. While this is substantial growth over previous levels, there must be in the vicinity of two hundred thousand children in pre-K–2, the grades targeted by Cookshop. Even if the program reaches its current goal of ten thousand students, it will be reaching only about 5 percent of those in the target grades.

The additional barriers posed by equipment, facilities, and staff skills have proven especially formidable. When I asked David Berkowitz about the prospects for a system-wide return to "scratch" cooking, he was blunt: "That's not going to happen." He went on to explain that fire safety regulations now required a kind of ventilation for stoves, called an Ansel system, that would necessitate extensive remodeling, not only of kitchens but of entire schools, and that he did not see the resources for such equipment installation in the foreseeable future. "I grew up with scratch cooking," he said; "I think it is fabulous. I wish we could do it. It's not realistic." Nevertheless, the system is gradually retraining its workers to build the culinary skills necessary to produce the new menus, and there is clearly a spirit of innovation and hope. "At the end of the day," said Ted Spitzer, whose consulting firm was hired to assess the School Food Plus effort, "the most important thing is to change attitudes, to make them believe that change is possible," and he was enthusiastic about the amount of attitude change that had taken place in New York.[11]

The New York story goes beyond attitude change, however, in the growing recognition that large urban school systems have enormous market power. New York has not only succeeded in getting products reformulated in a healthy direction for use in its own schools; in the process it has changed the food products available to other school systems as well. And if a single school system buys enough yogurt to command a product reformulation, think what a coalition of large urban systems could accomplish.

With that market power in mind and with support from the W.K. Kellogg Foundation, Toni Liquori has recently organized just such a coalition designed to help large urban systems use their buying power to enhance both the healthfulness of the products they procure and their impact on environmental sustainability. Working with experts from Michigan State University, School Food FOCUS (an acronym for Food Options for Children in Urban Schools) is enabling large urban systems to identify sustainable sources of healthy food within their regions and to share and promote practices that work.[12]

Controlling Competitive Foods

The effort to upgrade the healthfulness of the foods offered at school has not been confined to the reimbursable meal. All over the country, individual schools, districts, and in some cases states have begun to set limits on what can be offered for sale in the various venues that market "competitive foods." Los Angeles made news in 2002 by banning the sale of sodas, and many other school systems have since considered similar bans on sweetened beverages and "junk foods." As Karen Peterson and Mary K. Fox have reported, "between 2003 and 2005, more than 200 bills to limit the availability of competitive foods and/or to establish nutrition standards for foods sold on school campuses were introduced in state legislatures." The quantity of activity may overstate the trend, however, only 13 percent of them passed. "Major obstacles," the researchers report, "include resistance to state governance of issues that many see as being the purview of local school districts and parents, and with regard to competitive foods, potential negative impacts on a needed source of revenue."[13] By the time Congress undertook the 2004 Child Nutrition reauthorization process, competitive foods had become a fairly high-profile issue. The existence of "pouring rights" contracts that give one particular beverage company exclusive rights to sell drinks on a campus had made news in many communities and had even influenced school board elections in some. Many groups were urging Congress to do something about competitive foods, not only health activists, but also advocates of commercial-free education who argued that schools should be safe havens, places free from marketing to children.[14] What Congress actually did, which was to add a "wellness policy mandate" to the legislation, represented a last-minute compromise between nutrition advocates who wanted the law to give the secretary of agriculture the authority to regulate competitive foods sold in schools no matter when or where they were sold and lobbyists for the food industry who opposed such authority.[15] The legislation took a permissive approach: it required schools participating in the National School Lunch Program or the School Breakfast Program to establish policies governing all foods offered to children at school as well as physical education and opportunities for exercise, but it did not specify the content of these policies, respecting the tradition of local control of the schools.

What followed was a nationwide flurry of activity as wellness committees were formed, met, and hammered out recommendations and policies, national organizations both private and public tried to provide guidance and assistance, and the snack food industry set to work adjusting its product formulations—and especially its portion sizes—to existing and anticipated local standards. One-hundred-calorie servings of cookies and salty snacks became common, and schools began replacing soda with juice, water, and milk in vending machines. Here again, baked chips began to replace fried chips, and calorie counts and fat content declined.

In some states, legislatures got into the act, promulgating state minimum standards.[16] As you can imagine, with billions of dollars in snack purchases at stake these efforts were not—are not—without conflict. In California the soft drink industry succeeded in limiting the first statewide soda ban to elementary and middle schools. In Connecticut, the House debated for eight hours over a bill to eliminate sodas and junk food snacks from the state's schools, while some members displayed bottles of Coca-Cola on their desks. Michele Simon reports that more than $200,000 was spent, primarily by the soft drink industry, to lobby against the bill. It passed, only to be vetoed by the governor.[17] A substitute compromise bill, which the governor did sign, provides an extra per-meal reimbursement for meals in districts that decide to adopt the new state standards, a voluntary-with-inducements approach that food service organizations in other states have suggested as a model. In New York State, a bill specifying minimum standards for various categories of snack foods and beverages was supported by the American Cancer Society and the New York State Academy of Family Physicians and adamantly opposed not only by beverage and snack food industry groups but by the New York State School Boards Association and the New York School Nutrition Association.[18]

The New York bill was held in committee, and New York has yet to establish state standards, but quite a few other states have, and evidence is mounting that snack machines and a la carte lines stocked with such healthier—or at least less unhealthy—options as air-popped corn and whole-grain pretzels can generate almost as much money, and in some cases more, than those stocked with pastries and candy bars. As the restaurateur-turned-food-service-director Bertrand Weber explained to an interviewer from *Restaurants and Institutions,* "Sales dropped at first, but by the third week, they returned. All the healthful items—waters, 100% fruit juices, baked chips, trail mix, cookies, pretzels, beef jerky, carrot sticks, yogurt and smoothies—are available, plus we're soft-drink free."[19] I heard similar reports from other food service personnel. "Students complained at first, but they got over it" was the common assessment.

The wellness policy mandate directed school districts to consider all foods offered to children within the schools, with the result that wellness polices often addressed foods sold at school sporting events and bake sales and other fundraisers, the use of food items as rewards in classrooms, and with much publicity and controversy, the provision of foods by parents for in-class birthday parties and other celebrations. The resulting "cupcake wars" touched a nerve, with some parents arguing that in the face of mounting obesity and diabetes, stringent restrictions were needed and others calling such limits overzealous. "I've heard these parents referred to as 'food police' and even 'nutrition Nazis,'" declares Dr. Susan Rubin, the founder of Better School Food, in the documentary film *Two Angry Moms,* which records Rubin's campaign to improve the food in a Westchester County, New York, school district. "People think we're looking to take away the cupcakes at the birthday parties. That always comes up." There is a lovely scene in the movie of Rubin eating a cupcake with obvious pleasure and commenting, "If you're going to eat a cupcake, I'd rather see these. It is sugar and butter; there is no high-fructose corn syrup and no hydrogenated oil. It's not about the cupcakes." What it is about, for Rubin and the wellness committees with which she works, is getting rid of the trans fats, the poor quality oils, the high-fructose corn syrup, and the highly refined carbohydrates; increasing fresh fruit and vegetables, especially produce from local farms; serving more whole grains and beans; offering more vegetarian options; giving students more time for lunch; and paying attention to portion size in both the full meal and the snacks.[20] Although the wellness policy mandate grew directly out of the controversy over competitive foods, it ended up directing the attention of concerned parents and food system activists to the reimbursable meal as well. Historians looking back at the "school food revolution" of this era are likely to point to the wellness policy mandate as a taproot for change.

The mandate and its aftermath have revealed one of those fault lines that often divide our society, deep differences in the understanding of troubling social conditions that result in profoundly different recipes for their solution. One segment of the food service community sees the remedy for energy-dense diets, for "too much fat and salt," in the genius of the American food-processing industry. In this vision, school food service will use its enormous market power to induce industry to reformulate products and adjust portion sizes to reduce the proportion of offending ingredients: leaner quesadillas and reduced-fat corn dogs, complete with Child Nutrition labels specifying exactly what portions of the meal plan they supply. An alternative diagnosis, with an alternative vision is also out there, competing for attention and endorsement. The taro patch described at the beginning of this chapter is but one example of a whole host of efforts to help children develop healthy preferences by rebuilding their connection with the sources of their food. The goal is appreciation of healthy food and real pleasure in its consumption. As Marion Kalb, the director of the national Farm to School Program of the Community Food Security Coalition, put it, "I'm kind of hoping that we stick with school food long enough to get away from what shouldn't be there to what should be there, because I think there's a lot of emphasis on 'let's not have this stuff in the school' and not nearly enough on what healthy things kids will eat. So that's my long term, that we change that perspective from the no's to the yes."

Changing the Children

Getting from the no's to the yes, many food service professionals argue, will require more than just offering better food. "We couldn't just put out better food and expect the children are going to choose to eat it," Doug Davis, child nutrition director for the Burlington, Vermont, schools, told me. "We need to . . . get into the classroom, show kids that food doesn't come from the grocery store." With better funding, he said, the schools could offer more fresh fruits and vegetables, "but just putting them out there isn't going to put them into the belly of the child. We have. . . . to have kids taste things and try things and prepare things and touch things and serve things, because then they are selling it to their own peers and that's where the change has to come from, not just school food service putting out a better product." Nutrition education was always intended to be a part of the SMI, and there are lively posters, guides, and other materials available from USDA, but some communities have undertaken strategies that go well beyond what is usually signified by the term "nutrition education"; they have taken on the daunting task of transforming children's food preferences and even their entire relationship to food. Cooking with Kids (CWK) one such project in Santa Fe, New Mexico, puts it this way: "Many of us were fortunate to grow up with parents and grandparents, neighbors and friends who cooked and gardened, sharing with us the value and pleasure of food. Growing, cooking, and eating fresh foods became a cherished part of our lives. Today, most children do not have this experience. We believe that hands-on experience with fresh, healthy foods is an important part of learning how to take care of yourself. Children embrace these experiences instinctively, with enthusiasm and willingness in every class we teach."[21]

In the food education classroom in the Sweeney Elementary School in Santa Fe, I observed and helped out a bit while Anna Ferrier, a CWK food educator, taught fourth graders to make Pizza Margherita on a hot plate. She began with a background lesson involving the origins of pizza in general and Pizza Margherita in particular and the nature, both nutritional and biological of the major components of the dish: wheat, basil, tomatoes, and mozzarella cheese. She showed the students that the color scheme matched the Italian flag, which one student described as "like the Mexican flag without the bird." Then she divided the students into three work teams, each supervised by an adult. One team made dough, another prepared the toppings, while my team made a huge salad of lettuce, purple cabbage, and grated carrots with dressing. In brief waiting periods while the dough was setting and later when the pizza was cooking, students completed the lessons in their "food journals," structured workbooks developed by the CWK staff to contribute to the achievement of specified state standards. When the pizzas were done, children were asked to put their food journals under their seats to prevent them from acquiring food stains, and the adults served the children "like a restaurant." Nearly everyone ate what we produced, and with obvious enjoyment.

Later in the week, the students would encounter the same menu in the school cafeteria. Repetition of the CWK menus in the school meal is an essential element of the program for two reasons. First, for many children, trying a new food is a scary proposition; seeing the same food in the cafeteria soon after they have prepared it themselves in class gives them an opportunity to reinforce their own bravery and adventuresome eating. It harnesses the excitement of participation in preparation to build a student's repertoire. Research on food neophobia, the fear of eating something new, makes clear that repeated exposure is the key.[22] And by offering the CWK menus, the school food service has expanded its own repertoire and improved the health profile and palatability of food in the Santa Fe public schools. Because the CWK staff provides training as needed to cafeteria staff, the project helps to build skills as well, and over the years since its inception in 1996, the CWK program has been able to provide some tools—professional knives for each kitchen with appropriate knife cases, for example—to enhance the overall capability of the system to deal with fresh foods. Finally, in a multicultural community, the CWK menus enhance the cultural responsiveness and inclusiveness of the cafeteria fare; the lessons for grades 4–6 include a North African Tajine and a Mediterranean Vegetable Paella as well as Tamales with Red Chile Sauce.

The most complete integration of course-based food preparation and school food that I've seen is the food lab at Pacific Elementary School in Davenport, California. Davenport is a tiny town ("Elevation, 80, Population, 200" says the sign on Highway 1 along the coast south of San Francisco), and Pacific Elementary has about a hundred students in five grades. At Pacific, the fifth graders prepare the school lunch. The fifth graders are divided into five teams of four, one team for each weekday. Under the supervision of Stephanie Raugust, a restaurateur, educator, and lunch lady extraordinaire, each student team plans, prepares, and serves the food on its day. The day that I visited, the menu was New

England clam chowder, salad, rolls, and oatmeal cookies. The process began when a student arrived with the day's lunch count from the principal's office. The crew of fifth graders took the recipe for chowder, noted the number of servings that it would afford, and carried out a bit of arithmetic to see how many multiples of the recipe they would need. They were old hands at salad, and already knew about how much to prepare, but the oatmeal cookies also needed the math factor. They worked with remarkable speed and cheer in the small kitchen, cutting up potatoes and onions, tearing lettuce, scraping carrots, slicing radishes, some of which came from the school garden, and measuring and mixing the cookie ingredients. It was spring when I visited, and they had been at this since September, so they were at ease, but the pace was brisk. About twenty minutes before lunch was scheduled, a team of fourth graders descended upon the school's lunchroom, housed in a sunny enclosed porch, to set the tables: checkered tablecloths, real knives and forks (not plastic), real plates (not paper), and a small bouquet of flowers, again from the school garden, graced each table. When the rest of the children arrived, most teachers ate with students, and all tables had at least one adult. While they ate, the multitalented Ms. Raugust played a recording of one of the concertos from Vivaldi's Four Seasons on the sound system and explained a bit about the composer and the instruments played in the piece. A daily dose of music education enables the school to pay Ms. Raugust, a certified music educator, partly from instructional funds. Given the amount of math she oversaw and the running commentary about nutrition, food values, and the properties of various ingredients she had provided during the preparation phase, music educator does not quite capture her academic contribution.

John Dewey, in whose University of Chicago Laboratory School the children cooked and served lunch at least once a week, would have loved it. And the theory underlying "Food Lab" as the course is called, and "Life Lab," the garden-based curriculum developed at the University of California at Santa Cruz and in use in school gardens throughout the state, is very compatible with the ideas of the founder of pragmatism. Dewey understood that learning was facilitated when children were engaged in real tasks with real consequences. In *School and Society*, which has never been out of print since its publication in 1899, he wrote of the "difference that appears when occupations are made the articulating centers of school life . . . a difference in motive, of spirit and atmosphere. As one enters a busy kitchen in which a group of children are actively engaged in the preparation of food, the psychological difference, the change from more or less passive and inert recipiency and restraint to one of buoyant outgoing energy, is so obvious as fairly to strike one in the face."[23] Amen. But Dewey did not include cooking just to mobilize the energies of his pupils. As Louis Menand has written, "Dewey incorporated into the practical business of making lunch: arithmetic (weighing and measuring ingredients, with instruments the children made themselves), chemistry and physics (observing the process of combustion), biology (diet and digestion), geography (exploring the natural environments of the plants and animals) and so on. Cooking became the basis for most of the science taught in the school." Menand calls it "one of Dewey's curricular obsessions."[24]

If Dewey provides an impressive pedigree for a food-based pedagogy, however, he couldn't solve the practical problems faced by today's schools. Even with the implied support of the nation's most famous educator, don't expect to find a Cooking With Kids clone or a replication of the Pacific Elementary approach in every school. Just finding a period of several hours when a class of children can work together to prepare, serve, and consume a meal is difficult. The Santa Fe food educator Anna Ferrier told me that CWK had experimented with shorter periods but found it needed a full two hours to complete the lessons. That in itself makes such an approach incompatible with most secondary schools, where students change classes at forty-five or fifty minute intervals. And even in elementary schools where children are together for the entire day, devoting the time to the development of skills that do not lend themselves directly to standardized testing is a risk that many principals are unwilling to take. Ultimately, as CWK's founder, Lynn Walters, notes, our curricula are a reflection of what we value as a society.

Programs that involve actual meal preparation are not the only effort to develop children's willingness to try new fruits and vegetables. In Santa Fe, where CWK works closely with a farm to school program operated under the auspices of an organization called Farm to Table, Le Adams told me about the menu of farm visits, farmers in the classroom, and farmers' market tours, and an allied school gardening project, through which they try to nurture the connections between children and the sources of their food. Because I first learned about farm to school (or F2S) in the context of efforts to create new and expanded markets for small and mid-sized farmers, I didn't realize the extent to which F2S programs are also grounded in theories about how children learn and designed to improve children's health by expanding their appreciation for fruit and vegetables. As Jack Kloppenburg and Neva Hassanein have written, F2S "frequently involves the transformation of pedagogical practice as a necessary precursor to transforming lunch."[25] I'll return to the agriculture side of the F2S equation in a bit, but in many communities, the dominant motivation is the children's diet. "It is a myth that children won't eat healthy food," declares Mollie Nicholie, the coordinator of Growing Minds, the F2S part of the Appalachian Sustainable Agriculture Program. "If they have a connection to it—saw it growing on a farm, met the farmer who grew it, grew it themselves, or helped prepare it—they will eat it."[26]

Even skeptics have been convinced by such programs. The California anti-hunger advocate Ken Hecht told me that when the former superintendent of public instruction first proposed a garden in every school, "I was as skeptical and nasty about it as I could have been, and I was totally wrong. It's terrific. In many schools, the garden did introduce kids to vegetables and fruit and growing and dirt and get them to eat all kinds of things and get them to think about all kinds of things that never would have happened otherwise. No one knows how to do nutrition education, but this is one way that you get some of it done."

Emily Jackson, the founder of Growing Minds, sees school gardens not only as dynamic and engaging learning environments, but also as important entry points for F2S. "You hear over and over that children won't eat these things. . . . What I see pretty much across the board is, if they grow it, they eat it. And that translates to raw beets in the garden. You pull a beet, I don't know if it's all the red that they turn and that's why they like it, but they pretty much eat every single thing. It's not a problem to get them to taste or try." And once that willingness is nurtured in a school garden, it extends to new products brought to school by the farm to cafeteria part of farm to school—the purchase of locally grown foods by school food service. That procurement piece is essential if farm to school programs are to achieve their other major goal, expanding the market for local farm products, and thus helping to preserve farms and farming. This is the centerpiece of a cluster of goals and activities that are often labeled "sustainability."

SUSTAINABILITY

From an economic standpoint, the logic of "buy local" is easy to grasp. Buying directly from local farmers helps them to find stable markets, thus enabling them to remain in business, and keeps the money spent circulating in the local economy. In addition, as Marilyn Briggs, the former director of Nutrition Services for the California Department of Public Instruction has pointed out, "Healthy farms provide jobs, pay taxes, and keep working agricultural land from going to development," thus providing flood control and diversified wildlife habitat.[27] Scholars writing from a planning perspective have pointed out that F2S is important not just to the current viability of farming, but also to its future. "When students visit a farm or when local farmers, school staff, and PTA members collaborate to launch a farm-to-school program, a broader-based constituency can be established for understanding the importance of local and regional farming within the region as a whole."[28] The farm to cafeteria concept also embraces college and university dining services and purchases for hospital or other employee cafeterias, and is linked to farm to institution programs that promote local purchase for correctional facilities and rehabilitation centers. According to Marion Kalb, K–12 schools pose the greatest challenge for such efforts: "Budgets are the tightest, requirements are the tightest. Food service directors are just swamped." Figures published by the Center for Food Justice, which keeps track of F2S projects, indicate that there are now more than 2,000 F2S programs in 40 states; more than 8,700 K–12 schools in 2,035 districts are involved. That is less than 15 percent of the school districts in the United States, but it is more than five times the number that were participating when I began studying school food five years ago.[29]

Farm to school is such an appealing idea that it may be surprising that these numbers are not even higher, but when you take a closer look, the obstacles are numerous and daunting. In the first place, there may not really be any local agriculture. "I'm from a farm background," the child nutrition director from Grayling, Michigan, told me. "My brothers and my dad are farmers, . . . and so I'm very supportive of the concept. I don't see it working very well where I live and operate because we don't have a lot of production agriculture. The closest would be Trevor City, an hour away, where they produce cherries and other kinds of fruits. We have very little industry and agriculture in our county, unless you count tree farming. So for the location I'm in, its going to be tough." Then there is the growing season issue. In most of the country, the peak growing season does not coincide with the school year. In fact, the school year, with its extended summer vacation, was designed around the labor needs of the agricultural communities of the Northeast where free public education got its start; sociology textbooks routinely use this calendar as an example of "cultural lag." Whatever its antecedents, it means that most schools are not in session just when most fresh fruits and vegetables are available from local sources. "Our growing season is about twenty minutes long, maybe half an hour," the Burlington, Vermont, school food service director Doug Davis quipped; nevertheless he buys local whenever he can, building into his procurement contracts a preference for produce to be delivered within twenty-four hours after it is picked.

Once the basic supply issues are taken into account, the biggest challenge is probably price. Most school food service operations are not in a position to pay premium prices for local products. Fortunately, this is often less a problem than consumers who have shopped at high-end and boutique farmers markets may imagine. By eliminating the distributor or produce broker from the process and reducing the total transportation costs, farms can often afford to supply schools at competitive prices. "We often hear that local can be more expensive to procure," declared Bill Jordan, then a special assistant to the New York State commissioner of agriculture, "yet we have consistent experience that food service directors can spend the same amount in most product categories, and the farm to school effort has not led to higher costs; rather, more of the same food dollar spent gets retained by the farmer when the product is coming from more local sources. Increasing transportation costs," he pointed out, "have only strengthened this argument."

There is another category of costs, however, calculated in time rather than dollars and sometimes referred to as "transaction costs." Food service directors do not have the time to make dozens of calls looking for ripe produce. They need to be able to take care of a week's or a month's ordering with a single fax or phone call or online order form. "Foragers" who find farmers with ripe produce and connect them to schools have become a staple of the farm to school movement; they are often paid by nonprofit groups, with the hope that once relationships become institutionalized, the need for their intermediary services will decline. Le Adams in New Mexico was filling that role for some schools in Albuquerque and a charter school in Santa Fe, not only finding the fruits but picking them up and delivering them, along with information about their history and nutritional value and suggestions and instructions for various in-class projects. Her enthusiasm and dedication were infectious, but I wondered if a program that depends on that sort of extraordinary commitment is sustainable over time. A more typical forager works with a group of schools and tries to, in essence, aggregate produce much as a broker would. Perhaps it is not surprising that some farm to cafeteria programs have moved from such direct marketing to specifying local preference in their contracts with distributors.

When you source your food through a distributor, you basically place your order and expect it to arrive at the time and place agreed upon; that is precisely the service for which you are paying. As a Minnesota study of farm to school opportunities and barriers explained, "Such distributors offer a very standardized, streamlined procurement environment that is suited to the risk-averse and cost-conscious environment of most school districts."[30] Reliability is a major concern that surfaces in nearly every study of food service directors' concerns about farm to cafeteria. It was the single most frequently identified concern in a 2004 survey of New York State food service directors.[31] The early days of farm to cafeteria were full of stories of arrangements flummoxed when a particular farm or area encountered an untimely storm or an invasive pest. CWK co-director Jane Stacey said that the apple tasting scheduled for the week after my visit to Santa Fe had run into just such an instance of nature's caprice. "This next week we are doing apple tastings in 238 classrooms. Lynn had made all the arrangements for all these local apples, but then the hail storm came and now what about that? And who brings it and how do we get it and where does it go and what if they don't come and then you have to get the boxes back to them! It is extremely difficult to put things into systems." It would be inconvenient, to say the least, to reschedule a session for 238 classes, but it could probably be done. You cannot, however, reschedule lunch for another day. No wonder the school food environment is risk averse.

The administrative time of food service directors engaged in procurement is not the only issue, of course. If the director procures fresh food from local farms, someone will have to prepare it. Emily Jackson at Growing Minds encountered considerable resistance from frontline cafeteria workers. She explained that in many rural counties, "it's kind of a political thing to get working in a school," and school boards and principals get involved in hiring cafeteria workers. The food service director may have little or no say in the matter, and the folks that are hired are not necessarily skilled in cooking. "And so the child nutrition directors may be all for this, but their staffs aren't; it goes back to they don't cook fresh things at home so doing it at work wouldn't be a natural extension. They are just part of the whole culture of people out there, relying on superprocessed food. And why would they be any different than anybody else?" Jackson's solution was to write a grant proposal and raise money to take food service directors and cafeteria staff out to meet the farmers and see what was being grown. "We took all the staff in three counties out to farms, spent the morning out there talking to these different farmers about what it's like to be a farmer. . . . And then we brought them together for a lunch of locally grown food in a little Farm to School Cafeteria. And we acknowledged them and applauded them and made them feel they are a part of something bigger." The cafeteria managers are responsible for placing their orders, she explained, "and we thought that by having them meet the farmer and seeing the things they offer, when they sat down to order their food, they are going to see potatoes . . . and then the farmer, his face, and maybe his family, because we met the families and saw where they lived." Apparently, the strategy worked. "One of our local farmers, usually his main item was lettuce, and at first they grumbled about finding spiders in it or something. And now he had a problem with one of his greenhouses and all of his lettuce got fried and so he didn't have the lettuce, and now they're asking 'Where's Delain's lettuce?'"

The learning curve in farm to cafeteria has begun to move beyond a mindset that says, "here is our menu, what can we procure locally at a competitive price?" to one that says "tell me what you can grow locally, and we'll try to figure out how can we incorporate these foods into our menu." As Janet Brown has put it in the "Procurement" section of *Rethinking School Lunch*, "food service directors need to develop menus that accommodate what grows seasonally in a given region, and farmers need to grow a diversity of crops to serve more of the daily needs of the school food service."[32] The biggest accommodation, however, that farmers can make to the realities of school food is probably undertaking some of the labor intensive processing for which many schools have neither the skills nor the equipment. The leading example of such "further processing," as it is often called, is the New North Florida Coop, which collects collard greens, yams, and other foods from associated members, aggregates them into the quantities needed, washes and chops the collard greens, and delivers the produce to schools. This model has begun to be emulated around the country. Marion Kalb sees it as a key to the future of the movement: "I think that a lot of the future success of farm to school could rest with the ability of farmers to organize on the supply side, particularly doing minimal processing." Broccoli florets, instead of broccoli stalks, for example: "being able to kind of meet the schools where they are, I think, on the farm side, would add a lot to the sustainability." Looking on the school side, she stressed the need for "kitchens, and having equipment and those kinds of things."

Farm to school is not without its critics. Probably the most trenchant critique of what has been accomplished comes from one of the chief

proponents of the movement, Kate Adamick, who served as the first
director of New York City's School Food Plus collaboration. Adamick
has helped schools in several parts of the nation to add more locally
grown fresh foods to their menus. Asked at a conference recently if
there was any truth to the rumor that she had grown "weary" of farm
to school, she replied that "far too many schools are saying 'We've fixed
the school lunch program, we've got farm to school,' and when you dig
deeper, you find they have started getting their apples locally. You have
to fix the center of the plate," she declared. "If you have just replaced a
side with a local side, it's nice, but it doesn't solve the problem."

In addition, long-term anti-hunger activists sometimes express frustration with what they see as remedies more likely to have an impact
in wealthier communities. "I don't think there is anything wrong with
trying to get stuff that's local," the New York City hunger activist Kathy
Goldman told me. "It's the Alice Waters approach. It's nice. I don't object
to that. Really, who would object to that? Having good food, local food
or whatever else? . . . It's just so far from what the reality is for most
families and most kids, who are not high-income. To me, it's over there,"
she said, pointing off to the side. "There's got to be something between
McDonald's and that, and I would like to focus more on what goes in
between." In a city in which "literally hundreds of thousands of people
do not have access" to, do not live within walking distance of a real
supermarket, she continued, the emphasis on local procurement struck
her as marginal. "What happens in the South Bronx? What happens to
these places that you still can't buy any of that stuff. But you're telling me that the people in Washington Heights are going to start eating
locally? If it's cheaper [to buy] Washington State apples, they are going
to buy Washington State apples. It's money."

It's money in another sense as well. As Patricia Allen and Julie Guthman have pointed out, farm to school programs appear more likely
to be undertaken and sustained in affluent communities and are often
supported in part by grants from private foundations. Thus they may
increase rather than decrease the disparities between affluent and
impoverished school systems. Allen and Guthman argue that "rather
than concede the inevitable disparities of devolution, public funding and
state support should be used to effect improvement across the board for
all children, not just those who happen to be in 'progressive' or affluent schools."[33] Farm to school advocates replied that they were in fact
working for public support that would permit extending the benefits
more widely.[34] Pilot programs have been important in the history of

school food, providing innovators and advocates with the information they need to convince legislators to provide the "improvement across the board for all children" that Allen and Guthman urge. Meanwhile, it appears to me, the most urgent tasks for those who want to reduce disparities and promote the well-being of the nation's poorest children are the challenges of access and inclusion: making sure that quality programs are available to all children and that barriers of bureaucracy and stigma do not prevent their participation.

INCLUSION

As we saw in chapter 6, inclusion of low-income children in school food programs has two components: institutional participation and individual (family) participation. If the school does not offer the program, of course, no one can participate. But even when the program is available, as lunch is in more than 90 percent of public schools, and breakfast in nearly 85 percent of those serving lunch, if the application is not submitted or the certification process breaks down or the child is deterred by stigma or other social pressures or the price is too high or the lines are too long or the bus arrives late, the meal does not find its intended target. Again, in the Any Town food service director's words, "if they don't eat it, it doesn't do them any good," and although he was primarily talking about the need to offer foods with which children are familiar, his dictum applies equally well to the need to make sure that meals are truly accessible, socially and emotionally as well as physically and financially, to the children who need them.

Expanding Access

The first step is ensuring "institutional participation," and that activity, in recent years, has been focused almost exclusively on breakfast. In the early days of breakfast expansion, groups of parents organized to ask the local school food authority to start the program in their schools and devised a wide array of tactics to pressure them until they agreed. Once the "low-hanging fruit" was picked, however, activists turned to state mandates. In 2003, for example, a coalition of New Jersey groups succeeded in convincing the state legislature to mandate the provision of the School Breakfast Program in all schools where at least 20 percent of the students are eligible for free or reduced price meals. The law required implementation in elementary schools by the 2004–2005

school year and in secondary schools in 2005–2006. The results of the
state mandate were dramatic: participation soared by more than 39
percent, from 82,220 in 2003–2004 to 114,387 in 2004–2005.

A case study from New England can shed some light on just what
may be involved in winning a mandate, however. In Rhode Island, a
dedicated band of activists, organized as the Campaign to End Childhood Poverty in Rhode Island and based at the George Wiley Center in
Pawtucket, has worked for years to bring breakfasts without stigma to
Rhode Island children. In the 1980s, when research demonstrated the
positive impact of school breakfast on health, behavior, and academic
performance, a few Rhode Island communities initiated the program,
but in many, the school committees (as school boards are generally called
throughout New England) refused to do so. Like their counterparts elsewhere, they worried about bus schedules and labor costs, but as Henry
Shelton, the founder of the Wiley Center, told me, "I found over the years
in Rhode Island, the main arguments were philosophical, not financial."
School committee members thought that offering breakfast would break
up the family or that they had to set limits to what the schools would do.
"What's next?" they asked. "You want me to order beds?"

Thinking back to how the fight for breakfast began in Pawtucket,
where the Wiley Center is located, Shelton recalled, "we picked the
school with the highest number of children eligible for free and reduced
price," a school where the school nurse was enthusiastically in favor of
the program. The Campaign bought muffins and juice and handed them
through the fence to the nurse, who offered them to the children "so it
wasn't like total strangers feeding children. . . . And we got the press
to come, and it was a wonderful experience. The kids were fed, we ran
out of food." The school committee was convinced to start the federal
program on a pilot basis at that school and one other. "We've used the
pilot approach quite a bit over the years," Shelton explained. "Foot in
the door. Evaluate. It's working."

Expansion to other schools, however, did not come easily, particularly in Pawtucket. As the activist Maggi Burns-Rogers recalls, "we
kept going to the school committee and saying, 'You've got these two
programs at these two schools and there should be equity and if you
see that they are working there . . . , you should implement it in other
schools." Finally, the Campaign turned to the General Assembly and
secured a mandate that schools with 40 percent or more of students
eligible for free or reduced price meals had to offer the breakfast program. The local Pawtucket activists continued to hammer away at their

school committee, trying to expand the program to additional schools by showing up at meeting after meeting. And in the end, Burns-Rogers recalled, "it was funny, because every time we would go to the school committee and ask them to do this, . . . people that weren't too closely involved would say, 'What, are you going back to them again? You know they are going to say no.' And we would explain, 'We have to ask them so that they say no so that when we go back to the state, we can show how horrifically unreasonable they are.' If you have a school at 39 percent and the state says 40 percent and they won't voluntarily put it in that school, that gives us ammunition when we go back to the state to say, 'You must mandate it at the state because they will not do it.'"

This strategy eventually worked; the General Assembly lowered the mandate threshold to 20 percent, though the chair of the Assembly Finance Committee complained to Henry Shelton, "Well, first it was 40 percent, and now you want 20, and eventually, you're going to want everybody to have breakfast." Indeed, that was their goal, and in 2000, they succeeded in getting a law that breakfast be made available in every public school in the state—as Burns-Rogers put it, "what they feared all along. Hooray for us!" The Rhode Island school breakfast access story does not end with the statewide mandate, however. "As soon as we had the state mandate, . . . our next goal was immediately universal [free] breakfast," Burns-Rogers recalled. "We made the argument that some kids don't come into the breakfast program because it's perceived as being for the poor kids." She pointed out the contrast with the way adults treat themselves: "I've been to many meetings with school administrators or any kind of workshops; they always have coffee and donuts and nobody says, 'Show me your tax statement or your last paystub.' You just come in and you eat. You don't say: 'One bagel,' or 'You've already had your coffee.'"

The fight for universal programs basically repeated the whole cycle. The activists fought for a pilot. The school committee resisted, until one night there were suddenly enough votes to pass a pilot project. Opponents were taken aback and began talk of ending the pilot, but, as Beverly Laprade, who was simultaneously a school food service worker, a parent of two students in the Pawtucket public schools, and a school committee member pointed out, they really couldn't end the pilot "because it was such a complete success. The numbers went through the roof; the food contractor is making money hand over fist. Just like we predicted, teachers are happy, children are going into class ready to learn; behavior problems are down, and it's just like part of the norm now to walk into school and get breakfast."

In a repeat of the earlier process, breakfast advocates argued that since the universal pilot was successful, it should be expanded to other schools in the district. Meanwhile, they used the successful program in one district to argue for pilots in others and finally succeeded in securing the introduction of legislation mandating universal free breakfast in all schools with 40 percent or more free and reduced price eligibility. Although the prospects do not look bright in the face of the current state budget crisis, the group can take a great deal of pride in its accomplishments. When the Campaign to Eliminate Childhood Poverty in Rhode Island began its school breakfast work, the state ranked fiftieth on the Food Research and Action Center School Breakfast Scorecard, or, as the Wiley Center newsletter put it, "dead last." By 2007, it had risen to twenty-second, and participation had tripled; fourteen thousand more low-income Rhode Island children were eating school breakfast on a an average day.[35] For Rhode Island school food activists, however, such success does not signal a time to rest on their laurels. The Campaign to Eliminate Childhood Poverty has already set its sights on the next target: "And as we speak," Maggi Burns-Rogers told me, "our next goal is universal free lunch."

State mandates are clearly effective, but they are not always feasible. Advocates at the Vermont Campaign to End Childhood Hunger found a subtler approach that had a similar outcome. Dorigen Keeney recounted to me the steps that led to the passage of Vermont's Act 22. "When I took the job, the Campaign had been working on increasing access to school breakfast for ten years, so when I came on, there were seventy schools left in the state without breakfast, and they said to me, 'You are hired to do this, to increase access to school meals, but we don't think you're going to get many of the schools. We've been working on them and working on them and could never get them.'" She went on to explain some of the reality. "Working with schools as an advocate, you don't have a lot of authority. You cajole. You nag. You provide information. You think just general harassment will finally get them."

Eventually, the Vermont Campaign hit upon an idea to take its school breakfast expansion beyond nagging and cajoling: adjusting existing legislation. A law passed in 1972 provided that every public school in the state should have a school lunch program and that any school that did not want to do so could take the issue to their local town meeting for a vote. The Campaign's executive director, Robert Dostis, was also a representative to the state legislature, and he introduced a bill that basically added breakfast to the existing law. Schools that did not want to offer the program would be required to present the matter for a vote at the annual town meeting. "And we realized that, honestly, if you put a community in a position where they have to vote not to feed their kids, it's going to be a very difficult vote." Dostis believes that it was important that the proposal fell short of a mandate. "If we had asked for a mandate, specifically saying that every school must do this, that probably wouldn't have passed." The fact that the bill respected local control helped him recruit cosponsors from across the political spectrum and gain even wider support when it came time for a vote in the Republican-controlled House. "Not having a mandate was very helpful in that respect."

Wending its way through the legislature, the bill was weakened a bit; the final version, Act 22, called for town meetings to take up the matter once in regard to any school without the program, and then for it to be discussed and voted upon annually by school boards rather than returning to the town meeting each year. In the long run, the bill worked a bit differently than the advocates had imagined. While a few town meetings took up the issue and voted to start a program, many of the schools without programs simply decided to start offering breakfast rather than take the discussion public. By two years after the passage of the act, the Vermont Campaign estimated that twenty-eight additional schools had begun breakfast programs because of Act 22.

In California, advocates have succeeded in getting incentives rather than mandates. The state makes grants of up to $15,000 for nonrecurring breakfast start-up and expansion expenses, and it offers an additional reimbursement per meal, adjusted annually. In 2006–2007, the rate was $0.1563 per meal. In 2007, the state raised the per meal reimbursement to $0.2195 for all free or reduced price meals, conditional on the elimination of trans fats and deep-fat and flash frying. California advocates have tried cajoling, providing information, and helping with outreach on the one hand, and shaming on the other: publishing a list of the "top ten" schools in the state without breakfast, ranked by the number and percentage of free and reduced price eligible students. Slowly, they are overcoming resistance.[36]

Making It Convenient and Socially Acceptable

As we have seen in Rhode Island, for advocates, getting schools to offer breakfast is only the first step. Once a school has the program, local advocates often work to expand participation by helping to get the word out and also by making breakfast more convenient, and to reduce stigma by making it universal, free for all students. When schools convert to a universal program format, one might expect increases in participation among those who formerly paid full price, and these certainly do occur, but the greater increases are usually among those eligible for free and reduced price. As a result, converting to universal raises participation among the children who need the program most and who bring the greatest federal revenues into the community. In Rhode Island, where all schools now offer some form of breakfast, for example, in October 2007, in schools without universal breakfast the participation rate for children eligible for free and reduced price was 21 percent, but in schools with universal breakfast the rate was 32 percent, half again as great.[37] Making it universal is a primary agenda for local advocates.

Provision 2 is the vehicle most frequently used to convert to universal meals. As explained in chapter 7, this provision allows schools to collect applications in a base year, calculate the percentages of meals served in each payment category (free, reduced price, and full price) and then apply those percentages to the number of meals served in each subsequent year for reimbursement purposes while feeding all children free. Adopting Provision 2 for breakfast is much more likely to be financially feasible than for lunch, because of the historic image of breakfast as a program for the poor. Even though schools must make meals available free of charge to all children in the base year, actual participation often remains concentrated among the lower-income children who are already in the habit of eating breakfast at school, and the proportion of free and reduced price meals remains very high. Once those initial proportions are established, however, some schools make a concerted effort to draw other children into the program. As Doug Davis explained, "the following year, once the base year was established, we put breakfast in the classroom. We put breakfast in the hallway. . . . We do hot breakfast in the classroom. We have breakfast from 7 until 10 at some schools." And once breakfast was made more convenient and accessible, participation soared.[38]

That doesn't mean there were no obstacles. Davis explained to me a bit of what is involved in actually converting to breakfast in the classroom. "We . . . have very old buildings. We have three-story buildings. We have buildings with no elevators. We have buildings with carpeting. So I've heard all of the excuses as to why this will not work. I've been down that road and there are challenges, and there are ski bumps in that road." He credits the program's success to "a good working relationship with the administration and the teachers and the maintenance staff" and stresses the necessity for "an open dialogue with them based on what the food choices are. . . . Some buildings have carpeting and the teachers have said, 'I would rather not have cereal and milk in my carpet because once it spills, it stinks.' So sometimes, honestly, there are menus that change based on the floor coverings in a building."

Davis went on to describe more "bumps" and the solutions that had surmounted them, and then he talked about the importance of teachers: "Without support from the teachers, the program fails. . . . It went from them saying 'Oh, no, we can't do that. It won't work' to 'This isn't so terrible'—which is my favorite one—to 'Maybe this isn't such a bad idea' to actually being good. It took them a long time to actually change their comments from negative to positive." Some of the schools were still getting ready to move to breakfast in the classroom, but Davis was optimistic. "It's a no-brainer. It's good for kids. They are going to see behavior changes. I can't sit here and say they are going to test better, because I haven't even gone into that arena. But the kids are going to behave better. They are going to be more attentive. They aren't going to be hungry. They aren't going to have headaches."

Some systems that have implemented universal breakfast from the top down have been much slower to make the connection between making breakfast more accessible and increasing participation. In the nation's largest school system, universal free was instituted in 2003 by a decision from the top, New York City Schools Chancellor Joel Klein, after advocates and consultants pointed out the financial implications and feasibility. Participation rose after breakfast went universal, but it was not rising as fast as observers thought it should be. So, under the auspices of the Children's Defense Fund, the longtime anti-hunger advocates Kathy Goldman and Agnes Molnar began looking into the barriers to participation. Schedules were a problem. Inaccessible cafeterias were a problem. Attitudes were a problem, particularly the attitudes of principals. As Goldman tells it, after seeing school after school where the principal regarded the program as a burden or intrusion, she visited a school in the Bronx where an entirely different attitude prevailed. Concerned because he couldn't schedule the fifth graders for lunch until 12:30, the principal had mandated that they begin their school day in the cafeteria during the breakfast period, hoping that a hearty breakfast would see them though to lunch. Their teachers would meet them in the cafeteria instead of the classroom. "Because of that, the rest of the school comes and eats too. So there are hundreds of kids eating breakfast in that school. It's absolutely startling. You walk in there and you can't even believe your eyes." Curious about how the innovation had come about, Goldman asked the principal what had prompted him to do this. She was, she said, "waiting for this big educational lecture," but the principal replied, "You know, I noticed at the beginning of the year that the Chancellor was really very interested in the whole food issue, and so I decided I would do something that might bring that about. Can you do anything to have him notice me?" It was an answer that confirmed something that Goldman and Molnar had been saying for years: "We've suggested more than once that when the principals are rated, they should be rated on how they run their food program." As the old adage goes: "what gets measured, gets done."

Principals' attitudes, of course, are not the only factors. Michelle Mullins, a social work graduate student whose fieldwork centered on efforts to expand participation in the School Breakfast Program at selected schools in New York City, worked extensively with an old school building in Chelsea that housed five different small schools. The cafeteria was located on the top floor, six long flights above ground level. She suggested that bagged "Grab 'N' Go" breakfasts be offered at the entrances. The cafeteria manager and her supervisor felt that they did not have the staff to distribute them, but when a health class decided to undertake distribution as a class project, the pick-up breakfast was instituted. Participation rose, but not as much as anticipated, so the health class students surveyed their peers. They found that students objected to cold bagels and to the "mystery bag"—they wanted to be able to see what was inside. So a warm grab-and-go was offered, with the components laid out so that students could select their own, and participation rose again. The factor that proved crucial, Mullins reported, was adult encouragement and attention. "Besides just being able to meet the students' needs and bringing the breakfast to them, I think also what really helps is the support of the teachers, really just promoting it. The second day that we had the warm grab-and-go, there was a teacher at the front entrance of the school saying 'Hey, guys, we've got warm bagels today. Did you guys eat breakfast?' All of the food was gone in fifteen minutes. . . . And I think that's why the back entrance is doing so well, because we have a school aid who is really talking to students as they're walking in and promoting it." Six weeks into the warm grab-and-go, participation had risen from 60 students to 225. The story does not have a happy ending, however; one day the bags contained apples, and a rowdy student threw an apple through a window in the lobby, shattering the glass. The vice principal in charge of discipline ended the grab-and-go breakfast then and there.

Breakfast participation may soon show significant increases in New York, because the city instituted a pilot breakfast-in-the-classroom program in 2008. The anti-hunger activist Joel Berg, the director of the New York City Coalition Against Hunger, describes what he saw when he went to take a look at the program in operation.

> At one pilot site I visited, Public School 68 in the Bronx, . . . the pilot is working better than anyone could have anticipated. The school's principal told me that, before the pilot, an average of fifty kids came to school late every day, so many that she had to assign extra staff to write out late slips. When they started serving breakfast in their classrooms, kids came in early just for the meals, and now only about five kids a day are late—a 900 percent decrease in tardiness. The principal told me that absenteeism and visits to school nurses also dropped, and in the afternoons, kids fell asleep in the classrooms less frequently. This is obviously not only good nutrition policy but also good education policy.[39]

Grab-and-go breakfasts and breakfast in the classroom to make the breakfast more convenient, more physically accessible, and teacher and staff leadership to make them more emotionally or socially accessible work best where Provision 2 or some other device has been used to achieve universal free breakfast. In some states, however, advocates have taken a different approach. They have induced state legislatures to provide funds to eliminate the charge paid by students eligible for reduced price—often referred to as a copayment or co-pay. While thirty cents may not seem like a lot of money, cafeteria mangers frequently report that they are daily confronted with hungry students who just don't have it. In Maine, the legislature allocated money from the Fund for a Healthy Maine (its tobacco settlement money) to eliminate the breakfast co-pay for reduced price eligible children in public schools. In the State of Washington, the legislature appropriated funds to eliminate the co-pay at breakfast for all reduced price children in 2006, and then to remove the lunch co-pay for those in grades K–3 in 2007. An effort to extend the lunch benefit to pre-K and 4–12 was mounted in 2008, but was strongly opposed by the governor, and money was not included in the budget to fund the initiative. In Colorado, a new "Start Smart" program, modeled on a successful program in Denver, began reimbursing schools for the 30-cent co-pay in the 2007–2008 school year. And finally, in Vermont, the legislature has just added funds to the budget of the Department of Education to eliminate the 30-cent charge. According to Jo Busha, the state director of Child Nutrition Programs, quoted in the Barre Montpelier Times-Argus, "The students that are approved for reduced-price meals participated in the breakfast program at about half the rate of the students who get the program for free. . . . Food service members tell me that when a family's income goes up enough to kick them from the free program into the reduced program, the family's children participate less often. The assumption is being made that for many of them the money is the barrier." Anti-hunger advocates praised the state legislature for its sensitivity to the needs of working families struggling at the margin and its leadership in seeing and meeting needs, and pointed out that if formerly reduced price children begin to participate at the same rate as children eligible for free meals, an additional $280,000 in federal funds will flow into the state.[40]

These state efforts take on added significance in light of the SNA's national-level campaign for the elimination of the reduced price category, or rather its merger with the free category, discussed in chapter 6. Congress passed a provision authorizing a pilot project to eliminate the distinction in five states in 2004, but failed to fund it. The old distinction between authorization and appropriation continues to haunt child nutrition. Results from these state-funded programs should help generate pressure for the continuation—and funding—of such pilots at the federal level in the next round of Child Nutrition legislation.

The fact that most local inclusion efforts have been focused on breakfast should not obscure the persistence of very real inclusion issues at lunch. Maggi Burns-Rogers in Rhode Island is not alone among breakfast champions who hope to demonstrate the superiority of universal approaches and then move on to lunch. In the context of fiscal constraints, it seems a distant goal to many, but all over the country, I ran into advocates and school food professionals convinced that the whole program would run far better as a universal program. As Mary Ann McCann, who runs the excellent program in Taos, New Mexico, on a universal basis by using Provision 2, explained to me, "We lose anywhere from $34,000 to $40,000 every year because we don't collect from the paid and reduced students, but we don't have to do applications, either, and that's worth a million bucks. . . . Just not having to hound parents for those applications every year is just a godsend. Because they are a horrible thing. I hate it." Beverley Laprade summarized the advantages of a universal lunch: "Then there's no stigma either way. Everyone comes to school. Everybody gets their meal; everybody goes to English class; everybody's treated the same; everybody gets the same choice. You don't have to worry about being embarrassed, [having] the lady at the register saying, 'Oh, I'm sorry. You owe two lunches. You can't get that lunch. You have to get a peanut butter and jelly, and we'll bill your account at the end of the day.' I mean, that's kind of hard to take." Other than the sporadic use of Provision 2, there are few examples of successful local battles to obtain a universal free school lunch. In New York, Los Angeles, and several other large districts, however, advocates are beginning to organize to seek implementation of an alternate approach similar to the one used in Philadelphia (see chapter 7).

SCHOOL FOOD ECONOMICS

Needless to say, all of the efforts for school food reform at the local level take place within the context of local economic realities. Better food usually costs more; money is generally easier to come by in more affluent communities—but, in fact, in regard to school food, the money picture is a bit more complicated. The two ends of the spectrum, wealthy districts and very poor districts may have options that more economically diverse districts lack. Districts with very high levels of eligibility for free and reduced price usually have higher participation rates and greater total federal reimbursements as a proportion of overall revenues. In large urban districts where labor costs are high, this may still not be enough to pay for quality food, but in areas where labor costs are more modest, a high free and reduced rate can supply the needed resources, and strategies that expand participation make higher quality feasible. At the other end of the continuum, very affluent districts may be able simply to raise prices in order to pay for better food.

For the whole range of communities in between, however, large urban areas where labor costs are high and economically diverse communities where those who don't qualify for free or reduced price meals are still not affluent, the economics of school food reform just don't add up at current funding levels, especially in the face of mounting food and fuel costs. When meal prices are raised, free and reduced price eligible families are protected, but for those with incomes just over the line, price increases can cause hardships, sometimes causing them to forgo the healthier reimbursable meal. The "fall off the cliff" or notch problem discussed in chapter 6 comes into play, and some of the youngsters who need the meals most are priced out of the market. As Mary Kate Harrison put it, "I think we'd want to do everything we could to control costs before we have to raise prices, because there are many parents who have to struggle to pay that $1.50 for four kids every day." In these communities, improving school meals will almost certainly require a revision of the federal funding structure.

RECIPES FOR SUCCESS

Telling success stories is an important way to counteract the disabling myths that are rife in the world of school food, but telling success stories is also a hazardous business. It can create a false sense that the various problems associated with school food can be solved with just a little effort and creativity at the local level. In fact, I came away from my encounters with successful efforts to reform school food at the local level with very nearly the opposite impression. I found the individuals and groups working for school food change—both paid staff and parent and citizen activists—to be so extraordinary, so dedicated, patient, persistent, and creative that there seems to me little likelihood that more typical communities will achieve such improvements under current federal rules and within current funding constraints. The duration of some of these efforts is staggering. The Rhode Island school breakfast activists worked on expanding breakfast for ten years before they finally got a statewide mandate and have continued working for another decade to expand the use of universal. The cajoling and nudging and nagging by Vermont activists that Dorigen Keeney mentioned had been going on for years before she got involved. It has taken twelve years to get Cooking with Kids to its current level; as co-director Jane Stacey explained to me, "We have moved very slowly because our program is very labor-intensive and expensive and involves schlepping food around and storing it." In addition to persistence, a certain passion and intensity is necessary. As Ann Cooper explained when asked what personal attributes helped her most in her work in Berkeley, "I think that the quality that serves me the most is tenacity. Just this passion and bulldog tenacity—getting up everyday and telling everybody that we can do it and that we will do it."[41] In a word, I found the successful efforts to be heroic.

A champion with vision, stamina, and courage, and hopefully connections, influence, and clout, an organizational base, and adequate resources, not only financial but also interpersonal and sometimes technical: it's a tall order. These are admirable characteristics, and indeed I do admire the local initiatives and the groups and individuals that have created them. Meanwhile, however, there are fifty-five million children in school in the United States, and it appears that most of them don't live in communities where such extraordinary leadership has been mobilized around school food. If the ingredients for successful school meal reform at the local level were easy to come by, surely compliance with the Dietary Guidelines, required by law, would be fairly widespread, but as we have seen in chapter 4, SNDA-III found that only a quarter of elementary schools and a tenth of high schools served lunches that, on average, met the standard for fat. If these changes were readily made, surely more than one secondary school in five would offer a salad bar on a daily basis.

It shouldn't be so hard. One should not have to be a superhero, a magician, or a saint to get healthy, tasty food into the school cafeteria or to make school food truly accessible to children. Local heroes can lead the way and demonstrate the possibilities, but they cannot enable the National School Lunch and School Breakfast programs to reach their full potential at the aggregate level. Counting on saints and heroes is not good public policy. Congress has the ultimate responsibility for school food programs, and Congress needs to step up to the plate to enact changes in federal law that make local improvements much easier to achieve. In conclusion, then, let us look at the basic questions I believe we need to confront at the national level about our school food system.

CONCLUSION

School Food at the Crossroads

Many years ago the historian of science Thomas Kuhn altered our perception of the way in which change takes place in scientific knowledge. In *The Structure of Scientific Revolutions,* he argued that science does not proceed, as many imagine, by the gradual and orderly accretion of knowledge. Rather, he suggested, it proceeds by the accumulation of "anomalies," data that do not fit the dominant theories of the age, until some new model is proposed that does a better job than the old one of making sense of the facts. The result is a paradigm shift. I think public policy proceeds in somewhat analogous fashion. Programs are created and then adjusted and reformed; tinkering produces new regulations here and there, the anomalies accumulate, and eventually the gap between intention and performance becomes too large to tolerate. I believe that the time has come for a new paradigm in school food. What is required is a thorough reconsideration, not just incremental tinkering. We need to draw on the creativity and knowledge of a whole host of interested parties: school food service professionals, anti-hunger advocates, program administrators at the federal and state levels, environmental activists, educators and their unions, health promoters, parents, and students to design school food for a healthier America. I hope this book will further this much-needed conversation.

■

In the six decades since the National School Lunch Act was passed, nearly everything about the way we produce, distribute, and consume our food has changed. Our nation has far fewer, and much larger, farms; much of our meat and poultry is produced in confined animal feeding operations (factory farms). Our food system has shifted in the direction of highly processed shelf-stable packaged goods. Many more of our parents are in the labor force, and our households are contributing more hours of work and are thus preparing and eating fewer meals at home. We spend more than half of our food dollar on food consumed away from home. Fast food has swept the nation, and convenience has become a central concern for food shoppers. Frequent snacking has become the norm. Our children have money and have become the primary targets of massive food advertising campaigns. Deficiency diseases have given way to the health hazards of overconsumption. We have more cars and walk fewer miles. We are putting on weight.

Schools have changed as well. Our school days and our school years are longer, and our school systems are consumed with high-stakes testing. Systems of accountability and state curriculum standards dominate what is taught and the way in which the school day is organized. Lunch hours are short and getting shorter as "time on task" becomes the mantra. A financial squeeze, along with scheduling difficulties and disinvestment in equipment and open spaces, has eliminated much physical education, and only 16 percent of children typically walk or bike to school, down from nearly half in 1969. Many schools are located on the outskirts of towns and cities, where land to build them is cheaper, so bus transportation has increasingly become the way to get to school. A third of children ride the school bus to school, and half are driven in a private vehicle.[1] Immigration, integration, and mainstreaming have led to more diverse student bodies, though our schools remain far from fully integrated. The growth of private school education, itself a reflection of mounting inequalities of income and wealth, and the growing gap in per pupil expenditure between cities and suburbs have left some urban public school systems with student bodies overwhelmingly composed of low-income minority students.[2] A rise in school violence, the spread of weaponry, and the general preoccupation with terror have resulted in increased security measures and personnel—even schools patrolled by uniformed guards.

Meanwhile, every successive decade has left its mark on school food. Each new concern—farm surpluses in the 1930s, national defense in the 1940s, educating the baby boom in the 1950s, hunger in the 1960s, plate waste in the 1970s, fraud in the 1980s, fat in the 1990s, and food safety and childhood obesity in the new millennium—has produced a new set of rules but seldom eliminated any old ones. The result is a set of programs that thwarts itself at every turn, simultaneously overregulated and underresourced. We need a new paradigm for school meals, one that sees expenditures for school food as investments in the current and future health of our children. It is time to go "back to the drawing board," to take a whole new look at the way we feed out children at school.

Now is the time for such a fundamental reconsideration. The rising rates of food-related illnesses and mounting concern about childhood obesity have brought the topic of school food to public attention as never before. And this is not just an amorphous "concern"; it has generated a whole raft of organized campaigns, as we have seen, from school food personnel to parents to anti-hunger activists. Two "Angry Moms," the filmmaker Amy Kalafa and the holistic health practitioner Dr. Susan Rubin, have made a powerful film depicting the efforts of parents and concerned professionals in one community to improve the quality of school food, and have used it to launch a broader crusade: "It's a movie, it's a movement!" Better School Food, an organization headed by Rubin, has begun offering consultation via teleconference to parent and community groups. The Center for Ecoliteracy has developed an ever-evolving online guide for parents, school food service personnel, and school administrators. Foundations led by the Robert Wood Johnson Foundation and the W.K. Kellogg Foundation have begun investing substantial sums in efforts to achieve healthier food and fitness environments in schools and communities. The Alliance for a Healthier Generation, a project of the William J. Clinton Foundation, has contributed both funds and its substantial capacity to generate attention to the cause. Farm to school programs are proliferating around the nation, and a new project funded by the Kellogg Foundation, School Food FOCUS (Food Options for Children in Urban Schools) has embarked on an ambitious plan to reorient procurement in large city school systems toward health and sustainability. Several large city systems, including New York City and Los Angeles have hired executive chefs to lead efforts to improve the menu. Although, as I noted at the end of chapter 8, I do not believe that the larger problems of school food can be solved at the local level, one community at a time, the local success stories are crucial, because they help to dispel the crippling myths that have constrained efforts in the past—especially the "kids won't eat vegetables" approach to menu planning. And finally, we in the United States are not alone. Similar concerns and active movements for change have arisen in other countries, notably the United Kingdom, so we can learn from other successes and failures as well. In fact, Kevin Morgan and Roberta Sonnino at the University of Cardiff in Wales have just published *The School Food Revolution: Public Food and the Challenge of Sustainable Development,* in which they look at the potential of school "catering," as it is called in the United Kingdom, to foster the health of both the children and the ecosystem and to contribute to the creation of the "green state," profiling reforms in Rome, New York, and London as well as rural areas of the United Kingdom.[3] With all of this ferment at the state and local level, and all of the stimulation from abroad, has come a learning curve; more people know more about the realities of school food than ever before. Now is the time to harness this concern and growing sophistication in a national program redesign.

We should begin by acknowledging the substantial accomplishments of the National School Lunch and School Breakfast programs. School food has meant the difference between the distractions of hunger and the ability to concentrate for literally millions of American school children. It has served as a politically acceptable outlet for surplus agricultural commodities and thus a tool for managing the farm economy. It has provided family-friendly jobs for thousands of breadwinners, and it has offered a great convenience for millions of families stressed by increased work hours and complex lives. These accomplishments should not be ignored nor underestimated. But we must also acknowledge that school food falls far short of reaching its true potential.

The National School Lunch Act, as we have seen, was built on a thoroughly accidental foundation. School food as a means to promote health and educational achievement among our children is a little like G. K. Chesterton's famous dictum about Christianity: It has "not been tried and found wanting; it has been found difficult and left untried."[4] We have never tried to design a school food program with our children's health, both immediate and long-term, as its central goal, its clear priority. The well-being of children has always had to compete with other agendas: the disposal of farm commodities or the maintenance of segregation or the reduction of the federal budget deficit. It's time to see what we can do if we put children first.

I have been considerably humbled by my journey through the world of school food. Doing this right is harder than I thought. I don't think

I have all the answers, but I do believe that collectively, we have them, and now is the time to put our heads together to see if we can design a better approach to food at school. I believe we need an extended and inclusive national conversation about these programs. In order to get this conversation started, I'm going to describe what I see as the ideal school food program. I'm not talking pie in the sky here; the program I want to describe is not utopian. It is well within our capacities—if we want it—though it would certainly require a substantially larger investment than the one we have been making. I'm going to organize this description around a series of questions, of choices that I think we must make. Even if you do not agree with all elements of my vision, you may find the questions useful in articulating your own.

1. A program for all children or a program that prioritizes poor children?

This has been a central question from the beginning of school food programs. Some of the school food pioneers of the early 1900s took up the issue because compulsory school attendance laws had brought into the schools large numbers of children from very poor families, and they were often too hungry to learn. The leaders of the "school hygiene movement," on the other hand, saw school food as a remedy for adulteration and uncleanliness; they were concerned about the safety and healthfulness of the food available to middle-class children who bought food from street vendors or school custodians. They argued that "school feeding is essentially social in character, in that it recognizes a natural need of all children, rich and poor," and that it is "a proper function of the school because it utilizes a child's natural appetite to teach" healthy eating and thrift. They pointed out that "in creating a department to serve all children, the school has at hand without further expense all necessary machinery for caring for the undernourished child." Although the two groups cooperated to establish school lunchrooms, there was a certain tension between them. As one proponent of the school hygiene approach put it, the movement for food for the poor "regards this service as being primarily charitable in character, and to be handled by the schools on that basis only. It looks on the elementary service as a real but regrettable necessity imposed upon the authorities by the practical problem of providing food for exceptional children whose parents are too poor or too ignorant to do it for them."[5]

By the time the federal government entered the school lunch arena, the nation was in the grip of the Great Depression, and the needs of poor children were obvious and pressing. Further, the plan to use school food as a means of disposing of agricultural surplus required that schools give priority to poor children: farmers and farm incomes would not benefit if donated federal commodities simply replaced other purchases. World War II, however, focused attention on nutrition and health across the class spectrum. "Defense nutrition" was the term that captured the need for a strong and healthy population, and the National School Lunch Act was passed "as a matter of national security."

The NSLP was supposed to serve all children without regard to ability to pay, but without federal resources to absorb the costs of meals for poor children it functioned for its first quarter-century primarily as a subsidy for the relatively affluent. Distressed by the revelations in the late 1960s that the children who needed the meals most were the least likely to get them, Congress changed the priority by establishing the three-tier eligibility and reimbursement system now in use. While it has indeed made federally supported meals available to most of the nation's poorest children, it has proven to have the numerous unanticipated consequences examined in previous chapters. Cuts in basic support for all meals in the early 1980s and an intensified emphasis on accountability have gradually shifted the image of school food away from that of a program for all children and toward that of a program for poor children.

David Ellwood, in *Poor Support,* his seminal consideration of cash welfare programs, called the hard choices about the allocation of benefits the "targeting-isolation conundrum."[6] Society wants to use its limited resources wisely, he suggests, so it does not want to provide money or assistance to people who do not need it, but if the poor are singled out for differential treatment, the effect is to isolate them, thus reducing their likelihood of joining the mainstream. I thought about this conundrum again and again as I read students' and others' accounts of the stigma attached to school food: "Those who were provided with lunch, they were the only ones who actually ate the school food. . . . There was also a separate door for them to receive their lunch, and they had to eat in the cafeteria because the school dishes were not allowed outside. . . . The system for free lunches made the students who received them stand out, it divided the high school." The rise of competitive foods has aggravated this situation and intensified the stigma of school food, driving students with money into the a la carte lines or off campus and deterring some of those who are eligible for free and reduced price meals from claiming them. "The area where the standard school lunch was served, where almost only free lunch students ate, was pretty far away from where most everyone else ate and bought food. . . . I ate mostly candy, pizza, and cinnamon rolls. . . . I was eligible for free lunch but was embarrassed, and annoyed my mom for pizza money." Whether this system deters parents from applying or students from eating, or simply imposes a burden of shame on those who do use the program, it seems to me to have no place in the public schools of a democratic society.

The three-tier system is inextricably involved with the provision of a la carte and vending options in our schools. The "cool" foods were introduced in part to lure the middle-income youngsters back into the cafeteria after the defection of paying students in the wake of the Reagan era cuts. And they have become a crucial revenue source as the combination of federal reimbursements and "full price" meals has failed to enable food service operations to break even. Together, the three-tier system and the availability of competitive foods prevent school food programs from fully meeting any of their goals. School food cannot teach healthy eating if the cafeteria is full of a la carte items of questionable nutritional value. It cannot deliver nutritionally sound food to its middle-class customer base if the nutritionally regulated meal is shunned in favor of a trip to the snack shack or the convenience store. As students reach adolescence, school food cannot even deliver a much-needed free meal to those who would rather go hungry than be labeled as poor. We have tried a variety of technological "fixes" to what is essentially a human and social problem. Well-designed and carefully operated PIN or swipe-card systems in "cashless" cafeterias can protect the privacy of individual students, but they cannot eliminate the idea that some students eat free while others pay, and thus the stigmatization of the federally regulated lunch as "welfare food," and the students' desire to distance themselves from it.

We have given the three-tier system a real try, and it has generated no end of problems. We know there are students, literally millions of them, for whom the free meals are the difference between hunger and adequate food; going back on our promise to poor children is not the solution. We need to think about ways to eliminate the means test so that school food can lose its stigma. It is time to move to universal free school meals. This would benefit poor children who would no longer have to eat a meal seasoned by shame, and it would benefit middle-income children for whom healthy school meals could become the norm. It would benefit our overstressed, time-starved working families by taking one more task, and one more parent-child battleground, off the table. It would benefit food service staff, who could turn their attention from accounting to cooking. And in the long run it would benefit us all through savings in health care costs and better educational outcomes.

An adequately supported universal free program could eliminate the need for any a la carte sales. Schools could simply serve a variety of healthy foods. Think of meals at summer camps. The menu would no longer have to compete with fast-food clones. Without cashiers, the lines would move faster, so students could have more time to eat. The nightmare of record keeping and the potential for errors of certification and verification would be eliminated, and children whose parents are too proud or too distracted or too frightened or too selfish to apply would no longer be excluded. The frustrating notch problem—the situation of families whose incomes are just over the line, causing them to lose the entire benefit—would be eliminated, and with it the temptation to misreport income. The anomalies that derive from using a single standard for families living in areas with radically different costs of living would be history. Children would be assured access to the healthy food they need, even when an unusual circumstance stressed the family budget. As the current generation of high school teenagers graduates and moves on, the stigma would fade and the school meal would become the normal way to eat. It could also be integrated with the curriculum and finally realize its potential as an instrument of health education. At the same time, it could realize its potential as a unifying element in the school day, a shared meal with all that this implies. I'm thinking of those summer camp meals again. When I observed school meals in Sweden, which has had the universal approach in grades 1–9 since the 1930s (and in secondary schools at local option), the program had no taint of poverty. It was lunchtime; children flocked to the cafeteria and ate; in most cases, so did their teachers. There was nothing for sale, so differences in purchasing power were not on display. No one was defined by whether or not they could afford to bypass the lunch line, and as far as I could see, no one did.

My conviction that universal is a better way is rooted in three basic values related to schools: democracy, hospitality, and community. When I say democracy, I am expressing a widely held belief that our public schools should be incubators of democracy, places where democratic ideals and beliefs are built into the fabric of the day. I don't mean that students should elect the principal, nor—as I hope I have made clear—that they should dictate the menu or the curriculum, but I do mean that all students should be treated fairly, without regard to their race, gender, religious beliefs, sexual orientation, or social class. I am personally very troubled by reports of fees for participation in athletic teams, for example. All members of the school community should have equal access to its opportunities. We would never, I think, allow a system in which admission to an expensive academic course—one that requires laboratory supplies and equipment, like chemistry—was based on ability to pay. That we have been willing to do this with school food reflects, in part, I believe, our failure to perceive it as an integral part of education. (See below, question 3.)

While the idea that schools should be fair and democratic in their treatment of students is familiar to all, the notion that they should be hospitable may be less so, but stop and think about it. School remains for many children the first institution they encounter outside the home—the essential transition from the protected status of children in their own homes to the wider world, the first place where they regularly interact with strangers. This is why we want kindergarten classrooms to be brightly colored, to have pets and plants, to be welcoming. And what is more welcoming than a meal? You would not invite an acquaintance to your home, and then, when she arrives, ask her for proof of her household income in order to determine how much she should pay for refreshments. A school is not a home, but it is a midway institution, closer to home than, say, a place of employment. We can decide to increase the hospitableness of our schools by making school meals available to all. Personally, I believe this practice would go a long way toward countering the negative attitudes that are generated in some children by their first encounters with school. Better behavior, fewer referrals to the principal's office for disciplinary action, is the single most consistently reported outcome of universal breakfast in the classroom; I'm sure much of this is because fewer children are "hangry." But I suspect it also has to do with the attitudes of children toward teachers and toward school. A school that welcomes you with breakfast is less likely to be seen as enemy territory.

School as community may be even more difficult for some people to swallow than the notion of school hospitality. Nevertheless, I think it is exactly the right word for what ought to be possible, for what should be a goal. I am certainly not the first educator to aspire to the notion of the school as a learning community, and I won't be the last. Here is the way the superintendent of schools in Berkeley, California, envisioned the community-building potential of the lunch hour, after discussing the possibility for integrating the school meal with the curriculum:

> In addition, the lunch period provides an important time for the enjoyment of food, socializing, and building camaraderie. It is a time when the whole learning community can sit down together as a family. . . . So the community of learners becomes an extended family. I just see so much potential for good healthy school culture in the development of this notion. Perhaps these understandings and the lessons around food and culture will be the key to combat the horrible rise in diet-related diseases and obesity of school age children.[7]

While I recognize this aspiration is likely to be only partially achieved, at least we can eliminate policies that make it impossible, and that, it seems to me, is what the three-tiered eligibility for school food does in many situations. In a school in which everyone normally ate a meal prepared and served on site, lunch hour could become a time for clubs and interest groups, for informal faculty-student interaction, for academic support. One way to deal with the overcrowding in the cafeteria would be to have luncheon clubs in the library and in classrooms or laboratories. Eating together is the most basic form of human solidarity; sharing food and the rituals that go along with it define us as a species, or in the cogent phrasing of Felipe Fernandez-Armesto, "meals make us human."[8] I don't believe that universal alone will restore civility to our secondary schools; that would require ample time to eat, good food, adult engagement, a fundamental change of attitude, and much, much more. But while it is not sufficient, I do believe it is necessary.

The greatest barrier to the universal approach, of course, is the cost. I am going to discuss the whole issue of how to pay for my ideal school food program in section 5 below. The issue of paying for the children of the affluent, however, is not simply an issue of fiscal capacity. It gets at fundamental beliefs about the responsibilities of families and about fairness, and those I want to discuss here. The idea that feeding children, and thus paying for their food at school, is a parental rather than a societal responsibility runs very deep. As Alice Boughton said nearly a century ago, many people see free school meals as "a regrettable necessity . . . of providing food for . . . children whose parents are too poor or too ignorant to do it for them."[9] In this frame of mind, receipt of free meals at school is a sign of parental failure. But that is not the only way to look at it; another paradigm suggests that children are required by society to attend school, and since they are there during mealtime and need food in order to learn, food should be a part of the school day. The old pattern of "neighborhood schools," from which children walked home for lunch, has been obsolete for a long while. In most households, there is no adult at home to feed them, and many schools do not allocate adequate time to permit such a round trip. Schools are not the only institutions that have adopted a more instrumental approach to meal service along with modernization. Americans who visit hospitals in less developed nations are sometimes surprised to learn that families are responsible for bringing in food to supply the patient. The first large-scale charitable feeding program in New York City, the Municipal Soup House, was established by the Society for the Relief of Distressed Debtors to provide meals for the inmates of the debtors' prison, who were similarly reliant on families, friends, or benefactors to feed them. Now we take prison meals and hospital meals for granted, but where children are involved, a lingering notion says this is a family responsibility. "Brown-bagging" is of course an option for preserving family responsibility, but the reality is that relatively few children bring a lunch packed at home, only about 10 percent of those in the most recent SNDA survey. And many of the brown bags making their way to lunch contain what the child purchased from the corner store on the way to school, sometimes with the lunch money his parents thought would be spent on a healthy school meal.

Nevertheless, a universal free program means finding the resources to feed many children whose parents can certainly afford to do so without help, and that is an ideological as well as a financial barrier. When I interviewed Marianne Dania, she was the director of child nutrition for the Stockton, California, Unified School District; she has long been a fan of Provision 2 and is willing to try just about anything else she could do to reduce the stigma that sent too many of her students to what she calls the "roach coach," the wagon selling food outside the school door. When I asked her about a completely universal program, however, she couldn't imagine it. "You can't do it," she told me; "my girlfriend is a director in Marin County—those kids drive BMWs to school. They buy burritos for $5. She has 2 percent [of the students] free and reduced. You couldn't do universal free there. She's already running in the red." When I explained what I meant, a program similar to Sweden's where no money changes hands at all, where school meals are part of the budget, financed by a combination of national and local funds, she became more enthusiastic, but I think her first reaction will be the first reaction of many. The idea of paying for meals for "rich kids" bothers people.

The last time that legislation embodying a universal approach was introduced in Congress, some advocates, justifiably concerned about competing with other programs that serve impoverished Americans, characterized the proposal as one that would take scarce resources away from programs that support poor families and use them to aid those with incomes averaging above the median—a transfer of benefits from the poor to the middle class. And under the current rules governing the federal budgeting process, this could be the case. This is part of the reason that I am recommending a thorough reconsideration of school food, rather than a piecemeal or incremental effort. I believe that we need to make school food a regular part of the school day and take it out of the antipoverty category altogether, but I believe that in so doing, we must protect, and indeed make more effective, the poor child's entitlement to food. We need to move school food to a budget category where it does not compete with adequate funding for WIC or SNAP.

It is important to realize, however, that the great majority of the parents who would be helped financially by the advent of universal free school meals are not "rich." Rising health care and health insurance costs, mounting energy prices, rising college tuition costs and the need to save for future college expenses, and more recently, the disruption of the housing market and rising food prices have put many "middle income" families in a bind, as economists and social scientists have been telling us. Take a look at Theda Skocpol's *The Missing Middle;* in particular chapter 4, entitled "Our Children and Their Overstretched Parents," in which she argues: "Too much of today's debate focuses on issues about 'welfare' and the situation of (just a fraction of) the very poor. Not enough attention is paid to the broadly similar dilemmas faced by single or dual working parents of modest as well as impoverished means. . . . We need to focus on working parents, the key actors struggling with new challenges in our time, and find ways to deliver more material and social support directly to those parents so they can better nurture our children."[10]

Or take a look at Katherine Newman and Victor Chen's *The Missing Class,* which focuses on the "near poor," those between 100 percent and 200 percent of the federal poverty threshold. The school lunch and breakfast programs do help many but by no means all families in this category—lunches are free for those with incomes up to 130 percent and available at reduced prices for those with incomes up to 185 percent of the relevant federal thresholds. This leaves another group of approximately a million and a half children just above the cutoff with no benefit, and as we have seen in chapter 6, many families in the group eligible for reduced price need more help than they are getting.[11] Furthermore, the 200 percent of poverty figure that forms the ceiling of the group of hard-working families depicted by Newman and Chen is hardly a ticket to comfort and luxury. The fight over state income thresholds for S-CHIP, the children's health insurance program, revealed that substantial numbers of families with incomes three or even four times the poverty level had trouble finding affordable health insurance. There are 18.5 million children in families with incomes between the current cutoff for reduced price meals and the figure that represents four times the poverty line—more children than there are in families with incomes that make them eligible for reduced price or free. I am not saying that families in these income brackets are in such dire want that their children are going without food; I'm saying that they are not so well off that it is somehow a waste to provide school meals free.

Finally, income volatility and the erosion of social insurance and employer-provided benefits like health care and pensions have left millions of middle-income American families far less secure than their parents. As Jacob Hacker argues in *The Great Risk Shift*: "Economic insecurity isn't just a problem of the poor and uneducated, as most of us assume. Increasingly, it affects . . . educated, upper-middle class Americans—men and women who thought that by staying in school, by buying a home, by investing in their 401(k)s, they had bought the ticket to upward mobility and economic stability. Insecurity today reaches across the income spectrum, across the racial divide, across lines of geography and gender. It speaks to the common 'us' rather than to the insular, marginalized 'them.'"[12]

Hacker wrote this in 2006, while the economy was still expanding; as I write, a recession if not worse is well underway. The real meaning of economic insecurity is likely to be brought home to hundreds of thousands of families while this book makes its way through the editorial and production process. If we had universal free meals, at least families trying to hang onto their homes while they look for new employment could count on wholesome meals without stigma at school. And beyond the near term, the whole financial horizon looks uncertain and unpredictable. For scholars who study economic history, almost the only certainty is change. What will happen to American families if the world no longer uses the dollar as its currency standard? What will happen if climate change wipes out coastal assets and industries, and massive relocation and reallocation of activity are needed? The road ahead is difficult to discern. Universal free school meals could help to ease families and children through the various adjustments that we will surely have to make, even though none of us can quite predict just what they will be. It is a hedge against uncertainty.

My point is simple: while the objections to paying for school food for middle-income families tend to picture the Marin County kids in BMWs, the great majority of those who would benefit are families who could use the help. Furthermore, the history of social provision in the United States shows us again and again that universal programs are generally held to a higher standard than are programs restricted to poor people. Social Security offices have a better reputation for customer service—and even for office decor—than welfare offices. Programs for poor people, Alvin Schorr taught us decades ago, quickly become poor programs.[13] The fact that more affluent parents with political clout would have an immediate stake in the quality of school meals would be a good thing for all concerned. Nevertheless, the money has to come from somewhere; again, I shall return to the issue of how to pay for the program I am imagining in section 5 below.

The immediate cost of reimbursing schools for lunches is not the only barrier to moving to a universal approach. A second issue is cafeteria size, especially as it interacts with the timing of lunches. Many schools count on substantial numbers of children leaving the premises at lunch time in order to get the job done. If meals are free for all, presumably fewer children will leave (even if we do not close the currently open campuses, another move I would favor for many reasons). It would take substantial flexibility and creativity to solve these logistical problems— or a "stimulus package" built around new cafeteria space and equipment. But there are many possibilities. After all, the schools can in some way accommodate all of their students at once; they need not all be in one room. Auditoria could be pressed into service. Classrooms could serve as meeting grounds for clubs in which students and perhaps even faculty shared a meal while pursuing joint interests. Or more schools could implement the approach taken by Haverford County, Pennsylvania, where sixth graders can have lunch in the library and listen to a librarian read aloud from a novel by opting for the Literary Lunch Club. Fortunately, universal breakfast in the classroom has become sufficiently popular to dispel some of the anxieties about classrooms overrun with rodents or unmanageable janitorial burdens, but in order for such a radical departure to receive serious consideration, school lunch would have to become a valued part of the school day, as I discuss in section 3.[14]

And there are other barriers. Various interests benefit from food sales to school children—from principals for whom the revenues from vending machines may be the only discretionary funds at their disposal to neighborhood restaurants and convenience stores that ring up big sales at the lunch hour. Vendors of all sorts tend to believe that they have a "right" to any market that they have penetrated or at least a right to compete for customers. Any attempt in the United States to convert school food to a universal basis would mobilize support from those who supply school cafeterias and opposition from those who sell directly to students in competition with school meals. Competitive food, however, is not the only aspect of school food that has been pervaded by the market mentality.

2. "Customers" or students? A business or a social program?

There were no vending machines in the schools when I was a child, in part because children did not typically carry money—at least not enough money for a soda. A soda was a treat, not a beverage. Today, however, children do have money. They have their own money, to the tune of billions of dollars, and they influence the purchases of their parents, shaping the expenditure of billions more. No wonder food marketers have targeted children so relentlessly in their efforts to expand their markets and develop early-onset brand loyalty. The tendency to view children as little consumers, however, has migrated from the boardrooms of advertising agencies to the school kitchen. "Our kids are our customers," school food service personnel told me again and again; "we have to give them what they want."

A great deal of creativity and ingenuity has gone into marketing school food: branding, logos, mascots, themes, endorsements, taste tests, prizes, giveaways: all the ploys of modern marketing. There is nothing wrong with these strategies, especially if they help to overcome the stigma of school food discussed above. And a healthy respect for the youngster's ability to opt out has probably improved "customer service." If the business model makes lunchroom personnel friendlier and more cheerful, that is certainly a plus. But there are problems with conceiving of school children in school meal programs simply as "customers."

From the point of view of student health, the child-as-customer model places the crucial choices in the hands of children who are subjected to relentless advertising for some of the nation's least healthy foods. If I proposed, as an experiment, to subject a group of children to hours of advertising for salty, fried foods like potato chips or corn chips, advertising in which these products were associated with fun and popularity, and then to give these children a choice between an apple or a bag of chips, I assume that nowhere in the nation would the institutional review board, the university committee charged with the protection of human subjects in research, permit me to proceed with such research. But that is essentially what the current school food system does, at least with the children who have the money to buy either the apple or the chips. But let me be clear: the kids-are-customers model does not just apply to the competitive foods and a la carte items; it also applies to the federally reimbursable school meal. With the a la carte line selling chips and fries, school food menu planners feel great pressure to offer similar items on the main line. Spend an hour reading the advertisements in the school food service magazines, and you will see how thoroughly the customer-child has become the end target and how these customers are depicted as needing a whole host of tricks and blandishments: food in "fun" shapes and foods with artificial colors and foods with cute faces and foods in fancy containers. If we have reached the stage where children will not eat foods unless they are shaped like something else, or unless they turn your tongue blue, then we need to take a closer look.

There is an abdication of adult authority and responsibility here. Food service personnel to whom I spoke talked with considerable passion about the importance of choice, but choice does not have to mean unlimited choice; all choices are not equal. As a colleague pointed out, the school library offers choices, lots of them, but that does not mean that it stocks pornography. We can offer our children choices without giving in to advertising-induced preferences for unhealthy foods. What is sold or offered at school carries the school's implicit seal of approval. By adopting the kids-are-customers model, schools are surrendering one of the most powerful potential tools that adults have for helping children to develop healthy habits. We are perhaps the only species that has to teach its young what is edible—that relies on culture rather than instinct to shape food preferences. We cannot afford to forgo this powerful tool because of an admiration for "market forces" or a worship of choice. We need to be teaching our children the critical thinking skills and analytical abilities that will help them to cope with the partial truths and distortions of the advertising industry, but meanwhile, we are the adults; we need to limit the foods that can be marketed to children at school to those that are healthy. As the Minnesota chef Seth Bixby Daugherty said after visiting his son at school during the lunch period, "They're kids. They're not supposed to be making these decisions. We're the adults. We need to show them the way."[15] We need to set limits on what can be bought and sold at school, and we need to use school meals proactively to teach healthy habits. Al Scheider, the innovative food service director at Folsom-Cordova Unified School District in California, put it bluntly:

"You have to have the courage and the power to say, 'That's the food that I am offering today. Taste it. Go and eat.'"

I am not suggesting that school menus be planned without concern for the children's preferences; I think the taste tests and surveys are great, and a wise cafeteria manager keeps an eye on the garbage pail to see what is not being eaten. Anyone who has raised a child, however, knows that adults must model healthy behavior and adults must make the rules. Research suggests that many children actively fear unfamiliar foods and require repeated exposure and perhaps a bit of cajoling or peer pressure before getting up the nerve to try them. But the adult role models and the opportunities for cajoling are missing if the teachers shun the cafeteria and its food, and the positive peer pressure won't occur if the peers are buying snack foods.

Another problem with the kids-are-customers/school-food-is-a-business model is that it does not fit the realities of school food service. School food is not just a concession located in a public building, like a snack shop in a national park. It is confronted with all sorts of rules and regulations with which other food services do not have to comply. It must provide special meals for children with a wide array of disabilities and allergies. But school food service is not allowed to charge extra for such meals—neither the parents nor the government can be asked to pay more. These are surely legitimate expectations, requirements, for a program that receives public funds from a society committed to mainstreaming children with special needs. My point is not that food service should not have to do these things, but that school food service is not a business and telling it to "operate like a business" is a distortion of the reality.

There are many other ways in which school food departs from the norms of a business model. In the first place, food service managers have only limited control over labor costs, wages, and hiring procedures. They can certainly influence employee take-home pay by adjusting work hours, but they often cannot give any form of merit raises. On the other side of the ledger, many school food service operations do not set their own prices. They generally need the approval of the school board, and school boards are sometimes reluctant to approve a price increase, especially in election years. In any case, raising the prices tends to hurt those who are already hurting. They usually cannot change prices during the school year, but they also cannot adjust to rising costs by cutting down on portion sizes, which are specified in the federal regulations. In fact, as we have seen, they have to comply with a whole host of nutritional requirements and specifications, standards that clearly set them apart from the business model. Restaurants in New York City may now be required to eliminate trans fats, but few could stay in business if they had to meet the federal nutrient requirements for school food. I find myself with considerable sympathy for the school food service personnel who have been urged by school boards and by their professional association to "run the cafeteria like a business," and then made to feel like failed entrepreneurs when this prescription did not break even.

The business model of school food, and the relentless pressure to break even have gone a long way toward eroding what was once a good job for parents, particularly mothers. Many of the mature school food service workers whom I interviewed told me that they first got into cafeteria work because they wanted a job that would allow them to be off during their children's vacations and holidays. A group of school food directors that I interviewed in Vermont told me the same thing: "Mothers are really the best, my best workers, mothers who are working because they want the hours. They want to be home when their children are home," said one director. Surely we want such child-centered people in our school cafeterias. Marion Nestle has told me that among the many school food service operations she has visited, the single factor that correlates most reliably with children actually eating the food was whether or not the staff know the children's names. The low pay, however, makes it difficult for women who are the sole support of their families to stay in school food service: "Some of the people who work for me get food stamps. They are extremely low income." In a society in which so many children are living in households headed by a lone parent, it strikes me as bad social policy to replace relatively secure, unionized jobs on the school calendar, jobs with health insurance and pension plans, with low wage jobs characterized by "short hours" and inadequate income.

When the tyranny of the bottom line drives school systems to contract out their food service operations to profit-making management companies, corporate policies designed for profitability often supersede local school district policies in the labor arena, as well as in procurement. Some school districts have been able to protect the seniority of their front line workers and their union representation in the contracting-out process. Others have not, but over time, the private management approach generally shifts food service into the culture of private industry. We need to rethink the business model, not only because it doesn't fit the school food reality, but also because the civil service model has historically made major contributions to upward mobility in our society. We need a supply of decent jobs that are compatible with parenting, that build skill, that offer security and lead to careers.

From both the consumption and production perspectives, then, there is a great deal to be said for the original vision of the creators of the National School Lunch Program, who specified that federal funds and commodities should go only to nonprofit lunch programs. I doubt they could have foreseen the sorts of creative interpretation that have allowed the specific practice of contracting with private management firms or the more general conversion of school food service to a self-supporting "business" within the school system. Surely they could not have envisioned that school systems would be billing their food services for electricity and gas for the cafeteria or for payroll services and other "indirect costs." This practice of billing food service operations for such costs is more than an accounting practice; it reveals the extent to which school cafeterias are seen as alien to the educational mission of the school. Part of understanding whether the people who eat in the cafeteria are customers or students, whether school food is a business or a part of education, has to do with the extent to which school meals are integrated into the curriculum and regarded as part of teaching by teachers and principals.

3. An interruption or an integral part of the school day?

"It's this wasted half hour," the education professor Karen Evans Stout says of the typical American school lunch. "We don't use that time to teach a thing." Stout has studied lunch periods in both Europe and the United States and finds ours sorely wanting by comparison.[16] She is talking not just about the time students spend waiting in line, but the failure of American public education to harness this central human experience as an opportunity for teaching and learning. I say "public education," because it is clear that many private schools have long viewed the lunch hour as an important arena for socializing youngsters, for teaching them responsibility and civility and sensitivity, and for the development of social skills and other forms of "social capital." With very young children, public schools still assume that adults should be in charge and that children should be taught the basics of sharing and respect. Think back to All I Really Need to Know I Learned in Kindergarten. As children grow older, however, far too many schools leave them to their own devices, with only the harried commands of "lunch monitors" or even security guards to regulate their interactions. Think of the depictions of food fights in cafeterias or the emotional and sometimes physical intimidation and bullying that so often occur in that setting.

As Michele Lawrence, the superintendent of the Berkeley, California, public schools told an interviewer from the Center for Ecoliteracy, "I'm coming to realize that the lunch hour and the delivery of food to kids is an opportunity for learning that we have almost completely ignored and need to include. . . . I am realizing that we have an educational obligation . . . in that time every day called 'the lunch period' to consider what's happening to our learner. This is part of the day that educators traditionally think of as outside the formal educational process."[17] As a friend observed to me, many school administrators look at the cafeteria as the proverbial "black box," students go in hungry and, hopefully, come out fed, and what happens in between is a mystery.

The interruption model, school meals as an opportunity for adults to get away from children and for the latter to "let off steam," seems to me to confuse the cafeteria with the playground. It goes hand in hand with a dismissive attitude toward school food service staff, simultaneously undervaluing and underutilizing the contributions of an entire set of adults on the school premises who could be allies in the accomplishment of the school's basic mission. In many schools, school food personnel are regarded not as part of the educational team, but as "kitchen help," almost servants.[18] "You don't have legs" was how one food service director in Vermont put it: "You stand behind a counter. You don't have legs." Her implication was that you were seen as not fully human. Listing the things she would like to change, she said: "the status of the job, that it be an employee of the school in a way that has the same status as any other person in the school, instead of an add-on or a lower class citizen or something. That lunch-lady image, that's not valued." School food service directors in large cities often oversee departments with hundreds of employees and budgets of millions of dollars. They must have expertise in nutrition, management, procurement, and marketing. Many have masters degrees and some have doctorates. But school systems have been almost completely unable to see them as educators, clinging to the image of "Miss Beazly" from the Archie comics or other equally unflattering (and distorted) images. Students looking for a topic for a term paper or a master's thesis might take a critical look at the imagery of "cafeteria ladies" in American popular culture.

Given the extent to which our nation's health problems—and ever-escalating health care costs—are rooted in the way we eat, it is easy to imagine that we might rely upon our schools to model and teach healthy eating and on our school food service departments to take the lead in this endeavor, but it will not happen, I believe, until more principals and school administrators adopt the point of view articulated to me by James "Torch" Lytle, now a professor in the School of Education at the University of Pennsylvania, about his experience leading a large and highly successful inner city school in Philadelphia:

> When I say the faculty, I include everybody. The secret of University City High School was that the security guards and the secretaries and the food service people and custodial staff were all part of the faculty, and since they were more likely to come from the neighborhood and know the kids and know what the kids' lives were like, the fact that we really had a kind of cohesive adult community really made it possible to be a lot more responsive to the kids. . . . Those are the folks who know the kids better than anybody. And if you don't make them part of the staff and listen to them, you're going to miss a lot of what you need to know.

He credited the food service staff with playing a major role in heading off fights among the students before they reached the boiling point.

The learning opportunities being missed in far too many schools are not just those that have to do with social relations, with acceptable and desirable ways of treating other people in the cafeteria and beyond. There are also exciting, engaging possibilities for instruction in academic content that are too frequently left lying on the table. In my experience, nearly everyone is interested in food. Everyone gets hungry. Everyone has likes and dislikes. Many of us have "issues." The rise of food studies programs in colleges and universities has been rapid and immensely gratifying to those who have led it. There are now food-related courses in a whole host of disciplines, as well as interdisciplinary degree programs, and the proliferation of the food-related academic literature has been nothing short of spectacular. Yet this central shared human experience plays remarkably little role in most American K–12 school curricula.

Schools do not have to start from scratch to integrate food into our children's education. One of the joys of this research has been my encounter with food educators dedicated to empowering children to become healthier consumers through innovative curricula. If you visit the kitchen classroom located in the Edible Schoolyard at Berkeley's Martin Luther King, Junior, Middle School, the innovative garden-based learning project that engages students in planting, tending, harvesting, preparing, and eating food, you can see just how interdisciplinary, and just how exciting, food-based education can be. History, art, language, math, and biology all go into the lessons there. Antonia Demas, of the Food Studies Institute, has developed a wonderful hands-on curriculum for children in the elementary grades, while Isobel Contento and her colleagues at Teacher's College, Columbia have pioneered LIFE—Linking Food and the Environment—an inquiry-based science curriculum for grades 4–6. In chapter 8 we looked at the Cookshop and Cooking with Kids programs. The staff of the Philadelphia Food Trust offers workshops for teachers, helping them to design units across the curriculum—math, science, social studies—that help to instill appreciation for healthy food and simultaneously meet state-specified curricular standards. The models are out there. They have been tried, evaluated, and in many cases, proven effective from both an academic and a behavioral standpoint. That is, children have both learned new concepts and tried and appreciated new foods.

Both of my parents were teachers, so perhaps that is why I have such a strong conviction that education begins with engagement, that you start by harnessing children's inquisitive natures and by addressing their own most pressing concerns. As Alice Boughton put it nearly a century ago, "utilize a child's natural appetite to teach him." What is more pressing for a typical six-year-old than the question of "what's for lunch?" What is more pressing for a thirteen-year-old than the issues of appearance or athletic performance? And what seems to me an enormous missed opportunity brings me back to my plea for consideration of universal free school meals. If we had such an approach, if we could assume that nearly all children in school on a given day were going to have the same basic choices, then we could begin to integrate the menu into the curriculum and the lunch period into the educational mission. Our cafeterias could evolve from fast food markets to edible classrooms.

In order to maximize these opportunities, however, I think we need to draw teachers back into the cafeteria. It is not uncommon now for teachers to regard "cafeteria duty" as a sort of punishment or at least as an unwelcome assignment to be accepted as infrequently as possible. The atmosphere is really very different, however, where teachers sit with their students, as I saw them doing in the huge, bare dining halls of the United Talmudic Academies in Brooklyn. UTA is one of the school systems serving the Satmar Hassidic community, and both the schools and the students are overwhelmingly impoverished. The meal was simple, but the students appeared to relish it, and even though the acoustics and furnishings were far from ideal, a room filled with several hundred students maintained a noise level that permitted students to converse with each other and with their teachers. I saw teachers eating with their students in other places around the country—not patrolling the cafeteria, but sharing the meal—and these were almost always the places where the meal hour was the least stressful, the most relaxed, the most conducive to learning. Under my universal vision, I'd offer the meal free to any teacher who ate it with students in the cafeteria, or perhaps to any teacher who simply ate it in the cafeteria. In Sweden, teachers ate at tables with the younger students, but in the high schools, they tended to eat together in small groups dispersed throughout the room—close enough by to exert a calming influence, but far enough away to allow students some privacy for their own concerns.

4. A nutrition program or a food program?

Among the food and nutrition educators who have grappled with the challenge of teaching children healthy food habits, and increasingly in the general population as well, there is a mounting suspicion of the whole "nutritionist" paradigm, often expressed as "people don't eat nutrients; they eat food." Many believe that the entire nutritional analysis and education enterprise is flawed, misguided, and ineffective. We know more and more about nutrition, but our national diet gets less and less healthy. Affluence and convenience trump common sense. We follow specific pieces of nutritional advice—eat less fat or fewer carbs—but we don't follow them in ways that actually improve our health. "The problem with nutrient-by-nutrient nutrition science," declares the New York University nutritionist Marion Nestle, "is that it takes the nutrient out of the context of food, the food out of the context of diet, and the diet out of the context of lifestyle."[19] There has been a critical discourse within the field of nutrition for decades, but recently the journalist Michael Pollan has become the foremost critic of "nutritionism," a term he borrowed from the Australian sociologist Gyorgy Scrinis. Nutritionism is in fact an ideology, and like all ideologies, it is based on unexamined assumptions. According to Pollan, in nutritionism, "the widely shared but unexamined assumption is that the key to understanding food is indeed the nutrient. From this basic premise flow several others. Since nutrients, as compared to foods, are invisible and therefore slightly mysterious, it falls to the scientists (and to the journalists through whom the scientists speak) to explain the hidden reality of foods to us. To enter a world in which you dine on unseen nutrients, you need lots of expert help."[20] That expert help, however, Pollan says, has been based on science that is proving with increasing frequency to have been wrong, and even when the science has been sound, the nuances have been lost in translation. People trying hard to follow this nutrient-based expert advice have far too often seen their health deteriorate rather than improve.

Pollan contrasts such expert help with "tradition and common sense. Most of what we need to know about how to eat we already know, or once did until we allowed the nutrition experts and the advertisers to shake our confidence in common sense, tradition, the testimony of our senses, and the wisdom of our mothers and grandmothers."[21] His reference to grandmothers, and what he calls the "great-grandmother rule" ("don't eat anything your great-grandmother wouldn't recognize as food"), reminds me of something that Terry Shintani told me about his work with Native Hawaiians in the interview quoted in the introduction to this book: "One of the things I say is, eat the way your ancestors ate. And that becomes a very good teaching tool, because if . . . I'm in the community and I talk grams of monounsaturated fats, I'll lose them. Complex carbohydrates, etc. The community will remember things that are much more familiar. . . . I remember in one class, someone asked, 'Okay, can I eat fried fish?' and I said, 'Well, did your ancestors eat fried fish?' 'Oh, no, they didn't have frying pans. They didn't have frying oil.' They will never forget that."

I am not recommending that schools give up frying pans and oil, but I am recommending that we think more about foods and guidelines that are expressed in clear, memorable terms of foods rather than percentages of nutrients. Clearly this critique has implications for nutrition education in schools. I do think we need to teach children to read labels, for a host of reasons, including the remarkable prevalence of food allergies, but I don't think they need to be able to recite the DRIs (formerly known as RDAs) or calculate complex percentages of macronutrients in particular products. In my own life, I have found three pieces of food advice to have the most salutary effect on my diet: (1) "Five a day"—eat at least five servings of fruit and vegetables daily; (2) "Eat all parts of the plant: roots, stems, leaves, seeds, flowers, fruit," a guideline I learned from Joan Gussow when I audited her class a quarter-century ago, and (3) "Limit highly processed foods," what Pollan calls "edible food-like substances." I am not a vegetarian, but like most Americans, my diet could probably be improved by eating less meat, more plant foods, fewer added sugars, and less salt. These three simple guidelines—which speak of foods, not nutrients—help me to do that. And when I follow the first two, I have less appetite left over for the highly processed, packaged foods that I believe are undermining our health. Have you ever sat in a meeting, opening a snack picked up on the run—say a package of cookies—only to have a colleague peel an orange and fill the room with that wonderful citrus aroma, accompanied in my case, at least, by a touch of envy and a resolution to remember to carry a tangerine myself, next time? This is not a commercial for my favorite nutritional guidance; it is an effort to raise the issue of what works, and how we can best incorporate a knowledge of what works into the education that takes place in the cafeteria.

My concern about "nutritionism," however, is not limited to the nutrition education project. I believe we need to rethink the role of nutrition science in setting guidelines for school meals. I know that the federal nutrition standards that govern school food are carefully designed and well intended, but as far as I can see, they often backfire. The effort to simultaneously ensure certain minimums without exceeding ceilings for fat and saturated fat leads to excessive reliance on fortified factory foods and to replacing whole milk with sweetened, flavored low-fat milk. As we saw in chapter 4, there are so many slips twixt cup and lip that many of the actual meals real children eat appear sadly deficient from a common sense perspective, even though they may come from a menu that meets federal nutrition standards. Monochromatic meals are almost never well balanced, and monochromatic meals—golden chicken nuggets, golden fries, and a golden roll—were prevalent nearly everywhere I went. We might make an improvement in school food simply by specifying "leafy green" before "vegetable" and considering the reclassification of potatoes. Anyone who has ever watched weight will tell you that, despite their wonderful endowment of vitamin C, potatoes are "starchy" and belong in the category with bread or rice, not as a substitute for salad or collard greens. I have a feeling that many school cafeterias would actually serve healthier meals if "Eat Your Colors" were the primary standard.

Advocates of better school food have argued that the nutrition standards have been essential, not only in protecting the quality of meals but also in resisting efforts to further erode federal funding for school food.[22] When I asked Lynn Parker, until recently the director of FRAC's child nutrition advocacy, whether it might be time to reconsider calorie minimums in light of the rising rates of obesity, her answer was instructive: "Well, the concern remains that kids need calories to concentrate in school. Low-income kids, if they didn't have breakfast, if they are not going to have something substantial when they get home, then you are concerned that the lunch provide them with sufficient calories and you also want them to get the fruits and vegetables, and that requires a certain level of calories." It would create the possibility, she pointed out that "schools that want to reduce costs or companies that want to reduce costs per plate will produce meals that are significantly lower in calories that may not meet the needs of the kids who actually are eating the meals." She called it a "scary prospect," and went on to remind me that it was the one-third of RDA requirement "that protected us when the Reagan administration wanted to cut funding. . . . So there is something very valuable about having standards like that, in order to protect from budget cuts." I do not suggest that my own preliminary ideas are ready to be substituted for the ones currently in place. But I do urge a new look at what children are actually eating, and if others find it as troubling as I have, then we should go back to the drawing boards to find a better approach to defining what might be included in an official school lunch. In so doing, I hope that the emerging insights into the limits of nutritionism can be taken into account. It has clearly failed to solve our problems and has often obscured common sense and the sort of appreciation of foods—colors, textures, scents, and, of course, tastes—that served humanity for millennia as guides to the age-old question of what to eat.

5.   Pay now or pay later? A cost or an investment?

Somewhere we need to talk about how to pay for the healthier food we want to serve. Suppose, for a minute, that we added 50 cents to the federal reimbursement for all lunches—not just free and reduced price meals, but the "paid" meals as well—and 25 cents to each breakfast, thus allowing us to serve healthier meals without raising the "full" price. At five billion lunches and two billion breakfasts per year, that would cost $3 billion, even without the increase in participation that could be expected if meal quality improved and/or prices for paying students were lowered. And it does not in any way include the price tag for moving to a universal free approach. But what about $3 billion more per year? Can we afford it? It depends, I think, on whether it would make enough difference in what our children actually eat to slow down the increasing rates of diabetes and obesity and have an impact on eventual rates of cancer and heart disease. The long-term trend is toward greater and greater public participation in the financing of health care. In the long run, when the health costs of childhood obesity and early onset diabetes come home to roost, they will fall heavily on public systems. If we could be sure that these interventions would actually work, then the question would become, could we afford not to make this investment? A study by the Institute of Medicine reported estimates of national direct and indirect health care expenditures related to obesity and overweight in adults alone ranging from $98 billion to $129 billion annually, and this included many adults who were slim as youngsters.[23] These figures do not include the loss of work hours and earnings attributable to premature death, estimated at another $56 billion a year. Nor do they calculate the financial impact of the fact that obese Americans suffer higher rates of disability and early retirement.[24]

The other side of the equation, however, is the question of what improvements in actual food intake and prevalence of obesity we can expect from various levels of investment. This is trickier. The literature on current interventions is mixed and guarded. As a recent review of interventions summarized, "school-based obesity-prevention interventions have shown some success in changing eating and physical activity behaviors but have been less effective in changing body weight or body fatness."[25] As we saw in chapter 4, the rate of improvement in school meals as measured by the SNDA series has leveled off; I suspect we have made most of the improvements that we can make based on the SMI and local wellness policies.

My own assessment is that these marginal improvements are not enough. I do not believe we will have a significant impact on "diabesity" by replacing the sodas in the vending machines with sports drinks or even juice, nor fried chips with baked chips. Instead, we need to get rid of competitive foods altogether and with them the easy access to snacking through the day; we need adults to be regularly involved with children at mealtimes; and we need to serve fresh, healthy appetizing foods with a strong emphasis on what we know is missing from our children's diets: fruits and vegetables, and whole grains and legumes. If we can really change the way our children are eating—from the scenario in which only 2 percent met the federal recommendations in all five categories, while 16 percent met none, to a scenario where most children are eating a whole grain, a calcium source, and several fruits and vegetables at school every day—then I imagine that our investment will pay off.[26]

When you think about it, our current level of investment is actually fairly meager. When you take the federal reimbursement and subtract the costs that go to pay for administering the means test and ensuring "accountability," the amount available for food and labor is pretty paltry. The Cornell University nutritionist and farm to school activist Jennifer Wilkins has estimated that most schools have less than a dollar to spend on food for each meal, once labor and administrative costs have been subtracted.[27] It is a kind of magical thinking to believe that we can create healthy, palatable food at that level of expenditure. I was fascinated to learn that meals served at senior citizens centers in New York State typically cost between $5 and $8 to prepare and serve, or that the meals served to hungry guests at Holy Apostles Soup Kitchen in Manhattan work out to nearly $7 apiece, despite the fact that the kitchen relies on the free labor of forty to fifty volunteers each day.[28] Some schools do manage to serve healthy appealing food at current levels of reimbursement, because they have relatively low labor costs or exceptional talent or the very high participation rates that allow economies of scale. Nevertheless, I think that if we relaxed the nutrient-based standards and returned to a more common sense approach, there might be some savings accruable through serving simpler meals. I am not talking about counting ketchup as a vegetable, but I'd like to see more soup and sandwich lunches, or soup and salad bar lunches.

Some readers will laugh when they read "soup," and tell me that students won't eat soups or stews. I agree they probably won't eat soups or stews if they have the choice of the familiar and heavily advertised pizza and nuggets, but that in fact they probably can learn to eat soups and stews just fine if the vending machines are gone from the halls and the a la carte line disappears. Why this sudden pitch for soups and stews? Because we are discussing costs, and soups and stews are great for preventing waste. I cannot fathom how I could keep food waste to tolerable levels in my own home if I did not make soup or the occasional casserole, and in institutional settings, the possibilities for waste are enormous and consequently so are the possibilities of savings from avoiding waste. Anything that reduces waste will reduce the unit cost of providing meals.

Perhaps waste should be its own separate question (a wasteful program or a thrifty one?), but it seems to me that it is inseparable from the issue of cost, particularly in the context of discussion of a universal program. One of the most useful functions of prices is to deter waste; a professor in graduate school drove this home to me once by asking me how I would behave if photocopying were free. If school food were "free," how could we control waste? But I'm much less worried about this since I visited Camp Speers El-Ja-Bar, a YMCA Camp in northeastern Pennsylvania, for a summer lunch with campers in the 11–14 age group.

I've already mentioned the enjoyable common meal atmosphere of camp lunches and dinners, but the thing that impressed me most in that visit was the near absence of food waste. Youngsters could return for seconds, even thirds, but they were expected to eat everything they took. I asked the counselors how this norm, thoroughly familiar to me from my own clean-plate childhood but not so ubiquitous today, was enforced. "Oh," one said, "at the first meal we collect all the scraps and weigh them and post the figure as the 'Ort Report.' We do it every day, and we try to get it down to zero." Of course we cannot do that all the time in every cafeteria, but it does seem to me that we can enlist young people in reducing waste. Where an appeal to environmental protection won't work, we could offer incentives: a movie, an extra recess period, or some sort of healthy treat when the collective waste is reduced below some reasonable threshold. Classes could do research on solid waste management; schools could hold waste-reduction competitions among lunch shifts or areas of the cafeteria. School food service directors could put their creativity into waste reduction instead of spending it all on competing with fast food.

More important, perhaps, would be to import the fundamental principle of family style meals—take only what you will eat, and return for seconds if you are still hungry. Food is valuable; it represents the labor of farmers, processing-plant workers, cooks, and cafeteria staff as well as nature's underlying gifts to us. We should not be teaching our children to waste it, but to treat it with respect. A universal format, by removing the endless accounting, would make such family style service more feasible. Of course, waste reduction is desirable even if we do not convert to a universal format, but the possibility of universal certainly escalates the urgency of creating new strategies, not only because people are more likely to waste what they perceive as "free," but also because the numbers of students eating will almost certainly increase in a universal system. So the discussion of waste leads naturally enough back to the issue of universal and how to pay for it.

How can we pay for universal? From what pool of money, people ask me, do I imagine drawing the resources necessary to feed all our children at school? As Representative George Miller said when he introduced a bill providing for a universal option in Congress in 1992, "I fully appreciate, Mr. Speaker, that there will be those who say this is a great idea, but it is one we cannot afford given the size of our deficit." I would point out, however, that charging parents who can afford to pay does not make the meals cheaper in any fundamental sense; indeed, adding the cumbersome application, certification, verification, and accountability process and all of the costs associated with handling money makes the meals more expensive to provide. We are eating up much of the Section 4 subsidy for "full price" meals, squandering it on the tasks associated with the means test. It is not just the administrative cost at the local level, but also the state and federal oversight needed to control errors. "I have fourteen auditors for fourteen days," the director of one large urban system told me, describing a review process in which the state education agency audited her books while the federal auditors from the regional office watched them to make sure they were doing it correctly. "CREs [Coordinated Review Efforts] are expensive," she told me: "hotels, rental cars, meals, an exit interview every day, extensive preparation of records, all of that to find $75 worth of error." There is, indeed, "no such thing as a free lunch," but the question of who pays is a social choice that we need to reconsider.

A leaner, sleeker process would fund school meals from the proceeds of the federal income tax. Parents of higher income students would pay more through the progressive structure. Of course, those who are not parents would pay as well. To my mind, that makes sense. Most affluent societies find ways to help parents defray the costs of child rearing, because they recognize that people in all stages of life have a stake in promoting the healthy development of the next generation. Between the damage associated with inadequate diet and the need for a well-educated work force, school food seems almost the poster child for this argument. Who does not have a stake in the way we feed our children at school? If taxing non-parents is truly a sticking point, however, it would be possible to raise some of the funds for universal free school meals by reducing the dependent child tax exemption for parents with school-age children and incomes over, say, $150,000.[29]

After decades of conservative anti-tax ideology, however, taxation has been given such a bad reputation in the United States that we are unable to think straight about situations in which it makes sense. As Mimi Abramovitz and Sandra Morgen have written, "The rhetoric of the tax 'burden' has been used to undermine our understanding of the reciprocal relationship between taxpayers and governments that provide the public services essential to our national well-being. And anti-tax activists who rail against 'tax and spend' policies have used the rhetoric to deflect attention from a long overdue dialogue about an adequate and effective level of public services, ignoring the fact that a policy based on taxing fairly and spending wisely is always sound public policy."[30]

When the anti-tax pendulum swings too far, citizens find their private investment, even their lives, put in jeopardy by the failure to provide adequate public services, as in the Minneapolis bridge collapse that occurred in 2007. There is such a thing as too low a level of taxation. If the property tax is sufficiently low in my city, I may have enough money to buy a fancy new car, but if the city fails to fix potholes in a timely manner because it has inadequate revenue, then my fancy new car may be damaged, and I might have been better off with my old car and a smoother street surface. Most people "get it" about bridge and street maintenance, because a bridge is a collective good. Goods consumed individually are a harder sell, but there are other situations in which it is easy to see the value of public provision, even if the benefit is individualized. Garbage collection comes to mind. The most immediate benefit is clearly to the household, and there are municipalities that do not provide garbage collection, leaving it up to the homeowner to hire a carting service and pay the costs. Nearly all large cities, however, have determined that this individually consumable service has broader public implications—that others will be negatively affected if the homeowner fails to arrange adequate collection, that most of the methods a homeowner might use to reduce the volume of trash to be collected (burning paper in the back yard as we did when I was a child, for example) have negative consequences for the whole community, and that individually assessing homeowners based on the volume of waste they produce is inefficient and probably not feasible. There are many circumstances in which public expenditure—and thus taxation—works better than relying on individual and family fees. School food, I believe, is a situation in which public financing is simply more reasonable and efficient than trying to distinguish among levels of need and calibrate benefits accordingly.

One of the peculiarities of federalism is that even after we make a decision to fund some activity through public expenditure, we still have to decide which level of government can most appropriately and effectively handle a particular task. This leads, unfortunately, to endless rounds of finger-pointing and evasion; it allows political actors to support causes and proposals for which they do not expect to have to pay. Since school food in the United States has long been a federal program and since the federal government has a variety of revenue generating options, I imagine drawing the resources for universal, or most of them, from the federal treasury. If the history of school food in the United States had evolved differently, I might be proposing a more robust role for the states in funding this new approach, but school food has been a federal program long enough that I think a return to state responsibility at this point is wishful thinking. Further, the states typically vary at any given time in their capacity to take on new financial obligations, and many right now are reeling under revenue reductions associated with the end of the housing bubble or the evaporation of value from financial markets. Further, many states rely on sales taxes, which are regressive, as opposed to progressive income taxes.

Of course, school food was originally a local project in the United States, and a case could be made for increasing local contributions— were school finance not in a morass precisely because schools are supported by local tax revenues (generally property taxes), and thus schools in poor communities, where education might be expected to cost more, have the least to invest.[31] (This is another issue that I believe we must address, sooner or later, as a nation, since the days are long gone when the products of a particular school system are likely to remain in town. Geographic mobility gives us all a stake in the effectiveness of all our schools, but that is another topic, ably addressed by others.) But even if some form of combined local, state, and federal funding might be ideal from an accountability standpoint, and even by a "fairness" standard, school food has been a federal (USDA) program so long that I simply find it difficult to imagine turning the clock back to heavier reliance on state and local funding.

How much would universal cost? Once the proposal for universal free meals reaches the stage of actual legislation, the Congressional Budget Office (CBO) will "cost out" the measure far more accurately and precisely than I can do it, but I can use the results of earlier CBO calculations to provide a rough idea, a sort of back-of-the-envelope estimate. When Representative George Miller introduced his legislation for universal free meals in 1992, he proposed an optional program that could be selected by local areas. The CBO estimated that by 1998, the cost of his proposal would reach twice the "baseline cost"—that is, a 100 percent increase over the cost of simply continuing the existing program. The CBO further projected that implementing a total national universal program rather than Miller's optional approach would require an increase of about 120 percent over the baseline. Currently, we spend about $11 billion on lunch and breakfast combined; if the same ratio applied, funding a total national universal program would cost an additional $13.2 billion annually. Overall participation in the program (as a percentage of enrollment) is about six percentage points, or 10 percent, higher than it was in 1992, so the pool of students who might be added is smaller, making the total increase in cost more modest. Let's say that universal would cost an additional $12 billion annually.

Coincidentally, that is about the amount that the president's budget specifies for the conflicts in Iraq and Afghanistan for *each month* of fiscal year 2009.[32] And that's for current expenses. Realistically, if we include the long-term costs of debt service and of providing rehabilitation and care for veterans, the cost of our wars is much higher. I understand that we cannot simply, miraculously, redirect the expenditure from the wars in Iraq and Afghanistan to school food. My intent is to give some sense of the size of the funding increment that would be needed—the effective price tag—and to point out that there do seem to be ways of "finding" money if we really want to. The "bailout" funded in response to the banking crisis would have been enough to pay for a conversion to universal free school meals for more than half a century.[33]

Of course, this estimate presumes the current reimbursement rates, and I have just argued that these should be increased. What about the $3 billion more I discussed above?[34] If we move to universal, I believe that we will save substantial amounts so that better meals could be produced at the current reimbursement rates, but probably not enough to provide meals of the quality we would like to see. At a conference of food service personnel from large cities, I asked the directors sitting at my table which they would rather have, a 50-cent increase in reimbursement rates across the board, or universal free at the current levels. Their answer was immediate and unanimous: "Universal." In part this is a matter of principle, but they also anticipated enormous savings from removing the burden of determining eligibility, certifying, verifying and counting and claiming. USDA calculations made in the mid-1990s projected far more modest savings; a study prepared for Congress estimated that conversion to a universal format would save twenty-five million hours of paperwork that the department valued at $550 million, or 10 cents per meal. Converted to 2008 dollars, that would be $798 million.[35] It is difficult to know how to assess this estimate, as the report provided no information on how it was derived. The various no-fee pilots initiated in 1992 had reported considerably higher savings per meal—19 cents in Philadelphia, for example, even after paying for the demographic study.[36] The directors were also imagining economies from greater volume and more predictable participation, but my guess is that the discrepancy between the department's perceptions of the savings to be achieved (back in 1994) and the more recent expectations of the food service directors stems in part from the escalating demands for accountability in the interim and the antipathy of the directors to doing business in the stressful climate of uncertainty and suspicion that has been generated by the focus on "erroneous payments."[37]

But whether the added cost of better meals on a universal basis turns out to be $12 billion or $16 billion, we still need to think about potential sources for such expenditure. Since I cannot go back in time and avoid the Iraq war, where else could we find an additional $13 billion or $14 billion a year? One place would be to adjust the national tax burden to reflect our professed national work ethic. At present, we tax unearned income—capital gains—at far lower rates than we tax earned income except for the two lowest tax brackets. Long-term capital gains are taxed at 15 percent, the same as the incomes of people in the tax bracket from $7,150–$29,050. In 2005, net capital gains totaled $668 billion. If we taxed that at 20 percent instead of 15 percent, we could have another $33.4 billion annually to improve school food, reduce the deficit, invest in health and education, or help home buyers refinance their mortgages. This is not the place for a primer on tax reform, nor am I equipped to provide one.[38] I hope, however, that I have made my point that what seems at first like a very large sum is not so huge relatively. If indeed we financed improved universal free school meals by a change in the capital gains tax, it would serve a decidedly redistributive function, ameliorating a benefit already received by millions of poor children by removing the stigma and improving the quality and simultaneously assisting "near poor," lower-middle- and middle-income families, who are all feeling mounting stress in the current economy. With inequality at levels not seen since before the Great Depression, such redistribution seems welcome in its own right.

More simply, we could find the money for better school meals on a universal basis by taxing soft drinks. The Center for Science in the Public Interest has told the Senate Finance Committee that a tax of a penny an ounce—adding 12 cents to a typical can of soda or 16 to a bottle of sweetened iced tea—would raise $16 billion a year and have the beneficial side effect of reducing consumption of sweetened drinks. A smaller tax of 1 cent per (12 oz.) serving would raise $1.5 billion a year.[39] This is a sticky wicket to say the least, even setting aside the proven capacity of the soft drink industry to frustrate any legislation that threatens its profitability. In the first place, there is the slippery slope of telling other people how to eat. Soft drinks are one of the treats that low-income families have been able to afford, but they are a pleasure that carries both known and suspected health risks. As Susan Lynn Roberts, who is both a nutritionist and an attorney, has summarized, "they pose health risks both because of what they contain—sugar and caffeine—and what they replace in the diet."[40] Soft drink consumption is clearly associated with obesity, and thus with diabetes, and as Mark Winne has put it, obesity and diabetes are "a disaster that has cut a deeper and wider furrow through the lives of the poor than it has through those of the rich."[41] If the fundamental objective is to promote health and free our children from the burdens of a lifetime of managing weight and diabetes, then discouraging consumption is desirable, and a bit of telling people how to eat may be in order. The industry, after all, spends many billions of dollars each year to tell people that soft drinks will make their lives happier, increase their popularity with their peers, and give them energy. But there is a deeper issue that I find more troubling. Like any tax on food, a tax on soft drinks is regressive; it takes a bigger bite out of the budgets of the poor than those of the affluent. There is something a bit unseemly about funding the provision of free meals to the "non-poor" by a tax that falls most heavily on the poor, even though I am convinced that a universal program would serve the needs of the poor far better than the current three-tier approach. Perhaps we should be taxing soft drink advertising rather than soft drinks themselves.

Finally, of course, we could fund added investment in school food simply by reducing income guarantees and support payments to the producers of "basic commodities" including corn and soy. Many groups championed this cause in the recent Farm Bill discussions. You can see the glass as half full: the Dorgan-Grassley amendment that would have capped such payments at $250,000 per farmer received fifty-six votes in the Senate. Or half empty: even with majority support it failed because in the Senate a sixty-vote minimum is needed to avoid a filibuster and allow the amendment to move forward. Dorgan-Grassley would have saved $1.15 billion over five years, not enough to fix school lunch, but certainly a down payment on the fundamental shift in farm policy that we need if we are to produce for human health instead of simply to maximize profit. There is money in the Farm Bill that could be used to improve school food if we can ever escape from the vicious cycle of commodity payments—those same payments that promote the production of high-fructose corn syrup and make shelf-stable packaged foods both possible and profitable. So now we come full circle to the situation underlying the critique of school food: the food system, which leads me to the final question.

6. *A reflection of the American food system or a tool to change it?*

This is really a philosophical question about public sector procurement. Do we want to treat procurement as a purely business decision, suggesting a heavy reliance on low-bid contracts to supply school food service with everything from beverage containers to hamburger meat, or do we want to pay attention to the potential impact of procurement on such diverse agendas as animal welfare, solid-waste management, living wages for farm workers, and preservation of rural communities? Are there factors other than price that we want to take into account? As Roberta Sonnino and Kevin Morgan have put it, do we want best value or best values? "Real 'value for money,'" they assert, "needs to be buttressed by a broader, more sustainable metric, one that reflects a range of social and cultural values, rather than a single and narrowly defined economic value."[42] As a nation, we have already asserted the value of product safety, although the effectiveness of our safeguards is under heavy scrutiny in the wake of the latest meat recall and the rising frequency of *E. coli* 0157:H7 contamination. I was interested to learn that we have also already assigned a value to certain aspects of animal welfare. Questioned about an apparent discrepancy that forbids the processing of "non-ambulatory disabled cattle" for USDA purchases for school lunch, but allows them for meat to enter the general commercial supply, a federal spokesman asserted, "There is really no inconsistency. . . . Federal purchase requirements exclude meat from non-ambulatory animals based on animal welfare considerations, not food safety concerns." He went on to explain that USDA had adopted the regulations, according to the Washington Post, "in response to feedback from school lunch operators that the welfare of the animals was an emerging concern."[43]

A long-simmering dispute between advocates of farm to school programs and USDA has concerned the legality of specifying in bids for purchase of foods for school a preference for food originating locally (or within the state). As we have seen, the "buy local" movement, when it comes to school cafeterias, poses many logistical challenges for school food service operators, but advocates thought they had solved the legal question when Congress included language authorizing local preferences in the 2004 Child Nutrition Reauthorization. USDA, however, interpreted the language in such a way as to permit it to continue to forbid locality in a bid specification. The 2008 Farm Bill has made the language even more unequivocal. "Local" is now legal, not only for produce but also for meat and dairy products.

The question I am raising here, however, goes beyond mere specification of factors that must or may be taken into account to the notion of a conscious strategy to shift the food system. The activist and author Mark Winne summarized a strategy for me: "Through the institutions that we control as citizens, as taxpayers, let's use the buying power that we have to try to generate the markets that will bring about the social and the economic and the environmental ends that we are seeking." Several European countries are currently engaged in active discussions of the environmental and social aspects of school food procurement,[44] but let me give you an example that is close to home. Several years ago, my family physician closed up his Brooklyn office and moved to upstate New York to raise grass-fed beef. In a recent e-mail, he discussed the potential importance that a commitment by New York City schools to use such beef could make:

> There is increasing awareness of the fact that there are close to 3 million acres of unused or underused grassland in NY State. What is less well understood is that this is more than enough land to produce high-quality beef for all the consumers in New York City—without the Midwest, without feedlots, without corn and all its imbedded fossil fuels. It's a notion that is both obvious and challenging.
>
> Farmers are kind of slow to change and quite risk adverse, at least to new risks (they actually love the same old risks). Gearing up and investing capital in a new type of livestock production (which is really an old type of livestock production) will probably take a generation without the push of institutional support that school systems can provide. It would be the equivalent of the milk truck and the milk check they have relied upon.
>
> On a policy level, putting local meats in the cafeteria links several serious goals—healthy kids, upstate economic development, energy policy, environmental policy. It is really not just about school lunch, but rather how school lunch can be a catalyst for saving the upstate agriculture and shrinking the environmental footprint of livestock production.[45]

Although New York City, with its 800,000 school meals per day, has the economic power on its own to make a difference in upstate economic development, many smaller school systems do not have such clout. USDA has it, however, in the commodities it buys on behalf of schools (and other USDA food-distribution programs). In fact, as we have seen, the original federal participation in school food was a side effect of surplus commodity management efforts and very decidedly an effort to help farmers stay in farming. In recent years, however, the major federal commodity support programs, those that subsidize the production of corn, soybeans, and other "basic commodities" have been widely charged with fomenting some of the food system's major ills: those shelf-stable packaged goods again, based on cheap high-fructose corn syrup and soy isolates, for example. Looking at this record, many might be tempted to say that innovations such as farm to cafeteria or environmentally sensitive purchasing are better left to the local and state levels. It will be enough, they might argue, for Congress to make sure that USDA does not stand in the way of such efforts.

I keep thinking about those seven billion meals per year, however—and probably closer to ten billion if we implemented universal free and upgraded the quality of school food—and I see an instrument for preventive health and environmental conservation so powerful that I'm not sure we can afford not to use it. Suppose that we went beyond removing obstacles and actually rewarded use of food produced by sustainable methods—foods that did not destroy the land and pollute the waterways. Suppose we paid attention to social justice issues and human welfare—the way farm workers are treated, for example—as well as environmental and animal welfare. By creating and assuring a market for such responsibly produced foods, we could help producers to make the transition, and in so doing, we could make such foods more widely available and affordable, beyond school food, to all consumers.[46]

This potential for achieving a wider reorientation of the food system has strongly influenced my thinking about one of the other fundamental choices facing would-be school food reformers: Which federal department should operate the programs? Ann Cooper, whose pioneering work has transformed food service, first at the Ross School in East Hampton, New York, and more recently at the Berkeley Unified School District in California, raised this question for an audience of culinary professionals at their annual meeting in 2005 in the context of a panel on school lunch and childhood obesity:

> Here's my big thing. . . . I think the only way to solve this problem is to take the responsibility of school lunch away from the USDA. It doesn't belong there and it needs to go to CDC or Health and Human Services. And the reason I believe this is you can't be promoting industrial agriculture and school lunch at the same time. Of course it's a conflict of interest. Why do we have the lobbyists winning? . . . If you look at the little boxes

of milk in most schools now, there is sugar. Chocolate milk, the very first ingredient is high-fructose corn syrup. White milk, [sugar] is up on the ingredient list. Why? Because we have a . . . lobby. So, the USDA is incapable of handling both of these programs. We need the school lunch program to be a health program, not an agricultural commodity program, and I'm sure that I'll get beat on the head a lot for saying that, but I'm going to keep saying it because I think that's how we're going to solve the problem.

Many observers of the current state of school meals have urged moving the school food programs out of USDA, into the Department of Education or, more commonly, into the Health component of the Department of Health and Human Services. I am of two minds about this proposition. If we achieve universal free school meals, integrated into the curriculum and the school day, then perhaps the Department of Education could become a hospitable home, but the DOE that has been administering No Child Left Behind strikes me as a poor fit for the kind of imaginative school food program that we need. The DOE's focus on measurement, I believe, could further distort the program. The Health folks within HHS could certainly help to shape a much needed focus on healthy eating, but they are fairly deeply committed, professionally, to the nutrient-based approach to health, which, as I have suggested above, does not seem to serve us well. Either of these alternate homes would bring to school food a partial perspective; either could be an improvement, but neither necessarily would be one. Some critics believe that the entire Washington-based agricultural establishment is too beholden to commodity groups and other lobbyists to put the public interest first; in that context, a move to any other agency would at least shake up and disrupt what one observer recently called the "school cafeteria–industrial complex."[47] In time, we might see other "complexes" develop, but at least such a move would give us a breather in which we could put children's well-being first. There is merit in that argument. It is not an accident that political scientists used agriculture to illustrate the notion of the "iron triangle," the dense interlocking relationships among Congressional committees, the agencies they oversee, and the interests groups served (and sometimes regulated) by those agencies.[48]

Nevertheless, I believe that, despite its faults, a home in USDA may be the best hope for a school food program that is part of a national effort to reorient our whole food system toward the affordable, healthy, wholesome, sustainably produced, and delicious food we all need and desire. When the nation was founded, the vast majority of the population was engaged in agriculture—more than 90 percent.[49] Now the proportion is tiny, less than 2 percent of all employment,[50] but we all still eat. It is time to reorient our Congressional committees, our public policy, and our administering agencies from "agriculture" to "food." I can think of no better place to begin that process than with the food that we serve our children at school.

Notes

Introduction

1. Program data are available on the USDA website at www.fns.usda.gov/pd/cnpmain.htm.

2. Kim Seversen and Meredith May, "Growing Up Too Fat: Kids Suffer Adult Ailments as More Become Dangerously Obese," *San Francisco Chronicle,* May 12, 2002.

3. Katherine Ralston et al., *The National School Lunch Program: Background, Trends, and Issues,* USDA, Economic Research Service, ERR-61, July 2008, 31. The data vary a bit among studies. The Centers for Disease Control's School Health Policies and Programs Study (SHPPS) for 2006 reports that nationwide, 32.7 percent of elementary schools, 71.3 percent of middle/junior high schools, and 89.4 percent of senior high schools have a vending machine, school store, canteen, or snack bar where students can purchase food or beverages. See Centers for Disease Control, National Center for Chronic Disease Prevention and Health Promotion, "SHPPS 2006," Overview Fact Sheet retrieved from www.cdc.gov/HealthyYouth/shpps/2006/factsheets/pdf/FS_FoodandBeverages_SHPPS2006.pdf. The 2006 data represent a noticeable improvement over the 2000 SHPPS, which reported that 43 percent of elementary schools, 73.9 percent of middle/junior high schools, and 98.2 percent of senior high schools had such venues. See H. Wechsler et al., "Food Service and Foods and Beverages Available at School: Results from the School Health Policies and Program Study, 2000," *Journal of School Health* 71, 7 (2001): 313, 321.

4. The eligibility cutoff for free meals is set at 130 percent of the federal poverty line. In the 2008–2009 school year, a child from a family of four with an annual income at or below $27,560 would be eligible for a free meal. Schools will receive $2.57 for each such lunch served, and $1.40 for each breakfast. The threshold for reduced price is 185 percent of poverty, or $39,220 for a family of four. Under the current rates, schools will receive $2.19 for each reduced price lunch and $1.10 for each breakfast. These rates are updated annually as the consumer price index is adjusted. To make matters more complicated, there is a differential for schools that serve a high percentage of meals in the free and reduced price categories, but the standards and the amounts differ between breakfast and lunch. Thus, for breakfast, schools in which at least 40 percent of *lunches* served during the second preceding school year (i.e., two years earlier) were free or reduced qualify for "severe need" reimbursement rates: $1.68 instead of $1.40 for free meals, and $1.38 instead of $1.10 for reduced price.

For lunch, on the other hand, the schools where 60 percent of the lunches served in the second preceding year were free or reduced price are eligible for a modest increment of two cents per meal in all three categories, free, reduced price, and paid. Food Research and Action Center, "Income Guidelines and Reimbursement Rates for the Federal Child Nutrition Programs," available at www.FRAC.org.

5. See www.angrymoms.org/inner/about.html.

6. Kevin Morgan and Roberta Sonnino, *The School Food Revolution: Public Food and the Challenge of Sustainable Development* (London: Earthscan, 2008).

7. Mark Nord, Margaret Andrews, and Steven Carlson, *Household Food Security in the United States, 2007,* USDA, Economic Research Service, ERS Report 66, November 2008, Summary and 7. The language is careful here: As the report explains, "Children in most food-insecure households—even in most households with very low food security—were protected from reductions in food intake. However, in about 323,000 households (0.8 percent of households with children), one or more children were also subject to reduced food intake and disrupted eating patterns at some time during the year" (7).

8. "Hunger in Massachusetts Increases at an Alarming Rate," *Market Watch,* October 31, 2008. www.marketwatch.com/news/story/Hunger-Massachusetts-Increases-Alarming-Rate/story.aspx?guid={A8F2E9A2-52A5-4F70-9375-44055BD045A9}.

9. Bob Herbert, "Children in Peril," *New York Times,* April 21, 2009. Herbert reports on the case load increase and quotes Dr. Redlener.

10. J. Larry Brown, "Nutrition," in *Social Injustice and Public Health,* ed. Barry S. Levy and Victor W. Sidel (Oxford: Oxford University Press, 2006): 241–45. Katherine Alaimo, et al., "Food Insufficiency, Family Income, and Health in Preschool and School-Aged Children," *American Journal of Public Health* 91 (2001): 781–86.

11. For ages 6–10, Institute of Medicine, "Overview of the IOM's Childhood Obesity Prevention Study. Fact Sheet," September 2004; for ages 12–19, Trust for America's Health, *F as in Fat: How Obesity Policies Are Failing in America,* 2007 Report. Because it is difficult to measure body fat in large populations, the IOM and most other studies use the Body Mass Index (BMI) to count obesity. For adults, there is a unified generic table; for children, however, growth rates and body fat percentages are age- and gender-specific. Therefore, the CDC has developed a set of age- and gender-specific BMI norms, and children are considered obese if their BMI is at or above the ninety-fifth percentile, and overweight if their BMI is at or above the eighty-fifth percentile but below the ninety-fifth. Until recently, the medical and public health community generally avoided using the term *obesity* in regard to children in an effort to avoid stigmatizing them. In its major 2005 publication, *Preventing Childhood Obesity: Health in the Balance,* edited by Jeffrey P. Koplan, Catharyn T. Liverman, and Vivica I. Kraak (Washington, DC: National Academies Press, 2005), the IOM undertook to change the prevailing usage. Its committee of nineteen experts in the fields of child health, obesity, nutrition, physical activity, and public health chose the standards specified above and recommended the standardization of terminology:

The committee recognizes that it has been customary to use the term "overweight" instead of "obese" to refer to children with BMIs above the age- and gender-specific 95th percentiles. . . . Obese has often been considered to be a pejorative term, despite having a specific medical meaning. There have also been concerns about misclassification, as BMI is only a surrogate measure of body fatness in children as in adults. Furthermore, children may experience functional impairment (physical or emotional) at different levels of body fatness.

However, the term "obese" more effectively conveys the seriousness, urgency, and medical nature of this concern than does the term "overweight," thereby reinforcing the importance of taking immediate action. Further, BMI in children correlates reasonably well to direct measures of body fatness . . . , and high BMIs in children have been associated with many co-morbidities such as elevated blood pressure, insulin resistance, and increased lipids. . . .

It is important that government agencies, health care providers, insurers, and others agree on the same definition of childhood obesity. . . . To the extent possible, there should be concurrence on definitions and terminology. (80–81)

12. Mary Story, Karen Kaphingst, and Simone French, "The Role of Schools in Obesity Prevention," *The Future of Children* 16, 1 (spring 2006); issue on Childhood Obesity; available at www.futureofchildren.org.

13. See Abigail C. Saguey and Kevin W. Riley, "Weighing Both Sides: Morality, Mortality, and Framing Contests over Obesity," *Journal of Health Policy, Politics and Law* 30, 5 (2005): 869–921, for a fascinating discussion of the social, political, and cultural consequences of framing contests over excess body weight.

14. Kelly D. Brownell and Katherine Battle Horgen, *Food Fight: The Inside Story of the Food Industry, America's Obesity Crisis, and What We Can Do about It* (New York: McGraw Hill Contemporary Books, 2004), 7–10.

15. Action for Healthy Kids, Fact Sheet: "Childhood Obesity: The Preventable Threat to America's Youth," July 2008; available at www.ActionForHealthy Kids.org.

16. Brownell and Horgen, *Food Fight,* 141.

17. Food and Nutrition Service (FNS), U.S. Department of Agriculture; Centers for Disease Control and Prevention, U.S. Department of Health and Human Services; and U.S. Department of Education. FN p.3.S-374, *Making It Happen! School Nutrition Success Stories* (Alexandria, VA, January 2005), 16–17.

18. Eleanor Randolph, "The Big Fat American Kid Crisis . . . and 10 Things We Should Do about It," *New York Times,* May 10, 2006.

19. "Officials, Experts Grapple with School Lunch Problem," CNN.com International, December 11, 2003.

20. FNS et al., *Making It Happen,* 18.

21. Mary Duenwald, "A Conversation With: Marion Nestle; an 'Eat More' Message for a Fattened America," *New York Times,* February 19, 2002.

22. Action for Healthy Kids, "Childhood Obesity."

23. In the United Kingdom, these questions have garnered sufficient attention that Kevin Morgan has characterized the current era of school food reform as "the ecological era: sustainable provision and controlled choice," and argues that it may signal an important revitalization of the public domain. Morgan, "School Food and the Public Domain: The Politics of the Public Plate," *The Political Quarterly* 77, 3 (2006): 379–87. Despite the appeal of the argument

that local food can reduce the carbon footprint, however, it is worth noting that this is just the tip of the "carbon audit" iceberg when it comes to school food. In some cases, it turns out, the nearest source is not the closest to carbon neutral. "There are no no-brainers" in figuring out the environmental impact of food sources, my food coop's produce manager explained. Among the complexities of calculating greenhouse gas emissions are type and condition of vehicles, not just miles traveled, and the way food is grown and processed and packaged.

24. For a less enthusiastic description of the coalition, see Ron Haskins, "The School Lunch Lobby," *Education Next* 5, 3 (summer 2005); Hoover Institution online publication at www.hoover.org/publications/ednext/3219311.html.

25. Ralston et al., *National School Lunch Program: Background, Trends and Issues*.

26. "All you have to do is look at the leading causes of death in America," Dr. Shintani pointed out. "Number one is heart disease. It kills 30 percent of us. That's nutrition related primarily. Number 2 is cancer. That kills a quarter of us. I think it's 23 or 24 percent. . . . Number three cause of death is stroke; 7 percent of us die of stroke. Also diet related. You just add up those three and that's . . . 60 percent of the deaths already. And then you have diabetes climbing up the scale, and now you have kidney disease, a lot of which is diet related. You can go on and on, and that's just deaths. That's mortality." This is an excerpt from an interview that I conducted with Dr. Shintani on a research trip to Hawaii in January 2005. Unless otherwise specified, all interview excerpts are from my own research and will not be individually attributed.

27. Jennifer Nelson, "Is *That* Your Lunch?" *Family Circle*, November 1, 2006, 49.

28. Quoted in ibid.

1. School Food 101

1. I have changed the names and some identifying details for the staff members in the Any Town schools.

2. Anne Gordon et al., *School Nutrition Dietary Assessment III*, vol. 1: *School Foodservice, School Food Environment, and Meals Offered and Served* (Alexandria, VA: USDA, 2007), 62, 63.

3. W. I. Thomas and Dorothy Swaine Thomas, *The Child in America: Behavior Problems and Programs* (New York: Alfred A. Knopf, 1928), 571–72.

2. Food Fights

1. For a more detailed account of the origins of school food in the Progressive Era, its development during the Great Depression, and its institutionalization during World War II, see Susan Levine's comprehensive history of school lunch in the United States, *School Lunch Politics: The Surprising History of America's Favorite Welfare Program* (Princeton, NJ: Princeton University Press, 2008).

2. Ibid., 41.

3. For a detailed account of the pig slaughter and the development of the Federal Surplus Relief Corporation and its successor, the Federal Surplus Commodities Corporation, see Janet Poppendieck, *Breadlines Knee Deep in Wheat: Food Assistance in the Great Depression* (New Brunswick, NJ: Rutgers University Press, 1986).

4. Section 32 appears to have been the result of a rather capricious process. A permanent appropriation like Section 32 was unheard of at the time, and there have been only one or two others since. Normally such legislation would include an "authorization" for appropriation, but actual appropriations would have to be made in a separate process and would involve the House Ways and Means Committee. Section 32 was included in the amendments passed by the House in the normal form, an authorization. The provision had not been included in the Senate version, so it had to be resolved when the bill went to conference. As recalled later by its author, House Agriculture Committee Chair Marvin Jones, Senator John Bankhead, the Senate conferee, was unenthusiastic about the proposal and wanted first to take up an extension of a provision that he had authored. When Jones refused, Bankhead accused Jones of an inability to compromise. Jones replied with an offer of a trade: "If you let me write Section 32 like I want it, and agree to that, then I'll agree to extend your Bankhead provision when we get to it." When Jones teased the senior Senator about his own ability to compromise, Bankhead agreed to the deal. "So I sat down there," Jones recalls, "and I struck out 'there shall be authorized to be appropriated' and wrote 'there is hereby appropriated,' and I made it a permanent piece of law." Marvin Jones, "Speech Marking the 35th Anniversary of the Signing of the Agricultural Adjustment Act," May 15, 1968; Agricultural History Branch Records, United States Department of Agriculture. For a more complete account, see Poppendieck, *Breadlines,* 192–97.

5. USDA, Bureau of Agricultural Economics, *The School Lunch Program and Agricultural Surplus Disposal,* Miscellaneous Publication No. 467, October 1941, 17–20.

6. The historian Martha Swain provided a lively account of the WPA School Lunchroom Project to the NFSMI Child Nutrition Archives Colloquium in celebration of the sixtieth anniversary of the National School Lunch Act. I am grateful to her for providing me with a copy of her address, "The WPA with Heart: New Deal Feeding Programs for Children During the Great Depression and Wartime." See also Donald Howard, *The WPA and Federal Relief Policy* (New York: Russell Sage Foundation, 1943), 127–30.

7. In the era before school consolidation, this represented about two-fifths of the nation's schools. United States Congress. Senate, 79th Congress, 1st Session. Report No. 553, "Providing Assistance to the States in the Establishment, Maintenance, Operation and Expansion of School Lunch Programs," a Report to accompany S.962, 19.

8. Lydia Roberts, "Beginnings of the Recommended Dietary Allowances," *Journal of the American Dietetic Association* 34 (September 1958): 903–8.

9. The WFA also developed Type B and C meals; Type B was a cheaper, scaled-down version of Type A, and Type C was simply a half pint of fluid milk.

10. PL 396, June 4, 1946, 60 Stat 231. Quoted in Gordon Gunderson, *The National School Lunch Program: Background and Development,* FNS-63 (Washington, DC: U.S. Government Printing Office, 1971), 14–15.

11. Gunderson, *NSLP: Background,* 15, 16.

12. "Truman Approves School Lunch Bill," *New York Times,* June 5, 1946.

13. Agnes E. Meyer quoted in Thelma Flanagan, "School Food Services," in *Education in the States: Nationwide Development Since 1900,* ed. by Edgar Fuller and Jim B. Pearson, a project of the Council of Chief State School Officers (Washington, DC: National Education Association, 1969), 568.

14. Significant, but not as impressive as it may appear, since total school enrollment rose by 60 percent in the same period. The NSLP was serving about a quarter of the nation's schoolchildren in 1947, and just over a third in 1960. U.S. Department of Education, Institute of Education Sciences, National Center for Educational Statistics, *120 Years of American Education, A Statistical Portrait,* by Thomas Snyder (1993), 37. http://nces.ed.gov/pubsearch/pubsinfo .asp?pubid=93442.

15. The executive branch was even less generous; throughout the 1950s, USDA budget requests for the program ran substantially below the amounts actually appropriated by Congress.

16. Levine, *School Lunch Politics,* 103.

17. Deborah Stone, *Policy Paradox: The Art of Political Decision Making,* rev. ed. (New York: W.W. Norton, 2002), 154.

18. There is not room here for a comprehensive history, but fortunately, other scholars and observers have provided useful accounts. Three are by insiders who lived parts of the history they tell. The most widely cited is the pamphlet prepared by Gordon Gunderson, *NSLP: Background.* A particularly useful account is provided by Josephine Martin, "History of Child Nutrition Programs," in *Managing Child Nutrition Programs: Leadership for the Twenty First Century,* ed. by Josephine Martin and Martha T. Conklin (Gaithersburg, MD: Aspen Publishers, Inc., 1999), 29–86. The third is Thelma Flanagan's "School Food Services." The nutrition educator Antonia Demas has provided a briefer version in her short work, *Hot Lunch: A History of the School Lunch Program* (Trumansburg, NY: Food Studies Institute, 2000). An examination in depth of the politics of food assistance from Kennedy to Reagan by the political scientist Ardith Maney is *Still Hungry after All These Years: Food Assistance from Kennedy to Reagan* (Westport, CT: Greenwood Press, 1989). Levine's *School Lunch Politics* covers the history of school food in the United States from the Progressive Era through the Reagan years. Susan Lynn Roberts, "School Food: Does the Future Call for New Food Policy or Can the Old Still Hold True?" *Drake Journal of Agricultural Law* 7, 3 (fall 2002): 587–620, provides a brief summary of the early history, an overview of legislative developments, and a particularly useful account of the legal battles over competitive foods. Finally, in 1989 the House Education and Labor Committee released a document summarizing the history of child nutrition programs with an emphasis on the role of Section 4 (general) subsidies; widely referred to as "the Committee Print," it was reprinted in full as Kathleen Stitt, Mary Klatko, Mary Nix (on behalf of the American School Food Service Association), and Jean Yavis-Jones

(Congressional Research Service), "Child Nutrition Programs: Issues for the 101st Congress," *School Food Service Research Review* 13, 1 (1989).

19. Michael Katz, *The Undeserving Poor: From the War on Poverty to the War on Welfare* (New York: Pantheon Books, 1989), 89.

20. Lyndon Baines Johnson, *The Vantage Point: Perspectives of the Presidency, 1963–1969* (New York: Holt, Rinehart, and Winston, 1971), 74; quoted in David Zarefsky, *President Johnson's War on Poverty* (Tuscaloosa: The University of Alabama Press, 1986), 21.

21. Katz, *Undeserving Poor,* 90.

22. Maney, *Still Hungry,* 25. Gilbert Yale Steiner, *The Children's Cause* (Washington, DC: The Brookings Institution, 1976), 182.

23. Nick Kotz, *Let Them Eat Promises: The Politics of Hunger in America* (Englewood Cliffs, NJ: Prentice-Hall, 1969).

24. Steiner, *Children's Cause,* 184.

25. Maney, *Still Hungry,* 55.

26. Katz, *Undeserving Poor,* 90. Zarefsky, *President Johnson's War,* 36, and see 26–36.

27. Levine, *School Lunch Politics,* 108–12.

28. Maney, *Still Hungry,* 66.

29. Steiner, *Children's Cause,* 185–97.

30. PL 89–642. 89th Congress, October 11, 1966, 80 Stat. 885–90.

31. Although it might seem that hunger is basically a manifestation of poverty, in the United States, hunger has had an independent "career" as a social problem:

> in 1966 domestic hunger was not an issue; by 1967 it had become a matter of public interest and concern. The first date is important, for it suggests that the hunger issue was no mere epiphenomenon of poverty or poverty policy: the War on Poverty had been going on for two years without making the issue of serious food deprivation a central focus. Nor had hunger entered the policy lexicon via the food stamp program, enacted into law in 1964. What transformed hunger from a problem to an issue in its own right was a series of dramatic field investigations and reports of malnutrition that occurred in 1967 and 1968.
>
> Peter Eisinger, *Toward an End to Hunger in America*
> (Washington, DC: The Brookings Institution, 1998), 76

32. For more detailed retrospective accounts of the "discovery" of hunger, see Jeffery Berry, *Feeding Hungry People* (New Brunswick, NJ: Rutgers University Press, 1984); Peter Edelman, *Searching for America's Heart: RFK and the Renewal of Hope* (Boston: Houghton Mifflin, 2001), 48–58; and Ardith Maney, *Still Hungry,* 69–112. For a collection of contemporary sources, see U.S. Congress, Senate, Subcommittee on Employment, Manpower, and Poverty, Committee on Labor and Public Welfare, *Hunger in America: A Chronology and Selected Background Materials,* October 2, 1968, 90th Congress, 2nd Sess.

33. U.S. Congress, Senate Select Committee on Nutrition and Human Needs, "The School Lunch Problem," in *Studies of Human Need,* Committee Print (Washington, DC: U.S. Government Printing Office, June 1972), 64.

34. Quoted in Steiner, *Children's Cause,* 180.

35. The Committee on School Lunch Participation, *Their Daily Bread: A Study of the National School Lunch Program* (Atlanta: McNelley-Rudd Printing Service Inc., 1968), 17–20.

36. Ibid., 21.

37. Citizens Board of Inquiry into Hunger and Malnutrition in the United States, *Hunger USA,* with an introductory comment by Robert F. Kennedy (Boston: Beacon Press, 1968), 68.

38. Maney, *Still Hungry,* 104–11.

39. Josephine Martin counts "sixteen laws . . . enacted between 1970 and 1979 that would directly effect child nutrition programs." "History of Child Nutrition," 66.

40. Beginning in 1981, the frequency of update was reduced to once per year.

41. Citizens Board of Inquiry into Hunger and Malnutrition in the United States, *Hunger USA Revisited* (Atlanta: Southern Regional Council: n.d. [ca. 1973]), 11.

42. Charlene Price and Betsy Kuhn, "Public and Private Efforts for the National School Lunch Program," *Food Review,* May-August 1996, 54. Anne Gordon et al., *School Nutrition Dietary Assessment Study-III,* vol. 1, *School Foodservice, School Food Environment, and Meals Offered and Served* (Alexandria, VA: USDA, 2007) 32; hereafter cited as *SNDA-III.*

43. My calculations, based on USDA figures reported in Carl Chelf, *Controversial Issues in Social Welfare Policy: Government and the Pursuit of Happiness* (Newbury Park, CA: Sage Publications, 1992), 52–54.

44. George McGovern, Foreword to Kotz, *Let Them Eat Promises,* viii.

45. See Steiner, *Children's Cause,* 184–185, for a more extended discussion of this issue.

46. It is difficult to do justice to this substantial network or even its core national organizations without writing another book. An umbrella organization called NAHO, National Anti-Hunger Organizations, produced a "Blueprint to End Hunger" in 2003, and updated it in 2008 with thirteen national organizations as signers. Some of these organizations, like Bread for the World, the Alliance to End Hunger, and World Hunger Year, work on global as well as domestic hunger; some, like the Food Research and Action Center (FRAC) and Feeding America, focus squarely on hunger in America. Some work with particular constituencies: End Hunger Network mobilizes figures from the entertainment world; Share Our Strength elicits contributions from the restaurant industry; the Association of Nutrition Services Agencies (ANSA) focuses on organizations that provide nutritional support to people with AIDS and other life-threatening medical conditions. Mazon describes itself as "a Jewish Response to Hunger," and Bread for the World identifies itself as a "Christian citizens movement." Some, like Results or the Center on Budget and Policy Priorities (CBPP), work on other domestic poverty issues as well as hunger. World Hunger Year also works on broader food system issues. Some have service delivery components as well as advocacy. Feeding America, formerly known as America's Second Harvest, coordinates the receipt and distribution of food donations to a network of more than thirty-five thousand local soup kitchens and food pantries through its more

than two hundred affiliated food banks, and contributes to policy and lobbying efforts through its research division and its Washington office. The Society of Saint Andrew oversees gleaning projects and arranges for the distribution of harvested crops to feeding programs around the nation. The Congressional Hunger Center sponsors a leadership development program that helps to tie the network together by placing fellows in most of the organizations listed above and other organizations that work on hunger issues—first in a local community for six months, and then in Washington for a second six months. Several other organizations work regularly on hunger and food assistance issues but do not define themselves primarily as anti-hunger organizations: Catholic Charities, the Children's Defense Fund, the Coalition for Human Needs, the Community Food Security Coalition. For a valuable discussion of how these organizations interact and get along, see Eisinger, *Toward an End to Hunger,* esp. chap. 7, "The Anti-Hunger Advocacy Group Network." It is interesting to note that Eisinger's core list, compiled at least a decade ago, contains all but one of the NAHO members mentioned above, and one organization, Foodchain, that has since merged with Feeding America. In short, there has been remarkable longevity and stability at the core of the anti-hunger movement.

47. Levine, *School Lunch Politics,* 151.

48. Dorothy Pannell-Martin, *School Foodservice Management for the Twenty-First Century,* 5th ed. (Alexandria, VA: InTEAM Associates Inc., 1999), 8, 11.

49. Mimi Sheraton, "Lunches for Pupils Given Poor Marks," *New York Times,* May 19, 1976.

50. Mimi Sheraton, "School Lunch Utopia? No Impossible Dream," *New York Times,* May 20, 1976.

51. Demas, *Hot Lunch,* 24.

52. Martin, "History of Child Nutrition," 94.

53. Mimi Sheraton, "Fast Foods Sell School Lunches in Las Vegas," *New York Times,* January 19, 1978.

54. Deputy Administrator, AMS, to Thomas F. Baker, Assistant Secretary, American Bottlers of Carbonated Beverages, April 21, 1955. Letter. Thelma Flanagan Files, Child Nutrition Archive, NFSMI.

55. Thelma Flanagan, "Florida Educators Seeking to Solve Problem of 'The Untouched Plate,'" *The School Director,* December 1948, 15. Copy in Flanagan Files, NFSMI.

56. Violet Moore, *Atlanta Journal,* September 19, 1948, quoted by Flanagan, in ibid.

57. Marion Nestle, *Food Politics: How the Food Industry Influences Nutrition and Health* (Berkeley: University of California Press, 2002), 208. Nestle's summary of this controversy (207–13) is particularly lucid and helpful.

58. For a particularly informative account of the battle over competitive foods, see Susan Lynn Roberts, "School Food," 605–19.

59. Josephine Martin, quoted in Marian Burros, "A Victory for Vending; Can Vigilance Veto Junk Foods?" *Washington Post,* June 9, 1977, final edition.

60. The specified nutrients were protein, vitamin A, vitamin C, niacin, riboflavin, thiamin, calcium, and iron.

61. Jody Levin-Epstein, quoted in Mimi Sheraton, "'Junk Food' Plan Widely Criticized," *New York Times,* July 13, 1979.

62. Gussow quoted in ibid.

63. Clint G. Salisbury, "Make an Investment in Our School Children: Increase the Nutritional Value of School Lunch Programs," *Brigham Young University Education and Law Journal* (2004): 335–36.

64. Stockman quoted in Robert Pear, "Many Children Decide Not to Buy More Costly School Lunches," *New York Times,* October 21, 1981.

65. Pannell-Martin, *School Foodservice,* 126. Some of this decline was, in fact, due to shrinking enrollments; the growth in enrollments that had characterized the baby boom of the 1950s and 1960s leveled off in 1971 and actual enrollments decreased every year thereafter until 1984. Enrollment began to increase again in 1985 and has continued to grow since then. U.S. Department of Education, Institute of Educational Sciences, National Center for Education Statistics, Fast Facts, elementary/secondary, enrollment trends; http://nces.ed.gov/fastfacts/display.asp?id=65. Such declines contributed to a number of school funding issues. Much of the funding for schools comes from states on a per-pupil basis, and every time enrollment declines, a school finds itself in a financial bind, since many expenses do not decrease accordingly. It is a frustrating situation: expanding enrollment brings more funds but puts pressure on facilities; declining enrollment often leads to program cuts and layoffs.

66. One account says that the Reagan administration first thought that the new rules had been proposed by bureaucrats trying to protect their budgets— what President Reagan called the "Washington Monument Game," in which any proposed cut is immediately translated into its most egregious and unpopular impact; thus a reduction in funding to the National Park Service begets an announcement of the closing of the Washington Monument. "Washington Talk; Briefing," *New York Times,* September 28, 1981.

67. Robert Dole, Jesse Helms, Thad Cochran, S.I. Hayakawa, Rudy Boschwitz, Roger Jepsen, Paula Hawkins, and Mark Andrews to James A. Baker III, October 27, 1981. Letter reprinted in Appendix B of Stitt et al., "Child Nutrition Programs," 64.

68. Stitt et al., "Child Nutrition Programs," 36.

69. This would not be the last time a block grant approach to child nutrition programs was proposed—nor was it the first. No sooner had school meals been made a right and given "performance funding" than their cost and the growth of federal spending became controversial. In 1973 the Nixon administration prepared legislation to consolidate several programs into a child nutrition block grant, hoping to slow down the escalation of program costs and transfer more responsibility to the states. Under a block grant, each state would receive a specified amount of federal funding each year for child nutrition purposes, but it would have a great deal more latitude in how to use it. Anti-hunger advocates saw block grants as an end run around the guarantees so recently accorded to low-income children, and they opposed them vigorously. Congress rejected the approach in 1974, as it did in 1984.

70. Martin, "History of Child Nutrition," 76.

71. This is the same dairy surplus that provoked the Reagan administration's famous cheese giveaways, which in turn led to the creation of TEFAP (The Emergency Food Assistance Program). For an account, see Janet Poppendieck, *Sweet Charity? Emergency Food and the End of Entitlement* (New York: Penguin Books, 1999), 87–91, 98–100, 142–49.

72. USDA, Food and Nutrition Service, Office of Analysis and Evaluation, "1990 Farm Bill School Lunch Studies: Interim Report to Congress," 1991. Typescript, Marshall Matz papers, Child Nutrition Archive, NFSMI.

73. Laura S. Sims, *The Politics of Fat: Food and Nutrition Policy in America* (Armonk, NY: M.E. Sharpe, 1998), 75, 76.

74. Jane T. Wynn, ASFSA, to Ellen Haas, October 26, 1988. Letter, Marshall Matz papers, NFSMI.

75. Statement by Dr. Suzanne S. Harris, Deputy Assistant Secretary of Agriculture for Food and Consumer Services, in response to Recommendations Announced by Public Voice, August 25, 1988. Press release (1152–88), copy in Marshall Matz papers, NFSMI.

76. Philip M. Gleason, "Participation in the National School Lunch Program and the School Breakfast Program," *American Journal of Clinical Nutrition* 611 (1995, suppl.): s215.

77. Nestle, *Food Politics*, 192–93.

78. Dorothy V. Pannell, "Why School Meals Are High in Fat and Some Suggested Solutions," *The American Journal of Clinical Nutrition* 61, 1 (1995, suppl.): s245–46.

79. Sims, *Politics of Fat*, 85–87.

80. Ibid., 76–84.

81. *Congressional Record*, May 14, 1996, H4912.

82. Cooper and Holmes, *Lunch Lessons*, 38.

83. Sims, *Politics of Fat*, 87.

84. Eisinger, *Toward an End*, 72, 73.

3. Penny Wise, Pound Foolish

1. School Nutrition Association, *ANC Trend Survey, Top Line Report*, August 2004, 38–39.

2. Dorothy Pannell-Martin, *School Foodservice Management for the Twenty-First Century*, 5th ed. (Alexandria, VA: InTEAM Associates, Inc., 1999), 90.

3. Rob Tricchinelli, Capital New Service, "Maryland Junk Food Lunches Should Be Scrapped, Experts, Parents Say," *Southern Maryland Online*, September 18, 2007. http://somd.com/news/headlines/2007/6399.shtml.

4. Ibid.

5. Mike Hendricks, "Too Much Junk Food in Our Schools," KansasCity.com, August 14, 2007. www.kansascity.com/news/columnists/mike_hendricks/232176.html; retrieved August 16, 2007.

6. Donnis Badgett, "School Lunches of Yore," *The Bryan-College Station Eagle,* July 22, 2007. www.theeagle.com/stories/072207/columnists_2007072250.php.

7. Keith Reid, "School Cafeteria Choices More Unhealthy Than Nutritious," *Stockton Record,* Stockton, CA, March 25, 2007; retrieved from www.recordnet .com on March 26, 2007.

8. Pannell-Martin, *School Foodservice,* 126.

9. Denise Brown, *Prevalence of Food Production Systems in School Foodservice* (Oxford, MS: National Food Service Management Institute, R-75–04, 2004), 8.

10. School Nutrition Association, *Little Big Fact Book* (Alexandria, VA: School Nutrition Association, 2006); emphasis in original.

11. Robert Morast, "School Lunch, Anyone?" *Sioux Falls Argus Leader,* November 29, 2006. http://argusleader.com/20061129.html.

12. Lisa Belkin, "The School-Lunch Test," *New York Times Magazine,* August 20, 2006, 32.

13. Mont-Ferguson quoted in a personal communication from School Food FOCUS, September 21, 2007.

14. Reid, "School Cafeteria Choices."

15. Center for Science in the Public Interest, *Making the Grade: An Analysis of Food Safety in School Cafeterias* (Washington, DC: CSPI, 2007), 1. "School Lunch Over-Certification: ASFSA Warns Congress about Overzealous Income Rules, While School Lunch Safety Concerns Resurface in the Senate," *FoodService Director,* 16, 4 (April 15, 2003); retrieved July 21, 2005, via Lexis-Nexis Academic.

16. "In Wake of $4.5 mil. Judgment: School District Switches to Precooked Beef for Liability," *FoodService Director* 14, 5 (May 15, 2001): 10.

17. Andrew Martin, "Stronger Rules on Produce Likely after Outbreaks of E. Coli," *New York Times,* December 11, 2006. www.nytimes.com/2006/12/11/ washington/11fda.html.

18. Michael Jacobson, *Six Arguments for a Greener Diet* (Washington, DC: Center for Science in the Public Interest, 2006), 61.

19. Robert Tauxe quoted in Christopher Cook, *Diet for a Dead Planet* (New York: The New Press, 2004), 56.

20. F. Diez-Gonzalez et al., "Grain Feeding and the Dissemination of Acid-resistant *Escherichia coli* from Cattle," *Science* 281 (1998): 1666–68.

21. Daniel Imhoff, *Foodfight: The Citizen's Guide to a Food and Farm Bill* (Healdsburg, CA: Watershed Media, 2007), 91.

22. Michele Simon, *Appetite for Profit: How the Food Industry Undermines Our Health and How to Fight Back* (New York: Nation Books, 2006), xii. The USDA Economic Research Service estimates that there are about 320,000 packaged food products available to American consumers. James J. Corbett, "A Survey of New Food Product Introductions and Slotting Allowances in the New England Marketplace from a Food Broker's Perspective," *Journal of Food Distribution Research* 35, 1 (March 2004): 44.

23. Information Resources Inc. (IRI), "What Do Americans Really Eat," press release, February 10, 2003; retrieved August 8, 2008, from www.infores .com/public/global/newsEvents/press/2003/glo_new_021003.htm.

24. Steven Greenhouse, *The Big Squeeze: Tough Times for the American Worker* (New York: Knopf Doubleday, 2009), 6.

25. Penny McLaren, "What Are They Thinking? Tips and Tricks for Successful Marketing to Today's American Teenagers," *School Foodservice and Nutrition* 58 (June-July 2004): 60.

26. Teenage Research Unlimited, "Teens Spent $175 billion in 2003." Press release, January 9, 2004. Accessed at www.teenresearch.com/PRview.cfm?edit_id=168.

27. National Institute on Media and the Family, "Fact Sheet: Children and Advertising"; accessed at www.mediafamily.org/facts/facts_childadv.shtml.

28. Institute of Medicine, *Preventing Childhood Obesity: Health in the Balance,* edited by Jeffrey P. Koplan, Catharyn T. Liverman, and Vivica I. Kraak (Washington, DC: National Academies Press, 2005), 172.

29. Note that a la carte sales do not generate commodity entitlements, although commodities may be used to prepare foods to be sold a la carte.

30. Barry Yeoman, "Unhappy Meals," *Mother Jones* 28, 1 (January–February 2003): 41–42.

31. Penny McLaren, "Precious Commodities," *School Foodservice and Nutrition,* 59, 8 (September 2005). www.schoolnutrition.org.

32. Food Research and Action Center, *Commodity Foods and the Nutritional Quality of the National School Lunch Program: Historical Role, Current Operations and Future Potential* (Washington, DC: Food Research and Action Center, September 2008), esp. 39–40, quote at 39; this source provides an excellent discussion of fruits and vegetables in the commodity program. At this writing, however, the future of DOD-Fresh appears uncertain. In 2006, the Defense Department moved to outsource its procurement, storage, and delivery to commercial vendors. USDA and DOD continue to oversee program operations, but many observers are unconvinced that commercial distributors will live up to the high standards for which the DOD was famous.

33. USDA, Food and Nutrition Service, "White Paper: USDA Commodities in the National School Lunch Program," August 2007, 5; available at www.fns.usda.gov.

34. Ibid., 4, 5.

35. California Food Policy Advocates and Samuels and Associates, "Report on Nutrition Impact of Federal Child Nutrition Commodities on School Meals, working draft for review," October 15, 2007; available at www.cfpa.net.

36. Penny McLaren, "The Great Commodities Cleft," *School Foodservice and Nutrition,* August 2000; www.schoolnutrition.org.

37. See J. Amy Dillard, "Sloppy Joe, Slop, Sloppy Joe: How USDA Commodities Dumping Ruined the National School Lunch Program," *Oregon Law Review* 87: 221–58, esp. 248–50 for a highly critical account of the role of commodities in school food.

38. Malissa Marsden, "Industry 101," *School Foodservice and Nutrition* 59, 9 (October 2004): 24.

39. Ibid., 26.

40. Jack Kloppenburg, Jr., and Neva Hassanein, "From Old School to Reform School?" *Agriculture and Human Values* 23 (2006): 419.

4. How Nutritious Are School Meals?

1. Barbara Parks, *Junie B., First Grader: Boss of Lunch,* A Stepping Stone Book (New York: Random House, 2002), 17.

2. The dietary guidelines in use at this writing are those from 2000. The 2005 DGAs have not yet been translated into regulations (see below).

3. Under the National School Lunch Act, Provision 2, on the books since the late 1970s but not widely used until quite recently, permits schools to serve all children meals free, and provides reimbursements based on the proportion of meals served in each category—free, reduced price, and full price—in a base year. (This is the provision under which Any Town offers free breakfast; see chapter 1.) Provision 3 permits schools to serve all children free but receive reimbursements based on the amounts received in a base year, adjusted for inflation and changes in enrollment. Either of these provisions permits a school to collect the information needed to establish the individual child's eligibility only once every four years. These provisions reduce the paperwork and administrative burden. They are discussed in great detail in chapter 7. See the Provisions 1, 2 and 3 Fact Sheet from USDA at www.fns.usda.gov/cnd/Governance/prov-1-2-3/Prov1_2_3_FactSheet.htm.

4. Food Research and Action Center, *An Advocate's Guide to the School Nutrition Programs* (Washington, DC: FRAC, 2005), 170. Although the connotation is slightly different, the term School Food Authority is frequently used interchangeably with another element of the school food service lingo, Local Educational Authority, or LEA, basically a school board.

5. Jean B. Wellisch et al., *The National Evaluation of School Nutrition Programs, Final Report* (Santa Monica, CA: Systems Development Corporation, 1983). John A. Burghardt, Barbara Devaney, and Anne R. Gordon, "The School Nutrition Dietary Assessment Study: Summary and Discussion," *The American Journal of Clinical Nutrition,* 61 (suppl.): s252–57.

6. Anne Gordon et al., *School Nutrition Dietary Assessment Study-III,* vol. 1: *School Foodservice, School Food Environment, and Meals Offered and Served* (Alexandria, VA: USDA, 2007), 35; hereafter cited as *SNDA-III.*

7. Abt Associates, Inc., *Evaluation of the Nutrient Standard Menu Planning Demonstration: Summary of Findings* (Cambridge, MA: Abt Associates, Inc.: August, 1998), 6.

8. U.S. General Accounting Office, *School Lunch Program: Efforts Needed to Improve Nutrition and Encourage Healthy Eating* (Washington, DC: Government Printing Office, May 2003), 10.

9. Mary Kay Fox et al., *School Nutrition Dietary Assessment Study-II,* Final Report (Alexandria, VA: USDA, 2001), 76–82; hereafter cited as *SNDA-II.*

10. *SNDA-III,* Executive Summary, 14, 15.

11. *SNDA-II,* 158.

12. *SNDA-III,* Executive Summary, 13.

13. *SNDA-II,* 163.

14. *SNDA-III,* Executive Summary, 11.

15. Joanne Guthrie and Jean C. Buzby, "Several Strategies May Lower Plate Waste in School Feeding Programs," *Food Review* 25, 2 (summer-fall 2002): 39.

16. John Burghardt and Barbara Devaney, *The School Nutrition Dietary Assessment Study: Summary of Findings* (Alexandria, VA: USDA, 1993), 21.

17. Jean C. Buzby and Joanne Guthrie, *Plate Waste in School Nutrition Programs: Final Report to Congress,* USDA, Economic Research Service, E-FAN-02-009, March 2002.

18. U.S. General Accounting Office, *School Lunch Program: Cafeteria Managers' Views on Food Wasted by Students,* Report to the Chairman, Committee on Economic and Educational Opportunities, House of Representatives, GAO/RCED-96-191 (Washington, DC: Government Printing Office, July 1996).

19. Buzby and Guthrie, *Plate Waste,* Appendix A, "Plate Waste Measurement Techniques and Data," 7.

20. K. Bark, *What Are Montana Children Eating in the School Lunch Program? Results of a School Lunch Plate Waste Study in a Rural State* (Bozeman: Montana Team Nutrition Program, Office of Public Instruction, Montana State University, 1998). Cited in Buzby and Guthrie, *Plate Waste,* 7.

21. Katherine Ralston et al., *The National School Lunch Program: Background, Trends and Issues,* USDA, Economic Research Service, ERR-61, July 2008.

22. In addition, the term is typically used to embrace foods sold as fundraisers and foods distributed in classrooms as rewards or as part of celebrations.

23. U.S. Government Accountability Office, *School Meal Programs: Competitive Foods Are Widely Available and Generate Substantial Revenues for Schools,* GAO-05-563 (Washington, DC: Government Printing Office, August 2005), 14.

24. Institute of Medicine, *Preventing Childhood Obesity: Health in the Balance* (Washington, DC: The National Academies Press, 2005), 243.

25. Karen W. Cullen et al., "Effects of a la Carte and Snack Bar Foods at School on Children's Lunchtime Intake of Fruits and Vegetables," *Journal of the American Dietetic Association* 100, 12 (2000): 1482–86. Martha Y. Kubik et al., "The Association of School Food Environment with Dietary Behaviors of Young Adolescents," *American Journal of Public Health* 93, 7 (2003): 1168–73.

26. Martha Marlette, Susan B. Templeton, and Myna Panemangalore, "Food Type, Food Preparation and Competitive Food Purchases Impact School Lunch Plate Waste by Sixth Grade Students," *Journal of the American Dietetic Association* 105, 11 (2005): 1779–82.

27. National Research Council, *Recommended Dietary Allowances,* 8th rev. ed. (Washington, DC: National Academy Press, 1974), 2; quoted in Jeanne P. Goldberg, "The Recommended Dietary Allowances: Can They Inform the Development of Standards of Academic Achievement?" *Applied Measurement in Education* 11, 1 (1998): 98.

28. The Fresh Fruit and Vegetable Program started out as a pilot program in five states, and was later expanded to a total of eight states and three Indian Tribal Organizations (ITOs). In 2008, after another partial expansion and a conversion of the first eight states and three ITOs to permanent authorization, the program was authorized for all states, the District of Columbia, and the three ITOs. Funds are limited, however, to $48.8 million—the $40 million

newly appropriated plus some funds remaining from the earlier appropriation. Schools will apply in a competitive grant program.

29. Joanna Dwyer et al., "Fat-Sugar See-Saw in School Lunches: Impact of a Low Fat Intervention," *Journal of Adolescent Health* 32, 6 (June 2003): 428–35.

30. JoAnn Manson, "Behind the Headlines," interview with Bonnie Liebman, *Nutrition Action* 33, 3 (April 2008): 3–5.

31. Stanley Garnett, Director, Child Nutrition Division, "Incorporating the 2005 Dietary Guidelines for Americans into School Meals," memo SP-04-2008, December 17, 2007; available at www.fns.usda.gov/cnd/Governance/Policy-Memos/2008/SP_04–2008-OS.pdf.

32. David Beller, "Congress Who? USDA on track to improve school meals . . . six years late," Friday, April 18, 2008, post on The Fresh Journal, a blog available at http://thefreshjournal.blogspot.com/.

33. Abt Associates, *Evaluation of the Nutrient Standard Menu Planning Demonstration: Summary*, 6.

34. Abt Associates, *Evaluation of the Nutrient Standard Menu Planning Demonstration: Findings from the Formative Evaluation* (Cambridge, MA: Abt Associates, Inc., February 1997), 2–1.

35. Ibid., 3–10.

36. Amitai Etzioni, *Modern Organizations*, Foundations of Modern Sociology Series, Alex Inkeles, editor (Englewood Cliffs, NJ: Prentice Hall, Inc., 1964), 10.

5. The Missing Millions

1. School Nutrition Association, "Managing the Forces of Change," Child Nutrition Industry Conference, January 16–18, 2005, conference schedule, 4. This conference is an annual event.

2. Julie Eckman, "Say Good-bye to Back-to-School-Blues," *School Foodservice and Nutrition* 58, 8 (September 2004): 42–47.

3. Anne Gordon et al., *School Nutrition Dietary Assessment-III*, vol. 2: *Student Participation and Dietary Intakes* (Alexandria, VA: USDA, 2007), 35–36; hereafter cited as *SNDA-III* 2.

4. Philip M. Gleason, "Participation in the National School Lunch Program and the School Breakfast Program," *American Journal of Clinical Nutrition* 61 (1995, suppl.): s213–20.

5. *SNDA-III* 2: 6.

6. Ibid., 38.

7. Carol Ann Marples and Diana-Marie Spillman, "Factors Affecting Students' Participation in the Cincinnati Public Schools Lunch Program," *Adolescence* 30 (1995): 748.

8. John Burghardt et al., *The School Nutrition Dietary Assessment Study: School Food Service, Meals Offered and Dietary Intakes*, U.S. Department of Agriculture, Food and Nutrition Service, Office of Analysis and Evaluation, October 1993, 129.

9. Gleason, "Participation," s217.

10. Lake Snell Perry Associates, Inc., "Students, Parents, and the School Breakfast Program in California: A Report on Focus Group Findings," fall-winter 2004, 5; unpublished material supplied by California Food Policy Advocates.

11. Frederic B. Glantz et al., *School Lunch Eligible Non-Participants*, Final Report (Cambridge, MA: Abt Associates, December 1994): 3–11.

12. John Hess, "Restaurant Food: Frozen, Cooked, Then Refrozen and Recooked," in *The Feeding Web: Issues in Nutritional Ecology,* ed. by Joan Gussow (Berkeley, CA: Bull Publishing Co., 1978), 158.

13. Patrick White, "Warming up to Retherm," *School Foodservice and Nutrition* 59, 3 (March 2005): 80.

14. Glantz, *Eligible Non-Participants*, 3–13.

15. Ibid., 3–11.

16. This is the CDC's definition as reported in U.S. General Accounting Office, *Food Safety: Continued Vigilance Needed to Ensure Safety of School Meals,* GAO-02-669T (Washington, DC: Government Printing Office, April 30, 2002), 1.

17. U.S. General Accounting Office, *School Meal Programs: Few Instances of Foodborne Outbreaks Reported, but Opportunities Exist to Enhance Outbreak Data and Food Safety Practices* GAO 03-530 (Washington, DC: Government Printing Office, May 2003), 8–9.

18. U.S. GAO, *Food Safety,* 8.

19. Ibid., 15.

20. School Nutrition Association, "Talking Points on May 1, 2005, *Dateline* Segment on School Food Safety." Available to SNA members on the organization's website, www.schoolnutrition.org (sign-in required); accessed April 13, 2008.

21. Center for Science in the Public Interest, "Making the Grade: An Analysis of Food Safety in School Cafeterias," January 2007; available at www.cspinet .org.

22. School Nutrition Association, "SNA Writes to CSPI on School Food Safety," www.schoolnutrition.org/index.aspx?id = 2310; accessed February 16, 2007.

23. Laurel G. Lambert, Martha T. Conklin, and J.J. Johnson, "Parental Beliefs toward the National School Lunch Program Related to Elementary Student Participation," *The Journal of Child Nutrition and Management* 26, 2 (fall 2002), available at http://docs.schoolnutrition.org/newsroom/jcnm/02fal/lambert/; Laurel G. Lambert, Martha T. Conklin, and Mary Kay Meyer, "Parents' Beliefs toward Their Children's Participation in the National School Lunch Program: Results of Focus Group Discussion Guided by the Theory of Reasoned Action," *Topics in Clinical Nutrition* 16, 4 (2001): 11–20.

24. Glantz, *Eligible Non-Participants,* 3–17.

25. Marples and Spillman, "Factors," 749.

26. Anand Vaishnav, "School Lunches are No Picnic, Longer Student Breaks Advocated," boston.com, August 6, 2005; www.boston.com/news/local/massachusetts/articles/2005/08/06/school_lunches_are_no_picnic/. SNDA-III, on the other hand, found a mean of 31 minutes and little variation among school types. Anne Gordon et al., *School Nutrition Dietary Assessment-III,*

Vol. 1: *School Foodservice, School Food Environment, and Meals Offered and Served* (Alexandria, VA: U.S. Department of Agriculture, 2007), Table 3.2, 63; hereafter cited as *SNDA-III* 1.

27. Mark Bliss, "Students Race to Enjoy Meals," *Southeast Missourian,* Monday, December 11, 2006, retrieved from www.semissourian.com/story/promt/1180757.html.

28. Ibid.

29. Cara Kumari, "School Lunch Could Put Students' Health at Risk," November 22, 2005. KAKE 10 On Your Side, www.kake.com.

30. Brad Perriello, "Fast Food: Most Schools Pressed for Time to Let Students Eat Without Rushing," *The Eagle Tribune Online,* September 2005, http://ecnnews.com/cgi-bin/05/etarchivestory.pl?200509+fn-fn-lunch.rbp-20050906-fn.

31. Howell Wechsler et al., "Food Service and Foods and Beverages Available at School: Results from the School Health Policies and Programs Study, 2000," *Journal of School Health* 71, 7 (September 2001): 313–24.

32. California Department of Education, *Healthy Children Ready to Learn: Facilities Best Practices,* 2006, 5, 6; available online at www.cde.ca.gov/re/pn/fd/documents/hcrtlfacilities.pdf.

33. Claudia Probart et al., "Factors Associated with the Offering and Sale of Competitive Foods and School Lunch Participation," *Journal of the American Dietetic Association* 106, 2 (2006): 242–47.

34. Samuel G. Freedman, "A Queens High School With 3,600 Students, and Room for Just 1,800," *New York Times,* January 16, 2008.

35. Martha T. Conklin, Laurel G. Lambert, and Janet B. Anderson, "How Long Does It Take Students to Eat Lunch? A Summary of Three Studies," *The Journal of Child Nutrition and Management* 26, 1 (spring 2002); http://docs.schoolnutrition.org/newsroom/jcnm/02spring/conklin/.

36. Nancy S. Buergel, Ethan A. Bergman, Annaka C. Knutson, and Monica A. Lindaas, "Students Consuming Sack Lunches Devote More Time to Eating Than Those Consuming School Lunches," *Journal of the American Dietetic Association* 102, 9 (September 2002): 1283–84.

37. Mary Kay Meyer, "Top Predictors of Middle/Junior High School Students' Satisfaction with School Food Service and Nutrition Programs," *Journal of the American Dietetic Association* 100, 1 (January 2000): 100–102.

38. Barbara Polichetti, "School Lunch Quiet Policy: Not So Much Silent as Safe," *Providence Journal,* January 26, 2007.

39. Alfonso Sanchez and Luis Rene Contreras, *Relationship of the Physical Dining Environment and Service Styles to Plate Waste in Middle/Junior High Schools.* NFSMI Item no. R-58-02 (Oxford, MS: National Food Service Management Institute, February 2003), 4, 18, 19, 42.

40. Mary Kay Meyer and Martha T. Conklin, "Variables Affecting High School Students' Perceptions of School Foodservice," *Journal of the American Dietetic Association* 98, 12 (December 1998): Table 1, 1427.

41. *SNDA-III* 2: Table 2.7, 45.

42. This relationship was essentially confirmed by the 1992–93 SNDA-I; a multivariate regression analysis, which controls for other major factors, found

that among students not certified for free and reduced price, a participation rate of 48 percent when lunches cost $1.20 rose to 52 percent for meals priced at $0.80, and declined to 44 percent for meals priced at $1.60. According to the researchers, "This implies an elasticity of 0.25, which is lower than the elasticity found in previous studies." Gleason, "Participation," s215, s216.

43. *SNDA-III* 2: 44. Gleason, "Participation," s217.

44. Alice Jo Rainesville, "Nutritional Quality of Reimbursable School Lunches to Lunches Brought From Home," *The Journal of Child Nutrition and Management* 25, 1 (spring 2001): 13–18.

45. Further, open-campus options may be so enmeshed with other variables that their impact is obscured in statistical analyses. As one of my students wrote, "The campus was open, but our lunch period was only a half hour, so you had to have a car to go anywhere." In her school, the policy probably reduced participation among affluent students with cars more than among poorer students; where such students are a small part of the student body, the open-campus policy may appear to have only modest impact.

46. *SNDA-III* 1: 94–95.

47. Ibid., 94–98.

48. Tina Moore, quoted in Johnny Jackson, "Longer Lunch Periods, Less Time To Eat," *Clayton News Daily-Online,* Jonesboro, GA, August 2006; www.news-daily.com/local/local/_story_237215214.html; retrieved August 27, 2006.

49. USDA, Food and Nutrition Service, *Foods Sold in Competition with USDA School Meal Programs: A Report to Congress* (Washington, DC: Government Printing Office, January 12, 2001), 4.

6. Hunger in the Classroom

1. Kara Chalmers, "There's No Place Like . . . School," *Sarasota Herald-Tribune,* December 29, 2002; Sunday Charlotte edition.

2. Janet Poppendieck, *Sweet Charity? Emergency Food and the End of Entitlement* (New York: Penguin Books, 1999), 74.

3. Robert Hunter, *Poverty,* Harper Torchbooks edition, edited and with an introduction by Peter d'A. Jones (New York: Harper and Row, 1965; orig. pub. 1904), 217.

4. Mary E.L. Small, "Educational and Social Possibilities of School Lunches," *Journal of Home Economics,* December 1914, 437. Retrieved from HEARTH (Home Economics Archive: Research, Tradition, and History); available at http://hearth.library.cornell.edu.

5. John Spargo, *The Bitter Cry of the Children,* reprinted with a new introduction by Jules Chametzky (New York: Johnson Reprint Corporation, 1969; orig. pub. 1906), 77.

6. Quotes in William Reese, "After Bread, Education: Nutrition and Urban School Children, 1890–1920," *Teachers College Record* 81, 4 (summer 1980): 504.

7. Hunter, *Poverty,* 216.

8. J. Larry Brown et al., *The Economic Cost of Domestic Hunger,* June 5, 2007, 19; an analysis commissioned by the Sodexho Foundation, in partnership with the Public Welfare Foundation and Spunk Fund, Inc. Originally posted at www.sodexofoundation.org/hunger_us/, the report is no longer available; I accessed and printed it out November 3, 2007.

9. Sharman Apt Russell, *Hunger: An Unnatural History* (New York: Basic Books, 2005), 183.

10. Ibid., 182.

11. Brown et al., *Economic Cost,* 19, 20. See also John T. Cook and Deborah A. Frank, "Food Security, Poverty, and Human Development in the United States," *Annals of the New York Academy of Science* 40 (2008), 1–17.

12. Deborah Stone, *Policy Paradox: The Art of Political Decision Making,* rev. ed. (New York: W.W. Norton, 2002), 164.

13. Russell, *Hunger,* 1.

14. I wanted to know precisely who said this, so I did a search on the phrase. On only the first page of responses, it was attributed to Cicero, Socrates, "the Chinese," a Zen parable, and "Spanish class," as well as—in another formulation, "The best sauce is hunger"—to *Don Quixote.*

15. Russell, *Hunger,* 34.

16. A great deal of the hunger that exists in the United States is relatively episodic and short-term; it does not result in the stunting of growth and emaciation readily detectable in anthropomorphic (height/weight) measurements. It does not always result in the kinds of malnutrition revealed by blood tests, though it may produce what researchers call "subclinical malnutrition." Asking people if they are hungry is not likely to be accurate because of both the confusions of language and the shame associated with being hungry and failing to feed one's children well.

17. For an excellent account of the evolution of hunger measurement in the United States, see Peter Eisinger, *Toward an End to Hunger in America* (Washington, DC: The Brookings Institution, 1998), 9–35. For an enlightening explanation of the politics of hunger measurement, see Joel Berg, *All You Can Eat: How Hungry Is America?* (New York: Seven Stories Press, 2008), esp. chapter 1.

18. Mark Nord, Margaret Andrews, and Steven Carlson, *Household Food Security in the United States, 2007,* Economic Research Service ERS Report 66 (Washington, DC: USDA, November 2008), 4–7, 14.

19. Brown et al., *Economic Cost,* 11. See also R. Kleinman et al., "Hunger in Children in the United States: Potential Behavioral and Emotional Correlates," *Pediatrics* 101, 3 (1998); and Michael Murphy et al., "Relationship between Hunger and Psychosocial Functioning in Low-Income American Children," *Journal of the American Academy of Child and Adolescent Psychiatry* 37 (1998): 163–70.

20. Nord, Andrews, and Carlson, *Household Food Security,* 12, Table 3.

21. Some states mandate participation by all schools except those that successfully seek a waiver or exemption. Some mandate participation in breakfast by schools in cities over a certain size or in schools with specified levels of eligibility for free and reduced price meals.

22. *Congressional Record*, House (February 20, 1946), 1487.

23. Letter to the editor from Steven John and Lloyd Szulborski, *Brattleboro Reformer*, December 20, 2005.

24. Richard Hilton, *Schools Leaving the National School Lunch Program: Final Report* (USDA, Food and Consumer Service, Office of Analysis and Evaluation, 1997), 5–10, 24–26.

25. Citizens' Board of Inquiry into Hunger and Malnutrition in the United States, *Hunger USA, Revisited* (Atlanta: Southern Regional Council: n.d. [ca. 1973]), 28.

26. Robert Pear, "3.2 Million Students and 2,700 Schools Drop Out of National Lunch Program in Year," *New York Times*, November 1, 1982.

27. Institutional nonparticipation became an issue once again in the early 1990s, when representatives of the AFSFA testified before Congress that schools were withdrawing from the program because of the administrative burden. In response Congress directed USDA to conduct the study mentioned above, which concluded that the administrative burden was not a significant factor, but that schools withdrew primarily for financial reasons or when students desired menu items prohibited by USDA. Since it is almost impossible to imagine that schools would withdraw from the program over hard candy or gum, I took that to mean schools that were unwilling to give up the lucrative sale of soda. USDA pointed out that the number of schools in the program had actually risen during the period leading up to the study (1989–93), as had participation, but did not mention that the total number of schools in the nation had grown even faster.

28. These are my calculations, based on comparing school participation data provided to me by the USDA Food and Nutrition Service, Office of Analysis, Nutrition, and Evaluation, and data on numbers of schools, both public and private, published by the National Center for Educational Statistics. It is possible that the decline in the rate of public school institutional participation that I have calculated is wholly or partly a function of the subdivision of large high schools into "small schools" (sharing a common building) as part of the "small schools movement." Each of these schools has its own principal and may be counted by NCES as a separate "school," but typically a single kitchen and cafeteria accommodates all students in the building, so the entire building may be counted by the School Food Authority, and thus by USDA, as a single "school."

29. Sar Levitan, *Programs in Aid of the Poor*, 6th ed. (Baltimore: The Johns Hopkins University Press, 1990), 99.

30. See Sandra G. Affenito, "Breakfast: A Missed Opportunity," research editorial, *Journal of the American Dietetic Association*, April 2007, 565–69.

31. Ibid., 565.

32. "Many Adolescents Are Skipping Breakfast," *USA Today*, September 1, 2001.

33. "Presentation by Congresswoman Lynn Woolsey, 'The School Breakfast Program,'" *Proceedings of the Breakfast and Learning in Children: Symposium*, April 22, 1999; USDA Center for Nutrition Policy and Promotion, September 1999; available at www.cnpp.usda.gov/Publications/OtherProjects/SymposiumBreakfastAndLearning.pdf.

34. See, for example, Theresa Nicklas, Carol O'Neil, and Leann Myers, "The Importance of Breakfast Consumption to Nutrition of Children, Adolescents and Young Adults," *Nutrition Today* 39, 1 (2004): 30–39. As stated in the abstract of this article, the study found, "Approximately 16% of 10 year olds, 19% of 15 year olds, and 37% of 19–28 year olds reported skipping breakfast. During the first three cross-sectional survey periods of the Bogalusa Heart Study, the tendency for 10-year-old children to skip breakfast increased. With the introduction of a school breakfast, the percentage of children who skipped breakfast fell from 30% to 13%. A significantly higher percentage of children who skipped breakfast did not meet two-thirds of the Recommended Dietary allowance (RDA) for essential vitamins and minerals, compared to those who consumed breakfast. . . . The school breakfast consumed by the 10-year-olds contributed significantly more energy, protein, and carbohydrate than breakfast eaten at home."

35. Food Research and Action Center, School Breakfast Scorecard 2006 (Washington, DC: FRAC, December 2006), 2–6; and School Breakfast Scorecard 2007 (Washington, DC: FRAC, December 2007), 1–7.

36. These figures actually understate the amounts by using the conservative assumption that none of the additional students participating would be in programs that qualify for the extra "severe need" reimbursement, which is an extra $0.25 per meal in 2007. It is probably a tribute to the success of the scorecard project as well as the growing awareness of the importance of breakfast that the 2007 scorecard raised the target from 55 free or reduced price breakfasts for every 100 free or reduced price lunches to 60; seven states had met or surpassed the 55 percent goal. FRAC, Scorecard 2006, 8.

37. FRAC, Scorecard 2007, 6.

38. Ibid. The scorecard counts residential child care institutions and any other organizations authorized to participate in the programs as "schools" for the purposes of reporting.

39. FRAC, Scorecard 2006, 11.

40. Lyanne Melendez, "SF School Lunch Programs Losing Money," ABC7News.com, March 11, 2008.

41. Lana F. Flowers, "Income Guidelines Higher than Poverty Level for Reduced-Price Lunches," *The* (Springdale, AR) *Morning News,* July 22, 2007.

42. Frederic B. Glantz et al., *School Lunch Eligible Non-Participants,* final report submitted to U.S. Department of Agriculture, Food and Consumer Service, Office of Analysis and Evaluation, May 1996, 3–20.

43. Constance Newman, *The Income Volatility See-Saw: Implications for School Lunch,* ERR-23 (USDA, Economic Research Service, August 2006), iii.

44. Paul J. Strasberg, *School Food Authority Administration of National School Lunch Program Free and Reduced Price Eligibility Determination,* USDA, Food and Nutrition Service, Office of Analysis, Nutrition, and Evaluation, CN-03-AV (Alexandria, VA: USDA, 2003), 16. The study was not a nationally representative sample, but focused on fourteen very large school districts. Another study, based on a nationally representative sample and conducted in the 1980s, reported a much lower nonresponse rate, 10.1 percent. It is not clear whether the difference reflects the nonrepresentativeness of the smaller study or

some actual decrease in parents' propensity to respond to verification requests. For the 1980s study, see Robert St. Pierre, M. Puma, M. Battaglia, and J. Layzer, "Study of Income Verification in the National School Lunch Program: Final Report," prepared by Abt Associates for USDA, Food and Nutrition Service, 1990, esp. xiv–xvi.

45. USDA, Food and Nutrition Service, *NSLP Certification Accuracy Research: Summary of Preliminary Findings* (September 2003), 6.

46. Zoe Neuberger and Robert Greenstein, "What Have We Learned from the FNS' New Research Findings about Overcertification in the School Meals Programs?" (Center on Budget and Policy Priorities, November 13, 2003), 5.

47. For more about the Family Economic Self Sufficiency Project, a collaboration of Wider Opportunities for Women, the Ms. Foundation for Women, the Corporation for Enterprise Development, and National Economic Development and Law Center, go to www.sixstrategies.org/sixstrategies/self sufficiencystandardtoolkit.cfm.

48. All calculations are derived from the Self Sufficiency Standard for Pennsylvania, 2006. The self-sufficiency standards permit sophisticated computer modeling, and the New York City organization that operates the calculator, the Women's Center for Education and Career Advancement, modeled the 2007 situation for me to see if a family of one adult, one teenager, and two younger school-aged children could "afford" school lunch at the reduced price rate at various incomes between 130 percent and 185 percent of poverty, keeping in mind that New York City charges only 25 cents for the reduced price lunch. What they found is telling:

> The modeling shows that even with conservative expenses budgeted, the household is unable to afford the cost of reduced price school lunches, except in very limited circumstances. In most scenarios when the family is eligible for reduced price lunches, the family is facing a budget shortfall—their expenses are greater than their income. If the family is receiving all of the benefits for which it is eligible except a housing subsidy, the household can only afford reduced lunches if their income is between 178 and 184 % of the Federal Poverty level (FPL). In all other instances when the family is eligible for reduced price lunches, or when their income is between 130% and 177% of FPL, they are facing a budget shortfall and cannot afford them. However, if the same family does not receive a Child Care subsidy, there is no point at which they are eligible for and can afford reduced price lunches.

49. Quoted in School Nutrition Association, "Help Increase Access to School Meals: A Mini Toolkit"; suggestions posted on the SNA web site, www .schoolnutrition.org, November 17, 2003.

50. "SNA Calls for Greater Access to School Meals," press release, June 7, 2005; posted at www.schoolnutrition.org.

7. Free, Reduced Price, Paid

1. Frederic B. Glantz et al., *School Lunch Eligible Non-Participants,* Final Report, December 1994, 3–25.

2. Ibid., 3–21.

3. Carol Pogash, "Free School Lunch Isn't Cool, So Some Students Go Hungry," *New York Times,* March 1, 2008.

4. Murray Milner, Jr., *Freaks, Geeks, and Cool Kids: American Teenagers, Schools, and the Culture of Consumption* (New York: Routledge, Taylor and Francis Group, 2006), 5.

5. Ibid., 66–67.

6. Beverly Daniel Tatum, *Why Are All the Black Kids Sitting Together in the Cafeteria? and Other Conversations about Race,* rev. ed. (New York: Basic Books, 1999), esp. 52–74.

7. Glantz et al., *School Lunch Eligible Non-Participants,* 3–21.

8. U.S. Congress, Senate, *Hearings before the Select Committee on Nutrition and Human Needs.* Part 9, *Universal School Lunch Program.* Washington, DC, October 13, 1971, 2474, 2464.

9. Citizens' Board of Inquiry into Hunger and Malnutrition in the United States, *Hunger USA, Revisited* (Atlanta: Southern Regional Council, n.d. [ca. 1973]), 35–36.

10. Jean Yavis Jones, "Universal School Lunch Program: Background, Issues, and Analysis," memorandum, Congressional Research Service, January 3, 1992, 6–7; copy in the Child Nutrition Archive, NFSMI. In fact, protecting the dignity and privacy of children served free or reduced price meals had been a concern since the earliest days of federal participation in school feeding during the New Deal. The contracts that the Department of Agriculture required schools to sign in order to receive surplus commodities specified that children receiving free meals could not be required to work for them or discriminated against in any way. When the ad hoc New Deal program was converted to a cash indemnity basis during World War II, USDA again specified that there be no discrimination or differential treatment of children receiving free meals, and these protections were carried over into the NSLA. Once the schools were receiving per-meal reimbursements, however, and had to prove that the meals were served to income-eligible children, the task of protecting privacy became more daunting and lapses more frequent.

11. Annette Bomar Hopgood, "Surviving an External Review," in *Managing Child Nutrition Programs,* ed. by Josephine Martin and Martha Conklin (Gaithersburg, MD: Aspen Publishers, Inc., 1999), 238; and see the attached "Selected Chronology: USDA Review Initiatives in the School Nutrition Programs, 1975–1998," Appendix 8-A, 259–63.

12. "Background information" attached to letter from Sue Greig, president of the American School Food Service Association, to Patrick Leahy, Chairman of the Senate Agriculture Committee, February 10, 1992. NFSMI, Child Nutrition Archive, Marshall Matz Papers.

13. USDA, Food and Nutrition Service, *Erroneous Payments in the National School Lunch Program and School Breakfast Program: Summary of Findings,* November 2007. The figure of 48 percent is my calculation from amounts reported in the summary.

14. Philip Gleason and John Burghardt, Mathematica Policy Research, Inc., "The National School Lunch Program: Ensuring That Free and Reduced Price Meal Benefits Go to the Poor." *Issue Brief: Timely Information from Mathematica,* April 2005, no. 2; available at www.mathematica-mpr.com.

15. Paul Strasburg, "School Food Authority Administration of National School Lunch Program Free and Reduced Price Eligibility Determination," *Special Nutrition Report Series,* No. CN-03-AV (Alexandria, VA: USDA, Food and Nutrition Service, Office of Analysis, Nutrition and Evaluation, 2003).

16. Robert Pear, "Aid to Poor Faces Tighter Scrutiny," *New York Times,* February 5, 2003; Louis Freedberg, "Targeting School Lunches," SFGate.com, January 6, 2003.

17. Comments by Gaye Lynn MacDonald, president, American School Food Service Association (now the School Nutrition Association), "Food for Thought: How to Improve Child Nutrition Programs," in Hearing before the Subcommittee on Education Reform of the Committee on Education and the Workforce, U.S. House of Representatives, 108th Congress, 1st Session, July 16, 2003. Serial No. 108–27; available at www.access.gpo.gov/congress/house.

18. Zoe Neuberger and Robert Greenstein, "New Analysis Shows 'Over-certification' for Free or Reduced-Price School Meals Has Been Overstated," Center on Budget and Policy Priorities, July 15, 2003; available at http://www.cbpp.org/cms/index.cfm?fa=view&id=2035.

19. Testimony of Robert Greenstein, executive director, Center on Budget and Policy Priorities, before the Senate Agriculture Committee, March 4, 2003; available at http://agriculture.senate.gov/Hearings/greenstein.pdf.

20. Agnes Meyer, "School Lunches Should Be Free," address delivered October 22, 1946, before the National Conference of State School Lunch Officials; quoted in Thelma Flanagan, "School Food Services," in *Education in the States: Nationwide Development Since 1900,* ed. by Edgar Fuller and Jim B. Pearson (Washington, DC: National Education Association, 1969), 568.

21. Donna Boss, "The Elders Speak: Dr. John Perryman, ASFSA," *Food Management* 15, 7 (July 1981): 66.

22. U.S. Congress, Senate. *Hearings before the Select Committee on Nutrition and Human Needs,* Part 1, *Problems and Prospects;* December 17, 18, 19, 1968. (Washington, DC: U.S. Government Printing Office, 1969), 157.

23. American School Food Service Association, 1993 Legislative Issue Paper, "Invest in Children: Share the Universal Vision," January 1993. Copy in the Marshall Matz files, Child Nutrition Archive, NFSMI.

24. Congressman George Miller (D-CA), Statement on the Introduction of the Universal Student Nutrition Act, June 25, 1992; Extension of Remarks, *Congressional Record,* House, June 26, 1992, E2007.

25. Center on Budget and Policy Priorities, "Universal School Lunch: A Timely Idea?" April 1993, revised May 9, 1994, 6; memo, copy provided on request by CBPP.

26. USDA, Food and Nutrition Service, "Provisions 1, 2 and 3 Fact Sheet"; available at www.fns.usda.gov/cnd/Governance/prov-1-2-3-/Prov1_2_3_Fact Sheet.htm. The difference between the Provision 2 rules and those used in the pilots mentioned by CBPP is that under Provision 2, a school or district establishes the percentages of *meals served* in each reimbursement category in the base year; under the pilot "no-fee" projects, the intent was to establish the percentage of *children eligible* for each category of reimbursement. Thus under Provision 2, if only a few fully paid meals were actually served in the base year,

and a very large number of free and reduced price meals were served, then reimbursements in the subsequent years would reflect that pattern, even though participation among full price eligible children might be expected to grow as parents and children became accustomed to meals served free.

27. Less than one half of one percent is my calculation based on USDA, Food and Nutrition Service, *Paperwork Reduction Pilot Projects: Interim Report,* March 1994, ERIC document 383 097. See also USDA, Office of Analysis and Evaluation, Food and Nutrition Service, *Universal-Type School Meal Programs: Report to Congress,* June 1994, Washington, DC, U.S. Government Printing Office: 1994 300–119/00164.

28. USDA, Food and Nutrition Service, *Paperwork Reduction Pilot Projects.*

29. The GAO also reported to Congress about the no-fee pilots. See U.S. General Accounting Office, "Early Results of USDA's 'No-Fee School Meal Pilot Program,'" testimony before the Elementary, Secondary and Vocational Education Subcommittee, Committee on Education and Labor, House of Representatives, GAO/T-RCED-94–184, April 14, 1984.

30. The "no-fee" pilots were not the only approach to paperwork reduction that USDA decided to study. Tests of alternative application procedures, direct certification, and an enrollment-based approach to Provisions 1 and 2 were also slated for study. The enrollment-based approach fell through when participating sites either withdrew from the pilot or failed to implement such an approach. The alternative application procedures were in fact tested, but generated little interest. Direct certification has been widely implemented and subjected to extensive study since these initial pilot programs.

31. *New York Times,* September 30, 2005. I am grateful to Stephanie Burke for calling this to my attention.

32. Ann Savino, "Lunch Online," *The American School Board Journal* 184 (February 1997): 46–49.

33. "Teachers Nationwide Visit Richland Two for Lessons," News 19: *www.wltx.com* (Columbia, SC), February 28, 2007; www.wltx.com/news/story .aspx?storyid=47401.

34. Kelly Tyko, "Finger Imaging in Martin Schools Gets a Big Thumbs-up," TCPalm.Com (Florida), January 31, 2007; www.tcpalm.com/tcp/local_news/ article/0,2545,TCP_16736)5316320,00.html.

35. Rory Schuler, "ACLU Lauds Committee's Move to Ban the Scan," TauntonGazette.com, April 20, 2007. See also David Able, "Taunton Schools Scrap Fingerprint-Scanning Plans," Boston.com, April 20, 2007.

36. Elaine Allen-Emrich, "Brutal School Policy Upsets Child," *North Port Sun,* November 16, 2005; accessed at www.sunonline.com.

37. USDA, FNS Instruction 765–7 Rev. 2, "Handling Lost, Stolen, and Misused Meal Tickets"; copy supplied by California Food Policy Advocates.

8. Local Heroes

1. Jennifer Nelson, "Is *That* Your Lunch?" *Family Circle,* November 1, 2006.

2. Anne Gordon, et al., *School Nutrition Dietary Assessment-III. Volume 1: School Foodservice, School Food Environment, and Meals Offered and Served* (Alexandria, VA: USDA, 2007), 10–11.

3. Robert Gottlieb, *Environmentalism Unbound: Exploring New Pathways for Change* (Cambridge, MA: The MIT Press, 2001): 265–68; Mark Vallianatos, Robert Gottlieb, and Margaret Haase, "Farm to School: Strategies for Urban Health, Combating Sprawl, and Establishing a Community Food Systems Approach," *Journal of Planning Education and Research* 23 (2004): 414–17.

4. See Mary MacVean, "If You Build It, Children Will Come to the Salad Bar," *Los Angeles Times*, November 4, 2004.

5. See especially Ann Cooper and Lisa M. Holmes, *Lunch Lessons: Changing the Way We Feed Our Children* (New York: Collins, 2006).

6. "Chef Ann Interview on Danaroc.com," December 3, 2007; retrieved from www.chefann.com. For a lively account of the work at BUSD, see Burkhard Bilger, "The Lunchroom Rebellion," *The New Yorker*, September 4, 2006, 72–80.

7. Katherine Ralston et al., *National School Lunch Program: Background, Trends and Issues*, ERR-61, July 2008, 39.

8. American School Food Service Association, *Little Big Fact Book*. 2003, 7.

9. Mary MacVean, "Cooking with Class in Mind," *Los Angeles Times*, Sunday, June 22, 2008.

10. Market Ventures, Inc., *School Food Plus Evaluation. Interim Report: Phase 3, School Year 2005–2006*, April 12, 2007, 11–12.

11. For a lively account of school food reform in New York, see Kevin Morgan and Roberta Sonnino, *The School Food Revolution: Public Food and the Challenge of Sustainable Development* (London: Earthscan, 2005), esp. chapter 3.

12. The rising rate of childhood overweight and obesity has generated a number of targeted interventions aimed at reducing obesity rates among schoolchildren, involving not only changes in cafeteria food but also nutrition education and physical activity. These have usually been undertaken by relatively large-scale outside actors—the National Institutes of Health, for example, or large foundations. Thus they generally do not fall within the meaning of "local" as I have used it in this chapter. It is worth noting, however, that the research has shown results that researchers have characterized as "modest." See Karen E. Peterson and Mary Kay Fox, "Addressing the Epidemic of Childhood Obesity through School-Based Interventions: What Has Been Done and Where Do We Go From Here?" *Journal of Law, Medicine, and Ethics* (spring 2007): 116. For a recent meta-analysis of rigorous studies, see D.L. Katz et al., "Strategies for the Prevention and Control of Obesity in the School Setting: Systematic Review and Meta-Analysis," *International Journal of Obesity* 32 (December 2008): 1780–89.

13. Peterson and Fox, "Addressing the Epidemic," 118.

14. See for example the work of the Campaign for a Commercial Free Childhood at http://commercialfreechildhood.org.

15. This is the authority that the court had decided that the secretary did not have in *National Soft Drink Association v. Block*, which USDA lost in 1983.

16. For an excellent overview of efforts to regulate competitive foods, see Ellen Fried and Michele Simon, "The Competitive Food Conundrum: Can

Government Regulations Improve School Food?" *Duke Law Journal* 56 (2007): 1491–1539.

17. Ibid., 1518. For a more detailed account of the Connecticut battle, see Michele Simon, *Appetite for Profit: How the Food Industry Undermines Our Health and How To Fight Back* (New York: Nation Books, 2006), 230–33.

18. New York School Nutrition Association, "Two Legislative Action Alerts," May 2006; retrieved from the NYSNA website, www.schoolnutrition .org, June 16, 2006.

19. Margaret Sheriden, "Interface: Bertrand Weber: His Retail Flair Involves the Community in a Fresh Approach to School Foodservice," *Restaurants and Institutions,* February 1, 2005.

20. *Two Angry Moms,* "TAM Preview," available on the "Movie clips" section of the Two Angry Moms website at www.angrymoms.org/inner/ movie_clips.html. See also "Top 10 List for Better School Food," at www .betterschoolfood.org.

21. http://cookingwithkids.net/What_We_Believe/index.html. Sharing a love of food with children and helping them to understand where their food comes from, how it gets to them, and what they can do with it has become something of a cottage industry in the United States. There is the famous edible schoolyard at the Martin Luther King Middle School in Berkeley, California, courtesy of celebrity chef Alice Waters and the Chez Panisse Foundation, and now a sister edible schoolyard at the Samuel J. Green Charter School in New Orleans. There is the Cookshop program in the New York City schools pioneered by Toni Liquori when she was at the Community Food Resource Center, now an integral part of the menu planning process for the city's 800,000 meals per day. In Cookshop, children study, prepare, and consume the "vegetable of the month," and then encounter it again in the school cafeteria. There is the work of Antonia Demas at the Food Studies Institute including a curriculum called *Food Is Elementary,* which "educates children about nutrition by providing a positive experience of food and food preparation that is fun, hands-on, and sensory based." Both Liquori's and Demas's work helped to inspire and shape Cooking With Kids in Santa Fe, which has developed a whole series of classroom-based food preparation projects, again linked to cafeteria menus. There are innumerable school gardening programs, including hydroponics, hoop houses, and other approaches that extend the growing season and slip the surly bonds of climate to make school gardening a viable educational option, even in colder regions. Finally, there is a whole host of efforts to integrate food and nutrition education into the academic curriculum. The Food Trust in Philadelphia has developed popular workshops in which teachers, on their own time, learn methods for providing food-related content in math, social studies, language arts, and other programs. The Center for Ecoliteracy in Berkeley, CA, has created a broad array of resource materials available in print or via the web. Food Education Every Day (FEED) in Vermont offers workshops in which teachers devise curriculum, sometimes for graduate or recertification credit, and has posted the resulting teacher-designed units on its website. A complete science curriculum organized around food and nutrition has been developed for grades 4–6 by Isobel Contento and her colleagues at Teachers College Columbia, and food-loving educators

in a host of states have shown how food education can meet state-specified standards. This list is undoubtedly incomplete, and by the time this book is published, it will be more so, but you can find extensive resources and up-to-date information through the magic of your internet browser.

22. See the work of Leann Birch on children's food acceptance: Leann Birch, "Psychological Influences on the Childhood Diet," *Journal of Nutrition* 128, 2 (1998, suppl.): s407–10; Leann Birch and D.W. Marlin, "I Don't Like It; I Never Tried It: Effects of Exposure on Two-Year Old Children's Food Preferences," *Appetite* 3, 4 (1982): 353–60.

23. John Dewey, *The School and Society,* in John Dewey, *The Child and the Curriculum* and *The School and Society,* introduction by Leonard Carmichael, rev. ed. (Chicago: The University of Chicago Press, 1943), 15.

24. Louis Menand, *The Metaphysical Club* (New York: Farrar, Straus and Giroux, 2001). I am grateful to Professor Troy Duster for calling my attention to Menand's characterization of Dewey's incorporation of cooking into the curriculum of the Lab School. See Troy Duster and Alice Waters, "Engaged Learning across the Curriculum: The Vertical Integration of Food for Thought," *Liberal Education* 92, 2 (spring 2006): 42–47.

25. Jack Kloppenburg, Jr., and Neva Hassanein, "From Old School to Reform School?" *Agriculture and Human Values* 23 (2006): 418.

26. Ms. Nicholie is quoted on the "31 Days of Nutrition" page of the website of the Growing Minds Project, www.growing-minds.org.

27. Marilyn Briggs, "Rethinking School Lunch," in *Ecological Literacy: Educating our Children for a Sustainable World,* ed. by Michael K. Stone and Zenobia Barlow (San Francisco: Sierra Club Books, 2005), 245.

28. Vallianatos, Gottlieb, and Haase, "Farm to School," 414–23.

29. A guide published by the Community Food Security Coalition in March 2004 reported programs in 387 school districts in 22 states.

30. JoAnne Berkenkamp, *Making the Farm/School Connection: Opportunities and Barriers to Great Use of Locally-grown Produce in Public Schools.* Prepared for the Department of Applied Economics, University of Minnesota, January, 2006, 2; available at www.leopold.iastate.edu/research/marketing_files/Minnesota.pdf.

31. New York State Farm to School Coordinating Committee, "Potential for Farm-to-School in New York: Survey of K-12 School food Service Directors," summary of results, 2004; typescript provided by the New York State Department of Agriculture and Markets.

32. Janet Brown, "Five Successful Models of Procurement," Section 8, "Procurement," 6; in Center for Ecoliteracy, *Rethinking School Lunch Guide.* www.ecoliteracy.org/programs/rsl-guide.html. This is a web guide, rather than a book, so its sections can be accessed in any order and pages are numbered only within sections.

33. Patricia Allen and Julie Guthman, "From 'Old School' to 'Farm-to-School': Neoliberalization from the Ground Up," *Agriculture and Human Values* 23 (2006): 412.

34. Kloppenburg and Hassanein, "From Old School to Reform School?" 420.

35. "Wiley Universal Free Breakfast Organizing Pays Off: State Improves from 35th to 22nd in the Nation," *This Week at the George Wiley Center and the Rhode Island Campaign to Eliminate Childhood Poverty* 67 (March 13, 2006). The improvement from thirty-fifth to twenty-second in the title refers to the improvement over the previous year's performance on the 2005 FRAC School Breakfast Scorecard. The ranking of fiftieth mentioned in the text refers to 1993, when the Wiley Center campaign began.

36. See the Breakfast First website, www.breakfastfirst.org. And see Food Research and Action Center, *School Breakfast Scorecard 2008* (Washington, DC: FRAC, January 2009), 16, which reports modest gains.

37. *2008 Rhode Island KIDS COUNT Factbook,* 44. Published by Rhode Island Kids Count and available at www.rikidscount.org; accessed August 7, 2008.

38. Recall, however, that the reimbursement percentages remain the ones established in the base year. At one point, Davis said, he became concerned and spoke to his state director: "'We are going to be claiming more meals under the free category than we have applications on file, based on our percentage of participation.' And she went back to USDA, and USDA said, 'As long as the base year information was obtained correctly,' which it was, 'that's perfectly fine.'"

39. Joel Berg, *All You Can Eat: How Hungry Is America?* (New York: Seven Stories Press, 2008), 245.

40. Louis Porter, "State Hopes to Boost School Breakfast Participation," *Times Argus* (Barre-Montpelier, VT), May 7, 2008.

41. "Chef Ann Interview on Danaroc.com," December 3, 2007.

Conclusion

1. Mary Story, Karen Kaphingst, and Simone French, "The Role of Schools in Obesity Prevention," *The Future of Children* 16, 1 (spring 2006): 119, 128; issue on Childhood Obesity; available at www.futureofchildren.org.

2. See Jonathan Kozol, *The Shame of the Nation: The Restoration of Apartheid Schooling in America* (New York: Crown Publishers, 2005).

3. Kevin Morgan and Roberta Sonnino, *The School Food Revolution: Public Food and the Challenge of Sustainable Development* (London: Earthscan, 2008).

4. G.K. Chesterton, *What's Wrong With the World* (1910); found at www.wisdomquotes.com.

5. Alice Boughton, "Household Arts and School Lunches," in *Cleveland Education Survey* (Cleveland, OH: The Survey Committee of the Cleveland Foundation, 1916), 118–19.

6. David Ellwood, *Poor Support: Poverty in the American Family* (New York: Basic Books, 1988), 23.

7. Michele Lawrence, superintendent of the Berkeley (California) Unified School District, interviewed by Janet Brown, program officer, Center for Ecoliteracy, in *Rethinking School Lunch Guide,* chapter on Curriculum Integration, 8; available at www.ecoliteracy.org.

8. Felipe Fernandez-Armesto, "Meals Make Us Human," *The Guardian*, September 14, 2002.

9. Boughton, "Household Arts and School Lunches," 118–19.

10. Theda Skocpol, *The Missing Middle: Working Families and the Future of American Social Policy* (New York: W.W. Norton and Company, A Century Foundation Book, 2000), 104.

11. Katherine Newman and Victor Chen, *The Missing Class: Portraits of the Near Poor in America* (Boston: Beacon Press, 2007). And see United States Census, Current Population Reports, Annual Social and Economic (ASEC) Supplement, POV02, "People in Families by Family Structure, Age, and Sex, Iterated by Income-to-Poverty Ratio and Race," 2008; available at http:// pubdb3.census.gov/macro/032008/pov/new02_200.htm.

12. Jacob S. Hacker, *The Great Risk Shift: The Assault on American Jobs, Families, Health Care, and Retirement and How You Can Fight Back* (New York: Oxford University Press, 2006), 6.

13. Schorr was an articulate proponent of universal approaches wherever feasible. He saw them as a step toward overcoming the nation's polarities: "We are a deeply divided nation—we are divided between those who have and those who have not, between slums and suburbs, between those who feel competent and those who feel exploited. The national structure of income maintenance is not a small matter. It can be structured to deepen the schism by dealing with the poor in identifiably separate programs, or it can strike across such divisions and help heal them." Alvin L. Schorr, *Explorations in Social Policy* (New York: Basic Books, 1968), 299.

14. Another barrier to switching to universal may be found in the various uses to which the school meal applications are currently put. The percentage of students eligible for free and reduced price meals is used to calculate the "E-Rate"—the level of discount that the school and its libraries receive for internet access and telecommunications services. It is used to determine which schools qualify for funding under Title I (of the Elementary and Secondary Education Act), the federal government's main compensatory funding for schools that serve impoverished areas or students. It is used to determine which schools can be funded to provide free tutoring services to all their students in conjunction with No Child Left Behind (NCLB). The applications are also used to determine income categories for measuring group performance under NCLB, and thus a school's Adequate Yearly Progress score, which carries important sanctions for schools that fail. And state governments also use the percentage of free and reduced price eligibility to distribute compensatory funding under various programs. All in all, there is a great deal resting on a fragile base. While it is true that elimination of the application process under a universal program would cause a short-term scramble for other bases, it is also the case that with current data-gathering technology, there are almost certainly other approaches that are more accurate. Revising the measurements on which such allocations are made is a long overdue change.

15. Jane Laskey, "Bringing Life to School Lunches," *St. Cloud Times*, March 13, 2008.

16. Karen Evans Stout, quoted in Frances M. Berg, *Underage and Overweight: Our Childhood Obesity Crisis—What Every Family Needs To Know* (New York: Hatherleigh Press, 2005), 317.

17. Michele Lawrence, in *Rethinking School Lunch Guide,* Curriculum Integration, 7.

18. I believe that one reason school food service directors seem to be so cozy with their industry suppliers is that they get far more respect from those than from their educational colleagues.

19. Quoted in Michael Pollan, "Unhappy Meals," *The New York Times Sunday Magazine,* January 28, 2007, 44.

20. Ibid., 41.

21. Michael Pollan, *In Defense of Food: An Eater's Manifesto* (New York: Penguin Press, 2008), 13; "great-grandmother rule" at 148.

22. Food Research and Action Center, *Commodity Foods and the Nutritional Quality of the National School Lunch Program: Historical Role, Current Operations, and Future Potential* (Washington, DC: FRAC, September 2008), 19. See also Eileen Kennedy and Edward Cooney, "Development of the Child Nutrition Programs in the United States," *Journal of Nutrition* 131 (2001): S435.

23. Institute of Medicine, *Preventing Childhood Obesity: Health in the Balance* (Washington, DC: National Academies Press, 2005), 70–71.

24. Ron Haskins, Christina Paxson, and Elisabeth Donahue, "Fighting Obesity in the Public Schools," *The Future of Children,* policy brief, spring 2006, 2; available at www.futureofchildren.org.

25. Story, Kaphingst, and French, "The Role of Schools in Obesity Prevention."

26. Kelly D. Brownell and Katherine Battle Horgen, *Food Fight: The Inside Story of the Food Industry, America's Obesity Crisis, and What We Can Do about It* (New York: McGraw Hill, Contemporary Books, 2004), 141.

27. Jennifer Wilkins, "Students Deserve to Eat Better," *Albany Times Union,* September 3, 2006.

28. The meals at the soup kitchen are much larger than school meals, averaging between 2,000 and 2,500 calories per meal. They are intended to sustain guests for a 24-hour period if need be. Holy Apostles Soup Kitchen, *Annual Report, 2006;* available at www.holyapostlesnyc.org/soup_kitchen/audited_financial_statement.htm.

29. This idea was proposed by Marshall Matz, the general counsel of the School Nutrition Association, in 2002 under the name of "pay-go." As he explained, "This proposal would allow parents to 'pay' for school meals once a year through the IRS as opposed to daily at the school," by reducing the personal tax exemption for dependent children. In this system, only those whose income was so low that they paid no taxes would get "free" meals; others would pay progressively, since the actual dollar value of the child exemption rises with tax bracket. Exemptions, however, are now subject to a phase-out at high-income levels, so you might say that Congress has already enacted my idea of reducing the exemption for higher-income families.

30. Mimi Abramovitz and Sandra Morgen with the National Council for Research on Women, *Taxes Are a Woman's Issue: Reframing the Debate* (New York: The Feminist Press at the City University of New York, 2006), 13.

31. Jonathan Kozol, *Savage Inequalities: Children in America's Schools* (New York: Harper Perennial, 1993). See also *Funding for Justice; Money, Equity and the Future of Public Education* (Milwaukee: Rethinking Schools, 1997).

32. James Glanz, "The Economic Cost of War," *New York Times*, March 1, 2009.

33. I have deep reservations about a rebate-based stimulus package, so let me propose an alternative: I'll call it the Transition to Healthy School Meals/Investment in America's Future Stimulus Package. It would have five components. (1) A construction fund, with two parts. The first would finance the construction of additional kitchen space if needed to permit schools to prepare fresh food on site; the second would fund the construction of additional cafeteria space where needed to permit all public schools to have sufficient facilities to accommodate all students in a reasonable number of shifts and thus to offer lunch hours of sufficient duration. Such cafeterias should be designed with an eye to dual use as community centers. This would help stimulate the construction industry, one of the hardest hit by the current turmoil. (2) An equipment fund to permit the purchase or restoration of kitchen equipment (and cafeteria chairs and tables if needed). This should help the appliance and furniture industries, also hard hit. (3) A culinary training program to upgrade the skills of school lunch workers. This would build skills and thus earning potential, and it would provide jobs, both for trainers and for additional workers to help while permanent workers were receiving training. This should help the restaurant and food service industries, another sector likely to be hard hit as discretionary spending declines. (4) A farm to cafeteria development fund to permit schools to build relationships with farmers and to help farmers make the transition to planting specifically for schools. (5) An Adults in the Cafeteria stipend program to permit out-of-work and retired adults to eat with children in school cafeterias, thus promoting intergenerational sharing and reestablishing the waning art of dining.

34. And of course, if it would cost $3 billion to add 50 cents to every lunch and 25 cents to every breakfast at current participation levels, then it would cost more to do so at the participation levels that we could anticipate if the meals were served free.

35. USDA, Food and Nutrition Service, Office of Analysis and Evaluation, *Universal-Type School Meal Programs: Report to Congress,* June 1994.

36. USDA, Food and Nutrition Service, *Paperwork Reduction Pilot Projects: Interim Report,* March 1994, ERIC document 383 097, 13–17; available at www.eric.ed.gov/ERICDocs/data/ericdocs2sql/content_storage_01/0000019b/80/13/f1/75.pdf.

37. Michael Ponza, Philip Gleason, Lara Hulsey, and Quinn Moore, *NSLP/SBP Access, Participation, Eligibility, and Certification Study: Erroneous Payments in the NSLP and SBP,* vol. 1: *Study Findings.* Special Nutrition Programs Report No. CN-07-APEC/ USDA, Food and Nutrition Service, Office

of Research, Nutrition, and Analysis, November 2007; available at www.fns
.usda.gov/oane/MENU/published/CNP/Files/apecvol1.pdf.

38. You can find just such a primer in Abramovitz and Morgen, *Taxes Are
a Woman's Issue,* 31–44.

39. Michael Jacobson, Executive Director, Center for Science in the Public
Interest, "Health Care Reform: *Prevention* Is Essential." Senate Finance
Committee, Roundtable Discussion on Financing Comprehensive Health Care
Reform, May 12, 2009. Available on the web at http://cspinet.org/new/pdf/
mikejacobsontestimony.pdf.

40. Susan Lynn Roberts, "School Food: Does the Future Call for New Food
Policy or Can the Old Still Hold True?" *Drake Journal of Agricultural Law,* 3
(fall 2002): 601–2.

41. Mark Winne, *Closing the Food Gap: Resetting the Table in the Land of
Plenty* (Boston: Beacon Press, 2008), 186.

42. Morgan and Sonnino, *The School Food Revolution,* 191.

43. Christopher Lee, "Disparate Federal Rules in Spotlight," Washingtonpost
.com, Sunday, March 9, 2008. The "non-ambulatory" animals in question are
those that "went down" between an initial inspection, which they passed, and
the "knock box"; the regulations allow them to be processed for meat if a
second inspection reveals that the animal was not sick but had an injury such
as a broken limb.

44. See Kevin Morgan and Roberta Sonnino, "Empowering Consumers:
The Creative Procurement of School Meals in Italy and the UK," *International
Journal of Consumer Studies* 30 (2006): 19–25.

45. E-mail, Kenneth Jaffe, Slope Farms, to Janet Poppendieck, February 19,
2008.

46. Since I started this chapter by issuing a plea for a "return to the drawing
boards" to see what sort of school food program we would create if we placed
a clear priority on children's health and education, you may want to accuse me
of betraying my own principle here, by permitting other agendas to compete
for attention and investment. I want to make clear that I don't see it that way; I
think that this is all one agenda—healthier children.

47. Richard Kuhn, "Vegan Education and the Epistemology of Ignorance,"
op-ed, *News Blaze,* October 23, 2008; retrieved from http://newsblaze.com:80/
story/20081023143919zzzz.nb/topstory.html.

48. The agency that administers a federal program generally determines the
locus of its congressional oversight. In the House of Representatives, oversight
by the Committee on Education and Labor would continue if the school food
program moved to the DOE or to HHS, but in the appropriations process, school
food would now be a part of the DOE or HHS budget, and the subcommittee of
the Appropriations Committee would presumably change. That might be good,
since vestiges of the old "farmer's money" mindset are still easy to spot. In the
Senate, the Committee on Health, Education, Labor and Pensions would most
likely assume jurisdiction. There I'm not sure this is a good thing. The members
of the Senate Agriculture Committee have built up considerable expertise over
the years and have frequently shown themselves to be thoughtful and informed
champions of school food. Certainly their engagement with issues of nutrition

and health has been growing. The committee continues to be dominated by farm state senators, many of whom are passionate protectors of big agriculture, but the alternative agriculture movement has been making slow but steady inroads into the agribusiness model. If we were to move to a universal free program, we could bring to this equation all of the political muscle and savvy of the broad middle class, a force that might accelerate a much needed reconsideration of our fundamental agricultural policy framework. In other words, a universal free school meals program might focus the attention of a far larger segment of the citizenry on agriculture policy.

49. Gladys Baker et al., *Century of Service: The First 100 Years of the United States Department of Agriculture* (Washington, DC: Centennial Committee, U.S. Department of Agriculture, 1963), 1.

50. United States Farm and Farm Related Employment, 2002. Economic Research Service, USDA; data set retrieved from www.ers.usda.gov/Data/ FarmandRelatedEmployment/.

Abramovitz, Mimi, and Sandra Morgen with the National Council for Research on Women. *Taxes Are a Woman's Issue: Reframing the Debate.* New York: The Feminist Press at the City University of New York, 2006.

Abt Associates, Inc. *Evaluation of the Nutrient Standard Menu Planning Demonstration: Summary of Findings* (Cambridge, MA: Abt Associates, Inc.: August, 1998).

Alaimo, Katherine, Christine Olson, E.A. Frongillo, and Ronette Briefel. "Food Insufficiency, Family Income and Health in U.S. Preschool and School-Aged Children." *American Journal of Public Health* 91 (2001): 781–86.

Allen, Patricia, and Julie Guthman. "From 'Old School' to 'Farm-to-School': Neoliberalization from the Ground Up." *Agriculture and Human Values* 23 (2006): 401–15.

American School Food Service Association. *Little Big Fact Book.* Alexandria, VA, 2003.

Baker, Gladys, Wayne Rasmussen, Vivian Wiser, and Jane Porter. *Century of Service: The First 100 Years of the United States Department of Agriculture* (Washington, DC: Centennial Committee, U.S. Department of Agriculture, 1963).

Belkin, Lisa. "The School-Lunch Test." *New York Times Magazine,* August 20, 2006; available at www.nytimes.com/2006/08/20/magazine/20lunches.html.

Berg, Frances M. *Underage and Overweight: Our Childhood Obesity Crisis— What Every Family Needs To Know.* New York: Hatherleigh Press, 2005.

Berg, Joel. *All You Can Eat: How Hungry Is America?* New York: Seven Stories Press, 2008.

Berry, Jeffery. *Feeding Hungry People.* New Brunswick, NJ: Rutgers University Press, 1984.

Bilger, Burkhard. "The Lunchroom Rebellion." *The New Yorker,* September 4, 2006, 72–80.

Birch, Leann, and D.W. Marlin. "I Don't Like It; I Never Tried It: Effects of Exposure on Two-Year Old Children's Food Preferences." *Appetite* 3, 4 (1982): 353–60.

Boss, Donna. "The Elders Speak: Dr. John Perryman, ASFSA." *Food Management* 15, 7 (July 1981): 46–48, 66, and 70–74.

Boughton, Alice. "The Administration of School Lunches in Cities," a presentation to the Fourth International Congress on School Hygiene, Buffalo, NY, 1913; reprinted in *Journal of Home Economics* 6, 3 (June 1914): 213–18.

———. "Household Arts and School Lunches." In *Cleveland Education Survey.* Cleveland, OH: The Survey Committee of the Cleveland Foundation, 1916.

Brown, Denise. *Prevalence of Food Production Systems in School Foodservice.* Oxford, MS: National Food Service Management Institute, R-75-04, 2004.

Brown, J. Larry. "Nutrition." In *Social Injustice and Public Health,* edited by Barry S. Levy and Victor W. Sidel, 238–52. Oxford: Oxford University Press, 2006.

Brownell, Kelly D., and Katherine Battle Horgen. *Food Fight: The Inside Story of the Food Industry, America's Obesity Crisis, and What We Can Do about It.* New York: McGraw Hill, Contemporary Books, 2004.

Buergel, Nancy S., Ethan A. Bergman, Annaka C. Knutson, and Monica A. Lindaas. "Students Consuming Sack Lunches Devote More Time to Eating Than Those Consuming School Lunches." *Journal of the American Dietetic Association* 102, 9 (September 2002): 1283–84.

Burghardt, John, and Barbara Devaney. *The School Nutrition Dietary Assessment Study: Summary of Findings.* Alexandria, VA: U.S. Department of Agriculture, 1993.

Burghardt, John, Anne Gordon, Nancy Chapman, Philip Gleason, and Thomas Fraker. *The School Nutrition Dietary Assessment Study: School Food Service, Meals Offered and Dietary Intakes.* U.S. Department of Agriculture, Food and Nutrition Service, Office of Analysis and Evaluation, October, 1993.

Buzby, Jean C., and Joanne Guthrie. *Plate Waste in School Nutrition Programs: Final Report to Congress.* U.S. Department of Agriculture, Economic Research Service, E-FAN-02-009, March 2002.

Center for Ecoliteracy. *Rethinking School Lunch Guide: An Online Resource;* available at www.ecoliteracy.org.

Center for Science in the Public Interest. *Making the Grade: An Analysis of Food Safety in School Cafeterias.* Washington, DC: Center for Science in the Public Interest, 2007.

Center on Budget and Policy Priorities. "Universal School Lunch: A Timely Idea?" Washington, DC, April 1993; revised May 9, 1994.

Chelf, Carl. *Controversial Issues in Social Welfare Policy: Government and the Pursuit of Happiness.* Newbury Park, CA: Sage Publications, 1992.

Citizens Board of Inquiry into Hunger and Malnutrition in the United States. *Hunger USA,* with an introductory comment by Robert F. Kennedy. Boston: Beacon Press, 1968.

———. *Hunger USA Revisited.* Atlanta: Southern Regional Council, n.d. [ca. 1973].

Committee on School Lunch Participation. *Their Daily Bread: A Study of the National School Lunch Program.* Atlanta: McNelley-Rudd Printing Service Inc, 1968.

Conklin, Martha T., Laurel G. Lambert, and Janet B. Anderson. "How Long Does It Take Students to Eat Lunch? A Summary of Three Studies." *The Journal of Child Nutrition and Management* 26, 1 (spring 2002). http://docs.schoolnutrition.org/newsroom/jcnm/02spring/conklin/.

Cook, Christopher. *Diet for a Dead Planet.* New York: The New Press, 2004.

Cook, John T., and Deborah A. Frank. "Food Security, Poverty, and Human Development in the United States." *Annals of the New York Academy of Science* 40 (2008): 1–17.

Cooper, Ann, and Lisa M. Holmes. *Lunch Lessons: Changing the Way We Feed Our Children*. New York: Collins, 2006.

Corbett, James J. "A Survey of New Food Product Introductions and Slotting Allowances in the New England Marketplace from a Food Broker's Perspective." *Journal of Food Distribution Research* 35, 1 (March 2004): 44–50.

Cullen, Karen, J. Egan, T. Baranowski, E. Owens, C. de Moor. "Effects of a la Carte and Snack Bar Foods at School on Children's Lunchtime Intake of Fruits and Vegetables." *Journal of the American Dietetic Association* 100, 12 (2000): 1482–86.

Demas, Antonia. *Hot Lunch: A History of the School Lunch Program*. Trumansburg, NY: Food Studies Institute, 2000.

Dillard, J. Amy. "Sloppy Joe, Slop, Sloppy Joe: How USDA Commodities Dumping Ruined the National School Lunch Program." *Oregon Law Review* 87: 221–58.

Duster, Troy, and Alice Waters. "Engaged Learning across the Curriculum: The Vertical Integration of Food for Thought." *Liberal Education* 92, 2 (spring 2006): 42–47.

Dwyer, Joanna, Paul Michell, Claire Cosentino, Larry Webber, Julienne M. Seed, Deanna Hoelscher, M. Patricia Snyder, Mary Stevens, and Philip Nader. "Fat-Sugar See-Saw in School Lunches: Impact of a Low Fat Intervention." *Journal of Adolescent Health* 32, 6 (June 2003): 428–35.

Edelman, Peter. *Searching for America's Heart: RFK and the Renewal of Hope*. Boston: Houghton Mifflin, 2001.

Eisinger, Peter. *Toward an End to Hunger in America*. Washington, DC: The Brookings Institution, 1998.

Ellwood, David. *Poor Support: Poverty in the American Family*. New York: Basic Books, 1988.

Flanagan, Thelma. "School Food Services." In *Education in the States: Nationwide Development Since 1900*, edited by Edgar Fuller and Jim B. Pearson, 557–96. Washington, DC: National Education Association, 1969.

Food Research and Action Center. *An Advocate's Guide to the School Nutrition Programs*. Washington, DC: Food Research and Action Center, 2005.

———. *Commodity Foods and the Nutritional Quality of the National School Lunch Program: Historical Role, Current Operations, and Future Potential*. Washington, DC: Food Research and Action Center, September 2008.

———. *School Breakfast Scorecard 2006*. Washington, DC: Food Research and Action Center, 2006.

———. *School Breakfast Scorecard 2007*. Washington, DC: Food Research and Action Center, 2007.

Fox, Mary Kay, Mary Kay Crepinsek, Patty Connor, Michael Battaglia. *School Nutrition Dietary Assessment Study-II: Final Report*. Alexandria, VA: U.S. Department of Agriculture, 2001.

Fried, Ellen, and Michele Simon. "The Competitive Food Conundrum: Can Government Regulations Improve School Food?" *Duke Law Journal* 56 (2007): 1491–1539.

Glantz, Frederic B., Regina Berg, Diane Polcari, Ellen Sackoff, and Shelley Pazer. *School Lunch Eligible Non-Participants: Final Report*. Submitted to U.S.

Department of Agriculture, Food and Consumer Service, Office of Analysis and Evaluation, December 1994.

Gleason, Philip M. "Participation in the National School Lunch Program and the School Breakfast Program." *American Journal of Clinical Nutrition* 61 (1995, suppl.): s213–20.

Goldberg, Jeanne P. "The Recommended Dietary Allowances: Can They Inform the Development of Standards of Academic Achievement?" *Applied Measurement in Education* 11, 1 (1998): 97–105.

Gordon, Anne, Mary Kay Crepinsek, Renee Nogales, and Elizabeth Condon. *School Nutrition Dietary Assessment-III.* Vol. 1: *School Foodservice, School Food Environment, and Meals Offered and Served.* Alexandria, VA: U.S. Department of Agriculture, 2007.

Gordon, Anne, Mary K. Fox, Melissa Clark, Renee Nogales, Elizabeth Condon, Philip Gleason, and Ankur Sarin. *School Nutrition Dietary Assessment-III.* Vol. 2: *Student Participation and Dietary Intakes.* Alexandria, VA: U.S. Department of Agriculture, 2007.

Gottlieb, Robert. *Environmentalism Unbound: Exploring New Pathways for Change.* Cambridge, MA: The MIT Press, 2001.

Greenhouse, Steven. *The Big Squeeze: Tough Times for the American Worker.* New York: Knopf, 2008.

Gunderson, Gordon. *The National School Lunch Program: Background and Development.* FNS-63, Washington, DC: U.S. Government Printing Office, 1971.

Guthrie, Joanne, and Jean C. Buzby. "Several Strategies May Lower Plate Waste in School Feeding Programs." *Food Review* 25, 2 (summer-fall 2002): 36–42.

Hacker, Jacob S. *The Great Risk Shift: The Assault on American Jobs, Families, Health Care, and Retirement and How You Can Fight Back.* New York: Oxford University Press, 2006.

Haskins, Ron. "The School Lunch Lobby." *Education Next* 5, 3 (summer 2005); Hoover Institution online publication at www.hoover.org/publications/ednext/3219311.html.

Hess, John. "Restaurant Food: Frozen, Cooked, Then Refrozen and Recooked." In *The Feeding Web: Issues in Nutritional Ecology*, edited by Joan Gussow, 157–59. Berkeley, CA: Bull Publishing Co., 1978.

Hilton, Richard. *Schools Leaving the National School Lunch Program: Final Report.* U.S. Department of Agriculture, Food and Consumer Service, Office of Analysis and Evaluation, 1997.

Hopgood, Annette Bomar. "Surviving an External Review." In *Managing Child Nutrition Programs: Leadership for the Twenty-First Century*, edited by Josephine Martin and Martha T. Conklin, 237–63. Gaithersburg, MD: Aspen Publishers, Inc., 1999.

Howard, Donald. *The WPA and Federal Relief Policy.* New York: Russell Sage Foundation, 1943.

Hunter, Robert. *Poverty.* Harper Torchbooks edition, edited and with an introduction by Peter d'A. Jones. New York: Harper and Row, 1965; orig. pub. 1904.

Imhoff, Daniel. *Foodfight: The Citizen's Guide to a Food and Farm Bill.* Healdsburg, CA: Watershed Media, 2007.

Institute of Medicine. *Preventing Childhood Obesity: Health in the Balance.* Committee on Prevention of Obesity in Children and Youth, Food and Nutrition Board, Board on Health Promotion and Disease Prevention, edited by Jeffrey P. Koplan, Catharyn T. Liverman, and Vivica I. Kraak. Washington, DC: National Academies Press, 2005.

Jacobson, Michael. *Six Arguments for a Greener Diet.* Washington, DC: Center for Science in the Public Interest, 2006.

Jones, Jean Yavis. "Universal School Lunch Program: Background, Issues, and Analysis." Memorandum, Congressional Research Service, January 3, 1992.

Katz, David L., Meghan O'Connell, Valentine Yanchou Njike, Ming-Chin Yeh, and Haq Nawaz. "Strategies for the Prevention and Control of Obesity in the School Setting: Systematic Review and Meta-Analysis." *International Journal of Obesity* 32 (December 2008): 1780–89.

Katz, Michael. *The Undeserving Poor: From the War on Poverty to the War on Welfare.* New York: Pantheon Books, 1989.

Kennedy, Eileen, and Edward Cooney, "Development of the Child Nutrition Programs in the United States." *Journal of Nutrition* 131 (2001): s431–36.

Kleinman, R., M. Murphy, M. Little, M. Pagano, C. Wehler, and K. Regal. "Hunger in Children in the United States: Potential Behavioral and Emotional Correlates." *Pediatrics* 101, 3 (1998).

Kloppenburg, Jack, Jr., and Neva Hassanein. "From Old School to Reform School?" *Agriculture and Human Values* 23 (2006): 417–21.

Kotz, Nick. *Let Them Eat Promises: The Politics of Hunger in America.* Englewood Cliffs, NJ: Prentice-Hall, 1969.

Kozol, Jonathan. *Savage Inequalities: Children in America's Schools.* New York: Harper Perennial, 1993.

———. *The Shame of the Nation: The Restoration of Apartheid Schooling in America.* New York: Crown Publishers: 2005.

Kubik, Martha Y., Leslie A. Lytle, Peter J. Hannan, Cheryl L. Perry, and Mary Story. "The Association of School Food Environment with Dietary Behaviors of Young Adolescents." *American Journal of Public Health* 93, 7 (2003): 1168–73.

Lambert, Laurel G., Martha T. Conklin, and J.J. Johnson. "Parental Beliefs toward the National School Lunch Program Related to Elementary Student Participation." *The Journal of Child Nutrition and Management* 26, 2 (fall 2002); available at http://docs.schoolnutrition.org/newsroom/jcnm/02fall/lambert/.

Lambert, Laurel G., Martha T. Conklin, and Mary Kay Meyer. "Parents' Beliefs toward Their Children's Participation in the National School Lunch Program: Results of Focus Group Discussion Guided by the Theory of Reasoned Action." *Topics in Clinical Nutrition* 16, 4 (2001): 11–20.

Levenstein, Harvey. *Paradox of Plenty: A Social History of Eating in Modern America,* rev. ed. Berkeley: University of California Press, 2003.

Levine, Susan. *School Lunch Politics: The Surprising History of America's Favorite Welfare Program.* Princeton, NJ: Princeton University Press, 2008.

Maney, Ardith. *Still Hungry after All These Years: Food Assistance from Kennedy to Reagan.* Westport, CT: Greenwood Press, 1989.

Manson, JoAnn. "Behind the Headlines," interview with Bonnie Liebman, *Nutrition Action* 33, 3 (April 2008): 3–5.

Market Ventures, Inc. *School Food Plus Evaluation. Interim Report: Phase 3, School Year 2005–2006.* April 12, 2007.

Marlette, Martha, Susan B. Templeton, and Myna Panemangalore. "Food Type, Food Preparation, and Competitive Food Purchases Impact School Lunch Plate Waste by Sixth Grade Students." *Journal of the American Dietetic Association* 105, 11 (2005): 1779–82.

Marples, Carol Ann, and Diana-Marie Spillman. "Factors Affecting Students' Participation in the Cincinnati Public Schools Lunch Program." *Adolescence* 30 (1995): 745–53.

Marsden, Malissa. "Industry 101." *School Foodservice and Nutrition* 59, 9 (October 2004): 23–24, 26, 28, 30.

Martin, Josephine. "History of Child Nutrition Programs." In *Managing Child Nutrition Programs: Leadership for the Twenty-First Century,* edited by Josephine Martin and Martha T. Conklin, 29–85. Gaithersburg, MD: Aspen Publishers, Inc., 1999.

McLaren, Penny. "What Are They Thinking? Tips and Tricks for Successful Marketing to Today's American Teenagers." *School Foodservice and Nutrition* 58 (June/July 2004): 58–66.

Meyer, Mary Kay. "Top Predictors of Middle/Junior High School Students' Satisfaction with School Food Service and Nutrition Programs." *Journal of the American Dietetic Association* 100, 1 (January 2000): 100–102.

Meyer, Mary Kay, and Martha T. Conklin. "Variables Affecting High School Students' Perceptions of School Foodservice." *Journal of the American Dietetic Association* 98, 12 (December 1998): 1424–38.

Milner, Murray, Jr. *Freaks, Geeks, and Cool Kids: American Teenagers, Schools, and the Culture of Consumption.* New York: Routledge, Taylor and Francis Group, 2006.

Morgan, Kevin. "School Food and the Public Domain: The Politics of the Public Plate." *The Political Quarterly* 77, 3 (2006): 379–87.

Morgan, Kevin, and Roberta Sonnino. *The School Food Revolution: Public Food and the Challenge of Sustainable Development.* London: Earthscan, 2008.

Murphy, Michael, Cheryl Wehler, M. E. Pagano, M. Little, Ron E. Kleinman, and M. S. Jellinek. "Relationship between Hunger and Psychosocial Functioning in Low-Income American Children." *Journal of the American Academy of Child and Adolescent Psychiatry* 37 (1998): 163–70.

Nelson, Jennifer. "Is *That* Your Lunch?" *Family Circle,* November 1, 2006, 49–50, 52, 54–55.

Nestle, Marion. *Food Politics: How the Food Industry Influences Nutrition and Health.* Berkeley: University of California Press, 2002.

Newman, Constance. *The Income Volatility See-Saw: Implications for School Lunch.* U.S. Department of Agriculture, Economic Research Service ERR-23, August 2006.

Nord, Mark, Margaret Andrews, and Steven Carlson. *Household Food Security in the United States, 2007*. U.S. Department of Agriculture, Economic Research Service ERS Report 66, November 2008.

Pannell, Dorothy V. "Why School Meals Are High in Fat and Some Suggested Solutions." *The American Journal of Clinical Nutrition* 61, 1 (1995, suppl.): s245–46.

Pannell-Martin, Dorothy. *School Foodservice Management for the Twenty-First Century,* 5th ed., Alexandria, VA: InTEAM Associates Inc., 1999.

Peterson, Karen E., and Mary Kay Fox, "Addressing the Epidemic of Childhood Obesity Through School-Based Interventions: What Has Been Done and Where Do We Go From Here?" *Journal of Law, Medicine, and Ethics* 35 (spring 2007): 113–30.

Pollan, Michael. *In Defense of Food; An Eater's Manifesto.* New York: Penguin Press, 2008.

———. "Unhappy Meals." *The New York Times Sunday Magazine,* January 28, 2007, 38–47, 65, 67, 70.

Ponza, Michael, Philip Gleason, Lara Hulsey, and Quinn Moore. *NSLP/SBP Access, Participation, Eligibility, and Certification Study: Erroneous Payments in the NSLP and SBP.* Vol. 1: *Study Findings.* Special Nutrition Programs Report No. CN-07-APEC/ USDA, Food and Nutrition Service, Office of Research, Nutrition, and Analysis, November 2007; available at www.fns.usda.gov/oane/MENU/published/CNP/Files/apecvol1.pdf.

Poppendieck, Janet. *Breadlines Knee Deep in Wheat: Food Assistance in the Great Depression.* New Brunswick, NJ: Rutgers University Press, 1986.

———. *Sweet Charity? Emergency Food and the End of Entitlement.* New York: Penguin Books, 1999.

Probart, Claudia, Elaine McDonnell, Terryl Hartman, Elaine Weirich, and Lisa Baily-Davis. "Factors Associated with the Offering and Sale of Competitive Foods and School Lunch Participation." *Journal of the American Dietetic Association* 106, 2 (2006): 242–47.

Ralston, Katherine, Constance Newman, Annette Clauson, Joanne Guthrie, and Jean Buzby. *The National School Lunch Program, Background, Trends and Issues.* U.S.D.A., Economic Research Service, ERR-61, July 2008.

Reese, William. "After Bread, Education: Nutrition and Urban School Children, 1890–1920." *Teachers College Record* 81, 4 (summer 1980): 496–525.

Roberts, Lydia. "Beginnings of the Recommended Dietary Allowances." *Journal of the American Dietetic Association* 34 (September 1958): 903–8.

Roberts, Susan Lynn. "School Food: Does the Future Call for New Food Policy or Can the Old Still Hold True?" *Drake Journal of Agricultural Law* 7, 3 (fall 2002): 587–620.

Russell, Sharman Apt. *Hunger: An Unnatural History.* New York: Basic Books, 2005.

Saguey, Abigail C., and Kevin W. Riley. "Weighing Both Sides: Morality, Mortality, and Framing Contests over Obesity." *Journal of Health Policy, Politics, and Law* 30, 5 (2005): 869–921.

St. Pierre, Robert G., and Michael J. Puma. "Controlling Federal Expenditures in the National School Lunch Program: The Relationship between Changes in Household Eligibility and Federal Policy." *Journal of Policy Analysis and Management* 11, 1 (1992): 42–57.

Salisbury, Clint. "Make an Investment in Our School Children: Increase the Nutritional Value of School Lunch Programs." *Brigham Young University Education and Law Journal* 2004: 331–52.

Sanchez, Alfonso, and Luis Rene Contreras. *Relationship of the Physical Dining Environment and Service Styles to Plate Waste in Middle/Junior High Schools.* NFSMI Item no. R-58-02. Oxford, MS: National Food Service Management Institute, February 2003.

Savino, Ann. "Lunch Online." *The American School Board Journal* 184 (February 1997): 46–49.

Schlosser, Eric. *Fast Food Nation: The Dark Side of the All-American Meal.* Boston: Houghton Mifflin, 2001.

School Nutrition Association. *Little Big Fact Book.* Alexandria, VA: School Nutrition Association, 2006.

Simon, Michele. *Appetite for Profit: How the Food Industry Undermines Our Health and How to Fight Back.* New York: Nation Books, 2006.

Sims, Laura S. *The Politics of Fat: Food and Nutrition Policy in America.* Armonk, NY: M.E. Sharpe, 1998.

Skocpol, Theda. *The Missing Middle: Working Families and the Future of American Social Policy.* New York: W.W. Norton and Company, A Century Foundation Book, 2000.

Spargo, John. *The Bitter Cry of the Children,* with a new introduction by Jules Chametzky. New York: Johnson Reprint Corporation, 1969; orig. pub. 1906.

Steiner, Gilbert Yale. *The Children's Cause.* Washington, D.C.: The Brookings Institution, 1976.

Stitt, Kathleen, Mary Klatko, Mary Nix, and Jean Yavis-Jones. "Child Nutrition Programs: Issues for the 101st Congress." *School Food Service Research Review* 13, 1 (1989): 5–98.

Stone, Deborah. *Policy Paradox: The Art of Political Decision Making,* rev. ed. New York: W.W. Norton, 2002.

Stone, Michael K., and Zenobia Barlow, eds. *Ecological Literacy: Educating our Children for a Sustainable World.* San Francisco: Sierra Club Books, 2005.

Story, Mary, Karen Kaphingst, and Simone French. "The Role of Schools in Obesity Prevention." *The Future of Children* 16, 1 (spring 2006): 109–42; issue on Childhood Obesity; available at www.futureofchildren.org.

Trust for America's Health. *F as in Fat: How Obesity Policies Are Failing in America, 2007 Report;* available at http://healthyamericans.org/reports/obesity2007/obesity2007report.pdf.

U.S. Congress. Senate. 79th Congress, 1st Session. Report No. 553, "Providing Assistance to the States in the Establishment, Maintenance, Operation and Expansion of School Lunch Programs," a report to accompany S. 962, July 1945.

U.S. Congress. Senate. *Hearings before the Select Committee on Nutrition and Human Needs.* Part 9, *Universal School Lunch Program.* Washington, DC, October 13, 1971.

U.S. Congress. Senate. Select Committee on Nutrition and Human Needs. "The School Lunch Problem." In *Studies of Human Need,* Committee Print. Washington, DC: U.S. Government Printing Office, June 1972.

U.S. Congress. Senate. Subcommittee on Employment, Manpower, and Poverty, Committee on Labor and Public Welfare. *Hunger in America: A Chronology and Selected Background Materials,* October 2, 1968 (90th Congress, 2nd Session).

U.S. Department of Agriculture. Bureau of Agricultural Economics. *The School Lunch Program and Agricultural Surplus Disposal,* Miscellaneous Publication No 467, October 1941.

U.S. Department of Agriculture. Food and Nutrition Service. *Erroneous Payments in the National School Lunch Program and School Breakfast Program: Summary of Findings.* November 2007.

———. *Foods Sold in Competition with USDA School Meal Programs: A Report to Congress.* Washington, D.C.: Government Printing Office, January 12, 2001.

———. *Paperwork Reduction Pilot Projects: Interim Report,* March 1994. ERIC document 383 097, at www.eric.ed.gov/ERICDocs/data/ericdocs2sql/content_storage_01/0000019b/80/13/f1/75.pdf.

U.S. Department of Agriculture, Food and Nutrition Service; U.S. Department of Health and Human Services, Centers for Disease Control and Prevention; and U.S. Department of Education. *Making It Happen! School Nutrition Success Stories,* FN S-374. Alexandria, VA, January 2005.

U.S. General Accounting Office. *Food Safety: Continued Vigilance Needed to Ensure Safety of School Meals.* GAO-02-669T. Washington, DC: Government Printing Office, April 30, 2002.

———. *School Lunch Program: Cafeteria Managers' Views on Food Wasted by Students.* Report to the Chairman, Committee on Economic and Educational Opportunities, House of Representatives, GAO/RCED-96-191. Washington, DC: Government Printing Office, July 1996.

———. *School Lunch Program: Efforts Needed to Improve Nutrition and Encourage Healthy Eating.* Washington, DC: Government Printing Office, May 2003.

———. *School Meal Programs: Few Instances of Foodborne Outbreaks Reported, but Opportunities Exist to Enhance Outbreak Data and Food Safety Practices.* GAO 03-530. Washington, DC: Government Printing Office, May 2003.

U.S. Government Accountability Office. *School Meal Programs: Competitive Foods Are Widely Available and Generate Substantial Revenues for Schools.* GAO-05-563. Washington, DC: Government Printing Office, August 2005.

Vallianatos, Mark, Robert Gottlieb, and Margaret Haase. "Farm to School: Strategies for Urban Health, Combating Sprawl, and Establishing a Community Food Systems Approach." *Journal of Planning Education and Research* 23 (2004): 414–23.

Wechsler, Howell, N.D. Brener, S. Kuester, and C. Miller. "Food Service and Foods and Beverages Available at School: Results from the School Health

Policies and Program Study, 2000." *Journal of School Health* 71, 7 (2001): 313–24.

Wellisch, Jean B., S. Hanes, L. Jordan, K. Maurer, J. Reinholt, and J. VerMeersch. *The National Evaluation of School Nutrition Programs, Final Report.* Santa Monica, CA: Systems Development Corporation, 1983.

Winne, Mark. *Closing the Food Gap: Resetting the Table in the Land of Plenty.* Boston: Beacon Press, 2008.

Yeoman, Barry. "Unhappy Meals." *Mother Jones* 28, 1 (January-February 2003): 40–45, 81.

Index

Abramovitz, Mimi, 286
Abt Associates, Inc.: food quality and, 140, 143, 144; participation and, 180–81; SNDA-II and, 115, 120–21; stigma and, 191–92; time to eat and, 148–49
Adamick, Kate, 243
Adams, Le, 240
administrative burden: costs of, 204–5, 289–90; means-tested programs and, 188–89, 206; nonparticipation and, 179–83, 209–10; Philadelphia pilot project and, 212–13; three-tier benefit structure and, 198–206, 209, 212–15
adolescents. See children's preferences; student participation
Agricultural Adjustment Act. See Section 32 (Agricultural Adjustment Act)
a la carte items: cashier line for, 31; federal cutbacks and, 75; menu critiques and, 85–87; participation in school meals and, 157, 159; school budgets and, 28, 40–41, 89, 92–94, 135–36; stigma and, 195–98; "universal" approach and, 264, 270–71. See also competitive foods
Allen, Patricia, 243–44
Alliance for a Healthier Generation, 259
Alliance to End Hunger, 304n46
American culture: family eating habits and, 100–102; food trends in, 98–100
American School Food Service Association (ASFSA). See School Nutrition Association
America's Second Harvest, 304n46
ANSMP (Assisted Nutrient Standard Menu Planning), 81
anti-hunger advocacy, 60–61, 63; block grants and, 82–83, 306n69; core organizations and, 304n46; "hunger lobby" and, 63–64; local reform efforts and, 243; NuMenu approach and, 80; overcertification challenge

and, 204–5; school participation and, 173–75
anti-poverty advocacy, 58. See also anti-hunger advocacy
Any Town HS: breakfast program at, 32–37; kitchen experience in, 26–45; lunch prep at, 26–28; lunchtime activity at, 28–32; money versus nutrition dynamic at, 37–43; staff views on jobs in, 43–44
Any Town Little School: breakfast program, 35–37
application process, 180–81, 191–92, 198, 212, 215
ASFSA (American School Food Service Association). See School Nutrition Association
Assisted Nutrient Standard Menu Planning (ANSMP), 81
Association of Nutrition Services Agencies (ANSA), 304n46
Atlanta Journal, 69
average daily participation (ADP): goals for increasing, 133–35; growth in, 64–65

Babbage principle, 89–90, 91
Badgett, Donnis, 87
Balanced Budget and Emergency Deficit Control Act of 1985, 74–75
Bankhead, John, 301n4
Belkin, Lisa, 93
Beller, David, 128
Berg, Joel, 252
Berkowitz, David, 228, 229
Bernaro, Virg, 27, 85–86, 102
Better School Food, 259
biometrics, 217
"bite tax," 59
block grant approach, 75, 76, 82–83, 213, 306n69
Body Mass Index (BMI), 298n11
"bonus" commodities, 103, 106–7, 112
Botchford, Hawley, 162
Boughton, Alice, 266, 278

CALIFORNIA STUDIES IN FOOD AND CULTURE

Darra Goldstein, Editor

Text: 10/13 Sabon
Display: Franklin Gothic Demi
Compositor: BookComp, Inc.
Indexer: Marcia Carlson
Printer and binder: Sheridan Books, Inc.

Portland Community College